discover
EGYPT

ANTHONY SATTIN
MICHAEL BENANAV, MATTHEW D FIRESTONE, THOMAS HALL

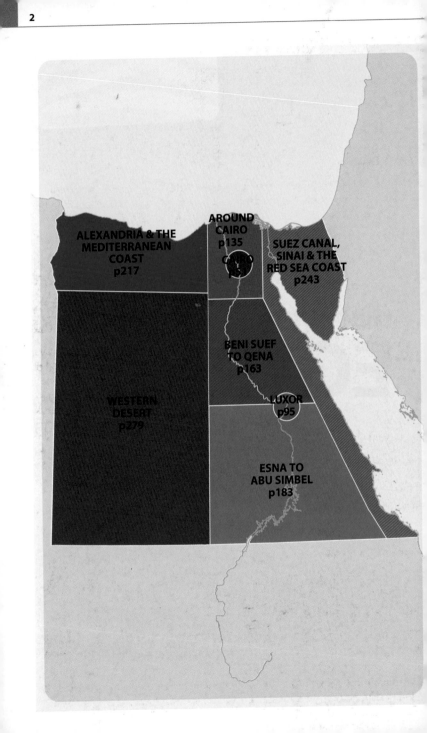

ALEXANDRIA & THE
MEDITERRANEAN
COAST
p217

AROUND
CAIRO
p135

CAIRO
p51

SUEZ CANAL,
SINAI & THE
RED SEA COAST
p243

BENI SUEF
TO QENA
p163

LUXOR
p95

WESTERN
DESERT
p279

ESNA TO
ABU SIMBEL
p183

DISCOVER EGYPT

Cairo (p51) The capital of Egypt is both an historical treasure trove and a fast-growing bundle of energy – chaotic but irresistible.

Luxor (p95) The long-time capital of ancient Egypt is being reshaped into the world's largest open-air museum.

Around Cairo (p135) Around the capital are early cities and pyramids, monastic retreats and a magical, palm-lined oasis.

Beni Suef to Qena (p163) Beyond the tourist trail, this part of the Nile is studded with tombs, temples and early churches.

Esna to Abu Simbel (p183) Awesome monuments, bustling towns and enchanting river scenes on this stretch of the Nile.

Alexandria & the Mediterranean Coast (p217) City of museums and cafes near clear-blue waters and endless beaches.

Suez Canal, Sinai & the Red Sea Coast (p243) Colonial architecture, Bedouin culture, and world-class diving in the Red Sea.

Western Desert (p279) This least visited region has beautiful oases surrounded by dunes and vast expanses of emptiness.

⬊ CONTENTS

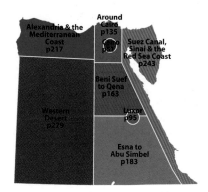

Around Cairo p135

Alexandria & the Mediterranean Coast p217

Cairo p51

Suez Canal, Sinai & the Red Sea Coast p243

Beni Suef to Qena p163

Western Desert p279

Luxor p95

Esna to Abu Simbel p183

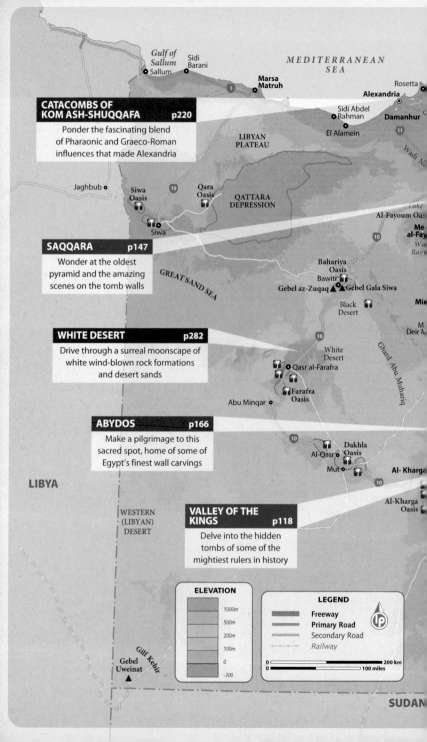

CATACOMBS OF KOM ASH-SHUQQAFA p220
Ponder the fascinating blend of Pharaonic and Graeco-Roman influences that made Alexandria

SAQQARA p147
Wonder at the oldest pyramid and the amazing scenes on the tomb walls

WHITE DESERT p282
Drive through a surreal moonscape of white wind-blown rock formations and desert sands

ABYDOS p166
Make a pilgrimage to this sacred spot, home of some of Egypt's finest wall carvings

VALLEY OF THE KINGS p118
Delve into the hidden tombs of some of the mightiest rulers in history

Gulf of Sallum
Sidi Barani
Sallum
Marsa Matruh
Rosetta
Alexandria
MEDITERRANEAN SEA
Sidi Abdel Rahman
Damanhur
El Alamein
LIBYAN PLATEAU
Wadi Na

Jaghbub
Siwa Oasis
Qara Oasis
QATTARA DEPRESSION
Lake
Al-Fayoum Oas
Me al-Fay
Wa Rayy
Siwa

GREAT SAND SEA

Bahariya Oasis
Bawiti
Gebel az-Zuqaq ▲ ▲ Gebel Gala Siwa
Black Desert
Mi
M Deir M

White Desert
Qasr al-Farafra
Farafra Oasis
Abu Minqar

LIBYA

Al-Qasr
Dakhla Oasis
Mut
Al-Kharga

WESTERN (LIBYAN) DESERT

Al-Kharga Oasis

Gilf Kebir
Gebel Uweinat ▲

ELEVATION
1000m
500m
200m
100m
0
-300

LEGEND
Freeway
Primary Road
Secondary Road
Railway

0 ———— 200 km
0 ———— 100 miles

SUDAN

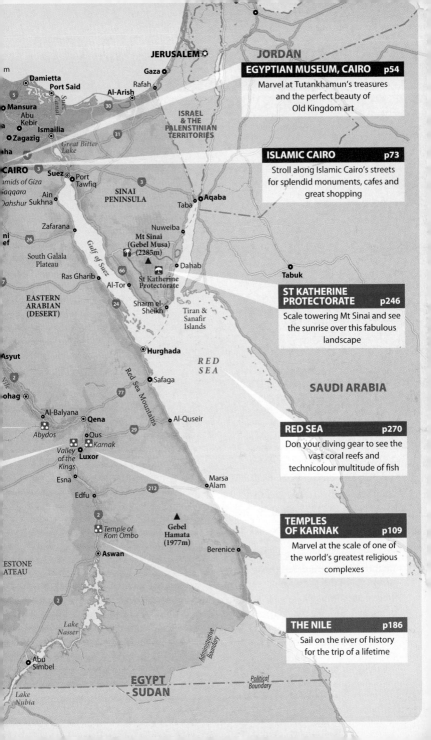

EGYPTIAN MUSEUM, CAIRO p54

Marvel at Tutankhamun's treasures and the perfect beauty of Old Kingdom art

ISLAMIC CAIRO p73

Stroll along Islamic Cairo's streets for splendid monuments, cafes and great shopping

ST KATHERINE PROTECTORATE p246

Scale towering Mt Sinai and see the sunrise over this fabulous landscape

RED SEA p270

Don your diving gear to see the vast coral reefs and technicolour multitude of fish

TEMPLES OF KARNAK p109

Marvel at the scale of one of the world's greatest religious complexes

THE NILE p186

Sail on the river of history for the trip of a lifetime

↘ THIS IS EGYPT

There are two predominant and clashing images of Egypt. One is a place of beauty and culture, the *Land of the Pharaohs* and tour brochures. The other is the Arab world's most populous nation, a struggling, noisy hive of energy, both frustrating and exciting.

Many visitors come to Egypt expecting the history – and the sun – and end up fascinated by the living culture. But the two are not mutually exclusive. The past has shaped the present and the present increasingly imposes on the past. By Egyptian terms, Cairo – whose original name is Al-Qahira, 'the Victorious' – is a newcomer, founded a mere 1000 years ago. But like most Egyptian towns and cities, it sits on ancient remains: Roman Babylon has been swallowed by its southern suburbs, most of ancient Heliopolis sits at the end of Cairo's airport runway and the Sphinx stares unseeing from the foot of the Pyramids in urban Giza.

Modern Egypt has some pressing concerns. With a population of over 80 million, limited farmland and a shortage of water, the challenges facing the country are enormous.

But Egyptians are nothing if not resourceful. Until recently there was little to Egypt beyond the thin south–north strip of the Nile, but the Aswan Dam has allowed some desert to be reclaimed (at what environmental cost remains to be seen), while the Red Sea and Mediterranean coastlines have been intensively developed.

In spite of the rapid change, Egyptians have held on to many of their traditional characteristics. They are playful people and love to laugh. They are rarely pushed to violence, having endured many a dictator and crisis over the millennia. And they are immensely hospitable.

> 'visitors come expecting the history and end up fascinated by the living culture'

Stunning monuments, vast deserts, coral-filled waters, characterful people – these are elements you can find in many countries, but in Egypt they are strung together in such a way as to make a journey here a memorable, perhaps even life-changing, experience.

⬂ EGYPT'S TOP
25 EXPERIENCES

1

⬂ PYRAMIDS OF GIZA

Although they're Egypt's most iconic images, nothing can prepare you for the sense of awe when first seeing the **Pyramids of Giza** (p79). Towering over both the urban sprawl and the desert beyond, these ancient monuments are at the top of every traveller's itinerary, and they never fail to amaze.

Matthew D Firestone, Lonely Planet Author

↘ THE NILE

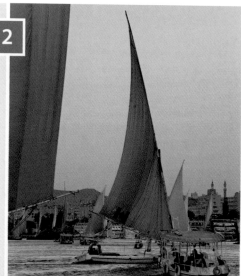

2

Floating on the **Nile** (p186) is always a magical experience. The water may have come from eastern Africa, but the experience, and the sounds that reach you wherever you are, are pure Egyptian. Watch the sun rise and set on the river and you come closer to understanding the spell the waterway held over ancient Egypt.

Anthony Sattin,
Lonely Planet Author

3

↘ LUXOR

Crowded and noisy it may be, and undergoing great change with the governor's development plan, but **Luxor** (p95) is still one of the most extraordinary places to visit. The largest open-air museum in the world, its well-preserved temples and tombs present images that will live long in your memory.

Anthony Sattin, Lonely Planet Author

1 RICHARD I'ANSON; 2 RICHARD I'ANSON; 3 IZZET KERIBAR

1 Camels at the Pyramids of Giza (p79); 2 Feluccas on the Nile, Aswan; 3 The Colossi of Memnon (p117) on Luxor's West Bank

↘ RED SEA

Egypt is more than sun, sand, pyramids and the Nile – the **Red Sea** (p270) is regarded as one of the premier scuba-diving destinations in the world. Whether you've logged hundreds of dives or you're looking to get certified, don't miss Egypt's remarkable underwater world and its incredible variety of coral and fish life.

Matthew D Firestone,
Lonely Planet Author

↘ RELAXING IN A MOSQUE

The quiet, shady arcades of a medieval mosque, such as **Al-Azhar Mosque** (p73), are the perfect places to take a break from modern Cairo – kick your shoes off and stay a while. The **Mosque of Ibn Tulun** (p77) has plenty of room, while the **Mosque of Al-Maridani** (p75) has a tree-filled courtyard.

Zora O'Neill, Lonely Planet Author

↘ SAQQARA & DAHSHUR PYRAMIDS

Everyone knows about *the* Pyramids, but they come with crowds and insistent touts. Savvy travellers head to the earlier and less-visited pyramids further south, particularly Saqqara's **Step Pyramid** (p148), the oldest pyramid in the world, and Dahshur's **Red Pyramid** (p154), the first true pyramid.

Matthew D Firestone, Lonely Planet Author

6

4 MARK WEBSTER; 5 PATRICK SYDER; 6 IZZET KERIBAR

4 Divers explore the Red Sea at Ras Mohammed National Park (p257); 5 Courtyard of Al-Azhar Mosque, Islamic Cairo (p73); 6 Step Pyramid of Zoser, Saqqara (p148)

↘ SIWA OASIS

It's impossible not to relax in Siwa (p299). With cold springs and palm groves to keep you cool in the day, and the best cafe/restaurant scene in the Western Desert at night, it's easy to spend enough time in Siwa to make the long drive there worthwhile.

Michael Benanav, Lonely Planet Author

7

8

⭘ EGYPTIAN CUISINE

Truth be told, Egypt doesn't have an haute cuisine, but sharing a table of freshly prepared mezze and a few drinks with friends is always a treat, and nowhere more so than at the excellent **Sofra** (p129) in Luxor, or the trendy **Abou El Sid** (p86) or **Sequoia** (p86) in Cairo.

Sylvie Franquet, Tour Leader

⭘ MT SINAI

9

Do not miss the sunrise from the top of **Mt Sinai** (p269), even though you have to climb through the night if you want to be at the summit in time. There are few mountains in the world that can top Sinai in terms of significance, a spot sacred to Jews, Christians and Muslims alike.

Matthew D Firestone,
Lonely Planet Author

7 JOHN ELK III; 8 FRANZ MARC FREI/LOOK-FOTO/PHOTOLIBRARY; 9 MARK DAFFEY

7 Houses in Siwa Oasis (p299); 8 Mezze bowls at a Cairo restaurant; 9 Rugged landscape surrounding Mt Sinai (p269)

10

⤵ EGYPTIAN MUSEUM, CAIRO

The Egyptian Museum (p54) is jokingly called the most important archaeological dig waiting to happen, as there are perhaps more exhibits in the
basement than above. What's on show, however, is spectacular, with room
after room of ancient treasures. Visit twice if you can.

Marie-Paule Gesquiere, Traveller, Belgium

⤵ TOMBS & TEMPLES

11

Wake before dawn on
Luxor's West Bank and
see the abode of death –
the Valley of the Kings
(p118), the Valley of the
Queens (p121) and Tombs
of the Nobles (p122) –
come to life. The Temple of
Hatshepsut (p117) and all
the other tombs are open
from 6am, at which time
most of the crowds are still
slumbering in their hotels.

↘ SHARIA AL-MUIZZ LI-DIN ALLAH

This wonderful Cairo **street** (p56), lined with medieval monuments and cutting right through the Fatimid city from **Bab al-Futuh** to **Bab Zuweila** (p74), and from there on to the **Mosque of Ibn Tulun** (p77), makes for a gorgeous afternoon walk. There's a wonder of Islamic art on every street corner.

Magdi Bouchra, Shopkeeper
on Sharia al-Muizz li-Din Allah

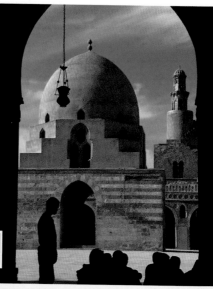

12

13

↘ ABYDOS

One of the most important, most beautiful and definitely the most mysterious of all ancient Egyptian temples is the **Temple of Seti I** (p179) at Abydos. **Abydos** (p166) was supposedly where the head of Osiris, the god of the dead, was buried and it was *the* place to be buried in ancient Egypt.

10 Golden statues at the Egyptian Museum, Cairo (p54); 11 Ramp at the Temple of Hatshepsut, Luxor (p117); 12 Mosque of Ibn Tulun, Islamic Cairo (p77); 13 Carved pillars at the Temple of Seti I, Abydos (p179)

14

➘ ASWAN SUNSET

Watch the sun set over **Aswan** (p201): there is something about the way the river is squeezed between rocks, the proximity of the desert, and the lonely burial places of the Aga Khan and of forgotten princes on the west bank, that makes the sunset here more poignant than anywhere else along the Egyptian Nile.

↘ SMOKING A SHEESHA

The bubbling *sheesha* (water pipe) is as essential to life in Egypt as the Nile itself. Keep it real with macho molasses-flavoured tobacco at a traditional **ahwa** (coffeehouse; p87) or go upscale with a cocktail of flavours including mint and apple or cappuccino at one of Cairo's numerous chic lounges.

Zora O'Neill, Lonely Planet Author

15

14 RICHARD I'ANSON; 15 ARIADNE VAN ZANDBERGEN

14 Feluccas sailing on the Nile at sunset, Aswan; 15 Two locals smoking *sheesha*

◥ TEMPLE OF HORUS, EDFU

Marvel at the most completely preserved ancient Egyptian temple and get lost in its inner chambers, all perfectly carved with sacred formulae, at Edfu's **Temple of Horus** (p198). Look out for the laboratory with its recipes for perfumes, or climb up on to the rooftop.

Hassan Hassaneen, Temple Guardian

16

17

⬐ COPTIC SITES

Seek out one of the old Coptic sites along the Nile, still used as churches, convents and monasteries. They tend to be overwhelmed on feast days, when thousands come to pray, but at other times they are sleepy places full of beauty and fascination, perhaps nowhere more so than in **Coptic Cairo** (p70).

⬐ AMUN TEMPLE, KARNAK

18

Feel tiny and be overwhelmed by the massive papyrus columns in the grand hypostyle hall at the **Amun Temple** (p109) at Karnak, which mimic the swamps along Egypt's riverbanks. Avoid the tour groups in the central lane and wander off to grasp the full scale and splendour of the place.

Mohamed Abd ar-Rahim, Guide

16 JOHN ELK III; 17 RICHARD I'ANSON; 18 RICHARD I'ANSON

16 Falcon statue at the Temple of Horus, Edfu (p198); 17 Mosaic at Coptic Cairo's Hanging Church (p71);
18 Pillars in the Hypostyle Hall in the Amun Temple, Karnak (p109)

⇘ DAHAB

Although it has expanded beyond its origins as a beachside hippy colony, **Dahab** (p264) is still ruled by independent travellers. Whether you're looking to dive the Red Sea, trek through the interior or spend days by the water, chances are you're going to get stuck here for longer than you planned.

Matthew D Firestone, Lonely Planet Author

19

20

⬊ ABU SIMBEL

Spend the night in **Abu Simbel** (p215) and visit the **Great Temple of Ramses II** (p215) after the day trippers have left or before they arrive. Explore the growing town and its attractions, not least local musician Fikri Kachef's simple hotel **Eskaleh** (p216), dedicated to all aspects of Nubian culture.

Rafael Wlodarski, Lonely Planet Author

19 CHARLES A FLYNN/PHOTOLIBRARY; 20 PATRICK SYDER

19 Camels on the beach, Dahab (p264); 20 Great Temple of Ramses II, Abu Simbel (p215)

21

⟩ SOUQS

Commercial insanity reigns in Egypt's **souqs** (p342), where bargaining is part of everyday life. Haggle for dusty antiques, alabaster vases, secondhand shirts, vintage sunglasses…or perhaps you'd like to buy a donkey?

Zora O'Neill, Lonely Planet Author

⟩ ST KATHERINE PROTECTORATE

Most tourists, day trip-pers from the resorts, climb **Mt Sinai** (p269) at dawn, visit the **monas-tery of St Katherine** (p268) and leave right away, but they are missing out on walk-ing in the spectacular World Heritage Site of **St Katherine Protectorate** (p246), with Byzantine ruins, high mountains, water pools, narrow can-yons and beautiful gar-dens, kept by the friendly Jebeliya Bedouin.

Zoltan Matrahazi, Trek Organiser

22

↘ LAKE NASSER

23

Nubia is like another country, a different landscape that was home to a separate nation. The Egyptian side of Nubia is mostly under water. The eerie, stark landscape of **Lake Nasser** (p215) is unlike anywhere else in the country, and decorated with the majestic temples at Abu Simbel.

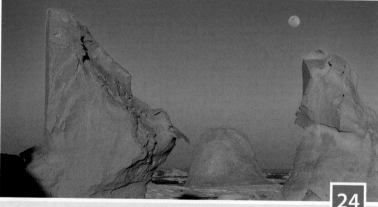

24

↘ FULL MOON, WESTERN DESERT

Night, especially in summer, comes like a liberating hero conquering the oppressive midday heat. It's a great time to explore the **Western Desert** (p279) – the full moon is so bright you can walk around without a torch!

Michael Benanav, Lonely Planet Author

21 JOHN ELK III; 22 JOHN BORTHWICK; 23 S TAUQUEUR/F1 ONLINE/PHOTOLIBRARY; 24 PETER M. WILSON/ALAMY

21 Food for sale at an Aswan souq; 22 St Katherine's Monastery, Sinai (p268); 23 Cruise ship passing Abu Simbel, Lake Nasser (p215); 24 Rock formations, White Desert area (p282) of the Western Desert (p279)

⬊ ALEXANDRIA'S PERIOD CAFES

Take a trip back in time and cultivate your sense of the city's cosmopolitan glory days by sipping a coffee in the magnificent establishments once frequented by literary lights like Durrell and Cafavy. Try the bar at the **Cecil Hotel** (p235) or coffee at **Athineos** (p233).

Thomas Hall, Lonely Planet Author

25

25 ARIADNE VAN ZANDBERGEN

The period charm of the Sofianopoulos Coffee Store, Alexandria (p233)

JUST THE HIGHLIGHTS

FIVE DAYS CAIRO TO LUXOR

Five days allows you to see the highlights from ancient Egypt
from the Old Kingdom pyramids near Cairo to the New Kingdom tombs and temples in Luxor. This itinerary is intense
sightseeing, but take a felucca on the Nile for some down tim

❶ CAIRO

Spend one day getting acquainted with Egypt's long history. Sta
with the **Egyptian Museum** (p54), which should take up the who
morning. After lunch at the **Citadel View** (p86) in **Al-Azhar Park** (p7
visit the **Mosque-Madrassa of Sultan Hassan** (p77) and the **Mosqu
of Ibn Tulun** (p77), before walking from **Bab Zuweila** to **Bab al-Futu
(p74) – stopping for some sightseeing, shopping, and tea and *sheesh*
(water pipe) along the way.

❷ PYRAMIDS & SAQQARA

Start the day early, arriving at the **Pyramids of Giza** (p79) before t
crowds. Try to get a ticket to go inside the **Great Pyramid of Khu
(Cheops)** (p79), take time to see the ancient boats at the **Solar Barqu
Museum** (p80) and visit the **Sphinx** (p81). Continue to Saqqara to se
the **Step Pyramid** (p148) and the surrounding complex. Have a picn
then explore the wonderful tombs near the Serapeum, including t
Tomb of Ptahhotep (p151). Back in central Cairo take a **felucca ri
(p125) on the Nile or enjoy dinner at a riverside restaurant. Travel
Luxor on the late-evening train (p92).

The avenue of sphinxes, Luxor Temple (p112)

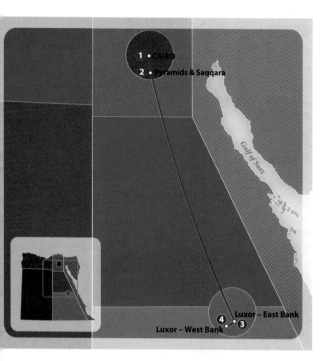

• LUXOR – EAST BANK

fter an early-morning check-in and breakfast, walk around the extraor-
nary **Temples of Karnak** (p109). Break for a traditional Egyptian lunch
Sofra (p129), then head for more monumental wonder at **Luxor
emple** (p112) before exploring **Luxor Museum** (p114). If you have the
ergy for a stroll after dinner, return to see Luxor Temple lit up after
rk, which reveals the wonderful detail on the carvings.

LUXOR – WEST BANK

n day four, take the ferry to the West Bank and hire a car, or opt for
bicycle if it's not too hot. Start with the magnificent **Valley of the
ings** (p118), taking in three or four tombs, before returning to the
pressive **Temple of Hatshepsut** (p117), temple of Egypt's most
mous female pharaoh. After lunch don't miss the wall paintings in
e less-visited **Tombs of the Nobles** (p122), from where you can then
alk to the temple of **Medinat Habu** (p123), which looks especially
unning in the afternoon light. Wind down with tea while enjoying
e sunset from **Maratonga Cafeteria** (p131), opposite the temple.
n the last day back on the East Bank, take in the curiosities of the
ummification Museum (p115) in the morning, leaving your after-
on free to go shopping for that perfect Egyptian souvenir.

THE OASES TOUR

TEN DAYS CAIRO TO LUXOR

This tour takes in the splendid oases of the Western Desert –
from Siwa, where Alexander the Great consulted the oracle,
down to Al-Kharga – with amazing desert scenery and plenty
of hot springs. You can bus between the oases, but the best
option is to drive yourself, or arrange a safari tour (see p310).

❶ SIWA OASIS

It's a nine-hour drive from Cairo to Siwa Oasis so have lunch and
swim on the way in **Sidi Abdel Rahman** (p239), arriving in Siwa in the
evening. On day two explore **Siwa Town** (p300) and cycle to Aghurmi
to visit the **Temple of the Oracle** (p301) and of **Umm Ubayd**. The
delve into the rock tombs of **Gebel al-Mawta** (p301) and take a di
in one of the hot springs, such as **Cleopatra's Bath** (p301). Settle in
a cafe in the town centre in the evening, and organise a trip into the
desert for the next day (p303). Spend the whole of day three wit
your guide in the spectacular dunes of the **Great Sand Sea** (p30!
stopping for a swim at the hot spring of **Bir Wahed** (p301).

❷ BAHARIYA OASIS

From Siwa drive to Bahariya Oasis on the fairly new desert road. It
a long drive, so in the evening take it easy with a stroll around the
town of **Bawiti** (p296). The next morning, visit Bawiti's **museum**
and the tombs of **Qarat Qasr Salim** (p297), leaving the afternoon
investigate some of the sights a little further afield, and the evenin
to bathe in a moonlit **hot spring** (p297).

Badr's Museum, Farafra Oasis (p295)

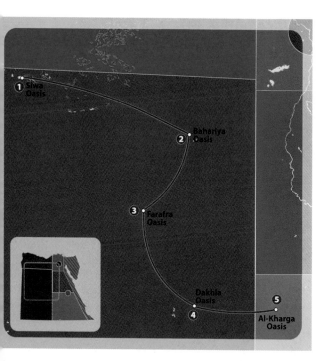

FARAFRA OASIS

ourney on to the oasis of Farafra on day six, via the dreamlike land-
ape of the **White Desert** (p282); excursions can be arranged in Bawiti
296) for those without their own vehicle. Wander around Farafra in
e evening and the next morning visit **Badr's Museum** (p295) for a
ste of traditional life in the oasis, before moving on to Dakhla.

DAKHLA OASIS

ter arriving in **Mut** (p292) in the afternoon, request to look inside
e **Ethnographic Museum**, and take a walk around the **old town**.
e picturesque must-see **Al-Qasr area** (p293), built over a Roman
te, is where you could spend most of day eight, and even spend
e night.

AL-KHARGA OASIS

rly the following morning, drive to the least scenic of the oases, the
pital of Al-Kharga. Browse the interesting selection of archaeological
ds at the **Museum of Antiquities** (p290), and visit the **Temple of
bis** (p291) and the intriguing **Necropolis of Al-Bagawat** (p290).
n the final day of your oases tour, take a car down the new road to
xor (three hours).

ULTIMATE NILE TRIP

TWO WEEKS CAIRO TO ABU SIMBEL

Egypt is the gift of the Nile, and so is this trip. Visit the fabulous sites of ancient Thebes and Aswan, and in between sail slowly in a felucca or dahablyya, stopping where the big cruis[ ] ships usually can't.

❶ CAIRO

Start your Egypt trip by getting a grip on 5000 years of Egyptian hi[s]tory with a morning visit to the **Egyptian Museum** (p54). Spend th[e] afternoon admiring the wonders of Islamic architecture with a wa[lk] in **Islamic Cairo** (p73), starting at the **Mosque of Ibn Tulun** (p77) an[d] **Gayer-Anderson Museum** (p77) and on to **Bab al-Futuh** (p74).

❷ PYRAMIDS & SAQQARA

On the second day arrange a taxi and start early at the **Pyramids** [of] **Giza** (p79), so you can get a ticket to go inside the **Great Pyrami[d] of Khufu (Cheops)** (p79). While here, go around the **Solar Barqu[e] Museum** (p80) and the **Sphinx** (p81). From Giza, follow the can[al] road past the palm groves to Saqqara, where you can gaze upon th[e] **Step Pyramid** (p148).

❸ LUXOR

Take an early flight to Luxor on day three and stop at the **Templ[e] of Karnak** (p109) on the way from the airport. Lunch at **Sofra** (p12[ ] before exploring **Luxor Temple** (p112) and the **Luxor Museum** (p11[ ] Preferably book yourself into a hotel on the West Bank and arrang[ ]

WAYNE WA[

Feluccas on the Nile, Aswan

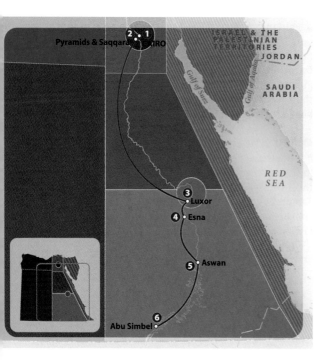

car or bike for touring the next day. Make the **Valley of the Kings** (p118) and the **Temple of Hatshepsut** (p117) your West Bank sightseeing priorities, and after lunch visit the **Ramesseum** (p119). It's worth spending another day on the West Bank, allowing plenty of time for some of the less-visited sights – start at the **Tombs of the Nobles** (p122), then walk to **Deir al-Medina** (p121). From there you can walk to the temple of **Medinat Habu** (p123).

THE NILE FROM ESNA

You can take a felucca trip any day, but most **dahabiyyas** (p309) set out from Esna (see p196) on Mondays. So start day six with a taxi to Esna (p195) and a visit to its temple and souq before boarding your boat. The next day, cruise to the site of **Al-Kab** (p197) and Edfu's well-preserved **Temple of Horus** (p198). The splendid quarries and chapels at **Gebel Silsila** (p199) make an excellent reason to step off the boat on day eight. The following day, moor on the banks near the unique temple of **Kom Ombo** (p200), and on day 10 sail on to Aswan.

ASWAN

Back on dry ground in Aswan the next day, check out the **Unfinished Obelisk** (p203) and head across to the island of **Philae** (p212) and its

delightful temple complex. Later, take to the water once again – th
time in a **felucca** (p206) sailing between the islands for a magical exp
rience of the river at Aswan. On day 12, take the public ferry across t
fascinating **Elephantine Island** (p203) and its **Aswan Museum**. Bac
in town, admire Nubian art and learn about Nubian culture throug
the exhibits at the **Nubia museum** (p203), and afterwards buy Nubia
handicrafts or other keepsakes at Aswan's **souq** (p208).

❻ ABU SIMBEL

For the last leg of your Nile journey, travel by taxi to **Abu Simb**
(p215) and check in to the **Eskaleh hotel** (p216). Enjoy a home-cooke
three-course lunch here – great fuel for a wander around the **Grea
Temple of Ramses II** (p215) after the crowds have returned to Aswa
later in the day. On the final day, relax in the town, or perhaps take
last look at the temple and its colossal Ramses statues.

CHRIS MEL

Great Temple of Ramses II, Abu Simbel (p215)

EGYPT'S BEST...

⬊ SCENIC JOURNEYS

- **Sailing the Nile** (p186) Float down the river of history.
- **Walking through Islamic Cairo** (p73) Cross the old city while sightseeing, shopping and sipping tea.
- **Driving the Western Desert** (p310) Slide gently down sand dunes and feel the exhilaration of arriving at a green oasis.
- **Diving the Red Sea** (p310) Discover some of the world's most amazing coral reefs and colourful marine life.
- **Trekking in Sinai** (p246) Join a Bedouin guide for a walk among the barren mountain tops and lush river valleys.

⬊ DESERT EXPERIENCES

- **Siwa Oasis** (p299) Hang out in sleepy Siwa Town and cycle around the palm groves.

- **Al-Qasr in Dakhla** (p293) Go back in time at the old settlement of Al-Qasr.
- **Cave of the Swimmers** (p310) Take a long desert trip to one of Egypt's most isolated destinations.
- **White Desert** (p282) Marvel at the bizarre rock formations sculpted by the wind.
- **Overnight stay** (p296) Gaze at the stars and sleep the sleep of the innocent in Bahariya Oasis.

⬊ NATURAL LIFE

- **Birdwatching** (p308) Get up early for some twitching in Aswan.
- **Lake Qarun** (p156) Row your boat on this salty lake.
- **Ras Mohammed National Park** (p257) Revel in some of the world's most colourful marine life.
- **Oases palm groves** (p279) Study the wonderful ecosystem of the Western Desert oases.

RICHARD I'AN

Cruisers line the banks of the Nile, Aswan (p201)

- **Great Sand Sea** (p305) Look for the rare gazelle in the dunes.

⬊ LESS-VISITED MUSEUMS

- **Mummification Museum** (p115) All you ever wanted to know about mummies at this Luxor museum.
- **Badr's Museum** (p295) Quirky collection illustrating local life in Farafra Oasis.
- **Ethnographic Museum** (p292) Lovely mudbrick house with objects from around Dakhla Oasis.
- **Coptic Museum** (p71) Find the connection between Pharaonic and Islamic Egypt in this wonderful Cairo museum.
- **Nubia Museum** (p203) Nubian art in all its splendour in Aswan.

⬊ SOUQS & SHOPS

- **Khan al-Khalili** (p73) Head to Cairo for the mother of all souqs.
- **Oum El Dounia** (p90) A great range of Egypt's best crafts and a bookshop, in Cairo.
- **Al-Khatoun** (p90) Quirky Egyptian crafts and local art in the capital.
- **Caravanserai** (p131) The friendliest crafts shop in Luxor, with fixed prices.
- **Aswan souq** (p208) The most exotic souq in Egypt.

⬊ LUNCHES

- **Citadel View** (p86) Egyptian menu and a view over Islamic Cairo.
- **Sofra** (p129) The best Egyptian food in Luxor.
- **Eskaleh** (p216) Fish caught from Lake Nasser and home-grown vegetables.
- **Adrére Amellal** (p304) Siwa Oasis delight serving delicious organic food in the garden.
- **Greek Club** (p236) Fresh fish and the best view in Alexandria.

⬊ HOTELS WITH CHARACTER

- **Old Winter Palace Hotel** (p128) Grand old colonial hotel with delightful gardens.
- **Al-Moudira** (p128) Stylish Eastern fantasy on the edge of the desert.
- **Adrére Amellal** (p304) Spartan, traditional-style chic set in its own oasis, plus blissful food.
- **Basata** (p267) Try this beach camp/ecolodge for ultimate relaxation.
- **Talisman Hotel** (p84) Downtown Cairo hotel with colourful rooms decorated in Egyptian style.
- **Al Tarfa Desert Sanctuary** (p293) A new level of style and luxury in the Western Desert.

THINGS YOU NEED TO KNOW

↘ AT A GLANCE

- **ATMs** Most international networks available; found in most tourist areas, harder in more off-beat places like the Western Desert
- **Bargaining** In most shops, markets and even hotels out of season
- **Credit cards** Visa and MasterCard widely accepted in midrange and upmarket hotels and larger shops
- **Currency** Egyptian pound
- **Language** Arabic; English is widely spoken in tourist areas
- **Tipping** For good service any-where (10%)
- **Visas** Available at the airport for European nationals and some other nationalities (see p357)

↘ ACCOMMODATION

- **Camping** There are many camps with simple beach huts in Dahab and further north along the Sinai coast.
- **Ecolodges** A number of new ecolodges have opened in Sinai, further south along the Red Sea coast and in the oases.
- **Hotels** (p344) There is a wide range of budget, midrange and top-end hotels in the main tourist areas, and smaller hotels in places further afield. Midrange hotels are usually of a decent standard but budget accommodation can be anything from flea-pit to character hotel.
- **Resorts** Find a large variety of resort hotels along the Red Sea coast and in Sinai.

IZZET KERIBA

Grand staircase in the Old Winter Palace Hotel, Luxor (p128)

ADVANCE PLANNING

- **Three months before** Start shopping around for a good deal on your flight, look into visa requirements and, if travelling in high season, book any domestic flights or sleeper trains.
- **One month before** Book your accommodation, a Nile cruise, diving classes or desert safaris.
- **One day before** Make reservations for restaurants in Cairo.

BE FOREWARNED

- **Check travel advisories** Check your government advisories for a current security report.
- **Mosques** Take off your shoes before entering a mosque.
- **Police convoys** Tourists still must travel in police convoy from Aswan to Abu Simbel.
- **Public holidays** Businesses and monuments close earlier during Ramadan and may open later.
- **Scams** Avoid hotel touts when arriving in bus or train stations.

COSTS

- **$40 to $50 per day** Simple but clean hotels, meals in Egyptian restaurants, public transport and admission fees; get more with a valid International Student Identity Card for admission discounts.
- **$50 to $100** Midrange hotels with private bathroom, good restaurants, taxis, admission fees and the occasional guided tour.

- **More than $100** Top-end hotels, top-notch dining, domestic flights and a few guided tours.

EMERGENCY NUMBERS

- **Ambulance** (☎ 123)
- **Fire** (☎ 180)
- **Police** (☎ 122)

GETTING AROUND

- **4WD** Essential for desert travel in the Eastern and Western Deserts.
- **Air** Domestic routes connect Cairo to the major cities and tourist centres.
- **Bicycle** Particularly ideal for touring around the West Bank in Luxor.
- **Boat** Dahabiyyas, feluccas and cruisers ply the Nile between Luxor and Aswan. There are cruisers on Lake Nasser.
- **Bus** Inexpensive buses connect Egypt's tourist hotspots, but need to be booked in advance.
- **Taxis** The best way through the chaos of Cairo, and to get around other cities.
- **Train** There is a good sleeper service between Cairo, Luxor and Aswan, and fast trains to Alexandria.

WHAT TO BRING

- **Cotton clothing** Bring light cotton clothing and a warmer layer for the evening.

- **Sunglasses, sunscreen and a hat** The sun is hot all year round.
- **A torch (flashlight)** To illuminate artwork in certain tombs.
- **Earplugs** For light sleepers. Cairo is a very noisy city, and dawn everywhere in Egypt is accompanied by the amplified voice of the muezzin calling the faithful to prayer.
- **Some toiletries** Contact-lens solution, roll-on mosquito repellent, tampons and contraceptives are available but with a limited choice of brands and often more expensive than at home.

↘ WHEN TO GO

- **Spring (March to May)** The temperatures are quite pleasant but desert winds (khamsin) and sudden rises in temperature are frequent.
- **Summer (June to August)** This is low season, as almost anywhere south of the Mediterranean is unbearably hot with temperatures soaring up to 40°C.
- **Autumn (September to November)** Perhaps the best time to travel, with sun in the day and cooler evenings.
- **Winter (December to February)** The tourist high season because temperatures in the south are pleasant. Cairo and the north can be quite cold.
- **Ramadan** During the Muslim month of fasting, many cafes and restaurants are closed during daylight hours, while sights and offices are open for reduced and sometimes erratic hours.

RICHARD I'ANSC

People in busy Khan al-Khalili, Islamic Cairo (p73)

GET INSPIRED

BOOKS

- **In an Antique Land** (Amitav Ghosh, 1992) An educational and entertaining account of the author's lengthy stay in a Delta village.
- **The Pharaoh's Shadow: Travels in Ancient and Modern Egypt** (Anthony Sattin, 2000) A wonderful search for 'survivals' of Pharaonic practices and traditions in the Egypt of today.
- **Letters from Egypt** (Lucie Duff Gordon) The journal of a solo woman traveller who lived in Luxor for from 1862 to 1869.
- **Cairo: The City Victorious** (Max Rodenbeck, 2000) An excellent history of Cairo.

FILMS

- **Death on the Nile** (1978) Based on an Agatha Christie novel.
- **The Spy Who Loved Me** (1977) The Pyramids, Islamic Cairo and Karnak provide glamorous backdrops for James Bond.
- **The Yacoubian Building** (2006) The onscreen adaptation of the best-selling Egyptian novel by Alaa al-Aswany.
- **The Night of Counting the Years** (Al-Momia; 1969) About the Gurnawi tomb raiders, this is one of the greatest Egyptian films ever made, directed by Shadi Abdel Salam and restored in 2009.

MUSIC

- **Umm Kolthum** Singer of love songs and *qasa'id* (long poems), and the most famous Arab singer of the 20th century. Her death in 1975 provoked nationwide grieving.
- **Ahmed Adawiyya** Politically subversive singer who dominated Egyptian popular culture during the 1970s.
- **Amr Diab** Egypt's best-known pop star, often described as the Arab world's Ricky Martin.
- **Mohammed Mounir** A cool Nubian musician who fuses traditional Arabic music with jazz.

WEBSITES

- **Al-Ahram newspaper** (http://weekly.ahram.org.eg) Online English-language newspaper.
- **Egyptian Tourist Authority** (www.egypt.travel) Egypt's official tourism site.
- **State Information Service** (www.sis.gov.eg) Tourist and cultural information.
- **Theban Mapping Project** (www.thebanmappingproject.com) Professor Kent Weeks' excellent website dedicated to the mapping of Thebes, and the Valley of the Kings.

CALENDAR

JAN FEB MAR APR

JANUARY

LUXOR MARATHON

In this popular annual marathon on the West Bank in Luxor, competitors start at the Temple of Hatshepsut and race around the main antiquities sites, including the Memnon Colossi, Tombs of the Nobles and Ramses III's temple at Medinat Habu. See www.egyptian marathon.com for dates.

CAIRO INTERNATIONAL BOOK FAIR

Held at the Cairo Exhibition Grounds over two weeks beginning in the last week of January, this is one of the major cultural events in the city. It draws massive crowds, but far more burgers, soft drinks and balloons are sold than books.

FEBRUARY–MARCH

ASCENSION OF RAMSES II   22 FEB

One of the two dates each year (see also October) when the first rays of the morning sun penetrate the entire length of the Great Temple of Ramses II at Abu Simbel (p215), illuminating the statues of the gods within the inner sanctum, to celebrate the ascension of the pharaoh on the throne.

INTERNATIONAL FISHING TOURNAMENT

This very popular fishing tournament is held in Hurghada, on the Red Sea coast, and attended by anglers from all over the world. See www.egaf.org.

MOULID AN-NABI

This is the birthday of the Prophet Mohammed and one of the major holidays of the year, during which the

Applauding participants in the Luxor Marathon (above)

CRIS BOURONCLE/AFP/GETTY IMAG

PLANNING YOUR TRIP

streets around the main mosques in towns and villages are a feast of lights and food. Special sweets are sold at stalls around the mosque. Holiday dates change each year according to the Islamic (Hejira) calendar – the *moulid* occurs mid-February in 2011 and 2012.

NITAQ FESTIVAL
This excellent festival organised by the main Downtown Cairo contemporary art galleries shows off this wonderful area, featuring two weeks of exhibitions, theatre, poetry and music at galleries, cafes and a variety of other venues. Held annually in February or March.

⇘ MAY

SOUTH SINAI CAMEL FESTIVAL
Camel races are an old sport for Bedouin and other nomads. In this race, which lasts the whole month, 250 camels take part with riders from 17 different Egyptian tribes. It may come as a surprise that the laid-back-looking camels can run up to 65 km/h (40 mph). See www.sinaiweekly.com/content/south-sinai-camel-festival.

⇘ JUNE

INTERNATIONAL FESTIVAL OF ORIENTAL DANCE
Held in Cairo, this is a festival of belly dancing in which famous Egyptian practitioners give showcase performances and workshops to international attendees. Check www.nilegroup.net for schedules.

CALENDAR

MARTIN KARIUS/ALAMY

Camel race in the desert

CALENDAR

| JAN | FEB | MAR | APR |

Evening in Islamic Cario's Khan al-Khalili (p73) during Ramadan

DBIMAGES/ALAM

JULY–AUGUST

RAMADAN

Observant Muslims fast for a whole month during daylight hours. People are tired, listless and hungry during the day, but they come back to life again when the sun goes down and they can feast and get festive. The Eid al-Fitr is a three-day feast that marks the end of Ramadan. Dates for the fast change each year according to the Islamic (Hejira) calendar so check in advance – Ramadan begins early August in 2010 and 2011, and late July in 2012

SEPTEMBER–OCTOBER

EXPERIMENTAL THEATRE FESTIVAL

Over 10 days this theatre festival attracts a broad selection of excellent interna-

tional theatre troupes. Check www.cdf -eg.org for this year's schedule.

PHARAOH'S RALLY

Similar to the famous Dakar Rally, this seven-stage, 3100km motor-vehicle (4WDs and bikes) race through the desert begins and ends at the Pyramids of Giza. Check www.rallyedespharaons .it for this year's dates.

BIRTH OF RAMSES   22 OCT

This is the second time in the year (see also February) when the sun's rays penetrate the inner sanctum of the Great Temple of Ramses II at Abu Simbel (p215).

NOVEMBER–DECEMBER

ARABIC MUSIC FESTIVAL

A 10-day festival of classical, traditional and orchestral Arabic music held at the

Cairo Opera House early in November. See www.cairoopera.org for schedule times.

EID AL-ADHA (EID AL-KEBIR; GREAT FEAST)

This festival celebrates the willingness of Abraham to sacrifice his son as an act of obedience to God. Those who can afford it buy a sheep to slaughter for the feast, which lasts for three days (many businesses reopen on the second day). Festival dates change according to the Islamic calendar – approximately mid-November 2010, early November 2011 and late October 2012.

100KM PHARAONIC RACE

This late-November race follows the route as described on a piece of rock found in 1977 by Egyptologist Ahmed Moussa. The story told of Pharaonic sol-diers running 100km from Saqqara to Fayoum Oasis, past a line of Pyramids. See www.egyptianmarathon.com for dates.

CAIRO INTERNATIONAL FILM FESTIVAL

This 14-day festival gives Cairenes the chance to watch a range of recent films from all over the world. The main attraction is that the films are all supposedly uncensored. Anything that sounds like it might contain scenes of exposed flesh sells out immediately. Held in November/December; check www.cairofilmfest.org for listings.

JTB PHOTO COMMUNICATIONS, INC/ALAMY

People gather to celebrate Eid al-Fitr, the end of Ramadan, Luxor

CAIRO

CAIRO

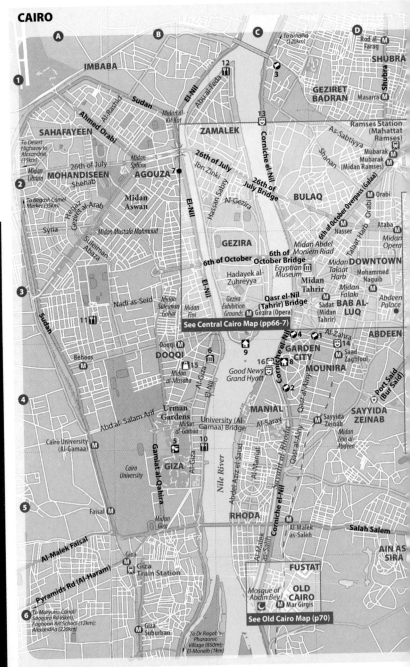

To Ismailia
(120km)

IMBABA

ZAMALEK

El-Nil
Al-Razzaq
Sudan
Abu-al-Feda

SAHAFAYEEN
Ahmed Orabi
Midan al-Kit Kat

To Desert
Highway to
Alexandria
(15km)

Midan
Lihtan
26th of July
Shehab
Midan
Sphinx
MOHANDISEEN
AGOUZA

To Birqash Camel
Market (35km)

Hegaz
Geziret al-Arab
Midan
Aswan

Syria
Suleiman
Abaza
Midan Mustafa Mahmoud

Nadi as-Seid
Midan
Suleiman
Gohar

GEZIRA

Ibn Zinki
26th of July

Corniche el-Nil

GEZIRET
BADRAN

SHUBRA

Rod al-
Farag

Masarra

Ramses Station
(Mahattat
Ramses)
As-Sabtiyya
Shanan

26th of July Bridge

BULAQ

6th of October Overpass (galaa)

Orabi
Nasser
Tabat Harb
Ataba

Midan Abdel
Moniem Riad
6th of October Bridge
Egyptian
Museum
Midan
Talaat
Harb
DOWNTOWN

Mohammed
Naguib

Hadayek al-
Zuhreyya
Midan
Falaki
BAB AL-
LUQ
Abdeen
Palace

Gezira
Exhibition
Grounds
Gezira (Opera)
Sadat
(Midan
Tahrir)

ABDEEN

See Central Cairo Map (pp66-7)

Al-Zahra

GARDEN
CITY
Saad
Zaghloul
MOUNIRA

Port Said
(Bur Said)

DOQQI
Midan
al-Missaha
Al-Giza
El-Nil

Good News
Grand Hyatt
MANIAL

Qasr al-Ainy
Qasr al-Ainy

SAYYIDA
ZEINAB

Sayyida
Zeinab
Midan
Zein al-
Abdeen

Urman
Gardens
University (Al-
Gamaa) Bridge
Al-Saray

Abd al- Salam Arif
Midan
al-Gamaa

Cairo University
(Al-Gamaa)

GIZA

Gamiat al-Qahira

Cairo
University

Qasr al-Ainy
Monorail Rhoda

Abdel Aziz el-Saud

Al Manial

Faisal

Midan
Giza

Nile River

RHODA

Al-Malek
as-Saleh

Salah Salem

AIN AS-
SIRA

Al-Malek Faisal

Giza
Train Station

FUSTAT

Pyramids Rd (Al-Haram)

Mosque of
Abdin Bey
OLD
CAIRO
Mar Girgis

To Maryuna Canal/
Saqqara Rd (6km);
Fagnoon Art School (12km);
Alexandria (220km)

Giza
Suburban

To Dr Ragab's
Pharaonic
Village (850m);
El-Moneib (1km)

See Old Cairo Map (p70)

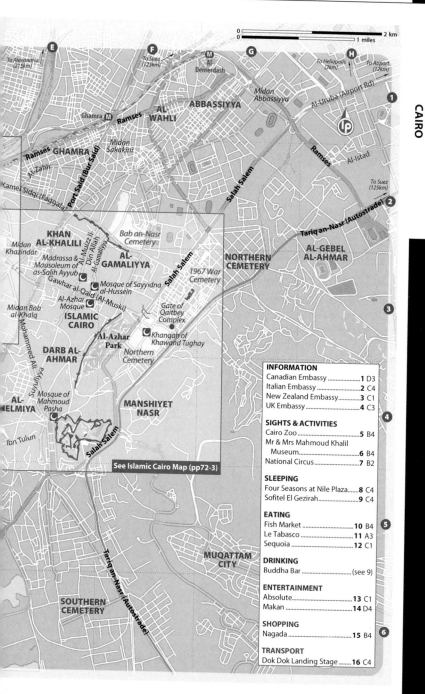

CAIRO

INFORMATION
Canadian Embassy 1 D3
Italian Embassy 2 C4
New Zealand Embassy.............3 C1
UK Embassy 4 C3

SIGHTS & ACTIVITIES
Cairo Zoo 5 B4
Mr & Mrs Mahmoud Khalil
  Museum..................................6 B4
National Circus.........................7 B2

SLEEPING
Four Seasons at Nile Plaza....8 C4
Sofitel El Gezirah.......................9 C4

EATING
Fish Market 10 B4
Le Tabasco 11 A3
Sequoia 12 C1

DRINKING
Buddha Bar ....(see 9)

ENTERTAINMENT
Absolute...................................13 C1
Makan 14 D4

SHOPPING
Nagada 15 B4

TRANSPORT
Dok Dok Landing Stage 16 C4

See Islamic Cairo Map (pp72-3)

CAIRO

HIGHLIGHTS

1 EGYPTIAN MUSEUM

BY SALIMA IKRAM, ARCHAEOLOGIST

This museum contains the world's premier collection of Egyptian antiquities. Its treasures include roomfuls of mummies – human and animal – delightful wooden models, sculptures, reliefs, and of course the fabled treasures from Tutankhamun's tomb. Regardless of how often I go, I notice something new each time. It is an endless source of entertainment and discovery.

HIGHLIGHTS

↘ SALIMA IKRAM'S DON'T MISS LIST

❶ PLANNING YOUR VISIT

If the museum is very crowded, go against the clock, skip the Old Kingdom galleries until later and start with the 1st floor to see the treasures of Tutankhamun. Good audio guides to the museum highlights are available at the entrance of the museum.

❷ ROYAL MUMMY ROOM

The extra admission charge here is steep but well worth it. The royals lie in glass showcases in a suitably tomblike environment and if you look closely you can see the wounds from which mar of these famous pharaohs died. Se I is perhaps the best-preserved roy mummy, but his son, Ramses II, show a fine profile and henna-dyed hair.

❸ MIDDLE KINGDOM MODELS

If you want to know how ancier Egyptians lived then there is no bette place to find out than in Rooms 32 an 27 on the 1st floor. These rooms a filled with wonderful models, foun in the tomb of Meketre, representin daily life about 4000 years ago, inclu

Clockwise from top: Popular mummy exhibit; Pharaoh Akhenaten in stone; Golden statues; The face of a Graeco-Roman mummy; Detail of an alabaster jar

g a model of Meketre's villa with fig
rden, a slaughter house, a loom, and
stable with cows.

GRAECO-ROMAN MUMMIES

oom 14 contains a sample of the ex-
uisite Fayoum Portraits. These must
e some of the earliest realistic por-
aits in history, and they look remarka-
y modern somehow. A dead person's
ce was painted on wood and then
aced over the Graeco-Roman mum-
y's embalmed face.

❺ ANIMAL MUMMIES

Children adore the animal mummies
in room 53, which I have curated. The
mummies here were either favourite
pet cats, dogs, monkeys and gazelles
or animals trained to hunt; or they are
the mummies of sacred animals believed to be inhabited by the spirit of
a god.

↘ THINGS YOU NEED TO KNOW

When to visit The museum is busy but lunchtime and late afternoons are a
ittle quieter Where to relax The cafeteria above the shop at the right of the
entrance The future The Grand Egyptian Museum near the Giza Pyramids is
due to open in 2012 See our author's review on p65

CAIRO

HIGHLIGHTS

2 SHARIA AL-MUIZZ LI-DIN ALLAH

BY ALAA ABDOU, JEWELLERY SHOP OWNER ON SHARIA AL-MUIZZ LI-DIN ALLAH

The tradition of jewellery making and working with precious stones is still very much alive in the alleys and the workshops off Sharia al-Muizz li-Din Allah, more than anywhere else in Egypt.

This street was the main street in medieval Cairo and has an incredible wealth of monuments.

HIGHLIGHTS

↘ ALAA ABDOU'S DON'T MISS LIST

❶ BAB AL-FUTUH

The best way to explore the old city is to start from **Bab al-Futuh** and walk to **Bab Zuweila** (p74), occasionally wandering off into the twisting alleyways. On weekdays it's buzzing with commerce, while on Sundays most shops are shut, so you can admire the monuments.

❷ MOSQUE OF AL-HAKIM

One of the oldest mosques in Cairo is the huge 11th-century **Mosque of Al-Hakim**, which was restored by Cairo's Ismaili community in the 1980s.

Towering above the city's mediev
walls are the oldest surviving mina
rets. The infamous Sultan al-Hakir
(985–1021) was notorious for patro
ling these streets, disguised and wit
his black slave, and when he found di
honest merchants they would be sodo
mised on the spot by his servant.

❸ BEIN AL-QASREEN

Bein al-Qasreen (Between the Tw
Palaces) is a reminder of the grea
Fatimid palaces that flanked th
street. The **Madrassa & Mausoleum**

Clockwise from top: Locals and travellers stroll Sharia al-Muizz li-Din Allah; Mosque of Al-Hakim; Streetside tomato seller; Coffee shop in the souq area of the Sharia al-Muizz li-Din Allah

CLOCKWISE FROM TOP: PHIL WEYMOUTH; ANDREW MCCONNELL/ROBERT HARDING TRAVEL/PHOTOLIBRARY; IAN CUMMING/AXIOM/PHOTOLIBRARY; PHIL WEYM(

arquq, the **Madrassa & Mausoleum** of **An-Nasir Mohammed** and the adrassa & Mausoleum of Qalaun ee p74) are some of the highlights.

① Bab al-Futuh
② Mosque of Al-Hakim
③ Bein al-Qasreen
④ Spice Market
⑤ Tarboosh (Fez) Maker

0 — 200 m
0 — 0.1 miles

Al-Benhawi · Bab an-Nasr Cemetery · Al-Galal · Al-Muizz li-Din Allah · Al-Gamaliyya · Bein al-Qasreen · Gawhar al-Qaid (Al-Muski) · **AL-GAMALIYYA** · **KHAN AL-KHALILI** · Mosque of al-Ashraf Barsbey · Mosque-Madrassa of Al-Ghouri · Al-Azhar · **Midan Al-Hussein** · Al-Muizz li-Din Allah · Bab Zuweila · **ISLAMIC CAIRO**

SPICE MARKET

n alley just south of the **Mosque of -Ashraf Barsbey** leads into a hidden pice market. Walk in and find fur-er to the right a small alley leading to the dusty place where spices are asted. Just follow your nose.

THE LAST FEZ MAKER

he area around the **Mosque-Madrassa** f **Al-Ghouri**, once the city's silk mar-et, is now taken over by shops selling ousehold goods and cheap clothing. n the right, 150m south of the mosque, Cairo's last **tarboosh (fez) maker**.

↘ THINGS YOU NEED TO KNOW

Best photo op From the minaret above Bab Zuweila **What to wear** Cover legs and shoulders and remove shoes at mosque entrances **Tips** Mosques are free to enter, but you should tip the caretaker **See our author's review of Islamic Cairo on p73**

HIGHLIGHTS

3

↘ THE PYRAMIDS

However much one has seen them in pictures, the **Pyramids of Giza** (p79) never fail to impress in reality, that is if you can handle the postcard sellers, tour buses and camel drivers. If you are fit and not claustrophobic, get one of the 300 tickets made available each day to enter the tomb chamber, otherwise walk around and take it all in. The restored **solar barques** (boats; p80) are also impressive.

4

↘ KHAN AL-KHALILI

The 14th-century warren of alleys that make up **Khan al-Khalili** (p73) was once the focus of Cairo's international trade. These days the main street is mostly occupied by shops selling tourist tat, but wander off it to find more authentic woven carpets, inlaid boxes, leatherware and gold. Break for lunch or a drink at **Mahfouz Coffee Shop** (p86).

5

↘ FISHAWI'S COFFEEHOUSE

The claim that it has never once closed since 1773 (except during Ramadan) may be exaggerated, but **Fishawi's** (p87) is still a great spot for people-watching. Busy day and night, it is the perfect place to stop for *shai* (tea) and *sheesha* (water pipe) and recover from an afternoon of shopping or a night on the town.

6

↘ MOSQUE-MADRASSA OF SULTAN HASSAN

The **Mosque-Madrassa of Sultan Hassan** (p77) is a wonder of Islamic architecture for its soaring height – all eyes go up to heaven. Barack Obama came here when he visited Cairo in 2009. Enjoy the perfect acoustics during the call to prayer in the adjacent mausoleum.

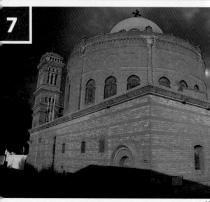

7

↘ COPTIC CAIRO

At the **Coptic Museum** (p71) admire the valuable collection of secular and religious artefacts, with early Christian reliefs suggesting that the Coptic cross developed from the Pharaonic *ankh* (key of life). Wander around the quiet lost-in-time alleys, where the Holy Family is believed to have once walked, and visit the old **churches** and **synagogue** (p71).

3 MASON FLORENCE; 4 FRANS LEMMENS; 5 IZZET KERIBAR; 6 IZZET KERIBAR; 7 SARA-JANE CLELAND

Camels at the Pyramids of Giza (p79); 4 Alleyway of Khan al-Khalili (p73); 5 Inside Fishawi's Coffeehouse (p87); Beautiful interior of the Mosque-Madrassa of Sultan Hassan (p77); 7 Church of St George, Coptic Cairo (p70)

CAIRO

THE BEST...

THE BEST...

↘ WAYS TO RELAX

- Take a **felucca** (p82) at sunset with some drinks and nibbles.
- Hang out in the **Marriott Garden Café** (p88).
- Take the **river bus** (p93) to **Coptic Cairo** (70) and wander around in this peaceful quarter.
- **Ride a horse** near the **Giza Pyramids** (p79).
- Sit down in the **courtyard of a mosque** (p75), always a great retreat from the hectic street scene.

↘ PLACES WITH A VIEW

- **Cairo Tower** (p79) Great view over the city.
- **Minarets of Mu'ayyad Mosque** Perched on top of **Bab Zuweila** (p74), they provide a view of the old city.
- **Citadel View** (p86) This restaurant in Al-Azhar Park has a magnificent view of the Cairo skyline.

- **Sofitel El Gezira** (85) Offering 360-degree views of the river.

↘ PLACES TO SMOKE A SHEESHA

- **Fishawi's Coffeehouse** (p87) For a smoke late afternoon or at dawn, as it never closes.
- **Mahfouz Coffee Shop** (p86) For a more upmarket smoke with a sandwich, and the cleanest toilets in the Khan.
- **Sequoia** (p86) For a hip outdoor *sheesha* with a vodka tonic rather than tea. There is a menu of tobacco flavours here.
- **Abou El Sid** (p86) For a funky restaurant experience with a *sheesha* to boot.

LEFT: PATRICK SYDER; RIGHT: IZZET KER

Left: Cairo Tower (p79); Right: In the courtyard of a mosque, Islamic Cairo (p73)

THINGS YOU NEED TO KNOW

↘ VITAL STATISTICS

- **Telephone code** (☎ 02)
- **Population** More than 20 million
- **Best time to go** October and November or March to May; December is very busy

↘ NEIGHBOURHOODS IN A NUTSHELL

- **Downtown** (p65) Busy area with Midan Tahrir and the Egyptian Museum at its centre.
- **Old Cairo** (p70) Ramshackle neighbourhoods with the small enclave of Coptic Cairo.
- **Islamic Cairo** (p73) The densely populated medieval heart of the city, including Khan al-Khalili.
- **Giza** (p79) On the west bank of the Nile, stretching 10km to the Pyramids.
- **Gezira** (p77) The northern half of Gezira Island is the affluent residential district Zamalek, with good shopping and restaurants; Cairo Tower and the Opera House are in the south.

↘ ADVANCE PLANNING

- **One month before** Book accommodation, particularly if travelling during European holiday periods.
- **One day before** Make reservations at the trendier restaurants.

↘ RESOURCES

- **Main tourist office** (Map pp66-7; ☎ 2391 3454; 5 Sharia Adly; ⏰ 8.30am-7pm)

- **Cairo Live** (www.cairolive.com) Online magazine with views on Cairo's cultural events, politics and general news.
- **Yallabina** (www.yallabina.com) Listings of the Big Mango's nightlife, with restaurant and bar reviews, concerts, events and films.
- **Croc** Free monthly entertainment listings flyer found at many restaurants and galleries.

↘ EMERGENCY NUMBERS

- **Ambulance** (☎ 123)
- **Fire service** (☎ 180)
- **Police** (☎ 122)
- **Tourist police** (☎ 2390 6028, emergency 126)

↘ GETTING AROUND

- **Taxi** The easiest way to get around and relatively cheap.
- **Walk** In Islamic Cairo and Coptic Cairo.
- **Taxi for the day** To get to the Pyramids and Saqqara.
- **Felucca** For a relaxing sail on the Nile River.

↘ BE FOREWARNED

- **Dress code** Cover arms and legs for walking around in Islamic Cairo and Coptic Cairo.
- **Baksheesh** Make sure you carry lots of small change as guards of sites rely on baksheesh (tips) to augment their salary.
- **Taxi rates** Fix a price before you ride, or take a yellow metered taxi.

DISCOVER CAIRO

This city has an energy, palpable even at three in the morning, like no other. It's the product of its 20 million inhabitants waging a battle against the desert and winning (mostly), of 20 million people simultaneously crushing the city's infrastructure under their collective weight and lifting the city's spirit up with their uncommon graciousness and humour.

One taxi ride can span millennia, from the resplendent mosques and mausoleums built at the pinnacle of the Islamic empire, to the 19th-century palaces and grand avenues (which earned the city the nickname 'Paris on the Nile'), to the brutal concrete blocks of the Nasser years – then all the way back to the days of the pharaohs, as the Pyramids of Giza hulk on the western edge of the city.

So embrace the apparent chaos, crack a joke and learn to look through the dirt to see the city's true colours. If you love Cairo, it will love you back.

CAIRO IN...

Two Days

Start day one with the exhibits at the **Egyptian Museum** (p65) then wander around Downtown, grabbing a cheap and delicious lunch at any of the local spots. In the afternoon, make your way to historic **Khan al-Khalili** (p73), and practise your haggling skills with the cheerful stall owners. Don't forget to have mint tea and a *sheesha* at **Fishawi's** (p87).

On day two hire a taxi for the day to take you to **Dahshur** (p153), **Memphis** (p146) and **Saqqara** (p147). In the afternoon visit the **Pyramids of Giza** (p79), then it's on to the **Citadel View** (p86) for dinner overlooking the medieval city.

Four Days

For days one and two, follow the Two Days itinerary.

Start day three by taking a taxi to the **Mosque of Ibn Tulun** (p77) and the **Gayer-Anderson Museum** (p77) in Islamic Cairo. Indulge in a bit of shopping at **Khan Misr Touloun** (p90) before going to Midan al-Hussein to visit historic **Al-Azhar Mosque** (p73) and the **Al-Ghouri complex** (p74). At sundown take an hour's **felucca ride** (p82).

On your last day take the river bus to explore **Coptic Cairo** (p70), then catch the metro back to Midan Tahrir. Walk over the Qasr el-Nil Bridge and stroll along the Nile to Zamalek for a late lunch and shopping. Stay in the area for a show at **El Sawy Culture Wheel** (p89) or head back down to Gezira for the **Cairo Opera House** (p88).

ISTORY

CAIRO

iro is not a Pharaonic city, though the esence of the Pyramids leads many believe otherwise. At the time the ramids were built, the capital of ancient ypt was Memphis, 20km southeast of e Giza Plateau.

The core foundations of the city of iro were laid in AD 969 by the Fatimid nasty. Construction began on the new pital, probably on purpose, when the anet Mars (Al-Qahir, 'the Victorious') was the ascendant; thus arose Al-Madina -Qahira, 'the city victorious', the pronun- ation of which Europeans corrupted to iro. The Fatimids were not to remain ng in power, but their city survived em and, under subsequent dynasties,

became a capital of great wealth, ruled by cruel and fickle sultans.

Cairo finally burst its walls, spreading west to the port of Bulaq and south onto Rhoda Island, while the desert to the east filled with grand funerary monuments. But at heart it remained a medieval city for 900 years, until the mid-19th cen- tury, when Ismail (1863–79), grandson of Mohammed Ali, decided it was time for change. For 10 years the former marsh became one vast building site as Ismail in- vited architects from Belgium, France and Italy to design and build a new European- style Cairo beside the old Islamic city.

Since the revolution of 1952 the popu- lation of Cairo has grown spectacularly, although at the expense of Ismail's vision. In the 1960s and 1970s, urban planners

HISTORY

CLOCKWISE FROM TOP LEFT: PATRICK SYDER; IZZET KERIBAR; EDDIE GERALD; RICHARD I'ANSON;

Clockwise from top left: Roof garden of the Gayer-Anderson Museum (p77); Inside Al-Azhar Mosque (p73); Church of St George, Coptic Cairo (p70); View of the Citadel, Islamic Cairo (p76);

concreted over the sparsely populated west bank of the Nile for desperately needed new suburbs. Luxe gated communities, sprawling housing blocks and full satellite cities, complete with malls and megastores, spring up from the desert every year: 6th of October City, New Cairo and others are the new Egyptian dream.

INFORMATION
BOOKSHOPS

American University in Cairo (AUC) Bookshop Downtown (Map pp66-7; ☎ 2797 5370; Sharia Mohammed Mahmoud; ⏱ 9am-6pm Sat-Thu); Zamalek (off Map pp66-7; ☎ 2739 7045; 16 Sharia Mohammed Thakeb; ⏱ 10am-6pm Sat-Thu, 1-6pm Fri) The best English-language bookshop in Egypt, with stacks of material on the politics, sociology and history of Cairo, Egypt and the Middle East.

Diwan (Map pp66-7; ☎ 2736 2578; 159 Sharia 26th of July, Zamalek; ⏱ 9am-11.30pm) Fabulous: English, French and German titles, from novels to travel guides to coffee-table books.

DANGERS & ANNOYANCES

In February 2009, Cairo was the scene of three separate acts of terrorism that were specifically aimed at tourists. Although none of the attacks were deemed sophisticated by Egyptian security officials, a 17-year-old French girl was brutally killed when a bomb exploded in Khan al-Khalili market. The second incident involved the stabbing of an American teacher in the face, while the third was a failed fire-bombing of a passing train on the Cairo metro. Overall security is currently good in the area but it's advisable to be aware of the history, and to check travel advisories before your trip.

Khan al-Khalili (p73)

Theft is not a big problem, but it pays be safe. Pickpockets are rare, but do som times operate in crowded spots such Khan al-Khalili, the Birqash camel marke the metro and buses. If anything does g stolen go straight to the tourist police.

Scams in Cairo are so numerous th there's no way to list them all. The wor scams afflicting Cairo are associated wit tours. Rather than making arrangemen in Cairo, you are almost always better o booking tours in the place you'll be ta ing them. Shopping scams are nearly a prevalent, but less nefarious. When you' in Downtown or Islamic Cairo, locals ma start walking next to you, offering he or chatting. These are usually touts wh want to direct you into shops where the earn a commission.

IGHTS
ENTRAL CAIRO
GYPTIAN MUSEUM

he **Egyptian Museum** (Map p65; ☎ 579 48; www.egyptianmuseum.gov.eg; Midan Tahrir, wntown; adult/student E£60/30; ⊗ 9am-6.45pm) one of the world's most important museums of ancient history and one of its eat spectacles. Here, the treasures of tankhamun lie alongside the grave ods, mummies, jewellery, eating bowls d toys of Egyptians whose names are st to history.

The **ground floor** of the museum is laid t roughly chronologically in a clockwise shion starting at the entrance hall.

The central atrium (Room 43) is filled ith a miscellany of large and small yptological finds. In the central cabinet ⊃ 8, the double-sided **Narmer Palette** is great significance. Dating from around 3100 BC it depicts Pharaoh Narmer (also known as Menes) wearing the crown of Upper Egypt on one side of the palette, and the crown of Lower Egypt on the other, suggesting the first union of Upper and Lower Egypt under one ruler. Egyptologists take this as the birth of ancient Egyptian civilisation and his reign as the first of the 1st dynasty.

Look for the three exquisite **black schist triads** (Room 47) that depict the pharaoh Menkaure (Mycerinus), builder of the smallest of the three Pyramids of Giza, flanked either side by a female figure. In the centre of Room 42 is one of the museum's masterpieces, a smooth, black, dioritic, larger-than-life-size **statue of Khafre (Chephren)**. The builder of the second pyramid at Giza sits on a lion throne, and is protected by the wings of the falcon god Horus. Slightly to the left

CAIRO

SIGHTS

EGYPTIAN MUSEUM

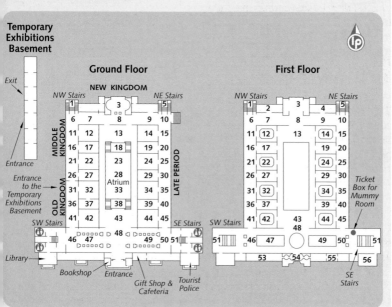

CAIRO

CENTRAL CAIRO

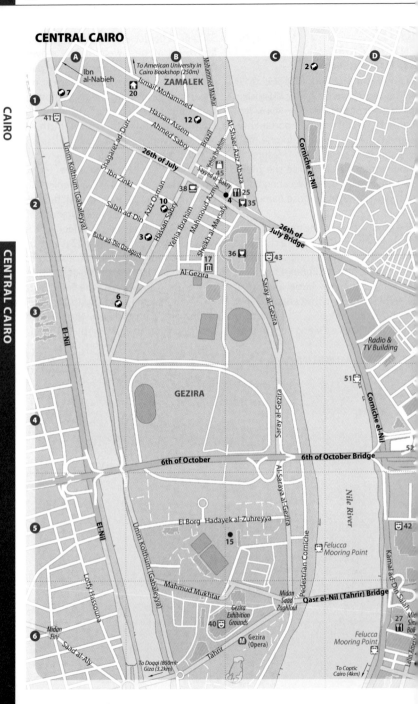

CENTRAL CAIRO

To American University in
Cairo Bookshop (250m)

ZAMALEK

Ibn
al-Nabieh

7

41

20

Ismail Mohammed

Hassan Assem

12

Ahmed Sabry

26th of July

Shagaret ad-Durr

Ibn Zinki

Umm Kolthum (Gabaleyya)

Salah ad-Din

Aziz Osman

Hassan Sabry

10

38

3

Baha ad-Din Qaragosh

Yehia Ibrahim

Mahmoud Azmy

Sheikh al-Marsafy

Sayyed al-Bakry

45

4

25

35

36

43

17

Al-Gezira

6

Saray al-Gezira

Mohammed Mazhar

Al-Shaer Aziz Abaza

Brazil

Corniche el-Nil

26th of
July Bridge

2

Radio &
TV Building

51

GEZIRA

EL-NIL

Saray al-Gezira

Umm Kolthum (Gabaleyya)

6th of October

6th of October Bridge

Al-Saraya al-Gezira

Nile River

Corniche el-Nil

52

El Borg

Hadayek al-Zuhreyya

15

Pedestrian Corniche

Felucca
Mooring Point

42

Lotfy Hassouna

Mahmud Mukhtar

Midan
Saad
Zaghloul

Qasr el-Nil (Tahrir) Bridge

Kamal ad-Din Salah

27

Nile
Sim
Boli

Midan
Finn

Saad al-Aly

Gezira
Exhibition
Grounds

40

Gezira
(Opera)

Tahrir

Felucca
Mooring Point

To Doqqi (850m);
Giza (3.2km)

To Coptic
Cairo (4km)

Latin America

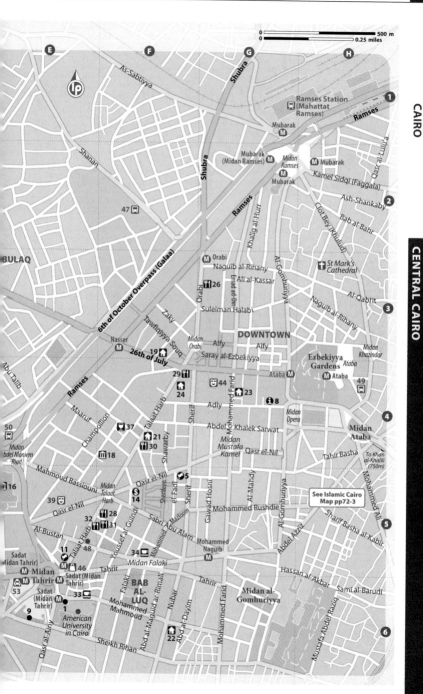

CAIRO

CENTRAL CAIRO

CAIRO

SIGHTS

in front of Khafre, the core of the stunning **wooden statue of Ka-Aper** (No 40) was carved out of a single piece of sycamore (the arms were ancient additions, the legs modern restorations). His eyes are amazingly lifelike, set in copper lids with whites of opaque quartz and corneas of rock crystal, drilled and filled with black paste to form the pupils. Nearby sits the **Seated Scribe** (No 44), a wonderful painted limestone figure, hand poised as if waiting to take dictation, his inlaid eyes set in an asymmetrical face giving him a very vivid appearance.

Room 32 is dominated by the beautiful **statues of Rahotep and Nofret** (No 27), a noble couple from the reign of Sneferu, builder of the Bent and the Red Pyramids at Dahshur. In a cabinet off to the left, a limestone group shows **Seneb**, 'chief of the royal wardrobe', and his family (No 39). Seneb is notable for being a dwarf: he sits cross-legged, his two children strategically placed where his legs would otherwise have been. Room 37, entered via Room 32, contains furniture from the Giza Plateau **tomb of Queen Hetepheres**, wife

of Sneferu and mother of Khufu (Cheops including a carrying chair, bed, bed can opy and a jewellery box.

Akhenaten (1352–1336 BC), the 'hereti pharaoh', ushered in a period of great a tistic freedom, as a glance around Roor 3 will show. Perhaps most striking of a is the **unfinished head of Nefertiti** (N 161), wife of Akhenaten. Worked in brow quartzite, it's an incredibly delicate an sensitive portrait and shows the quee to have been extremely beautiful – unlik some of the relief figures of her elsewher in the room, in which she appears wit exactly the same strange features as he husband.

Exhibits on the **1st floor** are groupe thematically and can be viewed in an order, but assuming that you've com up the southeast stairs, we'll enter th **Tutankhamun Galleries** at Room 4. The tomb and treasures of this pharaoh who ruled for only nine years during th 14th century BC (1336–1327 BC), wer discovered in 1922 by English archaeolo gist Howard Carter. The **pharaoh's lio throne** (Room 35) is one of the museum

CAIRO

SIGHTS

Mr & Mrs Mahmoud Khalil Museum (below)

PCL/ALAMY

⬎ IF YOU LIKE...

If you like the dusty chaos of the **Egyptian Museum** (p65) you may also like some of the city's smaller museums:

- **Museum of Islamic Ceramics** (Map pp66-7; ☎ 2737 3298; 1 Sharia Sheikh al-Marsafy, Zamalek; adult/student E£25/15; ⊗ 10am-1.30pm & 5.30-9pm Sat-Thu) A beautiful museum in a gorgeous 1924 villa, where the intricately carved walls are as fascinating as the colourful plates, tiles and even 11th-century hand grenades on display.

- **Museo Mevlevi** (Map pp72-3; Sharia Suyufiyya; admission free; ⊗ 8am-4pm) Centres on a meticulously restored Ottoman-era theatre for whirling dervishes. Downstairs, see the remains of the madrassa that forms the building's foundation; the thorough notes are a rare model of thoughtful excavation.

- **Umm Kolthum Museum** (Map p70; ☎ 2363 1467; Sharia al-Malek as-Salih, Rhoda; adult/student E£6/3; ⊗ 10am-5pm) Set in a peaceful Nileside garden, part of the Monastirli Palace, this museum is dedicated to the most famous Arab diva, Umm Kolthoum, and includes her famous sunglasses, a room with her music, and a film about her life.

- **Museum of Islamic Art** (Map pp72-3; ☎ 2390 1520; Sharia Bur Said) One of the world's finest collections of Islamic applied art: a trove of manuscripts, woodwork, textiles and astronomy instruments. Unfortunately it has been shut for restoration for several years, so check its current status before coming.

- **Mr & Mrs Mahmoud Khalil Museum** (Map pp52-3; ☎ 3338 9720; 1 Sharia Kafour, Doqqi; admission with ID card or passport only, adult/student E£25/12; ⊗ 10am-5pm Tue-Sun, 10am-3pm holidays) The 1940s politician Mohammed Mahmoud Khalil amassed one of the Middle East's finest collections of 19th- and 20th-century European work, including sculptures by Rodin and paintings by the likes of Delacroix, Gauguin, Toulouse-Lautrec, Picasso, Manet, Monet and Pissarro.

highlights. Covered with sheet gold and inlaid with lapis, cornelian and other semi-precious stones, the wooden throne is supported by lion legs.

Room 3 is the room everybody wants to see as it contains the pharaoh's golden sarcophagus and jewels; at peak times, prepare to queue. Tutankhamun's astonishing **death mask** has become an Egyptian icon. Made of solid gold and weighing 11kg, the mask covered the head of the mummy, where it lay inside a series of three sarcophagi. The mask is an idealised portrait of the young pharaoh; the eyes are fashioned from obsidian and quartz, while the outlines of the eyes and the eyebrows are delineated with lapis lazuli. No less wondrous are the two **golden sarcophagi**.

The **Royal Mummy Room** (adult/student E£100/50, ticket office beside stairs off room 50;

☾ 9am-6.20pm) houses the remains of som of Egypt's most illustrious pharaohs an queens from the 17th to 21st dynasties 1650 to 945 BC.

OLD CAIRO

Broadly speaking, Old Cairo incorporate the area south of Garden City down t the quarter known to foreigners as Copti Cairo. Most visitors head straight to th latter.

COPTIC CAIRO

Coptic Cairo is the heartland of Egypt's in digenous Christian community, a haven c tranquillity and peace that reveals layer of history. In this traditional part of Cair appropriate dress is essential. Visitor of either sex wearing shorts or showin their shoulders will not be allowed int churches or mosques. The easiest way c

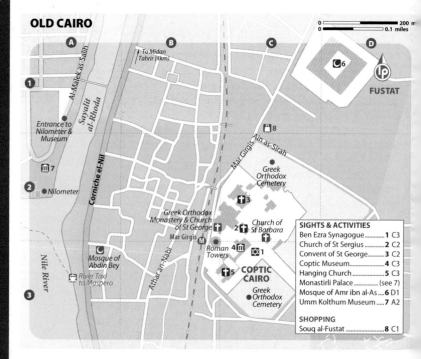

OLD CAIRO

0 — 200 m
0 — 0.1 miles

FUSTAT

Entrance to Nilometer & Museum

To Midan Tahrir (4km)

Al-Malek as-Salih

Sayalit al-Rhoda

Corniche el-Nil

Nilometer

Nile River

Mosque of Abdin Bey

River Taxi to Maspero

Athal an-Nabi

Greek Orthodox Monastery & Church of St George

Mar Girgis

Roman Towers

COPTIC CAIRO

Greek Orthodox Cemetery

Mar Girgis

Ain as-Sirah

Greek Orthodox Cemetery

Church of St Barbara

SIGHTS & ACTIVITIES		
Ben Ezra Synagogue	**1**	C3
Church of St Sergius	**2**	C2
Convent of St George	**3**	C2
Coptic Museum	**4**	C3
Hanging Church	**5**	C3
Monastirli Palace	(see 7)	
Mosque of Amr ibn al-As	**6**	D1
Umm Kolthum Museum	**7**	A2

SHOPPING		
Souq al-Fustat	**8**	C1

CAIRO

FACTORIA SINGULAR/AGE FOTOSTOCK/PHOTOLIBRARY

Children in the Hanging Church (below), Coptic Cairo

SIGHTS

etting here is by metro: trains run every
w minutes, and Mar Girgis station is right
utside the Coptic Cairo compound.

The **Coptic Museum** (Map p70; ☎ 2363
42; www.copticmuseum.gov.eg; Sharia Mar Girgis;
dult/student E£50/25; ☻ 9am-4pm), founded
1908, houses Coptic art from Graeco-
oman times to the Islamic era in a collec-
on drawn from all over Egypt. Reopened
fter thorough renovation in 2006, it is a
eautiful place, as much for the elaborate
woodcarving in all the galleries as for the
reasures they contain.

Just south of the museum on Sharia
Mar Girgis (the main road parallel with
he metro), a stone facade inscribed with
Coptic and Arabic marks the entrance to
he **Hanging Church** (Al-Kineesa al-Mu'allaqa;
Map p70; Sharia Mar Girgis; ☻ Coptic Mass 8-11am
ri, 9-11am Sun). Still in use for Mass and
y parishioners who come to pray over
collection of saints' relics and an icon
f Mary, this 9th-century (some say 7th-
entury) structure is called the Hanging or
uspended Church as it is built on top of
he Water Gate of Roman Babylon.

To get to the **Church of St Sergius** (Abu
Serga; Map p70; ☻ 8am-4pm), walk down the
lane that the Convent of St George is on,
following it around to the right. This is
the oldest church inside the walls, with
3rd- and 4th-century pillars. It is said to be
built over a cave where Joseph, Mary and
the infant Jesus sheltered after fleeing to
Egypt to escape persecution from King
Herod of Judea, who had embarked upon
a 'massacre of the first born'.

The 9th-century **Ben Ezra Synagogue**
(Map p70; admission free, donations welcome)
occupies the shell of a 4th-century
Christian church. In the 12th century the
synagogue was restored by Abraham Ben
Ezra, rabbi of Jerusalem – hence its name.
The adjacent spring is supposed to mark
the place where the pharaoh's daughter
found Moses in the reeds, and where Mary
drew water to wash Jesus.

Sharia Mar Girgis leads north past
Souq al-Fustat, a covered market with
quality crafts shops and a pricey cafe, to
the **Mosque of Amr ibn al-As** (Map p70;
Sharia Sidi Hassan al-Anwar, Old Cairo), the first

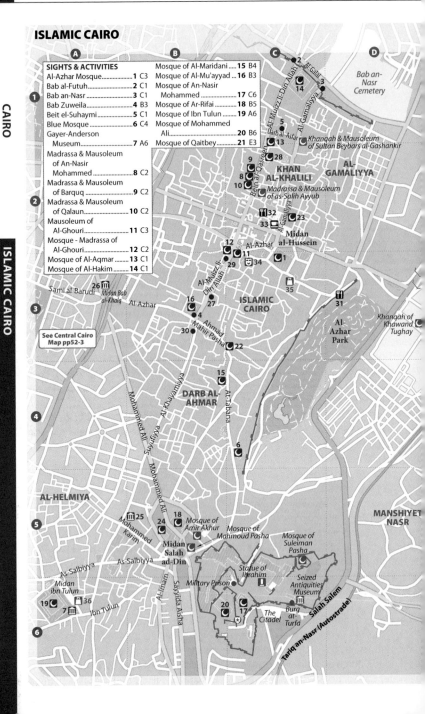

ISLAMIC CAIRO

SIGHTS & ACTIVITIES

Al-Azhar Mosque	1	C3
Bab al-Futuh	2	C1
Bab an-Nasr	3	C1
Bab Zuweila	4	B3
Beit el-Suhaymi	5	C1
Blue Mosque	6	C4
Gayer-Anderson Museum	7	A6
Madrassa & Mausoleum of An-Nasir Mohammed	8	C2
Madrassa & Mausoleum of Barquq	9	C2
Madrassa & Mausoleum of Qalaun	10	C2
Mausoleum of Al-Ghouri	11	C3
Mosque - Madrassa of Al-Ghouri	12	C2
Mosque of Al-Aqmar	13	C1
Mosque of Al-Hakim	14	C1
Mosque of Al-Maridani	15	B4
Mosque of Al-Mu'ayyad	16	B3
Mosque of An-Nasir Mohammed	17	C6
Mosque of Ar-Rifai	18	B5
Mosque of Ibn Tulun	19	A6
Mosque of Mohammed Ali	20	B6
Mosque of Qaitbey	21	E3

CAIRO

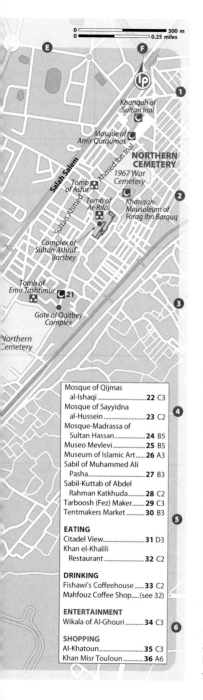

0 / 500 m
0 / 0.25 miles

Khanqah of Sultan Inal

Mosque of Amir Qurqumas

NORTHERN CEMETERY

Salah Salem

Ahmed Ibn Ihal

Tomb of Asfur

1967 War Cemetery

Sultan Ahmed

Tomb of Ar-Rifai

Khanqah-Mausoleum of Farag Ibn Barquq

Complex of Sultan Ashraf Barsbey

Tomb of Emir Tashtimur 21

Gate of Qaitbey Complex

Northern Cemetery

mosque built in Egypt, constructed in AD 642 by the general who conquered Egypt for Islam. The oldest section is to the right of the sanctuary; the rest of the mosque is a forest of some 200 different columns, the majority taken from ancient sites.

ISLAMIC CAIRO

Appropriate dress in this traditional part of Cairo is not just polite but necessary if you want to enter mosques, where legs and shoulders must be covered. Mosques are usually closed to visitors during prayer times.

SIGHTS

AL-AZHAR & KHAN AL-KHALILI

Founded in AD 970 as the centrepiece of the newly created Fatimid city, **Al-Azhar Mosque** (Gami' al-Azhar; Map pp72–3; Sharia al-Azhar; 24hr) is one of Cairo's earliest mosques and its sheikh is the highest theological authority for Egyptian Muslims. A madrassa was established in AD 988, growing into a university that is the world's second-oldest educational institution (after the University of al-Kairaouine in Fez, Morocco). At one time the university was one of the world's pre-eminent centres of learning, drawing scholars from Europe and across the Arab world, and it is still the most prestigious place to study Sunni theology.

One of the most sacred Islamic sites in Egypt, the **Mosque of Sayyidna al-Hussein** (Map pp72–3; Midan al-Hussein; closed to non-Muslims) is the reputed burial place of the head of Hussein, the grandson of the Prophet, whose death in Karbala, Iraq, cemented the rift between the Sunni and Shia branches of Islam.

Jaded travellers often dismiss **Khan al-Khalili** (Map pp72–3) as a tourist trap, and there's no ignoring the flotillas of tour buses parked on the square, and all the touts and tat that come with them. Open from early morning to sundown (except Friday morning and Sunday), the agglomeration of shops – many arranged around small courtyards, in the original medieval 'minimal' layout – stock everything from soap powder to semiprecious stones, not to mention stuffed-toy camels and alabaster pyramids. There are few specific things to see in the khan but **Fishawi's Coffeehouse** (Map pp72-3; 24hr except during Ramadan) in an alley one block west of Midan al-Hussein, is an absolute must (see p87).

FROM BAB AL-FUTUH TO BAB ZUWEILA

The square-towered **Bab an-Nasr** (Gate of Victory; Map pp72-3) and the rounded **Bab al-Futuh** (Gate of Conquests; Map pp72-3) were built in 1087 as the two main northern entrances to the walled Fatimid city of Al-Qahira. **Sharia al-Muizz li-Din Allah** (Sharia al-Muizz; Map pp72–3) which takes its name from the Fatimid caliph who conquered Cairo in AD 969, is the former grand thoroughfare of medieval Cairo, once chockablock with storytellers, entertainers and food stalls. See also p56.

About 250m south of Bab al-Futuh, the narrow lane **Darb al-Asfar** (Map pp72–3) runs east. The first few buildings you pass are part of **Beit el-Suhaymi** (Map pp72-3; Darb al-Asfar; admission E£25; 9am-5pm), a family mansion and caravanserai (merchants' inn) built in the 17th and 18th centuries.

Further south along the street, where the road splits, the **Sabil-Kuttab of Abdel Rahman Katkhuda** (Map pp72-3) is one of the iconic structures of Islamic Cairo, depicted in scores of paintings and lithographs. This one was built in 1744 by an emir notorious for his debauchery.

Today three great abutting Mamlu complexes line the west of the stree providing one of Cairo's most impre sive assemblies of minarets, domes an striped stone facades. First comes th **Madrassa & Mausoleum of Barquq** (Ma pp72–3). Enter through the bold blac and-white marble portal into a vaulte passageway. To the right, the inner cou has a colourful ceiling supported by fo porphyry Pharaonic columns. Barquq neighbour to the south is the **Madrass & Mausoleum of An-Nasir Mohamme** (Map pp72–3), built in 1304 by a Mamlu sultan both despotic and exceedingly a complished. Built in just 13 months, th 1279 **Madrassa & Mausoleum of Qalau** (Map pp72–3) is both the earliest and th most splendid of the three buildings. Th mausoleum, on the right, is a particular intricate assemblage of inlaid stone an stucco, patterned with stars and floral mo tifs and lit by stained-glass windows.

On the south side of Sharia al-Azha opposite the khan, the grand **Mosque Madrassa of Al-Ghouri** (Map pp72–3 with its red-chequered minaret, and th elegant **Mausoleum of Al-Ghouri** (Ma pp72–3) together form an exquisite mo ument to the end of the Mamluk era.

Further down on the left is the delica Ottoman-style **Sabil of Muhammed A Pasha** (Map pp72–3). Across the stree the red-and-white-striped **Mosque of A Mu'ayyad** (Map pp72–3), built on the si where its patron Mamluk sultan had earli been imprisoned, displays a particular grand entrance portal, dripping with st lactite vaulting. Built at the same time the northern gates (10th century), beau ful **Bab Zuweila** (Map pp72-3; adult/stude E£20/10; 8.30am-5pm) is the only remai ing southern gate of medieval Al-Qahir Visitors may climb the ramparts, whe some intriguing exhibits about the gate

CAIRO

Mosque of Al-Aqmar (below), Islamic Cairo

NICO TONDINI/ROBERT HARDING TRAVEL/PHOTOLIBRARY

SIGHTS

⬊ IF YOU LIKE...

If you like the **Mosque-Madrassa of Al-Ghouri** (p74) and the **Mosque-Madrassa of Sultan Hassan** (p77), you may want to explore these less visited mosques:

- **Mosque of Qijmas al-Ishaqi** (Map pp72-3; Darb al-Ahmar, Islamic Cairo) This mosque was built in the Mamluk period, around 1481. Don't be deceived by the plain exterior: inside are beautiful stained-glass windows, inlaid marble floors and stucco walls.

- **Mosque of Al-Maridani** (Map pp72-3; Darb al-Ahmar, Islamic Cairo) This 14th-century Mamluk mosque incorporates architectural elements from several periods: eight granite columns were taken from a Pharaonic monument; the arches contain Roman, Christian and Islamic designs; and the Ottomans added a fountain and wooden housing.

- **Blue Mosque** (Mosque of Aqsunqur; Map pp72-3; Darb al-Ahmar, Islamic Cairo) Built in 1347, this mosque gets its name from the combination of blue-grey marble on the exterior and the flowery Ottoman tiling.

- **Mosque of Qaitbey** (Map pp72-3; Northern Cemetery) Sultan Qaitbey's mosque in the Northern Cemetery, completed in 1474, is widely agreed to mark the pinnacle of Islamic building in Cairo. The true glory is the exterior of the dome, the intricacy and delicacy of which were never surpassed in Egypt.

- **Mosque of Al-Aqmar** (Map pp72-3; Sharia al-Muizz li-Din Allah) Built in 1125 by one of the last Fatimid caliphs, it is the oldest stone-facaded mosque in Egypt. Several features appear here that became part of the mosque builders' essential vocabulary, including *muqarnas* (stalactite) vaulting and the ribbing in the hooded arch. North of Khan al-Khalili.

CAIRO

SARA-JANE CLE

Mosque of Mohammed Ali, the Citadel

SIGHTS

↘ THE CITADEL

Sprawling over a limestone spur on the eastern edge of the city, the Citadel (Al-Qala'a) was home to Egypt's rulers for 700 years. Saladin began building the Citadel in 1176 to fortify the city against the Crusaders. Following their overthrow of Saladin's Ayyubid dynasty, the Mamluks enlarged the complex, adding sumptuous palaces and harems. This didn't stop Mohammed Ali – who rose to power when the French left – from demolishing them.

The fortress is dominated by the **Mosque of Mohammed Ali**. Modelled along classic Turkish lines, with domes upon domes, it took 18 years to build (1830–48), and its interior is all twinkling chandeliers and luridly striped stone. Note the glitzy clock in the central courtyard, a gift from King Louis-Philippe of France in thanks for the Pharaonic obelisk that adorns the Place de la Concorde in Paris. It was damaged on delivery and has yet to be repaired. Dwarfed by Mohammed Ali's mosque, the 1318 **Mosque of An-Nasir Mohammed** is the Citadel's sole surviving Mamluk structure. The interior is a little sparse because the Ottoman sultan Selim I had it stripped of its marble, but the old wood ceiling and *muqarnas* show up nicely, and the twisted finials of the minarets are interesting for their covering of glazed tiles, something rarely seen in Egypt. Facing the entrance of the Mosque of An-Nasir Mohammed, a mock-Gothic gateway leads to a grand terrace, with superb views.

To walk from Midan Ataba to the Citadel's entrance (about 4km), go straight down Sharia al-Qala'a and its continuation, Sharia Mohammed Ali, to Midan Salah ad-Din, then walk to Sharia Salah Salem via Sharia Sayyida Aisha. A taxi will cost E£12.

Things you need to know Map pp72-3; ☎ 2512 1735; Sharia Salah Salem; adult/student E£50/25; ☼ 8am-5pm Oct-May, 8am-6pm Jun-Sep, mosques closed during Fri prayers

istory are in place. The two minarets atop he gate, also open to visitors, offer one of he best available views of the area.

The 'Street of the Tentmakers', **Sharia l-Khayamiyya**, takes its name from the rtisans who produce the bright fabrics sed for the ceremonial tents at funerals, akes, weddings and feasts. Most artisans re found directly after Bab Zuweila, in he covered **tentmakers market** (Map p72–3).

HE CITADEL TO IBN TULUN

lassive yet elegant, the great structure of he **Mosque-Madrassa of Sultan Hassan** Map p72-3; Midan Salah ad-Din; admission E£25; 8am-5pm Oct-May, 8am-6pm Jun-Sep) is re- arded as the finest piece of early-Mamluk rchitecture in Cairo. It was built between 356 and 1363 by the troubled Sultan assan, a grandson of Sultan Qalaun; he ook the throne at the age of 13, was de- osed and reinstated no less than three mes, then assassinated shortly before he mosque was completed. Beyond the triking, recessed entrance, a dark pas- age leads into a square courtyard whose aring walls are punctured by four *iwan*s vaulted halls), one dedicated to teach- g each of the four main schools of Sunni lam. To the right, a bronze door leads to he sultan's mausoleum.

Opposite the grand mosque, the **Mosque of Ar-Rifai** (Map pp72-3; E£20) is onstructed on a similarly grand scale, egun in 1869 and not finished until 912. Members of modern Egypt's royal mily, including Khedive Ismail and King arouk, are buried inside, as is the last hah of Iran. Their tombs lie to the left of he entrance.

Walking west along busy Sharia as- albiyya eventually leads to the **Mosque f Ibn Tulun** (Map pp72-3; 8am-6pm), easily dentified by its high walls topped with neat crenulations that resemble a string of paper dolls. Built between AD 876 and 879 by Ibn Tulun, who was sent to rule the outpost of Al-Fustat in the 9th century by the Abbasid caliph of Baghdad, it is the city's oldest intact, functioning Islamic monument. Ibn Tulun drew inspiration from his homeland, particularly the an- cient Mosque of Samarra (Iraq), on which the spiral minaret is modelled. He also added some innovations of his own: ac- cording to architectural historians, this is the first structure to use the pointed arch, a good 200 years before the European Gothic arch.

Through a gateway to the south of the main entrance of the mosque, the quirky **Gayer-Anderson Museum** (Beit al-Kritliyya, the House of the Cretan Woman; Map pp72-3; ☎ 2364 7822; Sharia ibn Tulun; adult/student E£30/15, video E£20; 9am-5pm) gets its current name from John Gayer-Anderson, the British major and army doctor who restored the two adjoining 16th-century houses between 1935 and 1942, filling them with antiqui- ties, artwork and knick-knacks acquired on his travels in the region. You may find the interior familiar – the museum was used as a location in the James Bond film *The Spy Who Loved Me*. Across the street, Khan Misr Touloun (see p90) is a good handicrafts emporium.

ZAMALEK & GEZIRA

Uninhabited until the mid-19th century, Gezira (Arabic for 'island') was a narrow strip of alluvial land rising up out of the Nile. After he built modern-day Downtown, Khedive Ismail dedicated his energy to a great palace on the island, with the rest of the land as a royal garden. During the development boom of the early 20th cen- tury, the palace grounds were sold off, while the palace was made into a hotel (now the core of the Cairo Marriott).

JOHN WARBURTON-LEE PHOTOGRAPHY/ALA

Green grass and pleasant water pool, Al-Azhar Park

↘ AL-AZHAR PARK

Islamic Cairo's eastern horizon changed substantially when Al-Azhar Park opened in 2005. With funds from the Aga Khan Trust for Culture, what had been a mountain of centuries' worth of collected garbage was transformed into a beautifully landscaped swath of green, the city's first (and only) park of significant size. It's hard to convey just how dramatically different the park is from any other public space in Cairo: a profusion of gardens, emerald grass, even a lake (part of a larger public water-supply system) cover the grounds, while ambient Arabic music drifts softly from speakers, and fountains bubble in front of sleek modern Islamic architecture. In addition to a couple of small cafes and an open-air theatre (El Genaina), there's the excellent Citadel View restaurant here (see p86) capitalising on the park's awesome views across the medieval city and beyond – a sunset visit is essential.

Things you need to know Park (Map pp72-3; ☎ 2510 7378; www.alazharpark.com; admission E£10; ☀ 9am-midnight); El Genaina Theatre (☎ 2362 5057; www.mawred.org)

The northern third of the island is the stylish residential district of Zamalek (Map pp66–7); the rest, still called Gezira, is largely occupied by sports clubs and parks. A leafy neighbourhood of old embassy mansions and 1920s apartment blocks, Zamalek has few tourist sites, but it's a pleasant place to wander around and an even better place to eat, drink and shop.

Gezira (Map pp66–7) is best approache across Qasr el-Nil Bridge from Mida Tahrir, a popular strolling spot for couple at sunset. This brings you to **Midan Saa Zaghloul**, presided over by the statue o tarbooshed Mr Zaghloul himself, a 1930 nationalist leader. Off the west side of th *midan* (square), the well-groomed **Gezir Exhibition Grounds** are dominated b the **Cairo Opera House** (p88). North o he Cairo Opera House and Ahly Stadium, he **Cairo Tower** (Burg Misr; ☎ 2735 7187; haria el-Borg; admission E£60, child under 6 free, ideo E£20; ☺ 8am-midnight) is the city's most amous landmark after the Pyramids. he 360-degree views from the top are learest in the late morning, after the haze urns off, or late afternoon.

PYRAMIDS OF GIZA

: was neither an obsession with death, nor fear of it, that led the ancient Egyptians o build such incredible mausoleums as the yramids. Rather it was their belief in eter-al life and their desire to be at one with the osmos. The complex also provided a con-tant visible reminder of the eternal power f the gods, as well as the absolute power f the pharaoh for whom it was built.

Ongoing excavations on the Giza lateau are providing more evidence hat the workers were not the slaves of Hollywood tradition, but a highly or-anised workforce of Egyptian farmers. During the annual flood season, when the Nile covered their fields, the same farm-rs could have been redeployed by the ighly structured bureaucracy to work on he pharaoh's tomb.

It can be a bit of a shock to visit the Giza Plateau (Map p80; adult/student E£50/25; ☺ 8am-4pm winter, to 6pm summer) and realise hat the sandy mound that's home to the Pyramids is actually plonked in the mid-lle of the congested city suburb of Giza. With battalions of buses, armies of touts nd legions of visitors from every part of he globe – all to a soundtrack of gargling amels and cries of 'Buy postcards?' – the ourist scene at the Pyramids is intense.

CAMELS & HORSES

f you're particularly interested in riding, iring a horse from one of the village tables is a far better option than tak-ing one at the Pyramids. General expat opinion holds that the best stables near the Sphinx are **NB** (☎ 3382 0435), owned by Naser Breesh, who's praised for his healthy steeds and good guides; his place can be tricky to find: head down the street by the Sphinx poster off the main square where horses are gathered, or ask for di-rections to the Sphinx Club, as the stables are just behind it. **MG** (☎ 3385 3832) and **AA** (☎ 3385 0531), near the coach park, are both decent as well.

GREAT PYRAMID OF KHUFU (CHEOPS)

The oldest pyramid in Giza and the larg-est in Egypt, the **Great Pyramid of Khufu** (Map p80; adult/student E£100/50) stood 146m high when it was completed around 2570 BC. After 46 windy centuries, its height has been reduced by 9m. About 2.3 mil-lion limestone blocks, reckoned to weigh about 2.5 tonnes each, were used in the construction.

Tickets, sold at the main entrance, are limited to 300 per day: 150 on sale start-ing at 7.30am and 150 at 1pm. There isn't much to see inside the pyramid, but the experience of climbing through the an-cient structure is unforgettable – though impossible if you suffer the tiniest degree of claustrophobia.

Past the entrance, on the north face, a passage descends to an unfinished tomb (usually closed) about 100m along and 30m deep in the bedrock. Before you reach this, about 20m after the entrance, another passage, 1.3m high and 1m wide, ascends for about 40m to reach the Great Gallery, an impressive area 47m long and 8.5m high.

As you continue through the Great Gallery, notice how precisely the blocks in the ceiling fit together. In the 10m-long King's Chamber at the end, the walls are

CAIRO

SIGHTS

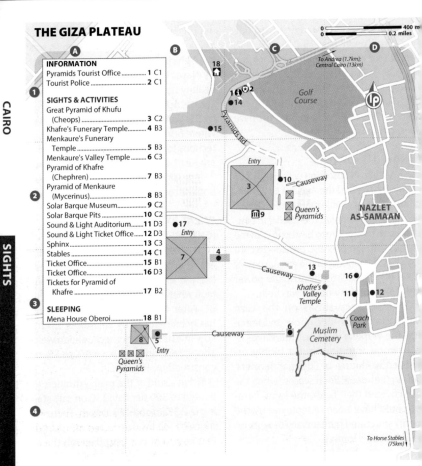

THE GIZA PLATEAU

built of red granite blocks. Outside, on the eastern side of the pyramid, three small structures some 20m high resemble pyramid-shaped piles of rubble. These are the Queens' Pyramids, the tombs of Khufu's wives and sisters.

South of the Great Pyramid is the fascinating **Solar Barque Museum** (Map p80; adult/student E£50/25; 9am-4pm Oct-May, 9am-5pm Jun-Sep). Five pits near the Great Pyramid of Khufu contained the pharaoh's solar barques (boats), which may have been used to convey the mummy of the dead pharaoh across the Nile to

the valley temple, from where it wa brought up the causeway and into th tomb chamber. One of these ancien cedar-wood vessels, possibly the oldes boat in existence, was unearthed in 1954 It was carefully restored from 1200 piece of wood and encased in a glass museun to protect it from damage from th elements.

PYRAMID OF KHAFRE (CHEPHREN)
Southwest of the Great Pyramid, th **Pyramid of Khafre** (Map p80; adult/studen E£30/15) seems larger than that of his fa

er, Khufu. At just 136m high, it's not, but stands on higher ground and its peak still capped with a limestone casing. ver the centuries, this casing has been tripped for use in palaces and mosques, xposing the softer inner-core stones to he elements.

The chambers and passageways of his particular pyramid are less elaborate han those in the Great Pyramid, but are lmost as claustrophobic. Back outside, to he east of the pyramid, are the substan- al remains of **Khafre's funerary temple** (Map p80) and the flagged paving of the auseway that provided access from the ile to the tomb.

YRAMID OF MENKAURE (MYCERINUS)

t 62m (originally 66.5m), this pyramid (Map p80) is the smallest of the trio. 'utside the pyramid you'll see the exca- ated remains of **Menkaure's funerary emple** and, further east, the ruins of his **alley temple**, less excavated.

HE SPHINX

nown in Arabic as Abu al-Hol (Father of error), the feline man was dubbed the phinx by the ancient Greeks because it esembled the mythical winged monster ith a woman's head and lion's body who et riddles and killed anyone unable to nswer them. The Sphinx was carved from he bedrock at the bottom of the cause- ay to the Pyramid of Khafre; geological urvey has shown that it was most likely arved during this pharaoh's reign, so it robably portrays his features, framed y the *nemes* (striped headcloth worn by oyalty).

As is clear from the accounts of early rab travellers, the nose was hammered ff sometime between the 11th and 5th centuries, although some still like

DONALD C. & PRISCILLA ALEXANDER EASTMAN

The Sphinx (left)

to blame Napoleon for the deed. Part of the fallen beard was carted off by 19th-century adventurers and is now on display in the British Museum in London.

SOUND & LIGHT SHOW

The Sphinx narrates the somewhat cheesy **sound and light show** (☎ 3385 2880; www .soundandlight.com.eg; admission E£75), but it's neat to be able to see the Pyramids so dramatically lit.

GETTING THERE & AWAY

By far the most straightforward way to go is in a yellow metered taxi from the rank on Midan Tahrir. It's usually about E£20, the same price you'd be lucky to bargain a black-and-white-cab driver down to – plus you get air-con.

ACTIVITIES
FELUCCA RIDES

One of the most pleasant things to do on a warm day is to go out on a felucca, Egypt's ancient broad-sail boat, with a supply of beer and a small picnic just as sunset approaches. The best spot for hiring is the Dok Dok landing stage (Map pp52–3) on the corniche in Garden City, across from the Four Seasons. Subject to haggling, a boat and captain should cost about E£30 per hour irrespective of the number of people on board; your captain will appreciate additional baksheesh (possibly in liquid form).

CAIRO FOR CHILDREN

Cairo can be exhausting for kids, but there is much they will enjoy. Most children will enjoy pretending to be a pirate on a Nile felucca, gawking at the treasures of Tutankhamun in the Egyptian Museum (p65), investigating the Pyramids of Giza (p79) and Dahshur (p153), as well as the maze of Khan al-Khalili (p73).

The **National Circus** (Map pp52-3; ☎ 3347 0612; Sharia al-Nil, Agouza, near the Zamalek Bridge; admission E£30-50; ☺ box office 11am-10pm, performances 10pm-midnight) is a traditional circus with clowns, acrobats, lions and tigers and lots of glitter. Not far away, children can feed the hippos, see countless kinds of camels – and meet lots of local kids – at the **Cairo Zoo** (Guineenat al-Haywanet; Map pp52-3; ☎ 3570 8895; Midan al-Gamaa, Giza; admission 50pt; ☺ 9am-4pm).

The theme park **Dr Ragab's Pharaonic Village** (off Map pp52-3; ☎ 3571 8675; www .pharaonicvillage.com; 3 Sharia al-Bahr al-Azam, Corniche, Moneib; per person from US$15; ☺ 9am-6pm Sep-Jun, 9am-9pm Jul & Aug) is cheesy but offers a child-friendly glimpse of what life in ancient Egypt would have been like, with a boat trip past actors in Pharaonic costumes, a playground and an art centre where kids can make mir reed boats.

Fagnoon Art School (off Map pp52-3 ☎ 3815 1014; Saqqara Rd, Sabil Umm Hashim per day E£25; ☺ 10am-7pm) is a wonder ful art centre in the fields between Giz and Saqqara. Children can slosh pain around, model clay, work with wrough iron or print and paint on textiles, all in th shadow of the Saqqara step pyramid.

Overlooking Islamic Cairo, Al-Azhar Par (p78) is home to one of the few children playgrounds in the central city.

TOURS

Innumerable companies and indi viduals offer tours of sights within an around Cairo. We recommend Sala Muhammad's **Noga Tours** (☎ 012 31 8446; www.first24hours.com), as he employ excellent English-speaking guide: Egyptologists and drivers. Mohame Anwar's specialised **museum tour** (☎ 012 340 7724) also have a goo reputation.

FESTIVALS & EVENTS

For general information on public ho days, see p351. For more on countrywid festivals, see p46.

Arabic Music Festival (www.cairooper .org) Held at the Cairo Opera House i November.

Cairo International Film Festival (ww .cairofilmfest.org) At the Cairo Opera Hous in November/December.

Moulid an-Nabi Birthday of Prophe Mohammed, 12 Rabi al-Awwal (se p352 for dates). A citywide party wit sweets and kids in new clothes, but i the week beforehand, Midan al-Hussei is the venue for the most intense Su zikrs (long sessions of dancing, chantin and swaying carried out to achieve one ness with God).

CAIRO

SLEEPING

Demonstrations of traditional fishing, Dr Ragab's Pharaonic Village (opposite)
CHRISTINE OSBORNE

ham an-Nassim First Monday after Coptic aster. Literally meaning 'sniffing the breeze' e to welcome spring), it's a ritual that came om Pharaonic tradition via the Copts, and celebrated by all Cairenes, who picnic at he zoo, in parks, by the Pyramids and on verbanks and even traffic islands.

LEEPING

airo has a few gem hotels, and something r every budget, but it certainly pays to nop around before the start of your trip, nd make reservations in advance when-ver possible. Breakfast is usually included the rate at budget and midrange ho-ls, and prices are somewhat negotiable, specially in the summer, when tourists e fewer.

UDGET
ension Roma (Map pp66-7; ☎ 2391 1088; ww.pensionroma.com.eg; 4th fl, 169 Sharia ohammed Farid, Downtown; s/d with shared athroom E£60/96, d/tr with shower E£123/162) un by a French-Egyptian woman with npeccable standards, the Roma brings

dignity, even elegance, to the budget-travel scene. Towering ceilings, dark wood floors and filmy white curtains create a feeling of timeless calm. Evening meals are an option. Book ahead, as the place is very popular with repeat guests, many of whom could afford to stay at more ex-pensive hotels but prefer the old-Cairo atmosphere here.

Hotel Luna (Map pp66-7; ☎ 2396 1020; www .hotellunacairo.com; 5th fl, 27 Sharia Talaat Harb, Downtown; r E£110-150, with shared bathroom E£100; ☒ ☐) The owner of this modern, backpacker-friendly place is one of the most fastidious in the city, and his spar-kling rooms offer many small comforts, such as bedside lamps and bath mats. In the newer 'Oasis' wing, even the paint and furniture are colour-coordinated in sooth-ing pastels – a rare sight indeed in Egypt. Excellent shared kitchen too.

MIDRANGE
Carlton Hotel (Map pp66-7; ☎ 2575 5022; www.carltonhotelcairo.com; 21 Sharia 26th of July, Downtown; s/d half board from US$28/42; ☒ ☐)

The rooms at this old-fashioned place near Cinema Rivoli are reasonably priced (and the staff often seem ready to make a deal), but vary in size and degree of dilapidation. The ones that have been renovated have shiny white paint, clean wooden floors, satellite TV and private bathrooms.

Hotel Osiris (Map pp66–7; ☎ 2794 5728; http://hotelosiris.free.fr; 12th fl, 49 Sharia Nubar, Downtown; s/d from €25/30; 🖭 💻) On the top floor of a commercial building, the Osiris' rooms enjoy views across the city. The French-Egyptian couple who run the place keep the tile floors and white walls spotless, and the pretty hand-sewn appliqué bedspreads tidily arranged on the supercomfy mattresses. Breakfast, served on a side terrace or the roof, involves fresh juice and crepes and omelettes.

Talisman Hotel (Map pp66–7; ☎ 2393 9431; www.talisman-hotel.com; 5th fl, 39 Sharia Talaat Harb, Downtown; s/d from US$85/95; 🖭 💻) Thanks to double-pane windows, Downtown traffic is a distant memory once you're inside this luxurious cocoon, one of the only real boutique hotels in the city. The 24 rooms are an impeccable m of Egyptian handicrafts, rococo furnitur and jewel-tone colours.

Hotel Longchamps (Map pp66–7; ☎ 273 2311; www.hotellongchamps.com; 5th fl, 21 Shar Ismail Mohammed, Zamalek; s US$54–62, d US$78–8 🖭) The old-European-style Longchamp has a residential feel. Rooms are spaciou and well maintained, and guests gather chat on the peaceful, greenery-covere rear balcony around sunset, or lounge i the restaurant (where alcohol – and a fu breakfast buffet – is served).

TOP END

Four Seasons at Nile Plaza (Map pp52– ☎ 2791 7000; www.fourseasons.com/cairon 1089 Corniche el-Nil, Garden City; r from US$36 🖭 💻 🛋) Of the two Four Seasons prope ties in Cairo (the other is the First Residenc in Giza), this one may be marginally le posh, but it has a much handier location you can walk to the Egyptian Museum i about 15 minutes. Rooms are nothing sho of impeccable, with lavish bathrooms fit f

Taxis and colonial-style buildings, central Cairo

royalty, and enormous picture windows that open out to the river.

Sofitel El Gezirah (Map pp52-3; ☎ 2737 3737; www.sofitel.com; Sharia al-Orman, Gezira; r from US$225; ✂ ✄ ▢ ☻) While it was something of the runt of the upmarket hotel litter for many years, the Sofitel has at long last been completely overhauled, and its interior is now an impressive mix of French and local styles. There are superb panoramas to be had from its plush rooms, though even non-guests can stop by and enjoy the views while having a drink at the floating bar on the Nile.

Mena House Oberoi (Map p80; ☎ 3377 3222; www.menahouseoberoi.com; Pyramids Rd, Giza; r garden wing from €150, r palace wing from €195; ✄ ▢ ☻) Built in 1869 as Khedive Ismail's hunting lodge, the stately Mena House offers two time warps in one: the public areas sport dazzling Islamic decoration and perpetually smell of jasmine, but the grandest palace-wing rooms are *Arabian Nights,* with whimsical tapestry bedspreads and opulent mirrors. You really have to go for a Pyramids view in the palace wing as rooms in the new garden wing are dully modern.

EATING

At one end of the spectrum are the scores of street carts, *kushari* counters, and fruit-and-veg markets where the majority of Cairenes feed themselves. And Egyptian minichains often serve some of the most delicious and cheap meals you'll have. Look for them along the main avenues in Downtown and Zamalek.

Cairo's upmarket dining scene is as trendy and sophisticated as any – most swank dining options are at the luxury hotels, and the chefs are usually imported straight from the relevant country, along with all the ingredients. At lunchtime feel free to stop by unannounced, though dinner reservations are generally recommended. Many restaurants tend to double as bars and nightclubs.

BUDGET

El-Abd Bakery (Map pp66-7; 35 Sharia Talaat Harb, Downtown; pastries E£1-6; ☘ 8am-midnight) For pastries head for Cairo's most famous bakery, easily identified by the crowds of people outside tearing into their sweets and savoury pies. There's another branch on the corner of Sharia 26th of July and Sharia Sherif.

At-Tabei ad-Dumyati (Map pp66-7; ☎ 2575 4211; 31 Sharia Orabi, Downtown; dishes E£2-10; ☘ 7am-1am) About 200m north of Midan Orabi, this place offers some of the cheapest local meals in Cairo. Start by picking four salads from a large array, then order *shwarma* or *ta'amiyya,* along with some lentil soup or *fuul.*

MIDRANGE

Felfela Restaurant (Map pp66-7; ☎ 2392 2833; 15 Sharia Hoda Shaarawi, Downtown; dishes E£15-40; ☘ 8am-midnight) Attracting tourists, coach parties and locals since 1963, Felfela is an institution that can deliver a reliable, if not wildly delicious, meal and good service. A bizarre jungle theme rules the decor, but the food is straight-down-the-line Egyptian and consistently decent, especially the mezze and grilled chicken.

Café Riche (Map pp66-7; ☎ 2392 9793; 17 Sharia Talaat Harb, Downtown; dishes E£15-40; ☘ 9am-1am) This narrow restaurant was the favoured drinking spot of Cairo's intelligentsia. It's a bit less lively now, but nonetheless a reliable and nostalgic spot to enjoy a meal (even a European-style breakfast) and a glass of wine, surrounded by framed portraits of Cairo luminaries on the wood-panelled walls.

CAIRO

EATING

CAIRO

DRINKING

Khan el-Khalili Restaurant & Mahfouz Coffee Shop (Map pp72-3; ☎ 2590 3788; 5 Sikket al-Badistan, Khan al-Khalili; snacks E£10-20, mains E£15-50; ☺ 10am-2am) The luxurious Moorish-style interiors of this restaurant and adjoining cafe are a popular haven from the khan's bustle and hassle. The place may be geared entirely to tourists but the food is reasonably good, the air-con is strong and the toilets are clean.

Citadel View (Map pp72-3; ☎ 2510 9151; Al-Azhar Park; entrées E£10-20, mains E£20-75; ☺ noon-1am) Eating at this gorgeous restaurant – on a vast multilevel terrace, with Cairo's elite seated around you and the whole city sprawled below – feels almost like visiting a luxury resort. Fortunately the prices are not so stratospheric, and the food, all traditional Egyptian grill items, is quite good.

Abou El Sid (Map pp66-7; ☎ 2735 9640; 157 Sharia 26th of July, Zamalek; mezze E£12-25, mains E£25-70; ☺ noon-2am) Cairo's first hipster Egyptian restaurant, Abou El Sid is as popular with tourists as it is with upperclass natives looking for a taste of their roots – Omar Sharif has been known to savour the chicken with *molokhiyya* (stewed leaf soup), but you can also enjoy a sugarcane-and-tequila cocktail at the big bar, or a postprandial *sheesha*. It's all served amid hanging lamps, kitschy gilt 'Louis Farouk' furniture and fat pillows. Reservations are a must.

Sequoia (Map pp52-3; ☎ 2576 8086; 3 Sharia Abu al-Feda, Zamalek; mezze E£15, mains E£35-80, minimum Sat-Wed E£50, Thu & Fri E£75; ☺ 1pm-1am) At the very northern tip of Zamalek, this sprawling Nileside lounge is a major scene, with art exhibits by Townhouse Gallery, low cushions for nursing a *sheesha* and everything from Egyptian-style mezze to sushi on the menu, washed down with a healthy bar list. Bring an

extra layer – evenings directly on the water can be surprisingly cool.

Andrea (off Map p80; ☎ 3383 1133; 59 Tir'at al-Maryutia, Giza; entrées E£5-15, mains E£20-25; ☺ 10am-1am) Take a trip to the country at this restaurant 1.5km north of Pyramids Rd on the west side of Maryutia Canal. At the entrance women pat out bread dough and tend the spit-roasted chicken the place is justly famous for. There's little else on the menu aside from this and salads, but everything is slow-roasted, which gives you ample time to enjoy a few Stellas.

TOP END

Bird Cage (Map pp66-7; ☎ 2795 7171; Semiramis InterContinental, Corniche el-Nil, Garden City; mains E£45-105; ☺ noon-1am) Spicy means *spicy* at Cairo's best Thai restaurant, a soothing wood-panelled space that's a favourite with wealthy Cairenes.

Sabaya (Map pp66-7; ☎ 2795 7171; Semiramis InterContinental, Corniche el-Nil, Garden City; mezze E£15-30, mains E£50-110; ☺ 7.30pm-1am) Lebanese cuisine is Egypt's most common 'ethnic' food, but it's rarely done as well as it is here, where the diverse and delicate mezze come with fresh-baked pillows of pita, and mains such as *fatte* are served in individual cast-iron pots.

Fish Market (Map pp52-3; ☎ 3570 9693; Americana Boat, 26 Sharia el-Nil, Giza; dishes E£25-60; ☺ noon-2am) After selecting some of the finest and freshest seafood in town from the large display counter, most guests tuck into delicious mezze while their fish is simply but expertly cooked. With its wonderful Nile views, laid-back feel and efficient service, this permanently docked boat-turned-restaurant is a hidden gem.

DRINKING

Cairo isn't a 'dry' city, but locals tend to run on caffeine by day, available at both

LUXOR

LUXOR – EAST BANK

LUXOR – EAST BANK

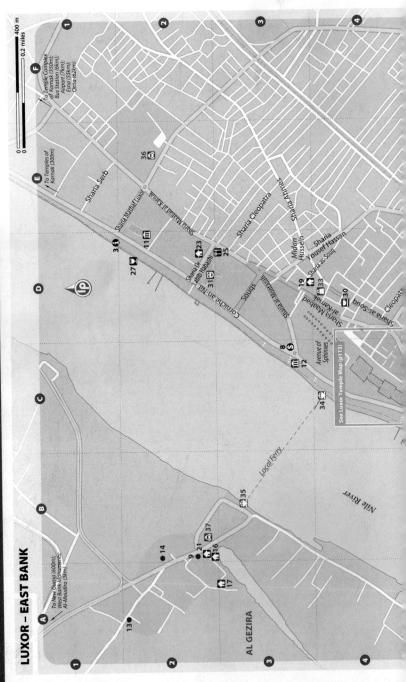

To New Gurna (600m);
West Bank Monument;
Al-Moudira (3km)

To Temple Complex
of Karnak (350m);
Bus Station (6km);
Airport (7km);
Esna (55km);
Qena (62km)

To Temples of
Karnak (300m)

Sharia Serb

Sharia Mathaf (Luxor)

Sharia Mashadd al-Karnak

Sharia Dr
Labib Habachi

Corniche an-Nil

Sharia al-Mahatta

Souqs

Sharia Cleopatra

Sharia Ahmes

Midan
Hussein

Sharia
Yousef Hassan

Sharia Maabad
al-Karnak

Sharia as-Souq

Sharia as-Souq

Avenue of
Sphinxes

See Luxor Temple Map (p113)

Local Ferry

Nile River

AL GEZIRA

400 m
0.2 miles

3
11
27
36
23
25
31
19
33
30
8
12
34
35
37
21
16
9
14
17
13

LUXOR – EAST BANK

SLEEPING
Al-Gezira Hotel 16 B2
Hotel Sheherazade 17 A3
Iberotel Luxor Hotel 18 B6
Nefertiti Hotel 19 D3
New Pola Hotel 20 B7
Nile Valley Hotel 21 B2
Old Winter Palace Hotel 22 C5
Philippe Hotel 23 D2
EATING
1886 Restaurant (see 22)
Arkwrights Gourmet Food 24 B7
As-Sahaby Lane (see 19)
Oasis Café 25 D3
Sofra 26 D6
DRINKING
Cocktail Sunset 27 D2
Kings Head Pub 28 B7
Metropolitan Café & Restaurant 29 B5
New Oum Koulsoum Coffee Shop 30 D4
ENTERTAINMENT
Hotel Mercure 31 D2
Tutotel Partner Hotel 32 B6
SHOPPING
Habiba 33 D4
TRANSPORT
EgyptAir (see 22)
Ferry Landing East Bank 34 C4
Ferry Landing West Bank 35 B3
Service Taxis 36 E2
Taxi Parking Lot 37 B2
Taxis 38 C5
Upper Egypt Bus Co Office 39 D5
INFORMATION
AA Gaddis Bookshop 1 C5
Aboudi Bookshop 2 C5
Corniche Tourist Office 3 D1
International Hospital 4 C7
Main Tourist Office 5 D5
Passport Office 6 B7
Thomas Cook (see 22)
Tourist Police 7 E5
Western Union 8 C3
SIGHTS & ACTIVITIES
Aladin Tours (see 19)
Bicycle Rental 9 B2
Hod Hod Suleiman 10 D7
Luxor Museum 11 D2
Mummification Museum 12 C3
Nobi's Arabian Horse Stables 13 A2
Pharaoh's Stables (see 22)
QEA Travel Agency 14 B2
Sky Cruise of Egypt 15 A8
Sharia al-Mahatta
Sharia Mohammed Farid
Sharia Ahmed Orabi
Sharia al-Manshiya
Ramses
Midanal-Mahatta
Train Station
Sharia Salahadin Ayyubi
Corniche an-Nil
Sharia Salah ad-Din
Sharia Televizyon
Khalid ibn al-Walid
Sharia al-Medina al-Munawwara
Sharia Khalid ibn al-Walid
To 7 days
7 ways (450m)

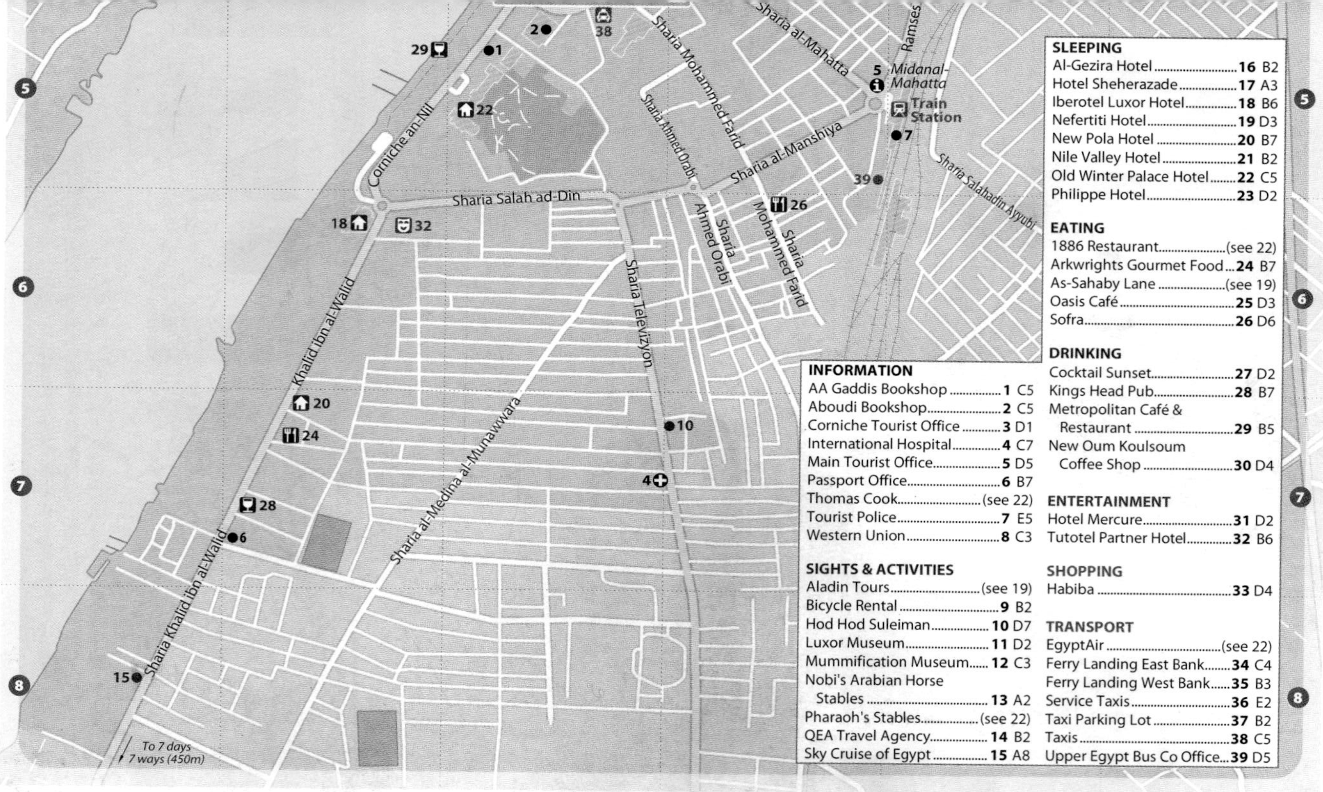

LUXOR

HIGHLIGHTS

HIGHLIGHTS

1 | TEMPLES OF KARNAK

BY JANE AKSHAR, CO-OWNER OF FLATSINLUXOR.CO.UK

Karnak is the largest religious structure in the world and needs time, after all it took thousands of years to build. The sun rises between the pylons, obelisks pierce the sky, there are echoing halls of massive pillars and endless inscriptions. There are also hidden delights: the open-air museum and the Temple of Khonsu.

⬊ JANE AKSHAR'S DON'T MISS LIST

❶ MAKING SENSE OF IT

With so many additions, the site can be very confusing. There are three complexes here, dedicated to the Theban triad of Amun, Mut and Khonsu, but most visitors concentrate on the main temple complex of Amun. In general the further you go into the complex the older the structures.

❷ GREAT COURT

Behind the first pylon is the Great Court with the **Temple of Seti II**, where the sacred barques of Mut, Amun and

Khonsu were held before the Ope Festival. During this important fertilit festival, the barque shrines of thes Theban gods were taken in a proces sion from Karnak to Luxor Temple.

❸ GREAT HYPOSTYLE HALL

Most tour groups stand in the mai passage, so venture further into th hall to find a quiet place, where yo can take in the grand scale of the fo est of tall columns, and find some c the original colours. Imagine, like th ancient Egyptians did, that this wa

Clockwise from top: Sound and light show at Karnak; Huge papyrus pillars in the hypostyle hall; Giant Scarab (p112) at the Karnak site; White Chapel of Sesostris I; Stone reliefs in Amun Temple Enclosure (p109)

...e a papyrus swamp on the banks of ...e Nile.

temple. The nice thing is that you can walk through the floodlit temple at night, before sitting down in the seating area near the Sacred Lake.

OPEN-AIR MUSEUM

...ost visitors miss the **open-air museum** (extra tickets at main ticket office, adult/ ...dent E£25/15; 6am-5.30pm summer, to ...30pm winter), but I have spent hours ...ere. I love the magnificent **White ...hapel of Sesostris I**, which is one of ...e oldest monuments in Karnak. Also ...onder over the many statues found ...n site.

SOUND & LIGHT SHOW

...e sound and light show (238 ...00; www.soundandlight.com.eg; adult/stu- ...nt E£100/60) is a 1½-hour kitsch affair, ...lling the history of Thebes and of ...e pharaohs who extended Karnak

☑ THINGS YOU NEED TO KNOW

When to visit The temple is quieter and the light is best early morning **Best photo op** From the southeastern corner of the hypostyle hall **Where to relax** The cafeteria by the sacred lake **For good luck** Walk seven times clockwise around the Giant Scarab **See our author's review on p109**

HIGHLIGHTS

2 | MEDINAT HABU TEMPLE

BY KHAIRY IBRAHIM, OWNER OF CARAVANSERAI SHOP

This temple was built over older shrines, includin◄ a temple built by Hatshepsut. This spot was always sacred, and even a Muslim sheikh is burie◄ in a corner. I was born in front of the temple, anc it has a lot of good memories as I used to play ir it as a child.

↘ KHAIRY IBRAHIM'S DON'T MISS LIST

❶ THE PERFECT TEMPLE

This is one of the few ancient temples in Egypt that has been completely excavated, and one of the best preserved. Because large parts of the ceiling are intact, the wall decoration and much of the original colours have been well preserved, giving a taste of what all temples must have looked like.

❷ THE ENTRANCE GATE

The entrance, known as the Syrian Gate, is unusual for Egypt, as it was modelled after a western Asiatic fortress. On the walls to the right a◄ captives from Syria, Palestine and oth◄ Mediterranean countries, to the left a◄ Nubians and Libyans. The stairway ◄ unfortunately closed, because th◄ rooms above the gate are decorate◄ with carvings of the pharaoh with h◄ harem.

❸ FIRST PYLON

On the first massive pylon you can s◄ Ramses III destroying his enemies ◄ battle, holding them by the hair. Th◄ loyal scribes are doing the account◄

Clockwise from top: Pharaoh's Palace at the Funerary Temple of Ramses III (p124), Medinat Habu; Hieroglyphs; Relief of Ramses III; Depiction of an ancient religious ceremony; Wall carving detail

CLOCKWISE FROM TOP: GORDON SINCLAIR/THE TRAVEL LIBRARY/PHOTOLIBRARY; IZZET KERIBAR; ARIADNE VAN ZANDBERGEN; ARIADNE VAN ZANDBERGEN; IZZET KER◄

unting chopped-off hands and nitals.

WINDOW OF APPEARANCES

mses III's palace, where it seems he ed to come for R&R, was to the left the first court. At the back were the oms for his harem, and between the lace and the court was the Window Appearances, where Ramses III ap- ared to his subjects.

❺ WALKING AROUND THE TEMPLE

In the afternoon light it is blissful to walk around the outer walls of the temple to see various scenes of the pharaoh spear fishing in the marshes and hunting. There are several other and older monuments, as well as a small sacred lake.

↘ THINGS YOU NEED TO KNOW

When to visit The light on the temple is soft and magnificent late afternoon **Best photo op** From a corner in the Second Court **Where to relax** Mara- onga Cafeteria, opposite the temple **See our author's review on p123**

HIGHLIGHTS

3

⬊ TOMBS OF THE NOBLES

Glimpse scenes of the good life of an ancient Egyptian aristocrat – so good they
wanted it represented on their tomb walls hoping it would continue after death –
in the **Tombs of the Nobles** (p122). Nestled in the Theban hills, there are more
than 400 tombs from the 6th dynasty to the Graeco-Roman period but only 15
or so tombs, the most exquisite ones, are open to the public.

4

⬊ LUXOR TEMPLE AT NIGHT

At night **Luxor Temple** (p112) is open until 10pm and beautifully lit. Marvel at
the architecture and the magnificent scenes carved on the walls. Look out for the
the **Colonnade of Amenhotep III**, showing the Opet Festival procession. During
this festival, cult images of the Karnak gods were carried along the avenue of
sphinxes, stopping for ceremonies on the way, or taken by boat up the Nile.

↘ LUXOR MUSEUM

The **Luxor Museum** (p114) is one of Egypt's most charming museums, with a small but perfectly displayed collection of objects and statuary found in and around Luxor. The new annex gives a wonderful insight into the might and know-how of the Egyptians during the New Kingdom period.

↘ STAY ON THE WEST BANK

Most of Luxor's hotels are on the East Bank, but, increasingly, small budget or midrange hotels are opening on the West Bank, with more character and offering a quieter stay closer to the local people. The most stylish are the intimate **Beit Sabée** (p127) and the larger **Hotel Sheherazade** (p127).

↘ EGYPTIAN CUISINE AT SOFRA

Many visitors have dinner at their hotel but it's worth venturing out to **Sofra** (p129) for an authentic Egyptian meal in very pleasant surroundings. Start with a table full of delicious mezze (salads and dips) and finish off the evening with some Egyptian sweets, mint tea and a perfumed *sheesha* (water pipe).

3 JOHN ELK III; 4 IZZET KERIBAR; 5 WAYNE WALTON; 6 JEAN DOMINIQUE DALLET/ALAMY; 7 BECCA POSTERINO

Scenes from the Tomb of Nakht (p122); 4 Obelisk at Luxor Temple (p112); 5 Pharaoh relief, Luxor Museum 114); 6 Luxury hotel Al-Moudira (p128); 7 Felafels – typical Egyptian fare

LUXOR

THE BEST...

⬂ PLACES TO RELAX

- The well-kept **Old Winter Palace Hotel gardens** (p128) offer a welcome retreat from the busy town.
- Imagine yourself in the courtyard of a secluded Moorish palace at **Al-Moudira** (p128).
- See the sun set behind the Theban hills from a **felucca on the Nile** (p125).
- **Ride a horse** (p124) through the fields around the West Bank monuments.
- After the hectic sightseeing in Luxor, relax on a **dahabiyya** (p132) trip to Aswan.

⬂ PLACES WITH A VIEW

- From **Maratonga Cafeteria** (p131) for a view of Medinat Habu.
- From the **New Oum Koulsoum Coffee Shop** (p130) for a view of the souq.
- From the rooftop of **Nile Valley Hotel** (Map pp96–7) for a view of the Nile and Luxor Temple.

⬂ WAYS TO WORK UP A SWEAT

- **Haggling** with the *hantour* drivers (p133) for a ride on the East Bank.
- **Walking** over the hill from the Valley of the Kings (p118) to the temple of Deir al-Bahri (p117).
- **Visiting** the Valley of the Kings (p118), one of the hottest places on earth, at midday.
- **Cycling** (p133) around the sights on the West Bank.

LEFT: ANDERS BLOMQVIST; RIGHT: PATRICK

Left: Passage to Ramses IV's tomb, Valley of the Kings (p121); Right: West Bank, Luxor

THINGS YOU NEED TO KNOW

⬏ VITAL STATISTICS

- **Telephone code** (☎ 095)
- **Population** 451, 350
- **Best time to go** October and November and March to May; December is very busy

⬏ NEIGHBOURHOODS IN A NUTSHELL

- **Luxor City** The centre of Luxor around the Luxor Temple (p112), including Sharia as-Souq, Sharia al-Mahatta and Sharia Maabad al-Karnak, is a bustling area.
- **Karnak** The area around Karnak Temple (p109) has several hotels.
- **West Bank** (p115) Al-Gezira village, near the ferry landing, has several midrange hotels; most of the monuments are further west.

⬏ ADVANCE PLANNING

- **One month before** Book accommodation, particularly if travelling during European holiday periods.
- **One day before** Book your dawn balloon ride over the West Bank monuments.

⬏ RESOURCES

- **Antiquities Inspectorate ticket office** (Map p116; main road, 3km inland from ferry landing; ⏾ 6am-5pm) Go to the office first to buy your tickets for most sights on the West Bank.
- **Main tourist office** (Map pp96-7; ☎ 237 3294; Midan al-Mahatta; ⏾ 8am-8pm) Helpful and sells tickets for the Karnak sound and light show.

- **Luxor Egypt** (www.luxoregypt.org) Official travel guide for Luxor city.
- **Luxor News** (luxor-news.blogspot .com) Jane Akshar's interesting blog about archaeological finds in Luxor.

⬏ EMERGENCY NUMBERS

- **Ambulance** (☎ 123)
- **Police** (☎ 237 1500, 237 3845)
- **Tourist police** (☎ 237 6620)

⬏ GETTING AROUND

- **Hantour** Take a *hantour (calèche)* for a scenic ride.
- **Bicycle** Around the West Bank, if you have time.
- **Taxi** Organise one for the day to get around the West Bank monuments.
- **Ferry** To cross the Nile between the two banks.

⬏ BE FOREWARNED

- **Heat** It can get very hot, so always carry sunscreen, sun hat and water.
- **Baksheesh** Bring small change. Guards at the West Bank sites might offer small services, such as lighting up wall carvings for you with a mirror, and will always expect a tip (baksheesh) to augment their meagre salary.

DISCOVER LUXOR

The city's governor would like you to know that Luxor is the world's greatest open-air museum, but that comes nowhere near describing this extraordinary place. The mid-19th-century traveller Florence Nightingale described it as 'the deathbed of the world' and likened to the writings of Shakespeare – somewhere one learned the origin and meaning of many things one took for granted. And whatever your interests, it is one of the few places in the world that truly deserves to be called unforgettable.

Although the modern East Bank city has grown rapidly in recent years, the setting is still breathtakingly beautiful, the Nile flowing between the modern town and the West Bank necropolis, backed by the enigmatic Theban escarpment. Scattered across the landscape is an embarrassment of riches, from the temples of Karnak and Luxor in the east, to the temples of Deir al-Bahri and Medinat Habu, the Colossi of Memnon and the Valley of the Kings in the west.

HISTORY

Palaeolithic tools found in the Theban hills indicate that there have been human settlements in the area for at least half a million years, but Thebes (ancient Waset) only became important in the Middle Kingdom period (2055–1650 BC). The 11th-dynasty Theban prince Montuhotep II (2055–2004 BC) reunited the country, moved his capital to Thebes and increased Karnak's importance as a cult centre to the local god Amun with a temple dedicated to him. Montuhotep's funerary temple at Deir al-Bahri served as an inspiration for Queen Hatshepsut's temple 500 years later. The 12th-dynasty pharaohs (1985–1795 BC) moved their administrative capital back north to Al-Lisht, situated about 30km south of Memphis, but much of their immense wealth from expanded foreign trade and agriculture, and tribute from military expeditions made into Nubia and Asia, went to the priesthood of Amun and Thebes, which remained the religious capital. This 200-year period was one of the richest times throughout Egyptian his-

tory, which witnessed a great flourishir of architecture and the arts, and maj advances in science.

After the Second Intermediate Peric (1650–1550 BC), when much of Egy was ruled by Asiatic tribes known as th Hyksos, it was the Thebans again, und Ahmose I, who drove out the foreigr ers and unified Egypt. Because of h military victories and as the founder the 18th dynasty, Ahmose I was deifie and worshipped at Thebes for hundred of years. This was the beginning of th glorious New Kingdom (1550–1069 BC when Thebes reached its apogee. It wa home to tens of thousands of peopl who helped construct many of its gre monuments.

Amenhotep III (1390–1352 BC) wa probably the greatest contributor of a to Thebes. He continued to accumulat wealth from foreign expeditions an spent vast sums on building, incluc ing substantial additions to the temp complex at Karnak, his great palac Malqata, on the West Bank, with a larg rbour for religious festivals and the rgest memorial temple ever built. Very tle of the latter is left beyond the so-lled Colossi of Memnon, the largest onolithic statue ever carved. His son nenhotep IV (1352–1336 BC), who later named himself Akhenaten, moved the ipital from Thebes to his new city of khetaten (Tell al-Amarna), worshipped ie god only (Aten the solar god), and ought about dramatic changes in art id architecture. The temples in Thebes ere closed until his death, but the owerful priesthood was soon after re-stated under Akhenaten's successor, itankhamun, who built very little but ecame the best-known pharaoh ever hen his tomb was discovered full of easure in 1922. Ramses II (1279–1213 C) may have exaggerated his military ctories, but he too was a great builder id added the magnificent hypostyle hall Karnak, other halls to Luxor Temple, id built the Ramesseum and two mag-ficent tombs in the Valley of the Kings r himself and his many sons.

The decline of Pharaonic rule was mir-rored by Thebes' gradual slide into in-significance: when the Persians sacked Thebes, it was clear the end was nigh. Mudbrick settlements clung to the once mighty Theban temples, and people hid within the stone walls against maraud-ing desert tribes. Early Christians built churches in the temples, carved crosses on the walls and scratched out reliefs of the pagan gods. The area fell into obscurity in the 7th century AD after the Arab inva-sion, and the only reminder of its glorious past was the name bestowed on it by its Arab rulers: Al-Uqsur (The Fortifications), giving modern Luxor its name.

By the time European travellers arrived here in the 18th century, Luxor was lit-tle more than a large Upper Egyptian village, known more for its 12th-century saint, Abu al-Haggag, buried above the mound of Luxor Temple, than for its half-buried ruins. Napoleon arrived in 1798 and the publication of the *Description de l'Egypte,* did manage to revive interest in Egypt. European exhibitions of mummies,

LUXOR

HISTORY

IZZET KERIBAR

emple of Hatshepsut at Deir al-Bahri (p117)

jewellery and other spectacular funerary artefacts from Theban tombs (often found by plundering adventurers rather than enquiring scholars) made Luxor an increasingly popular destination for travellers. By 1869, when Thomas Cook brought his first group of tourists to Egypt, Luxor was one of the highlights. Mass tourism had arrived and Luxor regained its place on the world map. Most recently, Dr Zahi Hawass, the secretary-general of the Supreme Council of Antiquities, has stated that this tourism is the greatest threat to the Egyptian monuments, and that if nothing is done they will be destroyed in less than 100 years. Many plans and projects to protect and manage the sites are under way, and Luxor is now a city in flux: on both banks, huge swaths of houses and in places entire villages are being demolished to clear the areas around the historical sites.

INFORMATION

AA Gaddis Bookshop (Map pp96-7; ☎ 238 7042; Corniche an-Nil; ☽ 9am-10pm Mon-Sat, 10.30am-10pm Sun, closed Jun & Jul)

Aboudi Bookshop (Map pp96-7; ☎ 237 3390; next door to AA Gaddis, Tourist Bazaar, Corniche an-Nil; ☽ 8am-10pm)

Ambulance (☎ 123)

International Hospital (Map pp96-7; ☎ 228 0192/4; Sharia Televizyon)

Tourist police (Map pp96-7; ☎ 237 6620; Midan al-Mahatta)

DANGERS & ANNOYANCES

Luxor is often considered the hassle capital of Egypt, and although the governor is cleaning up the town in every possible way, the scams and hassle remain, so much so that several package tour hotels tell their clients it is too dangerous to leave their hotel. The most common scams are asking for extra baksheesh

at the monuments, overcharging for *calèche* (horse-drawn carriage) or feluc[e] charging European prices for taxi rid[e] and touts in the souq or station targe[t]ing new arrivals. A frequent scam is th[e] taxi or *calèche* drivers tell tourists the[re] is a local souq which is less touristy th[an] the souq behind the Luxor Temple. Th[ey] then drive around town and pull up at t[he] same old souq. The tourist office or t[he] tourist police will need a written repo[rt] from you if anything happens, and will [?] to take action.

In recent years Luxor has also becom[e a] known destination for female sex touris[m] popular with some often-older Weste[rn] women looking for sex with your[g] Egyptians. Because of this, individu[al] women travellers looking for nothi[ng] more risqué than an ancient temple [at] a desert sunset can find themselves s[e]riously hassled. Another alarming ne[w] trend is for taxi or *calèche* drivers to off[er] prostitutes to foreign clients.

SIGHTS – EAST BANK

Luxor's East Bank is still a busy provinc[ial] city, despite the presence of an eve[r] increasing number of tourists. The gove[r]nor has made huge efforts to clean up t[he] town centre but not everyone is happ[y] Many locals feel that their interests hav[e] been placed second in the drive to boo[st] tourism, and have raised concerns ov[er] the relocation and compensation effort[s] The project to clear the 3km-long alley [of] the sphinxes between the two temple[s] has been the most controversial.

The city centre, where hotels, bars an[d] restaurants are concentrated, is eas[ily] walkable when the heat is not intens[e] At its heart is Luxor Temple, an elega[nt] architectural masterpiece, its courtyar[d] and sanctuaries dedicated to the Theba[n] triad, Amun, Mut and Khonsu. Rather tha[n]

ANDERS BLOMQVIST

Central court, Karnak (below)

tart here, it makes sense to visit the awe-inspiring temple complex of Karnak early n the morning. Here, for more than 1500 ears, pharaohs vied for the gods' attention by outdoing each other's architectural feats. Luxor Temple can be visited ter and is even open at night.

Complementing the monuments are wo excellent museums. Luxor Museum, urrently the best-designed museum in he country, as a fascinating collection of rtefacts discovered in this antiquities-rich rea. The nearby Mummification Museum lisplays animal and human mummies and xplains in detail how ancient Egyptians erfected the embalming process.

EMPLES OF KARNAK

More than a temple, **Karnak** (Sharia Maabad l-Karnak; adult/student E£65/40; 🕐 6am-5pm ct-Apr, to 6pm May-Sep) is an extraordinary omplex of sanctuaries, kiosks, pylons nd obelisks dedicated to the Theban ods and the greater glory of pharaohs. verything is on a gigantic scale: the site overs over 2 sq km, large enough to con-

tain about 10 cathedrals, while its main structure, the Temple of Amun, is the largest religious building ever built. This was where the god lived on earth, surrounded by the houses of his wife Mut, and their son Khonsu, two other huge temple complexes on this site. Built, added to, dismantled, restored, enlarged and decorated over nearly 1500 years, Karnak was the most important place of worship in Egypt during the New Kingdom. New Kingdom records show that the priests of the Temple of Amun had 81,000 people working in or for the temple, owned 421,000 head of cattle, 65 cities, 83 ships and 276,400 hectares of agricultural land, giving an idea of its economic, as well as spiritual, significance. It was called Ipet-Sut, meaning 'The Most Esteemed of Places'; Karnak is its Arabic name meaning 'fortified settlement'.

The most important place of worship was the massive **Amun Temple Enclosure** (Precinct of Amun; Map pp110–11), dominated by the great Temple of Amun-Ra, which contains the famous hypostyle

AMUN TEMPLE ENCLOSURE

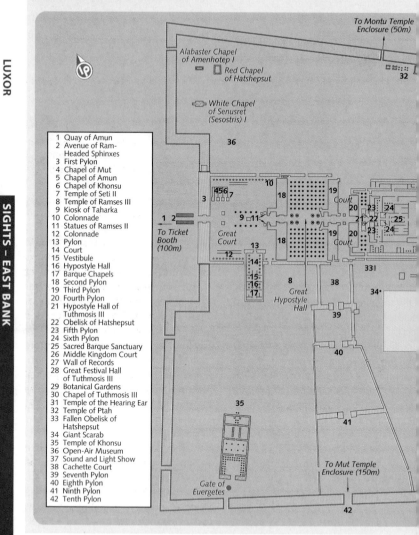

To Montu Temple
Enclosure (50m)

Alabaster Chapel
of Amenhotep I

Red Chapel
of Hatshepsut

32

White Chapel
of Senusret
(Sesostris) I

36

1 Quay of Amun
2 Avenue of Ram-
  Headed Sphinxes
3 First Pylon
4 Chapel of Mut
5 Chapel of Amun
6 Chapel of Khonsu
7 Temple of Seti II
8 Temple of Ramses III
9 Kiosk of Taharka
10 Colonnade
11 Statues of Ramses II
12 Colonnade
13 Pylon
14 Court
15 Vestibule
16 Hypostyle Hall
17 Barque Chapels
18 Second Pylon
19 Third Pylon
20 Fourth Pylon
21 Hypostyle Hall of
  Tuthmosis III
22 Obelisk of Hatshepsut
23 Fifth Pylon
24 Sixth Pylon
25 Sacred Barque Sanctuary
26 Middle Kingdom Court
27 Wall of Records
28 Great Festival Hall
  of Tuthmosis III
29 Botanical Gardens
30 Chapel of Tuthmosis III
31 Temple of the Hearing Ear
32 Temple of Ptah
33 Fallen Obelisk of
  Hatshepsut
34 Giant Scarab
35 Temple of Khonsu
36 Open-Air Museum
37 Sound and Light Show
38 Cachette Court
39 Seventh Pylon
40 Eighth Pylon
41 Ninth Pylon
42 Tenth Pylon

To Ticket
Booth
(100m)

Great
Court

Great
Hypostyle
Hall

Court

Court

To Mut Temple
Enclosure (150m)

Gate of
Euergetes

hall, a spectacular forest of giant papyrus-shaped columns. On its southern side is the Mut Temple Enclosure, once linked to the main temple by an avenue of ram-headed sphinxes. To the north is the Montu Temple Enclosure, which hon-

oured the local Theban war god. Mos of what you can see was built by th powerful pharaohs of the 18th to 20t dynasties (1550–1069 BC), who spen fortunes on making their mark in thi most sacred of places. As almost ever

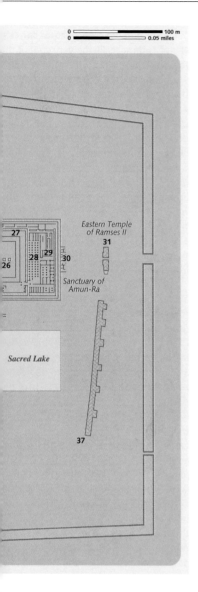

0 ⸻ 100 m
0 ⸻ 0.05 miles

Eastern Temple of Ramses II

27
28 29
26 30
31

Sanctuary of Amun-Ra

Sacred Lake

37

The **Quay of Amun** was the dock where the large boats carrying the statues of the gods moored during the festivals. On the east side is a ramp sloping down to the processional **avenue of ram-headed sphinxes** which leads to the massive unfinished **first pylon**, built by Nectanebo I of the 30th dynasty. On the inside is a massive mudbrick construction ramp, onto which the blocks of stone for the pylon were dragged up with rollers and ropes. When Napoleon's expedition visited there were still blocks on the ramp.

Behind the first pylon lies the **Great Court**, the largest area of the Karnak complex. To the left is the **Temple of Seti II** with three small chapels that held the sacred barques of Mut, Amun and Khonsu during the lead-up to the Opet Festival. In the southeastern corner (far right) is the well-preserved **Temple of Ramses III**, a miniature version of the pharaoh's temple at Medinat Habu. The temple plan is simple and classic: pylon, open court, vestibule with four Osirid columns and four columns, hypostyle hall with eight columns and three barque chapels for Amun, Mut and Khonsu. At the centre of the court are two rows of five columns. Only one still stands 21m tall with a papyrus-shaped capital, and a small alabaster altar at the middle: all that remains of the **Kiosk of Taharka**, the 25th-dynasty Nubian pharaoh. The **second pylon** was begun by Horemheb, the last 18th-dynasty pharaoh, and continued by Ramses I and Ramses II, who also raised three colossal red-granite **statues** of himself on either side of the entrance; one is now destroyed.

Beyond the second pylon is the awesome **Great Hypostyle Hall**, one of the greatest religious monuments ever built. Covering 5500 sq metres – enough space

pharaoh left his or her mark here, it can feel like a crash course in the evolution of ancient Egyptian artistic and architectural styles. Wandering through this gigantic complex is one of the highlights of any visit to Egypt.

to contain both Rome's St Peter's Basilica and London's St Paul's Cathedral – the hall is an unforgettable forest of 134 towering papyrus-shaped stone pillars. Originally, it would have been brightly painted – some colours remain – and roofed, making it pretty dark away from the lit main axis. The hall was planned by Ramses I and built by Seti I and Ramses II.

Beyond the **fourth pylon** stands one of the two magnificent 30m-high obelisks erected by Queen Hatshepsut (1473–1458 BC) to the glory of her 'father' Amun. The other is broken but the upper shaft lies near the sacred lake. The **Obelisk of Hatshepsut** is the tallest in Egypt, its tip originally covered in electrum (a commonly used alloy of gold and silver).

Obelisk of Hatshepsut, Karnak (above)

The original **sacred barque sanctuary** of Tuthmosis III, the very core of the temple where the god Amun resided, was replaced by a granite one, that was built and decorated with well-preserved painted reliefs by Alexander the Great's successor and half-brother: the fragile, dim-witted Philip Arrhidaeus (323–317 BC). East of the shrine of Philip Arrhidaeus, is the oldest known part of the temple, the **Middle Kingdom Court**, where Sesostris I built a shrine, of which the foundation walls have been found. On the northern wall of the court is the **Wall of Records**, a running tally of the organised tribute the pharaoh exacted in honour of Amun from his subjugated lands.

South of here is the **sacred lake**, where, according to Herodotus, the priests of Amun bathed twice daily and nightly for ritual purity. On the northwestern side of the lake is part of the **Fallen Obelisk of Hatshepsut** showing her coronation, and a **Giant Scarab** in stone dedicated by Amenhotep III to Khepri, a form of the sun god.

LUXOR TEMPLE

Largely built by the New Kingdom pharaohs Amenhotep III (1390–1352 BC) and Ramses II (1279–1213 BC), this **temple** (Map p113; Corniche an-Nil; adult/student E£50/30; 6am-9pm Oct-Apr, to 10pm May-Sep) is a strikingly graceful monument in the heart of the modern town. Visit early when the temple opens, before the crowds arrive or later at sunset when the stones glow. Whenever you go, be sure to return at night when the temple is lit up, creating an eerie spectacle as shadow and light play off the reliefs and colonnades.

The temple, also known as the Southern Sanctuary, was once the dwelling place of Amenemopet, the ithyphallic Amun of the Opet, and was largely built for the Opet

LUXOR TEMPLE

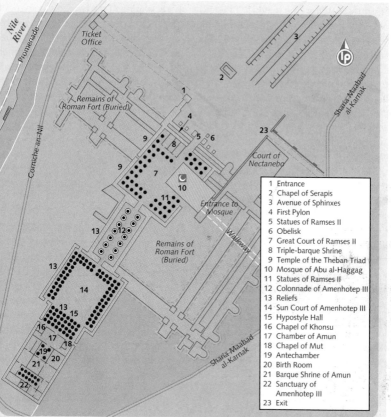

0   60 m

1	Entrance
2	Chapel of Serapis
3	Avenue of Sphinxes
4	First Pylon
5	Statues of Ramses II
6	Obelisk
7	Great Court of Ramses II
8	Triple-barque Shrine
9	Temple of the Theban Triad
10	Mosque of Abu al-Haggag
11	Statues of Ramses II
12	Colonnade of Amenhotep III
13	Reliefs
14	Sun Court of Amenhotep III
15	Hypostyle Hall
16	Chapel of Khonsu
17	Chamber of Amun
18	Chapel of Mut
19	Antechamber
20	Birth Room
21	Barque Shrine of Amun
22	Sanctuary of Amenhotep III
23	Exit

lebrations, when the statues of Amun, ut and Khonsu were annually reunited ring the inundation season with that Amun of Opet. In ancient times the mple would have been surrounded a warren of mudbrick houses, shops d workshops which now lie under e modern town, but after the decline the city people moved into the – by en – partly covered temple complex d built their city within it. In the 14th ntury, a mosque was built in one of the terior courts for the local sheikh (holy an) Abu al-Haggag. Excavation works, begun in 1885, have cleared away the village and debris of centuries to uncover what can be seen of the temple today, but the mosque remains and has recently been restored after a fire.

In front of the temple is the beginning of the **avenue of sphinxes** that ran all the way to the temples at Karnak 3km to the north, which is now being entirely excavated. The massive 24m-high **first pylon** was raised by Ramses II and decorated with reliefs of his military exploits, including the Battle of Kadesh. The pylon was originally fronted by six colossal **statues** of Ramses II, four seated and two standing, but only two of the seated figures and one standing remain, and a pair of pink granite **obelisks**, of which one remains and the other stands in the Place de la Concorde in Paris. Beyond lies the **Great Court of Ramses II**, surrounded by a double row of columns with lotus-bud capitals, the walls of which are decorated with scenes of the pharaoh making offerings to the gods. Over the southeastern side hangs the 14th-century **Mosque of Abu al-Haggag**, dedicated to a local sheikh, entered from Sharia Maabad al-Karnak, outside the temple precinct.

Beyond the court is the older splendid **Colonnade of Amenhotep III**, built as the grand entrance to the Temple of Amun of the Opet. South of the Colonnade is the **Sun Court of Amenhotep III**, once enclosed on three sides by double rows of towering papyrus-bundle columns, the best preserved of which, with their architraves extant, are those on the eastern and western sides. Beyond lies the **Hypostyle Hall**, the first room of the original Opet temple, with four rows of eight column each, leading to the temple's main room. The central **chamber** on the axis south of the Hypostyle Hall was the cult sanctuary of Amun, stuccoed over by the Roman in the 3rd century AD and painted with scenes of Roman officials. Through the chamber, either side of which are **chapel** dedicated to Mut and Khonsu, is the fou columned **Antechamber**, where offering were made to Amun, and immediate behind it the **Barque Shrine of Amun** rebuilt by Alexander the Great, with relie portraying him as an Egyptian pharaoh

LUXOR MUSEUM

This wonderful **museum** (Map pp96-7; ☎ 2 0269; Corniche an-Nil; adult/student E£80/4 ⏱ 9am-1pm & 4-9pm Oct-Apr, 9am-1pm & 5-10p May-Sep) has a beautifully displayed colle tion, from the end of the Old Kingdo right through to the Mamluk perio mostly gathered from the Theban ten ples and necropolis.

The ground-floor gallery has sever masterpieces including a well-preserve

Interior of the tomb of Tuthmosis III, Valley of the Kings (p123)

mestone **relief of Tuthmosis III (No 140)**, an exquisitely carved **statue of Tuthmosis** I in greywacke from the Temple of Karnak (No 2), an alabaster **figure of Amenhotep** I protected by the great crocodile god Sobek (No 155) and, one of the few examples of Old Kingdom art found at Thebes, **relief of Unas-ankh (No 183)**, found in his tomb on the West Bank.

A new wing was opened in 2004, dedicated to the glory of Thebes during the New Kingdom period. The highlight, and the main reason for the new construction, is the two **royal mummies**, Ahmose (founder of the 18th dynasty) and the mummy some believe to be Ramses I (founder of the 19th dynasty and father of Seti I), beautifully displayed without their wrappings in dark rooms. Other well-labelled displays illustrate the military might of Thebes during the New Kingdom, the age of Egypt's empire-building, including chariots and weapons.

Back in the old building, moving up via the ramp to the 1st floor, you come face to face with a seated **granite figure** of the legendary scribe Amenhotep (No 4), son of Hapu, the great official eventually deified in Ptolemaic times and who, as overseer of the pharaoh's works under Amenhotep (1390-1352 BC), was responsible for many of Thebes' greatest buildings. One of the most interesting exhibits is the **Wall of Akhenaten**, a series of small sandstone blocks named *talatat* or 'threes' by workmen – probably because their height and length was about three hand lengths – that came from Amenhotep IV's contribution at Karnak before he changed his name to Akhenaten and left Thebes for Tell al-Amarna.

A ramp back down to the ground floor leaves you close to the exit and beside a black-and-gold wooden head of the cow deity Mehit-Weret, an aspect of the goddess Hathor, which was also found in Tutankhamun's tomb. On the left just before the exit is a small hall containing 16 of 22 statues that were uncovered in Luxor Temple in 1989. All are magnificent examples of ancient Egyptian sculpture but pride of place at the end of the hall is given to an almost pristine 2.45m-tall quartzite statue of a muscular Amenhotep III, wearing a pleated kilt.

MUMMIFICATION MUSEUM

Housed in the former visitors centre on Luxor's Corniche, the **Mummification Museum** (Map pp96-7; ☎ 238 1501; Corniche an-Nil; adult/student E£50/25; 🕙 9am-1pm & 4-9pm Oct-Apr, 9am-1pm & 5-10pm May-Sep) has well-presented exhibits explaining the art of mummification. On display are the well-preserved mummy of a 21st-dynasty high priest of Amun, Maserharti, and a host of mummified animals. Vitrines show the tools and materials used in the mummification process – check out the small spoon and metal spatula used for scraping the brain out of the skull. Several artefacts that were crucial to the mummy's journey to the afterlife have also been included, as well as some picturesque painted coffins. Presiding over the entrance is a beautiful little statue of the jackal god, Anubis, the god of embalming who helped Isis turn her brother-husband Osiris into the first mummy.

SIGHTS – WEST BANK

The West Bank is a world away from the noise and bustle of Luxor town on the East Bank. Taking a taxi across the bridge, 6km south of the centre, or crossing on the old ferry, you are immediately in the lush Egyptian countryside, with bright green sugar-cane fields along irrigation canals and clusters of colourful houses, all against the background of the desert and the Theban hills. Coming towards the end of the cultivated land you start to notice huge sandstone blocks lying in the middle of fields, gaping black holes in the rocks and giant sandstone forms on the edge of the cultivation below. Magnificent memorial temples were built on the flood plains here, where the illusion of the pharaoh's immortality could be perpetuated by the devotions of his priests and subjects, while his body and worldly wealth, and the bodies of his wives and children, were

laid in splendidly decorated hidden tomb excavated in the hills.

It is planned that every site will hav its own visitors centre and ticket offic but at the time of writing the **Antiquitie Inspectorate ticket office** (Map p116; ma road, 3km inland from ferry landing; ☼ 6am-5pm near Medinat Habu, still provided all tick ets except for the Temple at Deir al-Bah and the Valley of the Kings. Check ther first to see which tickets are available, an which tombs are open.

Above all, bring plenty of water (thoug it is available at many of the sights) an

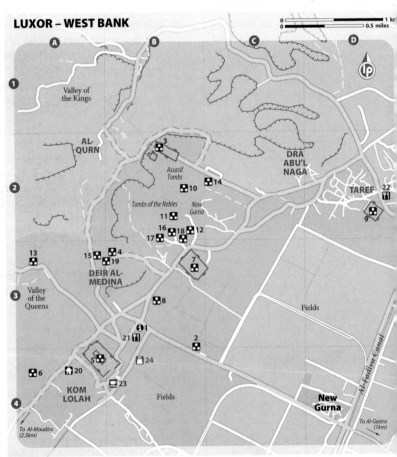

LUXOR – WEST BANK

a sun hat. Small change for baksheesh is much needed too, as guardians rely on tips to augment their pathetic salaries – a few Egyptian pounds should be enough for them to either leave you in peace, or to open a door or reflect light on a particularly beautiful painting. A torch (flashlight) can come in handy.

COLOSSI OF MEMNON

The two faceless Colossi of Memnon (Map p116) that rise majestically about 18m from the plain are the first monuments tourists see when they visit the West Bank. The enthroned figures have kept a lonely vigil over the changing landscape, and few visitors have any idea that these giants were only a tiny element of what was once the largest temple built in Egypt, Amenhotep III's memorial temple,

believed to have covered an area larger than Karnak. Some tiny parts of the temple remain and more is being uncovered by excavation; the colossi are the only large-scale elements to have survived. The Greeks and Romans considered it good luck to hear the whistling sound emitted by the northern statue at sunrise, which they believed to be the cry of Memnon greeting his mother Eos, the goddess of dawn. She in turn would weep tears of dew for his untimely death. All this was probably due to a crack in the colossus' upper body, which appeared after the 27 BC earthquake. As the heat of the morning sun baked the dew-soaked stone, sand particles would break off and resonate inside the cracks in the structure. After Septimus Severus (193–211 AD) repaired the statue in the 3rd century AD, Memnon's plaintive greeting was heard no more.

DEIR AL-BAHRI

The eyes first focus on the dramatic rugged limestone cliffs that rise nearly 300m above the desert plain, a monument made by nature, only to realize that at the foot of all this immense beauty lies a man-made monument even more extraordinary, the dazzling **Temple of Hatshepsut (Map p116; adult/student E£30/15; ☾ 6am-5pm)**. The almost modern-looking temple blends in beautifully with the cliffs from which it is partly cut, a marriage made in heaven.

Continuous excavation and restoration since 1891 have revealed one of ancient Egypt's finest monuments, but it must have been even more stunning in the days of Hatshepsut (1473–1458 BC), when it was approached by a grand sphinx-lined causeway instead of today's noisy tourist bazaar, and when the court was a garden planted with a variety of exotic trees and perfumed plants – the ancient Egyptians called it *Djeser-djeseru*, 'Most Holy of Holies'. Deir al-Bahri has been designated as one of the hottest places on earth, so an early morning visit is advisable, also because the reliefs are best seen in the low sunlight.

If the design seems unusual, it featured in fact all the things a memorial temple usually had, including the rising central axis and a three-part plan, but had to be adapted to the chosen site almost exactly on the same line with the Temple of Amun at Karnak, and near an older shrine to the goddess Hathor. The temple was vandalised over the centuries: Tuthmosis III removed his stepmother's name whenever he could Akhenaten removed all references to Amun, and the early Christians turned it into a monastery, Deir al-Bahri ('Monastery of the North'), and defaced the pagan reliefs.

A large ramp leads to the two upper terraces. The best-preserved reliefs are on the **middle terrace**. The reliefs in the north colonnade record Hatshepsut's divine birth and at the end of it is the **Chapel of Anubis**, with well-preserved colourful reliefs of a disfigured Hatshepsut and Tuthmosis III in the presence of Anubis Ra-Horakhty and Hathor. The wonderfully detailed reliefs in the **Punt Colonnade** to the left of the entrance tell the story of the expedition to the Land of Punt to collect myrrh trees needed for the incense used in temple ceremonies. There are depictions of the strange animals and exotic plants seen there, the foreign architecture and strange landscapes as well as the different-looking people. At the end of this colonnade is the **Hathor Chapel**, with two chambers both with Hathor-headed columns. On the north wall is a faded relief of Hatshepsut's soldiers in naval dress in the goddess's honour. Beyond the pillared halls is a three-roomed chapel cut into the rock, now closed to the public, with reliefs of the queen in front of the deities, and with a small figure behind the door of Senenmut, the temple's architect and some believe Hatshepsut's lover.

VALLEY OF THE KINGS

Once called the Great Necropolis of Millions of Years of Pharaoh, or the Place of Truth, the **Valley of the Kings** (Wadi Biban al-Muluk; Map p116; www.thebanmapping project.com; adult/student for 3 tombs excl Ramses VI, Ay & Tutankhamun E£80/40, Tomb of Ay available from the Antiquities Inspectorate office near Medinat Habu E£25/15, Tomb of Ramses VI E£50/25, Tomb of Tutankhamun E£100/60; 6am-4pm winter, 6am-5pm summer) has 63 magnificent royal tombs from the New Kingdom Period,

ROBERT HARDING PICTURE LIBRARY LTD/ALAMY
Chamber in the tomb of Seti I (p120)

The Ramesseum (below)

IZZET KERIBAR

↘ IF YOU LIKE...

If you like **Deir al-Bahri** (p117), then you'll also like some of the other surviving mortuary temples:

- **Temple of Seti I** (Map p116; tickets from the Antiquities Inspectorate office; adult/student E£30/15; ☉ 6am-5pm) The temple sees few visitors, despite its picturesque location near a palm grove and recent restoration after being severely damaged by floods in 1994. The walls of the columned portico at the west facade of the temple, and those of the hypostyle court beyond it, contain some superbly executed reliefs.
- **The Ramesseum** (Map p116; tickets from the Antiquities Inspectorate office; adult/student E£35/20; ☉ 6am-5pm) The Ramesseum is famous for the scattered remains of fallen statues that inspired the English poet Shelley's poem 'Ozymandias', using the undeniable fact of Ramses II's mortality to ridicule his aspirations to immortality.
- **Temple of Merenptah** (Map p116; adult/student E£15/10) Merenptah succeeded his father Ramses II in 1213 BC and ruled for 10 years. In the 19th century, the 'Israel Stele', now in the Egyptian Museum in Cairo, was found here, which is the only known Egyptian text to mention 'Israel' (which Merenptah claimed to have defeated). At the small **museum** near the entrance, the history of the temple is illustrated with text, plans and finds from excavations.

550–1069 BC), all very different from each other. The secluded site enclosed by steep cliffs was easy to guard and, when seen from the Theban plain, appears to be the site of the setting sun, associated with the afterlife by ancient Egyptians. The tombs have suffered great damage from treasure hunters, floods and, in recent years, from mass tourism: carbon dioxide, friction and humidity produced by the average of 2.8g of sweat left by each visitor have affected the reliefs and the pigments of the wall paintings. The Department of Antiquities has installed dehumidifiers and glass screens in the worst-affected tombs, and introduced a rotation system for opening some tombs to the public while restoring others.

As befits such an important pharaoh, **Seti I** (1294–1279 BC), son and heir of Ramses I, has one of the longest (137m) and most beautiful **tombs** (KV 17) in the valley. Its discovery by Giovanni Belzoni in 1817 generated almost the same interest as the discovery of Tutankhamun's tomb a century later. The tomb is indefinitely closed for restoration (ongoing since 1991), but soon there should be a replica of this tomb including the missing parts now in foreign museums (www.factum -arte.com/eng/con servacion/seti/seti_ en.asp).

The **Tomb of Tutankhamun** (KV 62) is small and bears all the signs of a rather hasty completion and inglorious burial. The son of Akhenaten by a minor wife, he ruled briefly (1336–1327 BC) and died young, with no great battles or buildings to his credit, so there was little time to build a tomb. The Egyptologist Howard

Carter slaved away for six seasons in the valley, excavating thousands of tonnes of sand and rubble from possible sites, believing that he would find the tomb of Tutankhamun intact with all its treasures. The first step was found on 4 November 1922, and on 5 November the rest of the steps and a sealed doorway came to light. The tomb's priceless cache of treasures, although it had been partially robbed twice in antiquity, vindicated Carter's dream beyond even his wildest imaginings. Four chambers were found crammed with jewellery, furniture, statues, chariots, musical instruments, weapons, boxes, jars and food – even the late discovery that many had been stuffed haphazardly into the wrong boxes by necropolis officials 'tidying up' after the ancient robberies does not detract from their dazzling wealth. Most of the treasure is in the Egyptian Museum in Cairo, a few pieces are in Luxor Museum, and only Tutankhamun's mummy in its gilded wooden coffin is in situ.

LEFT: THE ART ARCHIVE/ALAMY; RIGHT: JIM HENDERSON/AL

Left: Paintings in the Chapel of Anubis (p118); Right: Statue head of Hatshepsut, Temple of Hatshepsut (p117)

Deir al-Medina (Monastery of the Town) on Luxor's West Bank (below)

ANDERS BLOMQVIST

↘ IF YOU LIKE...

If you like the **Valley of the Kings** (p118) and the **Tombs of the Nobles** (p122), then you'll also like these other very different tombs:

- **Deir al-Medina** (Monastery of the Town; Map p116; tickets from the Antiquities Inspectorate office; adult/student E£30/15, extra ticket for Tomb of Peshedu adult/student E£15/10; ⊙ 6am-5pm) Many of the workers and artists who created the royal tombs lived and were buried here. Archaeologists have uncovered more than 70 houses in this village and many tombs, the most beautiful of which are now open to the public. Some of the small tombs have exquisite reliefs.

- **Valley of the Queens** (Biban al-Harim; Map p116; tickets from the Antiquities Inspectorate office; adult/student E£35/20) These tombs belonged to queens of the 19th and 20th dynasties and other members of the royal families, including princesses and the Ramesside princes. Hailed as the finest tomb in the Theban necropolis – and in all of Egypt for that matter – the **Tomb of Nefertari** was completely restored and reopened in 1995, but closed again until further notice.

- **Assasif tombs** (Map p116) This group of tombs located near Deir al-Bahri belonged to 18th-dynasty nobles, and 25th- and 26th-dynasty nobles under the Nubian pharaohs. The area is under excavation by archaeologists, but the **Tomb of Kheruef** (adult/student E£30/15; ⊙ 6am-4.30pm Oct-Apr, to 5pm May-Sep) and of **Pabasa** (adult/student E£25/15; ⊙ 6am-5pm) are open to the public, if rarely visited. Tickets are available at the ticket office of Deir al-Bahri.

The paintings in the burial chamber of the **tomb of Ramses IV** (KV 2; 1153–147 BC) have deteriorated, but there is a wonderful image of the goddess Nut, stretched across the blue ceiling, and it is the only tomb to contain the text of the Book of Nut, with a description of the daily path taken by the sun every day. The most visited tomb in the valley is the **Tomb of Ramses IX** (KV 6; 1126–1108 BC), with a

LUXOR

FRANS LEMMENS

Scenes of daily life in the Tomb of Nakht (below)

⭦ TOMBS OF THE NOBLES

The tombs in this area are some of the best, but least visited, attractions on the West Bank. Where the pharaohs decorated their tombs with cryptic passages from the Book of the Dead to guide them through the afterlife, the nobles, intent on letting the good life continue after their death, decorated their tombs with wonderfully detailed scenes of their daily lives.

Only 15 or so tombs are open to the public – they are divided into five groups and each requires a separate ticket.

The beautiful and highly colourful wall paintings in the **Tomb of Menna** and the **Tomb of Nakht** emphasise rural life in 18th-dynasty Egypt. The **Tomb of Ramose**, a governor of Thebes under Amenhotep III and Akhenaten, is fascinating because it is one of the few monuments dating from that time, a period of transition between two different forms of religious worship. The exquisite paintings and low reliefs show scenes in two different styles from the reigns of both pharaohs, depicting Ramose's funeral and his relationship with Akhenaten.

The most interesting parts of the **Tomb of Sennofer**, overseer of the Garden of Amun under Amenhotep II, are deep underground in the main chamber. The ceiling there is covered with clear paintings of grapes and vines, while most of the vivid scenes on the surrounding walls and columns depict Sennofer and the different women in his life, including his wife and daughters and his wet nurse. The **Tomb of Rekhmire**, governor under Tuthmosis III and Amenhotep II, is one of the best preserved in the area. In the first chamber, to the extreme left, are scenes of Rekhmire receiving gifts from foreign lands.

Things you need to know Map p116; tickets from the Antiquities Inspectorate ticket office; ⏱ 6am-5pm

vide entrance, a long sloping corridor, a large antechamber decorated with the animals, serpents and demons from the Book of the Dead, and then a pillared hall and short hallway before the burial chamber. Although the **tomb of Ramses VI's** (KV 9; 1147–1143 BC) plastering was not finished, its fine decoration is well preserved, with an emphasis on astronomical scenes and texts. The burial chamber is beautifully decorated, with a superb double image of Nut framing the books of the day and of the night on the ceiling. Ramses III (1184–1153 BC), the last of Egypt's warrior pharaohs, built one of the longest tombs in the Valley of the Kings. The **tomb of Ramses III** (KV 11), started but abandoned by Sethnakht (1186–1184 BC), is 125m long, much of it still beautifully decorated with colourful painted sunken reliefs featuring the traditional ritual texts (Litany of Ra, Book of Gates etc) and Ramses before the gods.

Hidden in the hills between high limestone cliffs and reached only via a steep staircase that crosses an even steeper ravine, the **tomb of Tuthmosis III** (KV 34) demonstrates the lengths to which the ancient pharaohs went to thwart the cunning of the ancient thieves. As secrecy was of utmost concern, Tuthmosis III (1479–1425 BC) chose the most inaccessible spot and designed his burial place with a series of passages at haphazard angles and fake doors to mislead or catch potential robbers.

MEDINAT HABU

Ramses III's magnificent memorial temple of **Medinat Habu** (Map p123; tickets from the Antiquities Inspectorate office nearby; ⏰ 6am-5pm) is perhaps one of the most underrated sites on the West Bank. With the Theban mountains as a backdrop and the sleepy village of Kom Lolah in front, it is a won-

derful place to spend a few hours late in the afternoon.

The site was one of the first places in Thebes to be closely associated with the local god Amun. At Medinat Habu's height there were temples, storage rooms, workshops, administrative buildings and accommodation for priests and officials. It was the centre of the economic life of Thebes for centuries and was still inhabited as late as the 9th century AD, when a plague was thought to have decimated the town. You can still see the mudbrick remains of the medieval town that gave

MEDINAT HABU   0 ⬛━━ 30 m

- Osiris Complex
- Barque Shrine
- Great Hypostyle Hall
- Victorian-Era Graffiti
- Second Court
- Second Pylon
- Window of Appearances
- First Court
- Pharaoh's Palace
- First Pylon
- Reliefs of Ramses Battling the Libyans
- Relief of the Scribes Counting the Hands & Genitals of Enemies
- Tomb Chapels of the Divine Adorers
- Sacred Lake
- Syrian Gate
- Brick Wall
- Outer Wall
- Entrance
- Hall
- Ptolemaic Pylon

the site its name (medina means 'town' or 'city') on top of the enclosure walls.

The original **Temple of Amun**, which was built by Hatshepsut and Tuthmosis III, was later completely overshadowed by the enormous **Funerary Temple of Ramses III**, the dominant feature of Medinat Habu. Ramses III was inspired in the construction of his shrine by the Ramesseum of his illustrious forebear, Ramses II.

You enter the site through the unique **Syrian Gate**, a large two-storey building modelled after an Asiatic fortress. The well-preserved **first pylon** marks the front of the temple proper. Ramses III is portrayed in its reliefs as the victor in several wars. Most famous are the fine **reliefs** of his victory over the Libyans (recognisable by their long robes, sidelocks and beards). There is also a gruesome scene of scribes tallying the number of enemies killed by counting severed hands and genitals.

To the left of the **first court** are the remains of the **Pharaoh's Palace**; the three rooms at the rear were for the royal harem. There is a window between the first court and the Pharaoh's Palace known as the **Window of Appearances**, which allowed the pharaoh to show himself to his subjects.

The reliefs of the **second pylon** feature Ramses III presenting prisoners of war to Amun and his vulture-goddess wife, Mut. Colonnades and reliefs surround the **second court**, depicting various religious ceremonies.

GETTING THERE & AROUND

Most tourists cross to the West Bank by bus or taxi via the bridge, about 7km south of town. But the river remains the quickest way to go. The *baladi* (municipal) ferry costs E£1 for foreigners (less for locals) and leaves from a dock in front of Luxor Temple. To hire a private taxi, expect to pay between E£150 and E£250 per day, depending on the season, the state of tourism and your bargaining skills. Cycling around the West Bank sights is also an option (see p133).

ACTIVITIES
BALLOONING

Hot-air ballooning to see the sun rise over the ancient monuments on the West Bank and the Theban mountains is a great way to start the day. **Hod Hod Suleiman** (Map pp96-7; ☎ 237 0116; Sharia Omar Ali, off Sharia Televizyon), **Sky Cruise of Egypt** (Map pp96-7; ☎ 237 6515; Sharia Khalid ibn al-Walid) and **Sindbad Balloons** (☎ 010 330 7708; www.sindbadballoons.com) all offer early morning flights at varying prices, often depending on how many people are taken on board. Expect to pay from €80 to €150 per person, although it should be possible to bargain, particularly out of season.

DONKEY, HORSE & CAMEL RIDES

Riding a horse, a donkey or a camel through the fields and seeing the sunset behind the Theban hills is a wonderful thing to do. The boys at the local ferry dock on the West Bank offer donkey and camel rides for about E£30 to E£40 for an hour, but beware. There are many reports of women getting hassled, and of overcharging at the end.

Excellent horses can be found at **Nobi's Arabian Horse Stables** (Map pp96-7; ☎ 23 0024, 010 504 8558; www.luxorstables.com; approx per hr E£30; ☺ 7am-sunset), which also provides riding hats, English saddles and insurance. Nobi also has 25 camels and as many donkeys at the same price, and organises longer horse riding and camping trips into the desert or a week from Luxor to Kom

WAYNE WALTON

esostris I holding two *ankh*, Luxor Museum (p114)

mbo along the West Bank. Call ahead
book, and he can arrange a hassle-
e transfer to make sure you arrive at the
ht place, as often taxi drivers will try
d take you to a friend's stable instead.
ound the corner is **Pharaoh's Stables**
ap pp96-7; ☎ 231 0015; ☒ 7am-sunset) with
rses, donkeys and camels (all E£30 to
35 per hour).

LUCCA RIDES
ke a felucca from either bank, and sail
r a few hours, catching the soft after-
on light and the sunset, cooling in the
ernoon breeze and calming down after
htseeing. Felucca prices range from
30 to E£50 per boat per hour, depend-
g on your bargaining skills.

A popular felucca trip is upriver to
Banana Island, a tiny isle dotted with
palms about 5km from Luxor. The trip
takes two to three hours. Plan it in such
a way that you're on your way back in
time to watch a brilliant Nile sunset from
the boat.

TOURS

Because of the bargaining and hassle involved, some people may find independent travel challenging at times, and a day
tour in an air-conditioned bus, taking in
the main sights, might be just the thing.
Several of the more reliable travel agents
are all near to each other, next door to the
Old Winter Palace Hotel.

Aladin Tours (Map pp96-7; ☎ 237 2386, 010
601 6132; http://nefertitihotel.com/tours; Nefertiti Hotel, Sharia as-Sahbi, East Bank) This very
helpful travel agency, run by the young,
energetic Aladin, organises sightseeing
tours in Luxor and around as well as in
the Western Desert, plus boat trips and
ferry tickets to Sinai.

QEA Travel Agency (Map pp96-7; ☎ 231
1667; Al-Gezira, West Bank) A different approach from this British-run agency that
runs tailor-made tours in and around
Luxor, as well as further afield to the
Red Sea or the Western Desert. A per-
centage of its profits go towards chari-
table projects in Egypt.

RIVER TOURS TO ABYDOS & DENDARA

The **Iberotel Luxor Hotel** (Map pp96-7;
☎ 238 0925; www.iberotel-eg.com; Sharia Khaled
ibn al Walid) organises day cruises from
7am to 7pm on the *Lotus Boat* to Dendara
from US$60, including lunch, tea, guide
and admission fees. The **Nefertiti Hotel**
(Map pp96-7; ☎ 010 601 6132; www.nefertitihotel
.com/tours; Sharia Sahbi) also organises day
cruises to Dendara.

Celebrating the Moulid of Abu al-Haggag

KICCA TOMMASI/IMAGESTATE/PHOTOLIB

FESTIVALS & EVENTS

The town's biggest traditional festival is the **Moulid of Abu al-Haggag**. One of Egypt's largest *moulid*s (saints' festivals), it is held in honour of Luxor's patron sheikh, Yousef Abu al-Haggag, a 12th-century Iraqi who settled in Luxor. The *moulid* takes place around the Mosque of Abu al-Haggag, the town's oldest mosque, which is built on top of the northeastern corner of Luxor Temple. It's a raucous five-day carnival that takes place in the third week before Ramadan.

In February each year a **marathon** (☎ 02-2260 6930, 012 214 8839; www.egyptian marathon.com) is held on the West Bank. It begins at Deir al-Bahri and loops around the main antiquities sites before ending back where it began.

SLEEPING

Luxor has a wide range of hotels for all budgets. Most package-tour hotels are on the East Bank, and so are the shops, restaurants and the hectic town life. The West Bank is developing at a fast rate and is cer-

tainly no longer as rural as it once was. B it is still a tranquil place, where the pa of life is much slower and where evening are more often than not blissfully quie Prices for many hotels drop considerab in summer; prepare to bargain. At all cos avoid the hotel touts who may pounce you as you get off the train or bus – the will get a 25% to 40% commission f bringing you into the hotel, but that w be added to your bill. Many hotels in t budget and midrange bracket offer fr or cheap transfers from the airport or tra station, so to avoid touts and bargainir with taxi drivers call ahead and arrang to be picked up.

BUDGET

Luxor has a good selection of budg places. Many boast both roof gardens ar washing machines. The budget hotels the West Bank are particularly good val much quieter and often offering a mo authentic meeting with locals.

Nefertiti Hotel (Map pp96-7; ☎ 237 2 www.nefertitihotel.com; Sharia as-Sahabi, bt

aria Maabad al-Karnak & Sharia as-Souq, East
nk; s/d/tr US$9/13/16; ⚅ 🖥) No wonder
is hotel is popular with our readers: the
oms are simple but cosy, the small pri-
te bathrooms are spotless, the breakfast
good and served on the roof terrace,
d the staff is super friendly. On Saturday
d Wednesday nights there is a folkloric
ow, with dinner (E£75), dervish danc-
g and snake charming, at the rooftop
staurant.

Al-Gezira Hotel (Map pp96-7; ☎ 231 0034;
w.el-gezira.com; Gezira al-Bayrat, West Bank;
/tr E£80/120/150; ⚅) Different in style, as
s in a modern building overlooking the
h and fertile agricultural land in the vil-
e of Gezira al-Bayrat, this hotel is very
ch a home away from home. The 11
sy and homey rooms are pristine, all
th private bathrooms, overlooking the
e or a branch of the Nile. Management
d staff are friendly and efficient, and the
stairs rooftop restaurant, where break-
t is served, has great Nile views as well
cold beer (E£12) and good traditional
yptian food.

IDRANGE

xor has an ever-growing selection of
drange hotels on both banks, often
tering to families. If you are looking for
otel with character, then check out the
all mudbrick, traditional-style hotels
the West Bank. The East Bank hotels
often slick, modern places, popular
h budget and adventure-tour groups.
ere are some excellent bargains in this
tegory, with good facilities at attrac-
e rates. Out of season some incredibly
eap packages can be found, including
hts from the UK.

ST BANK

w Pola Hotel (Map pp96-7; ☎ 236 5081;
w.newpolahotel.com; Sharia Khalid ibn al-Walid;

s/d US$20/30; ⚅ 🖥 📺) Great views and a
small rooftop pool make the New Pola
an excellent bargain. The decor is kitsch
but the 81 air-con rooms are spotless and
come with minibars, satellite TV and private bathrooms; half also have Nile views.
The staff is very friendly and many clients
are return customers.

Philippe Hotel (Map pp96-7; ☎ 237 2284,
012 922 0336; www.philippeluxorhotel.com;
Sharia Dr Labib Habashi; s US$20-22, d US$29-36;
⚅ 📺) Near the Corniche, the Philippe is
immensely popular with budget tours,
offering comfortable and clean rooms
with satellite TV, private bathrooms and
air-con. The style is rather impersonal, but
it is good value, and there is a roof terrace with a small pool. Front rooms are
the best: most have small balconies and
receive plenty of light.

WEST BANK

Hotel Sheherazade (Map pp96-7; ☎ 231
1228, 012 212 3719; www.hotelsheherazade.com;
Al-Gezira; s/d/tr E£150/220/230, flat E£300; ⚅)
Mohammed Sanusy dreamt of building
this place for several years, and he takes
great pride in his hotel. The 17 comfortable and spacious rooms are decorated
with local colour and furnishings and all
have en suite bathrooms. The Moorish-
style building is surrounded by a garden.
Three-course meals are also available for
E£40 per person.

Beit Sabée (Map p116; ☎ 010 632 4926,
010 570 5341; info@beitsabee.com; Kom Lolah; d
€40-70, with air-con €50-80; ⚅) More like a
house than a hotel, Beit Sabée has appeared in design magazines for its cool
use of Nubian colours and local furnishings with a twist. Set in a traditional-style
two-storey mudbrick house, the eight
bedrooms with en suite bathrooms are
effortlessly stylish, and breakfast is served
in the courtyard or on the roof.

TOP END

Luxor has many four- and five-star hotels, all, with one notable exception, run by international hotel chains. Most are much cheaper when booked on the internet.

Old Winter Palace Hotel (Map pp96–7; ☎ 237 1197; www.sofitel.com; Corniche an-Nil, East Bank; old wing r €180–350, ste €420–890, new wing pavilion r €108–120, ste €325; ⌧ ⌧ ⌧) The Old Winter Palace was built to attract the aristocracy of Europe and is one of Egypt's most famous historic hotels. A wonderfully atmospheric Victorian pile, it has high ceilings, lots of gorgeous textiles, fabulous views over the Nile, an enormous garden with exotic trees and shrubs, a huge swimming pool, table-tennis tables and a tennis court. The rooms vary in size and decor, but are very comfortable, and the food is excellent as is the service.

Al-Moudira (off Map p116; ☎ 012 325 1307; www.moudira.com; Daba'iyya, West Bank; r €220, ste €270; ⌧ ⌧ ⌧ ⌧) Al-Moudira is a true luxury hotel, with an individuality that is missing from so many other hotels in Luxor. A Moorish fantasy of soaring vaults,

pointed arches and enormous dome surrounded by lush green and birdsor the hotel has 54 rooms grouped togeth around small courtyards. Each room different in shape, size (all are very lar though) and colour, each with its ov hand-painted *trompe l'oeil* theme a with antiques found throughout Egyp The public spaces are even more spe tacular with traditional *mashrabiy* (wooden lattice) work combined wi work by contemporary 'orientalist' a ists. It's a long way from anywhere, b transport is fairly cheap.

EATING

Most people come to Luxor for mon ments and not for its fine cuisine – a go thing as most restaurants, particularly the hotels, are pretty mediocre. Howev the food is gradually getting better, wit few restaurants upping the standards doing what Egyptians do best: cook ho est traditional Egyptian food. Outside t hotels few serve alcohol or accept crec card payment; exceptions are noted in t

Hypostyle hall at the Ramesseum (p119)

views. Unless otherwise noted, restaurants tend to open from about 9am until midnight.

RESTAURANTS
AST BANK

asis Café (Map pp96-7; ☎ 012 336 7121; aria Dr Labib Habashi; mains E£15-60; ✆ 10am-pm; ⊠) Set in a renovated 1930s build-g right in the centre of town, with jazz oftly playing, smoking and nonsmok-g rooms, the *New Yorker* to read and iendly staff, this is the perfect place for inch, to linger over a good morning tte or to spend the afternoon reading. he food is good too, with an extensive runch menu and a regular menu of in-rnational dishes, including pastas (E£20 to E£30), grilled meats (E£47 to E£60), fill-g sandwiches (E£25), daily specials on e blackboard and a wide selection of astries.

Sofra (Map pp96-7; ☎ 235 9752; www.sofra m.eg; 90 Sharia Mohammed Farid, off Sharia -Manshiya; mains E£20-55; ✆ 11am-midnight) ofra remains our favourite restaurant in uxor. Located in a 1930s house, away om all the tourist tat, it is as Egyptian can be, in menu and decor, and even price. The house is filled with antique rniture, chandeliers and traditional corations, all simple but cosy and very steful. The menu is large, featuring all e traditional Egyptian dishes, such as uffed pigeon and excellent duck, as well a large selection of salads, dips (E£4) d mezze. Alcohol is not available, but ere are delicious fresh juices on offer, d *sheesha* afterwards.

As-Sahaby Lane (Map pp96-7; ☎ 236 09; www.nefertitihotel.com/sahabi.htm; Sharia -Sahaby, off Sharia as-Souq; mains E£35-60; 9am-11.30pm) Great easygoing alfresco staurant in the lane running between souq and the street to Karnak Temple.

Fresh and well-prepared Egyptian dishes like *tagens* (stews cooked in earthenware pots) are served as well as good pizzas and salads. The young staff is very friendly, always ready to help or up for a chat. This terrace is a great place to watch the world go by, or relax from shopping in the souq.

1886 Restaurant (Map pp96-7; ☎ 238 0422; Old Winter Palace Hotel, Corniche an-Nil; starters E£35-122, mains E£60-190; ✆ dinner only; ⊠) The 1886 is the gourmet restaurant in town, serving inventive Mediterranean-French food and a few Egyptian dishes with a twist, in a grand old-style dining room with very formal waiters. Guests are expected to dress up for the occasion – men wear a tie and/or jacket (some are available for borrowing) – and the food is superb and light.

WEST BANK

Restaurant Mohammed (Map p116; ☎ 012 385 0227; Kom Lolah; set menu E£20-40) With an outdoor terrace and laid-back atmosphere, Mohammed's is the perfect place to recharge batteries in the middle of a day exploring temples and tombs, or to linger in the evening. The menu is small but includes meat grills, delicious chicken and duck as well as stuffed pigeon, served with fries and excellent simple salads. Stella beer is available (E£10) and Egyptian wine.

Al-Moudira (off Map p116; ☎ 012 325 1307; Daba'iyya; mains E£75-95; ✆ 8am-midnight) In keeping with its flamboyant decor, Al-Moudira has the most sophisticated and the most expensive food on the West Bank, with great salads and grills at lunchtime and a more elaborate menu for dinner with a delicious Mediterranean-Lebanese cuisine. This is a great place for a romantic dinner in the courtyard, or by the fire in winter. Call ahead for reservations.

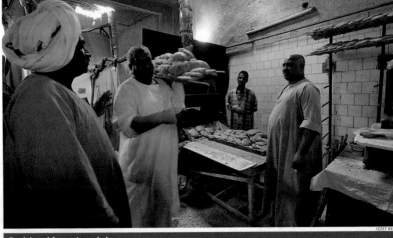

IZZET KEF

Fresh bread from a Luxor bakery

SELF-CATERING

On the West Bank try the food and fruit shops on the main street in Al-Gezira, or head for the wonderful weekly market **Souq at-Talaat** (Map p116; ☾ Tue mornings), in Taref opposite the Temple of Seti I. **Arkwrights Gourmet Food** (Map pp96-7; ☎ 228 2335; www.arkwrights-luxor.com; Sharia al-Mahdy, off Sharia Khaled ibn al-Walid, near St Joseph Hotel; ☾ 6am-midnight) is the place to stock up for a more sophisticated picnic, as they recently started doing packed lunches, freshly made sandwiches and salads to take away.

DRINKING
EAST BANK

Metropolitan Café & Restaurant (Map pp96-7; lower level, Corniche an-Nil) A pleasant, popular outdoor cafe, right on the Nile, in front of the Old Winter Palace Hotel. The perfect place to enjoy a sundowner, but apart from some snacks with the drinks, the food is pretty mediocre.

New Oum Koulsoum Coffee Shop (Map pp96-7; Sharia as-Souq; ☾ 24hr) Pleasant

ahwa (coffeehouse) right at the hea of the souq, on a large terrace with we come mist machines, where you ca recover from shopping and haggling in th souq and watch the crowds without an hassle. On the menu are fresh juices (E£ to E£15), hot and cold drinks and a goc *sheesha* (E£10) as well as 'profession Nespresso' coffee (E£15).

Kings Head Pub (Map pp96-7; ☎ 2 0489; Sharia Khaled ibn al-Walid; ☒) A relaxe and perennially popular place to hav a drink and shoot pool, the Kings Hea tries to capture the atmosphere of a English pub without being twee. Th laid-back atmosphere also means th women can come here without bei harassed.

Cocktail Sunset (Map pp96-7; ☎ 238 05 Corniche an-Nil, opposite Luxor Museum; ☒) C a pontoon, which rumour has it on belonged to King Farouk's father, on th Nile, this place is hugely popular for congenial atmosphere, cocktails and ic cold beers. There is a nice fashion sto on the 1st floor.

EST BANK

here are no real bars on the West Bank;
inking of alcohol is done at restaurants
not at all.

Maratonga Cafeteria (Map p116; ☎ 231
33; Kom Lolah; ⏰ 6am-11pm) This friendly
utdoor cafe-restaurant, in front of
edinat Habu, is the best place to sip
cold drink under a big tree after wan-
ering through Ramses III's magnificent
mple, or have a delicious *tagen* (E£35)
salad for lunch. The view is superlative
d the atmosphere is relaxing.

NTERTAINMENT

ith tourism booming in Luxor, the town
busy at night. The Temple of Luxor is
en until 10pm and worth seeing at
ght; the souq is open late as well and
ore lively at night than in the day.
owever, this is not exactly the place for
ibbing, even if you're into dancing to
tmoded disco music. The best discos
e at **Tutotel Partner Hotel** (Map pp96-7;
237 7990), one of the more popular op-
ns, while at **Hotel Mercure** (Map pp96-7;
238 0944; nonguest minimum E£50) the extra
arge covers you for watching the belly-
ncing show at 11.30pm too.

HOPPING

e whole range of Egyptian souvenirs is
ailable in Luxor town, but for alabaster
s best to head for the West Bank. Take
re when buying, as sometimes what
sses for stone is actually wax with stone
ips. Avoid going with a tour guide as
commission will invariably be added
your bill.

Habiba (Map pp96-7; ☎ 010 124 2026; www
bibagallery.com; Sharia Sidi Mahmoud, off Sharia
Souq; ⏰ 10am-10pm) Run by an Australian
man who loves to travel in Egypt
d who wants to promote the best of
yptian crafts, this tiny shop goes from

strength to strength. A world away from
what is available in the nearby souq.

Caravanserai (Map p116; ☎ 012 327 8771;
www.caravanserailuxor.com; Kom Lolah; ⏰ 8am-
10pm) This delightful shop, the only one
of its kind on the West Bank, is kept by
the friendly Khairy and his family in a
beautifully painted mudbrick house near
Medinat Habu. The shop has the beautiful pottery from the Western oases, plus
Siwan embroideries, amazing appliqué
bags and lots of other interesting crafts
that can be found almost nowhere else
in Egypt.

GETTING THERE & AWAY
AIR
EgyptAir (Map pp96-7; ☎ 238 0581; Corniche
an-Nil; ⏰ 8am-8pm) operates several daily

Shopkeepers in Luxor

flights between Cairo, Luxor and Aswan. There are four flights per week to Sharm el-Sheikh.

BUS

The **bus station** (off Map pp96-7; ☎ 237 2118, 232 3218) is out of town on the road to the airport, about 1km from the airport, but tickets for the **Upper Egypt Bus Co** (Map pp96-7; ☎ 232 3218, 237 2118; Midan al-Mahatta) buses can be bought at its office in town, south of the train station. A taxi from the town to the bus station will cost around E£25 to E£35, but check because some buses leave from the office near the train station. There are buses to all major towns in Egypt. **Superjet** (☎ 236 7732) runs buses from Luxor bus station at 8pm to Cairo via Hurghada.

CRUISER

There are numerous cruisers plying the waters between Luxor and Aswan. Most cruises starting from Luxor are a day longer than those starting from Aswan, partly because they are going against the Nile's strong current. If you want to spen longer in Luxor or are concerned abou cost, start from Aswan and head nort Prices vary considerably according to th time of year, the state of tourism, and ho you book.

M/S Sudan (☎ France 00 33 1 7300 818 www.steam-ship-sudan.com; 3-night cruise s from €750/990, 4-night cruise from €945/1265; ☒ The *Sudan* was built as part of Thoma Cook's steamer fleet in 1885 and wa once owned by King Fouad. It was als used as a set in the film *Death on th Nile*. It has been refurbished and offe 23 cabins, all with private bathroom, a con and access to the deck. It's unusu in that it has no pool, but it's also uniqu because it has so much history and cha acter, something sorely missing on mo cruisers.

M/S Sun Boat III (www.abercrombieke .co.uk; per person per night from US$575; ☒ ☒ Abercrombie & Kent's most intima cruiser is the beautiful *Sun Boat III,* wi 14 cabins and four suites decorated a contemporary Egyptian style, straig

Sunrise at Luxor

RICHARD I'A

t of a style magazine. The 11-night
nerary includes visits to Dendara and
ɔydos. Dinner on board is à la carte or
set menu with two European choices,
ɪd one Egyptian.

M/S Philae (www.oberoihotels.com; per
rson per night from €150; ⊠ ⊠) Designed
 resemble a Mississippi paddle boat,
e award-winning *Philae* runs four- and
-night cruises. Its interior is filled with
ɔod panelling and antiques, and all
ɔms have a balcony. The old-world feel
backed up by state-of-the-art water fil-
ation, a library and all the comforts of a
ɔod five-star hotel.

ELUCCA
ɔu can't take a felucca from Luxor to
wan; most feluccas leave from Esna
ɛcause of the Esna Lock. But unless you
ɪve a strong wind, it can take days to
ɔ more than a few kilometres in this
ɾection.

ɛRVICE TAXI
ɛ station for service taxis and minibuses
ɪap pp96–7) on the East Bank is on the
ɔrth side of Sharia Maabad al-Karnak,
ɛar Rezeiky Camp, 2km from the centre
 Luxor.

ɾAIN
ɪxor Station (Map pp96-7; ☎ 237 2018; www
ɪyptrail.gov.eg; Midan al-Mahatta) has left-
ɪggage facilities, plenty of cardphones
ɪd a post office.
 The **Abela Egypt Sleeping Train** (☎ 237
15, in Cairo 02-2574 9474; www.sleepingtrains
m) goes daily to Cairo at 9.40pm and
.50am (single/double including din-
ɛr and breakfast US$80/120, child four
 19 years US$45, nine hours). There
ɛ no student discounts available and
kets must be paid for in US dollars or
ɛuros.

GETTING AROUND
TO/FROM THE AIRPORT
Luxor airport is 7km east of town. A sign
at the airport announces the official tariffs
to get a taxi to different parts of Luxor,
between E£25 to E£50, but none of the
taxi drivers will accept these prices: the
asking price is often about E£70 to E£100
or more, and in low season when there is
not enough work a fight between drivers
may erupt. In short, it is a major hassle, so
if you want peace of mind ask the hotel
to arrange your transfer. There is no bus
between the airport and the town.

BICYCLE
The town lends itself to cycling, and dis-
tances on the generally flat West Bank are
just far enough to provide some exercise
but not exhaust (except when it's too hot).
Cycling at night is inadvisable given the
local habit of leaving headlights off.
 A good place to rent is from restaurant
7 days 7 ways (off Map pp96-7; ☎ 012 020
1876; www.bikerentalluxor.com; Sharia Sheraton;
⊗ 8am-11pm), which also organises cycling
tours around Luxor.
 You can take bikes across to the West
Bank on the *baladi* ferry (see p124). If
you're based on the West Bank, you can
find several bike rentals near the ferry
landing, or try renting from your hotel.

FELUCCA
There is a multitude of feluccas to take
you on short trips around Luxor, leaving
from various points all along the river.
How much you pay depends on your bargaining skills, but you're looking at about
E£20 to E£40 for an hour of sailing.

HANTOUR
Also called a *calèche,* these horse and carriages cost about E£20 to E£50 per hour
depending on your haggling skills (this is

LUXOR

GETTING AROUND

JOHN WARBURTON-LEE PHOTOGRAPHY/JULIAN LOVE/PHOTOLIB

A *hantour* (also called a *calèche*) passing Luxor Temple

where you really need them). Expect to pay about E£20 to get to Karnak.

TAXI

There are plenty of taxis in Luxor, but passengers still have to bargain hard for trips.

A short trip around town is likely to co· at least E£10. Taxis can also be hired f· day trips around the West Bank; expe· to pay E£150 to E£250, depending on t· length of the excursion and your barga· ing skills.

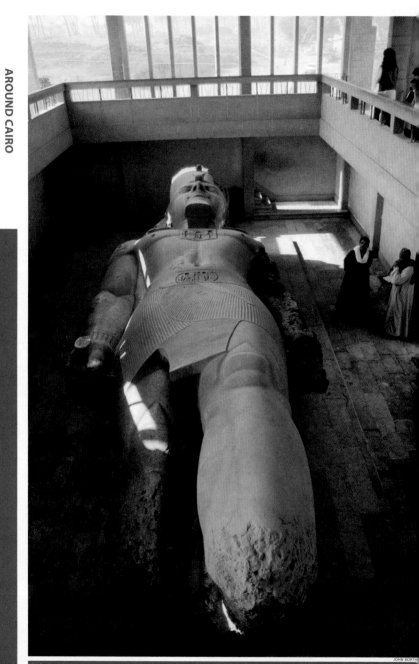

JOHN BORTH

Fallen limestone statue of Ramses II, Memphis museum (p147)

AROUND CAIRO

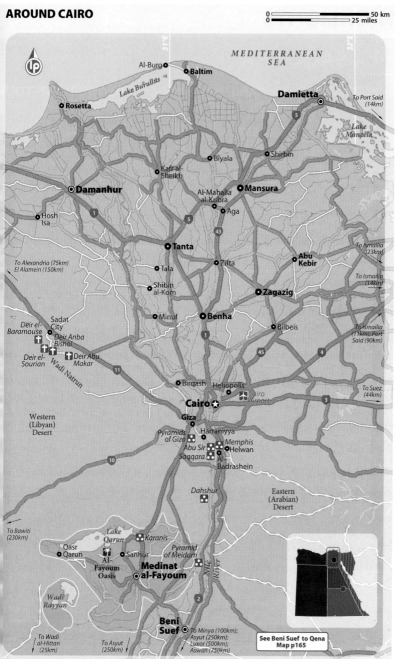

0 — 50 km
0 — 25 miles

MEDITERRANEAN SEA

Al-Burg
Baltim
Lake Burullus
Damietta
To Port Said (14km)
Rosetta
Lake Manzala
Biyala
Shirbin
Kafr al-Sheikh
Damanhur
Al-Mahalla al-Kubra
Mansura
Hosh Isa
Aga
To Ismailia (23km)
To Alexandria (75km)
El Alamein (150km)
Tanta
Zifta
Abu Kebir
To Ismailia (14km)
Tala
Shibin al-Kom
Zagazig
Minuf
Benha
Bilbeis
To Ismailia (11km); Port Said (90km)
Deir el-Baramouse
Sadat City
Deir Anba Bishoi
Deir Abu Makar
Deir el-Sourian
Wadi Natrun
Birqash
Heliopolis
Cairo Airport
To Suez (44km)
Western (Libyan) Desert
Cairo
Giza
Haraniyya
Pyramids of Giza
Abu Sir
Memphis
Helwan
Saqqara
Al-Badrashein
Dahshur
Eastern (Arabian) Desert
To Bawiti (230km)
Lake Qarun
Karanis
Qasr Qarun
Al-Fayoum Oasis
Sanhur
Pyramid of Meidum
Medinat al-Fayoum
Nile River
Wadi Rayyan
To Wadi al-Hittan (25km)
To Asyut (250km)
Beni Suef
To Minya (100km); Asyut (250km); Luxor (500km); Aswan (750km)

See Beni Suef to Qena Map p165

HIGHLIGHTS

1 SAQQARA

BY NABIL NAGUIB, EGYPTOLOGIST AND TOU GUIDE

Egypt has many monuments, but Saqqara stands out. This was the first time in history that human built a monumental structure in limestone. What was achieved by Pharaoh Zoser and his architect changed the world forever. It is important to remember that as you walk around the area.

⭢ NABIL NAGUIB'S DON'T MISS LIST

❶ THE COLONNADE

This is how you enter the Step Pyramid complex and it is a wonderful thing. There are 40 columns here, all original, in the shape of a bundle of papyrus or palm stems. It was the corridor that pharaohs and priests walked along as they approached the Heb-Sed Court.

❷ MASTABA OF TI

Ti was in charge of the Abu Sir pyramids nearby, and his wife was a priestess, so they were important. But the importance now is the quality of decora-

tion: here we can see people workin cooking, dancing, even watching o for crocodiles.

❸ MUSEUM OF IMHOTEP

Architects did not get much recogn tion in ancient Egypt, but Imhotep the exception and it is good that h was, for he was the one who mad the jump from the benchlike mastab tombs of earlier kings, to the Ste Pyramid of Zoser. Later generation worshipped him as a god. The ne **museum** (adult/student E£20/10; ⏰ 9a

Clockwise from top: Statue and wall carvings, Saqqara; Step Pyramid of Zoser (p148) up close; Exhibit at the Imhotep Museum (above); The tiers of the Step Pyramid of Zoser; Saqqara visitors centre and Imhotep Museum

30pm) at Saqqara is a great place to nderstand the extent of his genius. It located beside the ticket office.

INSIDE THE PYRAMID F TETI

eti's pyramid was built 300 years after oser's and, like his, was a step pyra- id cased in limestone. The outside as been quarried, but the inside has urvived and the burial chamber is in- ct, even with its basalt sarcophagus. s you can't go inside Zoser's, this akes a good substitute.

❺ TOMB OF PTAHHOTEP

Ptahhotep lived after Zoser and before Teti. As a high official, he lived the high life – in the paintings in his tomb you can even see him having his wig fitted and feet massaged.

⇘ THINGS YOU NEED TO KNOW

When to visit Spring and autumn are best, although April can be very windy **To avoid crowds** Saqqara is a very big site and it's usually possible to keep the crowds at a distance **See our author's review on p147**

HIGHLIGHTS

2

⬎ DAHSHUR

While the crowds get ever thicker around the Pyramids of Giza, the wonderful pyramids at **Dahshur** (p153) see few visitors. The Red Pyramid is the oldest of all the 'true' pyramids (as opposed to the Step Pyramid at Saqqara). What's more, you are likely to be alone when you step into its interior. Its twin, the Bent Pyramid, shows how the architects struggled to achieve perfection.

3

⬎ THE DESERT

It may not be a true oasis, but Al-Fayoum is still hemmed in by the desert. A short drive away from its fields and palm groves is the **Wadi Rayyan Protected Area** (p158), one of the most accessible areas of desert and a haven for migratory birds. A further 55km into the desert, **Wadi al-Hittan** (p158) is a Unesco World Heritage Site and home to fossilised whales.

4

⬎ WADI NATRUN

Ancient Egyptians came to this valley between Cairo and Alexandria to find natron, used in mummification. But since at least the 4th century, **Wadi Natrun** (p159) has been home to Copts, whose monasteries have provided a safe haven at times of persecution. The four surviving monasteries are a window into Coptic history and resilience.

5

⬎ TOMB OF MERERUKA

You don't have to go to Luxor to see wonderful tombs: Saqqara has plenty of them, including several from the time of Tutankhamun and Ramses II. One of the finest tombs belonged to the Old Kingdom vizier **Mereruka** (p152). The carvings are exceptionally beautiful and give an idea of how good the good life could be in ancient Egypt.

6

⬎ PALM GROVES

The landscape south of Giza is thick with palm groves. The area between Saqqara and Dahshur is particularly rich. While so much else in has been transformed in the past century, a drive along the north–south road between the two will give you classic views of palms and pyramids.

2 CHERYL FORBES; 3 SHANIA SHEGEDYN; 4 PETER M. WILSON/ALAMY; 5 JOHN ELK III; 6 S TAUQUEUR/F1 ONLINE/PHOTOLIBRARY

A taxi in front of the Red Pyramid, Dahshur (p154); 3 Looking out from a cafe at Wadi al-Hittan (p158); 4 Deir Anba Bishoi (p161), Wadi Natrun; 5 Reliefs in the Tomb of Mereruka, Saqqara (p152); 6 Pyramids and palm groves

THE BEST...

↘ WAYS TO EXPERIENCE THE DESERT

- Take a picnic and settle into the sands around Saqqara once you have seen the **Step Pyramid** (p148).
- Early Coptic hermits escaped the temptations of the world at **Wadi Natrun** (p159). Although much of the wadi is now farmed, the desert is never far away.
- Walk into the deep desert along trails laid out from **Wadi al-Hittan** (p158), the Valley of the Whales.

↘ PLACES WITH A VIEW

- Along the road between Saqqara and Dahshur there are great views of the pyramid fields. One of the best is from the ridge at **Memphis** (p146), beyond the agricultural land at the edge of the desert.
- The walkway above the **Great South Court** (p149) at Saqqara for a view of the Step Pyramid and to imagine the Heb-Sed (Jubilee) Festival.
- The ridge in front of the **Ptolemaic temple** (p157) of Qasr Qarun for a view of Lake Qarun and the desert.

↘ ANCIENT MONUMENTS

- Pharaoh Zoser's **Step Pyramid** (p148) was such an extraordinary leap of the imagination that the architect was later made a god.
- The fallen **statue of Ramses II** (p146), at Memphis, is one of the few remaining clues to the magnificence of the ancient capital.
- Dahshur's **Red Pyramid** (p154) is often overlooked but is almost as spectacular as the Great Pyramid at Giza.

DE AGOSTINI EDITORE/PHOTOLIBR

Frieze of cobras at the Great South Court, Saqqara (p149)

THINGS YOU NEED TO KNOW

✒ VITAL STATISTICS

- **Telephone codes** Memphis (☎ 02), Al-Fayoum (☎ 084)
- **Best time to go** Autumn and spring, though April can be the season of sandstorms; summer is blisteringly hot

✒ PLACES IN A NUTSHELL

- **Saqqara** (p147) The cemetery of Memphis, ancient Egypt's long-time capital.
- **Al-Fayoum Oasis** (p154) Not a true oasis, as it is connected to the Nile, but a lush, remote, desert-hemmed patch of land.
- **Wadi Natrun** (p159) A remote desert valley where early Christian hermits went to escape the temptations and persecutions of the world.

✒ ADVANCE PLANNING

- **Before going to Wadi Rayyan** Contact the Fayoum Tourism Authority (below) to check whether you need permission from the tourist police in Medinat al-Fayoum.

✒ RESOURCES

- **Fayoum Tourism Authority** (☎ 624 2313; Governorate Bldg, Sharia Saad Zaghloul, Medinat al-Fayoum) This is the place to come for guides to take you around the sites of Al-Fayoum Oasis.

- **Guardian's Egypt** (www.guardians .net) Has links to images and explanations of several pyramids and monuments around Cairo, with bulletins from Dr Zahi Hawass, the secretary-general of the Supreme Council of Antiquities.

✒ GETTING AROUND

- **Taxis** The best way of seeing the sights around Cairo. Fix a price (including petrol) and rent one for the day.
- **Tours** Many companies operating out of Cairo offer tours that take in Saqqara and other sights outside the city. See p82.

✒ BE FOREWARNED

- **Permits** There are travel restrictions in place in some parts of this area, either because it is a military zone or, as with Wadi Rayyan, because travel in the desert requires permission.
- **Pyramid access** While the sights at Saqqara are fully manned, you may need to look around for the guard to allow you access to some of the more out-of-the-way monuments.

ITINERARIES

THE PYRAMID FIELDS One Day

The many pyramids around Cairo make a great day out and have
story to tell: visit them in chronological order and you can see the wa
ancient architects worked from the basic mastaba to the comple
Great Pyramid at Giza.

Start at the beginning, at **(1) Saqqara** (p147). The Mastaba of T
gives an idea of the sort of structures that existed before pyramid
(and also has some fabulous decoration inside). The nearby Ste
Pyramid, the oldest of all pyramids, built around 2650 BC, evolve
from a mastaba.

From Saqqara, drive south to the **(2) Pyramid of Meidum** (p156
the 'Collapsed' Pyramid. Built around 50 years after the Step Pyramic
the Pyramid of Meidum earned its nickname because only the cor
of what was a 92m-high pyramid remains. Begun as a step pyramic
it was eventually cased with smooth, sloping sides.

The Meidum Pyramid may have been finished by Sneferu, wh
is also responsible for two of the most impressive structures a
(3) Dahshur (p153), which you will pass on your way back along
this same road to Cairo. The Bent Pyramid – also known as Sneferu'
Southern Pyramid – takes its name from the shift in angle of incline o
the pyramid's sides, thought to be due to a design flaw. The nearb
Red Pyramid, Sneferu's Northern Pyramid and the one in which th
great pharaoh was probably buried, is the world's oldest true pyramic
and one of the most impressive to enter. It is also one of the tallest o
all Egypt's pyramids – only the Great Pyramid at Giza, built by Sneferu'
son, Cheops, is taller.

VALLEY OF MONASTERIES One Day

Head to **(1) Wadi Natrun** (p159) for a unique encounter with earl
Christianity. This could be a day trip from Cairo or a stop en route t
Alexandria. The most easily accessed of the four monasteries in th
valley is **(2) Deir Anba Bishoi** (p161). Its oldest church dates back t
the 4th century and the time of St Bishoi. Two hundred years afte
that first monastery was founded, a breakaway group of monks buil
(3) Deir el-Sourian (p161), named after Syrian monks who lived her
at one time. This monastery has the most interesting church in th
valley, the 10th-century Church of the Virgin, with wonderful decora
tion, including an inlaid ebony door and painted murals.

DESERT ADVENTURE Three Days

Start by driving out of the Nile Valley and across the barren land
scape towards Al-Fayoum Oasis. Take a break at **(1) Karanis** (p156
to see the Graeco-Roman temples and museum before heading t

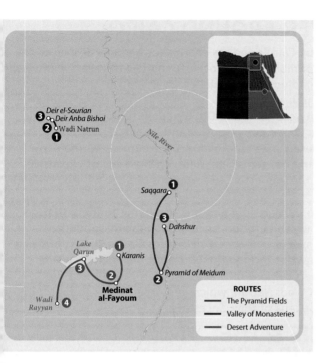

Medinat al-Fayoum (p154), stopping briefly to see the waterwheels nd to pick up a guide, if you want one), before spending the night on) **Lake Qarun** (p156). Enjoy the second day in the sands, visiting the **) Wadi Rayyan Protected Area** (p158) – you might find drinks and ven meals near the lake, but should come with your own supplies case the kiosks are shut. If you have a 4WD, you can continue on Wadi al-Hittan (p158) to see the fossilised whale skeletons, about km further south from Wadi Rayyan. Those who've come pre-ared for it could spend the night at the wilderness camp site here – therwise, head back to lodgings at Lake Qarun, returning to Cairo e following day.

DISCOVER AROUND CAIRO

Held hostage by Cairo's endless charms (or perhaps desperate to flee in search of more relaxed locales), too few travellers explore the capital's surrounding countryside.

On the southern edge of the city limits lies the city of Memphis, once the mighty capital of the Old Kingdom. Unfortunately, little remains of this famed city of power and wealth, though the surrounding desert pays eloquent visual testimony to the early pharaohs' dreams of eternal life. Here, on the edge of expansive sand seas, are the impressive necropolises of Saqqara, Abu Sir and Dahshur.

The southern outskirts of Cairo are also home to the lush oasis of Al-Fayoum, which harbours ancient monuments, abundant wildlife and a spectacular desert rich in fossils. Northwest of Cairo, memorable day trips include the Birqash camel market, where Sudanese traders dispose of the last of their camels; and the monasteries of Wadi Natrun, which lure urban Copts to follow in the pilgrimage footsteps of their ancestors.

MEMPHIS & THE EARLY PYRAMIDS

Although most tourists associate Egypt with the Pyramids of Giza, there were, at the time of writing, known to be 118 ancient pyramids scattered around the country, with more being discovered every few years or so. The majority of these monuments are spread out along the desert between the Giza Plateau and the oasis of Al-Fayoum, and include the must-see Step Pyramid of Zoser at Saqqara and the Red and Bent Pyramids of Dahshur.

MEMPHIS

Around 3100 BC, the legendary pharaoh Narmer (Menes) unified the two lands of Upper and Lower Egypt, and founded Memphis, symbolically on the spot where the Nile Delta met the valley. For most of the Pharaonic Period, Memphis was the capital of Egypt, though the seat of power was later moved to Thebes (now Luxor) during the era of the New Kingdom.

Originally known as *Ineb-hedj*, meaning 'White walls', the contemporary name of Memphis derives from *Men-nefer*, meaning 'Established and beautiful'. Indeed the city was filled with palaces, gardens and temples, making it one of the greatest cities of the ancient world. In the 5th century BC, long after its period of power, Greek historian and traveller Herodotus still described Memphis as 'a prosperous city and cosmopolitan centre'. Even after Thebes became the capital during the New Kingdom, Memphis remained Egypt's second city, and prospered until it was finally abandoned during the first Muslim invasions in the 7th century AD.

The foundations of the ancient city have long since been ploughed under, and even the enormous temple of the creator god, Ptah, is little more than a few sparse ruins frequently waterlogged due to the high water table. Today, there are

GORDON SINCLAIR/ALAMY

Zoser's Funerary Complex (p148)

w clues as to Memphis' former grandeur nd importance and, sadly, it's difficult to nagine that any sort of settlement once tood here.

Nonetheless, a visit to Memphis is orthwhile just to stand on the hallowed rounds of one of the world's greatest cit-·s. Furthermore, Memphis is home to a oteworthy open-air **museum** (Mit Rahina; dult/student E£30/15, parking E£5; ⏰ 8am-4pm :t-Apr, to 5pm May-Sep, to 3pm during Ramadan), rhich is built around a magnificent fallen olossal limestone **statue of Ramses II**.

IETTING THERE & AWAY
ne tiny village of Memphis is 24km south f Cairo and 3km from Saqqara. While it is rorth visiting as part of a tour of Saqqara nd Dahshur, only those seriously into gyptology would want to trek down here y public transport – getting to Memphis a pain in the neck and a lengthy process. nless you have plenty of time, enjoy dis-omfort or have overspent, we strongly commend taking a tour or hiring a taxi ·r a day instead.

SAQQARA
Covering a 7km stretch of the Western Desert, Saqqara, the huge cemetery of ancient Memphis, was an active burial ground for more than 3500 years, and is Egypt's largest archaeological site. Old Kingdom pharaohs were buried within Saqqara's 11 major pyramids, while their subjects were buried in the hundreds of smaller tombs found in the great necrop-olis. Not surprisingly, the name Saqqara is most likely derived from *Sokar*, the Memphite god of the dead.

Most of Saqqara, except for the Step Pyramid, was buried in sand until the mid-19th century, when the great French Egyptologist Auguste Mariette uncovered the Serapeum. Since then, it has been a gradual process of rediscovery: the Step Pyramid's massive funerary complex was not discovered until 1924 and it is still being restored. French architect Jean-Philippe Lauer, who began work here in 1926, was involved in its restoration for an incredible 75 years until he passed away in 2001.

THE PYRAMIDS OF ABU SIR & SAQQARA

ORIENTATION & INFORMATION

The main monuments are in an are around the Step Pyramid known as **Nort Saqqara** (adult/student E£50/25, parking E£ ☻ 8am-4pm Oct-Apr, to 5pm May-Sep, to 3p during Ramadan). About 1km south of th Step Pyramid is a group of monument known as South Saqqara, with no offici entry fee or opening hours as these ar rarely visited.

At North Saqqara, facilities includ toilets, drink stands and souvenir stall but you shouldn't expect anything b monuments and sand at South Saqqar. Before exploring either complex, check the ticket office to see which monument are open – this constantly changes.

SIGHTS
ZOSER'S FUNERARY COMPLEX
STEP PYRAMID

In the year 2650 BC, Imhotep, the pha aoh's chief architect (later deified) bu the Step Pyramid (Map p149) for Zoser. is Egypt's (and the world's) earliest ston monument, and its significance cann be overstated. Previously, temples wei made of perishable materials, whil royal tombs were usually undergroun rooms topped with mudbrick mast. bas. However, Imhotep developed th mastaba into a pyramid *and* built it hewn stone.

The pyramid was transformed fror mastaba into pyramid through six sep. rate stages of construction and alteratio With each stage, the builders gained co fidence in their use of the new mediu and mastered the techniques required t move, place and secure the huge block This first pyramid rose in six steps to height of 60m, and was encased in fir white limestone.

The Step Pyramid is surrounded a vast funerary complex, enclosed by

NORTH SAQQARA

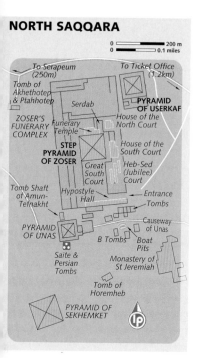

0 — 200 m
0 — 0.1 miles

To Serapeum (250m)
To Ticket Office (1.2km)
Tomb of Akhethotep & Ptahhotep
Serdab
PYRAMID OF USERKAF
ZOSER'S FUNERARY COMPLEX
Funerary Temple
House of the North Court
STEP PYRAMID OF ZOSER
House of the South Court
Great South Court
Heb-Sed (Jubilee) Court
Tomb Shaft of Amun-Tefnakht
Hypostyle Hall
Entrance Tombs
PYRAMID OF UNAS
B Tombs
Boat Pits
Causeway of Unas
Saite & Persian Tombs
Monastery of St Jeremiah
Tomb of Horemheb
PYRAMID OF SEKHEMKET

645m-long panelled limestone wall, and covers 15 hectares. Part of the enclosure wall survives today at a height of about 3m, and a section near the entrance was restored to its original 10m height.

The complex is entered at the south-eastern corner via a vestibule and along a colonnaded corridor into the broad hypostyle hall. The 40 pillars in the corridor are the original 'bundle columns', ribbed to resemble a bundle of palm or papyrus stems. The walls have been restored, but the protective ceiling is modern concrete. The roof of the hypostyle hall is supported by four impressive columns and there's a large, false, half-open ka door.

GREAT SOUTH COURT

The hypostyle hall leads into the Great South Court (Map p149), a huge open area flanking the south side of the pyramid,

with a section of wall featuring a frieze of cobras. The cobra, or uraeus, represented the goddess Wadjet, a fire-spitting agent of destruction and protector of the pharaoh. It was a symbol of Egyptian royalty, and a rearing cobra always appeared on the brow of a pharaoh's headdress or crown.

Near the base of the pyramid is an altar, and in the centre of the court are two stone B-shaped boundary markers, which delineated the ritual race the pharaoh had to run, a literal demonstration of his fitness to rule. The race was part of the Jubilee Festival, or Heb-Sed, which usually occurred after 30 years' reign, and involved the pharaoh's symbolic rejuvenation and the recognition of his supremacy by officials from all over Egypt.

North of the Heb-Sed Court are the **House of the South Court** (Map p149) and **House of the North Court** (Map p149), representing the two main shrines of Upper and Lower Egypt, and symbolising the unity of the country. The heraldic plants of the two regions were chosen to decorate the column capitals: papyrus in the north and lotus in the south.

The House of the South also features one of the earliest examples of tourist graffiti. In the 47th year of Ramses II's reign, nearly 1500 years after Zoser's death, Hadnakhte, a treasury scribe, recorded his admiration for Zoser while 'on a pleasure trip west of Memphis' in about 1232 BC. His hieratic script, written in black ink, is preserved behind perspex just inside the building's entrance.

SERDAB

A stone structure right in front of the pyramid, the serdab (a small room containing a statue of the deceased to which offerings were presented; Map p149) contains a slightly tilted wooden box with two holes drilled into its north face. Look

JIM HENDERSON/ALAN

The Black Pyramid (below), with the Bent Pyramid (p154) in the distance

◥ IF YOU LIKE...

If you like Saqqara's **Step Pyramid** (p148), you'll also like these other pyramids that litter the desert:

- **Pyramids of Abu Sir** (Map p148) The four pyramids of Abu Sir, which form the necropolis of the 5th dynasty (2494–2345 BC), have not survived as well as their neighbours at Giza and Saqqara, having been much quarried, but they still make a fascinating visit. The **Pyramid of Sahure** is ruined, but its large funerary complex can still be made out. The 45m high **Pyramid of Neferirkare**, Sahure's father, resembles the Step Pyramid only because its limestone casing has been removed. From here, you can sometimes see another 10 pyramids in the distance. Note that although Abu Sir is officially open, it doesn't see a lot of visitors and the guard may not always be here.
- **Black Pyramid** It's not nearly as well preserved as its neighbours, the Bent Pyramid and the Red Pyramid, but this crumbling towerlike Middle Kingdom structure at Dahshur (p153) is oddly attractive.
- **Pyramid of Pepi II** (Map p148) Pepi II was perhaps the longest-serving of all Egyptian pharaohs. His pyramid, in South Saqqara, can sometimes be entered. The outside seems little more than a pile of rubble, but the interior walls are decorated with passages from the Pyramid Texts.

through these and you'll have the eerie experience of coming face to face with Zoser himself. Inside is a near-life-size, lifelike painted statue of the long-dead pharaoh, gazing stonily out towards the stars. However, it's worth noting that this statue is only a copy – the original is in Cairo's Egyptian Museum.

PYRAMID & CAUSEWAY OF UNAS

What appears to be another big moun of rubble, this time to the southwest of Zoser's funerary complex, is actually th 2375–2345 BC Pyramid of Unas (Ma p149), the last pharaoh of the 5th dynast Built only 300 years after the inspired cre

tion of the Step Pyramid, this unassuming pile once stood 43m high.

From the outside, the Pyramid of Unas not much to look at, though the interior marked the beginning of a significant development in funerary practices. For the rst time, the royal burial chamber was ecorated, its ceiling adorned with stars nd its white alabaster-lined walls inscribed with beautiful blue hieroglyphs.

The aforementioned hieroglyphs are ne funerary inscriptions now known as ne Pyramid Texts, comprising 283 separate 'spells' chosen by Unas to protect is soul. The inscriptions include rituals, rayers and hymns, as well as lists of items, uch as the food and clothing Unas would equire in the afterlife. Unfortunately, deterioration of the interior led to the pyra- id's permanent closure in 1998.

OMB OF AKHETHOTEP
PTAHHOTEP

khethotep and his son Ptahhotep were enior royal officials during the reigns of Djedkare (2414–2375 BC) and Unas at the end of the 5th dynasty. Akhethotep served as vizier, judge, supervisor of pyramid cities and supervisor of priests, though his titles were eventually inherited by Ptahhotep, along with his tomb (Map p149). The joint mastaba has two burial chambers, two chapels and a pillared hall. The painted reliefs in Ptahhotep's section are particularly beautiful, and portray a wide range of animals, from lions and hedgehogs to the domesticated cattle and fowl that were brought as offerings to the deceased.

SERAPEUM

The Serapeum (Map p148), which is dedicated to the sacred Apis bull, is one of the highlights of visiting Saqqara. The Apis bulls were by far the most important of the cult animals entombed at Saqqara. The Apis, it was believed, was an incarnation of Ptah, the god of Memphis, and was the calf of a cow struck by lightning from heaven. Once divinely impregnated,

JIM HENDERSON/ALAMY

Pyramid of Sahure, Abu Sir (opposite)

the cow could never again give birth, and her calf was kept in the Temple of Ptah at Memphis and worshipped as a god.

The Apis was always portrayed as black, with a distinctive white diamond on its forehead, the image of a vulture on its back and a scarab-shaped mark on its tongue. When it died, the bull was mummified on one of the large travertine embalming tables discovered at Memphis, then carried in a stately procession to the subterranean galleries of the Serapeum at Saqqara, and placed in a huge stone sarcophagus.

The first Apis burial took place in the reign of Amenhotep III (1390–1352 BC), and the practice continued until 30 BC. The enormous granite and limestone coffins could weigh up to 80 tonnes each. Until the mid-19th century, the existence of the sacred Apis tombs was known only from classical references. But, having found a half-buried sphinx at Saqqara, and using the description given by the Greek historian Strabo in 24 BC, in 1851 Auguste Mariette uncovered the avenue leading to the Serapeum. However, only one Apis sarcophagus was found intact.

MASTABA OF TI

The Mastaba of Ti (Map p148) is perhaps the grandest and most detailed private tomb at Saqqara, and one of our main sources of knowledge about life in Old Kingdom Egypt. Its owner, Ti, was overseer of the Abu Sir pyramids and sun temples (among other things) during the 5th dynasty. In fact, the superb quality of his tomb is in keeping with his nickname, Ti the Rich. A life-size statue of the deceased stands in the tomb's offering hall (as with the Zoser statue, the original is in the Egyptian Museum). As men and women are seen working on the land, preparing food, fishing, building boats, dancing,

trading and avoiding crocodiles, their im ages are accompanied by chattering hierc glyphic dialogue, all no doubt familiar to during his career as a royal overseer: 'Hurr up, the herdsman's coming', 'Don't mak so much noise!', 'Pay up – it's cheap!'.

PYRAMID OF TETI

The avenue of sphinxes excavated b Mariette in the 1850s has again bee hidden by desert sands, but it once ex tended to the much earlier Pyramid of Te (Map p148). Teti (2345–2323 BC) was th first pharaoh of the 6th dynasty, and hi pyramid was built in step form and case in limestone. Unfortunately, the pyrami was robbed for its treasure and its stone and today only a modest mound remain The interior fared better, and is similar i appearance to that of the Pyramid of Una (p150). Within the intact burial chambe Teti's basalt sarcophagus is well preserved and represents the first example of a sar cophagus with inscriptions.

TOMBS OF MERERUKA & ANKHMAHOR

Near the Pyramid of Teti is the tomb (Ma p148) of his highest official, Mereruka, v zier and overseer of priests. It's the larg est Old Kingdom courtier's tomb, wit 32 chambers covering an area of 1000 s metres. The 17 chambers on the easter side belong to Mereruka, and include magnificent six-columned offering ha featuring a life-size statue of Mereruk appearing to walk right out of the wall t receive the offerings brought to him.

Other rooms are reserved for Mereruka wife, Princess Seshseshat (Teti's daugh ter), and their eldest son, Meriteti (whos name means 'Beloved of Teti'). Much of th tomb's decoration is similar to that of th Mastaba of Ti, with an even greater numbe of animals portrayed – look out for th ide-mouthed, sharp-tusked hippos as ou enter – along with a charming scene f domestic bliss as husband and wife are eated joyfully on a bed as Seshseshat lays them music on her harp.

Further east, the tomb (Map p148) of ne 6th-dynasty vizier and palace over-eer, Ankhmahor, contains more interest-ng scenes of daily life. Most unusual here re images of surgical procedures, earning ne tomb its alternative title, the Doctor's omb. As two boys are circumcised the ieroglyphic caption says, 'Hold him firmly o he does not fall'!

ETTING THERE & AWAY

aqqara is about 25km south of Cairo and best visited in a taxi, combined with a isit to Memphis and Dahshur.

ETTING AROUND

's easy to walk around North Saqqara, hough it can be a hot and sweaty slog hrough the sand to South Saqqara. It's lso possible to hire a camel, horse or onkey from near the Serapeum to take you on a circuit of the sites for between E£25 and E£50.

DAHSHUR

About 10km south of Saqqara in a quiet bit of desert is **Dahshur** (Map p137; adult/student E£25/15; 8am-4pm Oct-Apr, to 5pm May-Sep, to 3pm during Ramadan), an impressive 3.5km-long field of 4th- and 12th-dynasty pyramids. There were originally 11 pyramids at Dahshur, but only the two Old Kingdom ones, the incredibly striking Bent and Red Pyramids, remain intact, as well as three Middle Kingdom pyramid complexes.

Pharaoh Sneferu (2613–2589 BC), father of Khufu and founder of the 4th dynasty, built Egypt's first true pyramid here, the Red Pyramid, as well as an earlier version, the Bent Pyramid. These two pyramids are the same height, and together are also the third-largest pyramids in Egypt after the two largest at Giza.

ORIENTATION & INFORMATION

The Bent Pyramid, and its surrounds, is still a militarised zone, meaning that

JOHN ELK III

he Bent Pyramid, Dahshur (p154)

it can only be admired at a distance. Fortunately, the wonderful Red Pyramid is open to visitors, and penetrating its somewhat dank interior is a true Indiana Jones-esque experience.

Note that there are no facilities at Dahshur aside from a toilet that you may or may not be allowed to use.

SIGHTS
BENT PYRAMID
Experimenting with ways to create a true, smooth-sided pyramid, Sneferu's architects began with the same steep angle and inward-leaning courses of stone they used to create step pyramids. When this began to show signs of stress and instability around halfway up its eventual 105m height, they had little choice but to reduce the angle from 54° to 43° and begin to lay the stones in horizontal layers. This explains why the structure has the unusual shape that gives it its name. Most of its outer casing is still intact, and inside (closed to visitors) are two burial chambers, the highest of which retains its original ancient scaffolding of great cedar beams to counteract internal instability. About halfway towards the cultivation to the east are the ruins of Sneferu's valley temple, which yielded some interesting reliefs.

RED PYRAMID
The world's oldest true pyramid is the North Pyramid, which is better known as the Red Pyramid. It derives its name either from the red tones of its weathered limestone, after the better-quality white limestone casing was removed, or perhaps from the red graffiti and construction marks scribbled on its masonry in ancient times. Having learnt from their experiences building the Bent Pyramid, the same architects carried on where they had left off, building the Red Pyramid at the same

43-degree angle as the Bent Pyramid' more gently inclining upper section.

GETTING THERE & AWAY
The only way to visit Dahshur is by tax or organised tour, which can easily b combined with a visit to Memphis, Ab Sir and Saqqara.

AL-FAYOUM OASIS

This large semi-oasis, about 70km wid and 60km long, is an extremely ferti basin watered by the Nile via hundred of capillary canals and is home to mor than two million people. The region als harbours a number of important archaeo logical sites, particularly Qasr Qarun an the Pyramid of Meidum, as well as sceni Lake Qarun and Wadi Rayyan.

MEDINAT AL-FAYOUM
pop 515,000
The largest town on the Al-Fayoum Oas was a favourite holiday spot for 13th dynasty pharaohs, who built a series o pleasure palaces in the area. Centurie later, the Greeks, who believed the croc diles in Lake Qarun were sacred, called th area Crocodilopolis, and built a temple i honour of Sobek, the crocodile-heade god. During Ptolemaic and Roman time pilgrims came from across the ancien world to feed the sacred beasts. Thes days Medinat al-Fayoum (Town of th Fayoum) is a less-than-appealing mix o crumbling concrete, horn-happy dri ers, choking fumes, swirling dust an crowded streets.

ORIENTATION & INFORMATION
The Bahr Yusuf canal acts as the city main artery, and most commercial activ ties take place along it.

Located at the Governorate Building, e **Fayoum Tourism Authority** (☎ 634 13; Sharia Saad Zaghloul) can organise guides take travellers around the oasis's sites. om Al-Fayoum, you'll be looking at a st of around E£300 to E£400 for a guide d taxi for the day, which should allow u to visit the Pyramid of Meidum, Lake arun and Wadi Rayyan.

For more information on the oasis, btain a copy of *The Fayoum: History and uide* by R Neil Hewison (AUC Press).

The bus and taxi stations are a short ke from the city centre.

IGHTS

s far as sights go, there's the **Obelisk f Senusert**, which you'll pass coming in om Cairo at the centre of a roundabout the northeast of town. Although it oks lost among the cars and buses, s supposedly the only obelisk in Egypt ith a rounded top, and it also features a eft in which a golden statue of Ra was aced, reflecting the sun's rays in the four rections of the wind.

Fayoum is also famous for its **waterwheels**, which in total number more than 200, and have become a prominent symbol of the town. Since Pharaonic times, these devices have kept the town well irrigated despite its irregular topography of rolling hills and steep depressions. Although some of the rickety waterwheels look as if they were built thousands of years ago, the vast majority are modern constructions.

The **Governorate Building** (Sharia Saad Zaghloul; ☉ closed irregularly) houses a modest display on the history and fauna of the oasis.

SLEEPING & EATING
Palace Hotel (☎ 635 1222; Bahr Yusuf; s/d from E£65/80; ❀) Although it maintains a certain air of respectability, this ageing relic has seen better dynasties. The rooms themselves are clean if slightly musty, and you'll get a decent night's sleep if you're not too fussy.

Queen Hotel (☎ 634 6819; Sharia Minshaat Lutfallah; s/d from E£175/215; ❀) The Queen

MIDDLE EAST/ALAMY

aterwheels at Medinat al-Fayoum (above)

is undoubtedly the most comfortable option in town, which is one reason it can be difficult to get a room here. Even if you're not staying here, you could try the on-site restaurant, which serves comparatively decent food.

There are several very basic cafes and assorted eateries on the canalside road just west of the park.

GETTING THERE & AWAY
Buses to Cairo (E£6 to E£8, two to three hours) leave every half-hour from 7am until 7pm from the train station on the west side of Gamal Abdel Nasser Rd (the Cairo road). These buses take you to Ahmed Helmy bus station behind Cairo's Ramses train station, stopping en route at Al-Monieb station on Midan Giza.

GETTING AROUND
Green-and-white minibuses (25pt) cover all areas of Medinat al-Fayoum between the western and eastern bus stations.

KARANIS
At the edge of the oasis depression, 25km north of Medinat al-Fayoum on the road to Cairo, lie the ruins of ancient Karanis. Founded by Ptolemy II's mercenaries in the 3rd century BC, the town was once a mudbrick settlement with a population in the thousands. Today, little of the ancient city remains intact aside from a few walls, though Karanis is home to two well-preserved **Graeco-Roman temples** (adult/student E£32/16; 9am-4pm) in the southern part of town. The larger and more interesting temple was built in the 1st century BC, and is dedicated to two local crocodile gods, Pnepheros and Petesouchos.

The nearby **Museum of Kom Aushim** (Mathaf Kom Aushim; 650 1825; Cairo rd; adult/student E£16/8; 9am-4pm) has good displays of Old and Middle Kingdom objects,

including sacred wooden boats, Canopi jars, and wooden and ceramic statuette entombed to serve the deceased in th afterlife. Items from the Graeco-Roma period, which give context to Karanis, ar exhibited on the 1st floor.

To get here, catch one of the Cair bound buses from Medinat al-Fayour (E£5 to E£7).

PYRAMID OF MEIDUM
About 30km to the northeast of Medina al-Fayoum is the ruin of the first true pyr mid attempted by the ancient Egyptian namely the **Pyramid of Meidum** (adul student E£32/16; 8am-4pm). However, ther were serious design flaws and, sometim after completion (possibly as late as th last few centuries BC), the pyramid own weight caused the sides to collaps Today, only the core of the 'Collapsed Pyramid of Meidum stands, though i still an impressive sight to behold.

The guard at the nearby house will ur lock the entrance of the pyramid, fror where steps lead 75m down to the empt burial chamber. Note that there are no fa cilities at Meidum.

To reach the pyramid, take any ser ice taxi or bus running between Cair and Beni Suef, and ask to be dropped c at the Meidum turn-off (E£13 to E£15 From here you will still have about 6k to go but it can be difficult to get a lift. much better option is to hire a taxi fro Medinat al-Fayoum, and visit Meidum i conjunction with the surrounding pyr mids. Prices are highly negotiable but yc should aim between E£100 and E£200 fc the complete circuit excluding entry fee and baksheesh.

LAKE QARUN
Prior to the 12th-dynasty reigns c Sesostris III and his son Amenemhat III, th

JOHN BORTHWICK

The 'collapsed' Pyramid of Meidum (opposite)

-Fayoum region was entirely covered by ake Qarun. In an early effort at land rec- mation, however, both pharaohs dug a ries of canals linking Qarun to the Nile, d drained much of the lake. Over the ast few centuries, the lake has regained ome of its former grandeur due to the iversion of the Nile to create more agri- ultural land. However, since Lake Qarun resently sits at 45m below sea level, it as suffered from increasing salinity. emarkably, the wildlife has adapted, and day the self-proclaimed 'world's most ncient lake' supports a unique ecosys- m. There's a good chance you'll spot ountless varieties of birds here includ- g a large colony of flamingos.

At the western end of Lake Qarun, near e village of Qasr Qarun, are the ruins of ncient Dionysus, once the starting point r caravans to the Western Desert oasis Bahariya. Although little remains of this istoric settlement, a **Ptolemaic temple** dult/student E£32/16; ☉ 8am-4pm), built in 4 C and dedicated to Sobek, the crocodile- eaded god of Al-Fayoum, is still standing.

If you're feeling adventurous, you can go down to the underground chambers (be- ware of snakes), and up to the roof for a view of the desert, the sparse remains of Ptolemaic and Roman settlements, and the oasis.

SLEEPING

New Panorama Village (☎ 683 0746; s/d from E£250/275; ❌ ☒) True to its moniker, the premises are designed along the lines of an Egyptian village, albeit one with balcony-lined chalets that front the incongruous waters of this mirage-worthy desert lake. The restaurant specialises in fresh fish from the lake waters, and fresh fowl from the lake shores.

Helnan Auberge Fayoum (☎ 698 1200; www.helnan.com; r from US$75; ❌ ☒) This opu- lent colonial-style hotel, constructed in the late 1930s, was where world leaders met after WWII to decide on the borders of the Middle East. Later, it served as King Farouk's private hunting lodge, though these days it primarily caters to wealthy Cairene families looking for some fresh air.

GETTING THERE & AWAY

While Lake Qarun is accessible by public transport, it's recommended that you visit the area by private vehicle. Having the freedom provided by your own wheels will allow you to cruise around the lake, in addition to visiting the spectacular Wadi Rayyan Protected Area and Wadi al-Hittan.

WADI RAYYAN & WADI AL-HITTAN

The **Wadi Rayyan Protected Area** (per person US$3 plus E£5 per vehicle, camping per person E£10) is primarily a major nesting ground for both endemic and migrating birds, though it's also something of a weekend picnic spot for escaping Cairenes. Here, you'll also find a visitors centre as well as a couple of small cafes serving cold drinks and light meals.

Be advised that you technically need permission in advance from the tourist police in Medinat al-Fayoum to visit here, though in a pinch a little baksheesh can help smooth things over at any of the roadside checkpoints. Also, don't b surprised if you're given a police esco to the park entrance, who will also like expect baksheesh in return for the service.

Some 55km further south into th desert is Wadi al-Hittan (Valley of th Whales), where the skeletons of prim tive whales have been lying for about 4 million years. These fossilised remains a of *Archaeoceti,* a now extinct sub-order modern whales that has helped to she light on the evolution of land-based t sea-going mammals. Although still pa of the Wadi Rayyan Protected Area, th Valley of the Whales now receives add tional support from various agencies aft being declared a Unesco World Heritag Site in 2005.

The Valley of the Whales area is als home to a small network of walkin tracks leading out to more than a doze skeletons, in addition to a wildernes camp site complete with basic toile and fire pits.

Action at the Birqash Camel Market (opposite)

ETTING THERE & AWAY

e Wadi Rayyan Protected Area is not ccessible by public transport; you'll ei-er need your own vehicle, or hire a taxi Medinat al-Fayoum. Prices vary, but u can plan on E£150 to E£250 if you're st visiting Wadi Rayyan, and upwards E£300 to E£400 if you want to extend ur trip to Wadi al-Hittan.

HE ROAD TO LEXANDRIA

e Cairo–Alexandria Desert Hwy (known ually as the Desert Hwy) roughly sepa-tes the green fields of the Delta and e harsh sands of the Western Desert. eviously desolate, large swathes of the ea's prairie-type expanses have been eened to create farms, and several new tellite towns have been established in der to ease the population pressure Cairo. However, it's the desert life of e past that draws most tourists to this etch, namely the famous Birqash camel arket and the historic Coptic monaster- of Wadi Natrun.

RQASH CAMEL MARKET

ypt's largest **camel market** (souq al-maal; admission E£20; ☻ 6am-noon) is held at rqash, a small village 35km northwest Cairo. Like all Egypt's animal markets, e Birqash camel market is not for animal vers, nor for the faint of heart, but a visit re can make an unforgettable day trip. Hundreds of camels are sold here every y, most having been brought up the rty Days Rd from western Sudan to just rth of Abu Simbel by camel herders, d from there to the market in Daraw ee p209). Unsold camels are then hob-ed and crammed into trucks for the 24-ur drive to Birqash.

In addition to those from Sudan, there are camels from various parts of Egypt (in-cluding Sinai, the west and the south) and sometimes from as far away as Somalia. They are traded for cash or other livestock, such as goats, sheep and horses, and sold for farm work or slaughter.

While at the market, watch out for pickpockets. Women should dress con-servatively – the market is very much a man's scene, with the only female pres-ence other than the occasional traveller being the local tea lady.

Negotiations tend to take place early in the day, with the peak of action being between 7am and 10am, especially on Fridays.

GETTING THERE & AWAY

Using public transport, the cheapest way to get to Birqash, involves getting your-self to the site of the old camel market at Imbaba, from where microbuses filled with traders and potential buyers shuttle back and forth to Birqash.

The easiest way to get to and from the market is to hire a private taxi for the morning. The market is an easy half-day trip (one to 1½ hours) from Cairo, and one hour in the hot and dusty market is usu-ally enough for most people. The return trip will cost somewhere between E£75 and E£125, depending on your bargain-ing skills.

WADI NATRUN

Wadi Natrun, about 100km northwest of Cairo, was of great importance to ancient Egyptians, for this was where they found natron, a substance that was crucial to the mummification process. Natron comes from large deposits of sodium carbonate that are left when the valley's salt lakes dry up every summer. Today, natron is used on a larger scale by the chemical industry.

Wadi Natrun is primarily known for its historic Coptic Christian monasteries. Besides their solitude and serenity, the monasteries are worth visiting for the Coptic art they contain, particularly at Deir el-Sourian.

HISTORY

A visit to the monasteries of Wadi Natrun reveals clues to the survival of the Coptic Church, for the desert has long been the protector of the faith. It was there that thousands of Christians retreated to escape Roman persecution in the 4th century.

The focal point of the monasteries was the church, around which were built a well, storerooms, a dining hall, kitchen, bakery and the monks' cells. These isolated, unprotected communities were fortified after destructive raids in 817 by Arab tribes on their way to conquer North Africa. Of the 60 monasteries once scattered over the valley, only four remain.

The Coptic pope is still chosen fro among the Wadi Natrun monks, and m nasticism is experiencing a revival, wi young professional Copts once aga donning robes and embroidered hoo to live within these ancient walls in t desert.

INFORMATION

Each monastery has different openin times, with some closed completely du ing the three annual fasting periods (Len at Easter, Christmas and in August. Befo going, it is worth checking with their Cai residences that visits are possible.

As a general rule, you can visit all the monasteries without prior notice, t only exception being Deir Abu Mak Males wishing to stay overnight (wom are not allowed to do so) need writte permission from the monasteries' Cai residences:

Deir Abu Makar (☎ 02-2577 0614)
Deir Anba Bishoi (☎ 02-2591 4448)
Deir el-Baramouse (☎ 02-2592 2775)
Deir el-Sourian (☎ 02-2592 9658)

TRAVELPIXS/A

The domed roof of Deir Anba Bishoi (opposite)

SIGHTS

DEIR ANBA BISHOI

St Bishoi founded two monasteries in Wadi Natrun: this one and neighbouring Deir el-Sourian. **Deir Anba Bishoi** (☾ daily **ccl during Lents**) is built around a church that contains the saint's body, said to be perfectly preserved in its sealed, tubelike container. Each year on 17 July, the tube is carried in procession around the church. According to the monks, the bearers clearly feel the weight of a whole body. The church also contains the cell where St Bishoi tied his hair to the ceiling to stop himself sleeping during prayers.

DEIR EL-SOURIAN

About 500m northwest of Deir Anba Bishoi, **Deir el-Sourian** (☾ 3-6pm Mon-Fri, **9m-6pm Sat & Sun during Lents**) is named after wandering Syrian monks who bought the monastery from the Copts in the 8th century, and is the most picturesquely situated of the monasteries. Since the 16th century it has been solely occupied by Coptic monks. Its Church of the Virgin was built around a 4th-century cave that had been occupied by St Bishoi, and is worth visiting for its superb series of 11th-century wall paintings.

DEIR ABU MAKAR

Nearly 20km southeast of Deir Anba Bishoi, **Deir Abu Makar** (☾ daily but only by prior ar-**rangement, closed during Lents**) was founded around the cell where St Makarios spent his last 20 or so years. Structurally, it suffered more than other monasteries at the hands of raiding Bedouin, but it is famous as most of the Coptic popes over the centuries have been selected from among its monks.

DEIR EL-BARAMOUSE

Until recently, when a good road was built to Deir Anba Bishoi to the southeast, **Deir**

Inside Deir Anba Bishoi (left)
TRAVELPIXS/ALAMY

el-Baramouse (☾ Fri-Sun, closed during Lents) was the most isolated of the Wadi Natrun monasteries. These days more than 100 monks live here, and there are now six modern churches and a restored medieval fortress (not open to the public) within its compound. There are also remnants of 13th-century wall frescoes in its oldest church, the Church of the Virgin Mary.

SLEEPING

If you have both a Y-chromosome and the necessary written consent, then you're welcome to spend the night in any of the monasteries listed above. Since all four places are major destinations for Coptic Christians on religious pilgrimages, a night's stay is generally a sombre affair defined by regular prayer sessions. Even if you're not devout, it is good manners to attend these religious services, and to leave a generous donation with the monks at the time of your departure.

GETTING THERE & AWAY

You can catch a West Delta Co bus to the less-than-inviting town functioning as the gateway to the monasteries that goes by the grandiloquent name of Wadi Natrun City. These leave from Cairo's main bus station every 30 minutes between 6am and 10pm and cost E£5 to E£10. From the bus lot at Wadi Natrun City, you'll have to negotiate with a taxi driver to take you around the monasteries; expect to pay around E£20 per hour. On Fridays and Sundays when the monasteries are crowded with pious Copts, you can easily pick up a lift. The last bus back to Cairo leaves at 6pm.

A taxi from Cairo should cost about E£150 to E£200 there and back, including a couple of hours driving around the monasteries.

JERRY C

The fertile banks of the Nile, Minya (p174)

BENI SUEF TO QENA

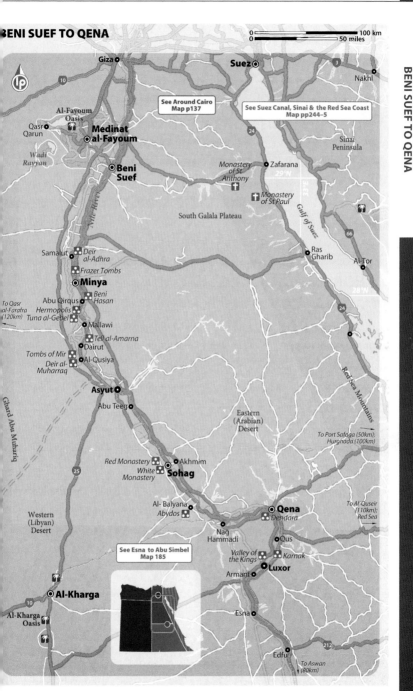

HIGHLIGHTS

1 | ABYDOS

BY HORUS, CO-OWNER OF THE HOUSE OF LIFE HOTEL, ABYDOS

Abydos was the holiest place in ancient Egypt. Fo this reason, Seti I built a very special temple for Osiris. Only here and in the tomb of Seti I in Luxo (p120) can you find such high-quality reliefs. Here you can still feel the atmosphere of the ancient Egyptian gods and goddesses.

⟍ HORUS' DON'T MISS LIST

❶ HYPOSTYLE HALL CARVINGS

Many carvings in temples along the Nile can seem clumsy or mass-produced, but the work in the hypostyle halls at Abydos have a delicacy and expressiveness about them, as though created by artists not masons. The work of Seti's craftsmen is evidence of one of the high point's of Egyptian art.

❷ TOMB OF OSIRIS (THE OSIREION)

There were shrines to the god Osiris the length of the Egyptian Nile, one for each province. According to leger each one marks a place where ti goddess Isis buried parts of the go dismembered body. But Abydos w always considered most special, whi was why so many people wanted to l buried here.

❸ THE GAP

Ancient Egyptians believed that ti hills beyond Abydos were the barri between the living and the dead. The is a gap in the hills you can see th allows you to walk through from or

Clockwise from top: Minaret at Abydos; Inside the Temple of Seti I (p179); Abydos columned halls; Local transport, Abydos; Intricate temple wall carvings

CLOCKWISE FROM TOP: UWE LANDGRAF/SHUTTERSTOCK; ROBERT HARDING PICTURE LIBRARY LTD/ALAMY; JOSEF NIEDERMEIER/IMAGEBROKER; MARKA/ALAMY; JOSEF NIEDERMEIER/IMAGEBF

de to the other. It's a long walk and, r the ancients, something you only d once. There was no coming back.

GRAVE OF OMM SETI

glishwoman Dorothy Eady believed e had lived previously in Abydos ring the reign of Seti I. 'Omm Seti', she was known, spent much of her ult life in Abydos, working for the tiquities service and dispensing formation on life in ancient Egypt. hen she died, she was buried in the esert beyond town. If you cannot find r grave (ask at the House of Life for rections, p180), you can find some of r spirit in the book she left behind. An Omm Seti museum is also being ilt near the Temple of Seti I (p179), ticipated to open in early 2011.

❺ WALK IN THE DESERT

The desert beyond the temple is beguiling. Walk around the remains of graves or, if the guards allow, head for the nearby temple of Ramses II. Much reconstructed, some of its fine carvings have survived.

↘ THINGS YOU NEED TO KNOW

When to visit The best time to visit Abydos is during spring or autumn **Where to relax** The cafeteria in front of the temple, or bring a picnic and head for the desert **What to read** Omm Seti's *Living Egypt* **See our author's review on p179**

HIGHLIGHTS

2

↘ TEMPLE OF HATHOR SECRETS

The **Temple of Hathor** (p180) at Dendara, one of the best preserved temples in Egypt, is packed with secrets and mysteries. Like Cleopatra, depicted on the temple's back wall, the cow-headed goddess Hathor was loved for her sense of fun, and her annual festival was one of the most popular. On the temple roof, look for the ancient zodiac and images telling of the conception of the god Horus.

3

↘ WRESTLING AT BENI HASAN

It's a cliché to say that so many things in Egypt remain unchanged from the time of the pharaohs, but in some ways it also happens to be true. For proof, look at the scenes of daily life in ancient Egypt painted on the walls of tombs in **Beni Hasan** (p177): grape picking, metal working, hunting and, yes, even wrestling.

↘ CARRIAGE RIDE IN MINYA

This part of Egypt used to be rich, as is obvious from the style and size of the old houses in the centre of **Minya** (p174). To get a taste of another time, try taking a leisurely ride around the town in a *hantour*, a horse-drawn carriage.

↘ HIDE OUT AT DEIR AL-MUHARRAQ

Coptic monasteries were strongholds as well as places of worship. They had to be because for much of their existence the monks had to protect themselves against threats from Bedouin tribes and by people of the valley. The 7th-century keep at **Deir al-Muharraq** (p178) gives an idea of how these two needs, of safety and sanctity, could be met.

↘ CONSIDER THE OSIREION

Of all the buildings in ancient Egypt, few have had archaeologists guessing as much as the **Osireion** (p180), behind the Temple of Seti I at Abydos. With its causeway, burial chamber and sarcophagus, it was assumed to be an Old Kingdom tomb, but it is now believed to have had a purely ceremonial purpose.

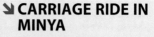

2 CHERYL FORBES; 3 SANDRO VANNINI/CORBIS; 4 CHRISTINE OSBORNE; 5 WORLD RELIGIONS PHOTO LIBRARY/ALAMY; 6 CHERYL FORBES

Columns and wall reliefs at the Temple of Hathor, Dendara (p180); 3 Tomb of Kheti, Beni Hasan (p177); 4 Minya yline; 5 Monk at Deir al-Muharraq (p178); 6 The Osireion, Abydos (p180)

THE BEST...

↘ WAYS OF GETTING ON THE NILE

- Take the **ferry** (p178) across the Nile to see the beautiful tombs at Beni Hasan.
- Sail a **felucca** (p176) or a **motorboat** from the tourist office in Minya to Banana Island.
- Travel to Dendara via a **river cruise** (p125) from Luxor to enjoy a quiet stretch of the river.

↘ KEY COPTIC SITES

- The complex of **Deir al-Muharraq** (p178), which includes a church said to have been consecrated in AD 60.
- The 4th-century **White Monastery** (p179) in Sohag, built using stones from pagan temples.
- The chapel of St Bishoi and St Bigol at the **Red Monastery** (p179), for its early frescoes.

↘ ANCIENT IMAGES

- The rare image of Cleopatra and her son Caesarion on the rear wall of the **Temple of Hathor** (p180) at Dendara.
- Carvings in the second hypostyle hall of the **Temple of Seti I** (p179) in Abydos are among the finest in Egypt.
- Hunting, wrestling and other scenes of daily life in the **tomb of Kheti** (p177) and the **tomb of Amenemhat** (p177) at Beni Hasan.

The smooth domes of the White Monastery, Sohag (p179)

THINGS YOU NEED TO KNOW

⬂ VITAL STATISTICS

- **Telephone codes** Minya (☎ 086), Sohag (☎ 093), Dendara (☎ 096)
- **Best time to go** Spring and autumn

⬂ PLACES IN A NUTSHELL

- **Beni Hasan** (p177) Fabulous painted tombs from the 11th and 12th dynasties.
- **Deir al-Muharraq** (p178) A Coptic monastery that goes back to the very beginnings of the Christian religion.
- **Abydos** (p179) One of the most sacred places in ancient Egypt, with superb carvings in its temple.
- **Dendara** (p180) One of the best preserved of all ancient Egyptian temples.

⬂ ADVANCE PLANNING

- **One month before** Book accommodation as the limited choice means some hotels do fill up.
- **One week before** Double-check with your embassy regarding travel restrictions in the area.

⬂ RESOURCES

- **Minya tourist office** (☎ 236 0150; Corniche an-Nil; ☺ 9am-3.30pm Sat-Thu)
- **Sohag tourist office** (☎ 460 4913; Governorate Bldg; ☺ 8.30am-3pm Sun-Thu) In the building beside the museum on Sohag's east bank. The office can help arrange visits to the monasteries.

⬂ EMERGENCY NUMBERS

- **Ambulance** (☎ 123)
- **Minya tourist police** (☎ 236 4527)
- **Sohag tourist police** (☎ 460 4800)

⬂ GETTING AROUND

- **Taxi** Great for a day trip to the area from Luxor, taking in the temples of Abydos and Dendara.
- **Train** To get to most major towns and cities in this region between Luxor and Cairo.

⬂ BE FOREWARNED

- **Travel restrictions** Although foreigners are no longer obliged to travel within armed police convoys, travel in the area can be slow and you may still be stopped when trying to leave train stations or at road blocks outside each town. If you're stopped you may be interviewed and then either put back on the train or taken to a hotel, where a guard may be placed to prevent you from leaving unescorted.

ITINERARIES

SOUTH FROM CAIRO One Day

If you want a taste of the stretch of country between Cairo and Luxo
but don't want to do the full tour, it should be possible to see som
sights in a day. The Nile south of the capital irrigates land that is ric
both in its soil and its history.

Start by catching an early train from Cairo to the provincial cap
tal of (1) Minya (p174) and taking a stroll around the town. Centr
Minya retains some of its old colonial elegance and the river here
quite inviting. You will then need to rent a taxi to drive you to th
ferry landing, from where a taxi can take you to the nearby tombs
(2) Beni Hasan (p177), and then on to the Coptic sights of (3) De
al-Muharraq (p178), before returning to Minya to catch the evenin
Cairo train.

NORTH FROM LUXOR One Day

Rent a taxi in Luxor for the day and drive north to visit two of th
best-preserved and most fascinating temples in Egypt, one from th
New Kingdom, the other from the time of the Ptolemies. Until recent
you had to travel out of Luxor as part of an armed police convoy, b
security has now been relaxed and you can travel north without th
problem. You are also likely to find yourself travelling without th
crowds that throng the sights between Luxor and Aswan.

Head first for the largely intact Temple of Hathor at (1) Denda
(p180) to explore its halls, crypts and chambers, and wonderf
hieroglyphs. From Dendara, continue on to (2) Abydos (p179), whe
you could happily spend the greater part of a day walking aroun
the limestone Temple of Seti I, and then walking a little way into th
desert, before returning to Luxor in the evening.

THE FULL TOUR Four Days

This tour is only newly possible: some parts of this region had been
limits to foreigners following Islamist terrorist attacks on tour boa
and buses in the early 1990s. As a result, there is very little touri
infrastructure and travelling in the region can be more difficult tha
in any other part of the country. Be prepared for basic hotels, close
restaurants and delays at checkpoints.

If you don't have your own vehicle, hiring a taxi is preferable – i
possible to complete this tour by train, but it will take much long
and you will still need to take taxis to get from the stations to th
sights.

Leaving Luxor in the morning, head first to the fabulous ancie
temples at (1) Dendara (p180) and then (2) Abydos (p179), driving
to the city of (3) Sohag (p178) before dark. The following day can

With broad tree-lined streets, a wide corniche and some great, if shabby, early-20th-century buildings, central Minya has retained the feel of a more graceful era.

SIGHTS & ACTIVITIES

Beyond the pleasure of walking around the town centre and watching the Nile flow against the background of the Eastern Hills, Minya doesn't have many sights. The new **Akhenaten Museum** on the east bank is heading towards completion. It will contain a collection of finds from the area, including from Akhenaten's capital, Tell al-Amarna. There is hope that when the museum officially opens, the German government will lend the exquisite bust of Akhenaten's queen, Nefertiti, even if only temporarily.

IVAN VDOVIN/JON ARNOLD TRAVEL/PHOTOLIBRARY

Statue of Meret Amun, Akhmim (below)

⇘ IF YOU LIKE...

If you like museums, you should look out for these museums in the region. In addition to these, some museums in the area are under construction or are completed but awaiting official opening ceremonies – it's worth checking in on progress when you pass through:

- **Mallawi Museum** (adult/student E£25/15; ⊗ 9am-3pm Sat-Tue & Thu, to noon Fri) This museum in Mallawi, 48km south of Minya, has a range of artefacts including tomb paintings, glassware, sculptures and pencil-thin ibis mummies, plus other finds from nearby Hermopolis and Tuna al-Gebel.
- **Sohag Museum** Once officially opened, this new riverside museum in Sohag (p178) will be home to a good collection of local antiquities.
- **Akhmim** On Sohag's east bank are the ruins of the ancient Egyptian town of Ipu. Among other interesting remains at this open-air museum there is an 11m-high **statue of Meret Amun** (adult/student E£20/10; ⊗ 8am-6pm), the tallest statue of an ancient queen to have been discovered in Egypt. Meret Amun was the daughter of Ramses II. A taxi from Sohag (p178) should cost around E£25 per hour, or you can take the microbus (E£2, 15 minutes).

Street scene, Minya (p174)

Hantours (horse-drawn carriages; per hr E£25 to E£35) can be rented for a leisurely ride around the town centre or along the corniche.

Motorboats (per hr E£50) and **feluccas** (per hr E£30) can be rented at the landing opposite the tourist office for trips along the river and to Banana Island.

SLEEPING & EATING

Dahabiyya Houseboat & Restaurant (☎ 236 3596/5596; Corniche an-Nil; s/d E£35/70) This old Nile sailing boat has been moored along the Corniche near the tourist office for many years, but recently refurbished, it is Minya's most unusual address, with a restaurant on the upper deck and accommodation below.

Aton Hotel (☎ 234 2993/4; fax 234 1517; Corniche an-Nil; s/d US$60/70; ✕ ☲) Still referred to locally as the Etap (its former incarnation) and still Minya's top hotel, the friendly, comfortable Aton is about 1km north of the town centre, on the west bank of the Nile and across the road from

the more expensive and less interesting Mercure Nefertiti.

Savoy Restaurant (Midan al-Mahatta dishes E£5-20), a busy corner restaurant serves good rotisserie chicken and kebab in the fan-cooled restaurant or you can take away.

GETTING THERE & AWAY
BUS

The **Upper Egypt Bus Co** (☎ 236 3721; Shari Saad Zaghloul) has hourly services to Cairo (E£12, four hours) from 6am. Foreigners are currently banned from the Asyut service. Buses leave for Hurghada at 10.30am and 10.30pm (E£50, six hours).

TRAIN

The **tourist office** (☎ 236 2722) in the station may be able to help with information. Trains to Cairo (three to four hours) have only 1st- and 2nd-class carriages and leave at 5.55am, 6.30am, 8.50am, 4.30pm (which goes on to Alexandria) and 6.50pm. Tickets in 1st-class cost E£35 to E£45, in 2nd-class E£29 to E£34.

Trains heading south leave fairly frequently, with the fastest trains departing from Minya between around 11pm and 1am.

BENI HASAN

The necropolis of **Beni Hasan** (adult/student E£30/20; 8am-5pm) occupies a range of east-bank limestone cliffs some 20km south of Minya. Many tombs remain unfinished and only four are currently open to visitors, but they are worth the trouble of visiting for the glimpse they provide of daily life and political tensions of the period.

TOMB OF BAQET (NO 15)

Baqet was an 11th-dynasty governor of the Oryx nome. His rectangular tomb chapel has seven tomb shafts and some well-preserved wall paintings. They include Baqet and his wife on the left wall watching weavers and acrobats – mostly women in diaphanous dresses in flexible poses.

TOMB OF KHETI (NO 17)

The tomb of Kheti, Baqet's son, has many vivid painted scenes that show hunting, linen production, board games, metalwork, wrestling, acrobatics and dancing, most of them watched over by the nomarch (local governor).

TOMB OF AMENEMHAT (NO 2)

Entered through a columned doorway and with its six columns intact, his tomb contains beautifully executed scenes of farming, hunting, manufacturing and offerings to the deceased, who can also be seen with his dogs.

TOMB OF KHNUMHOTEP (NO 3)

Khnumhotep was governor during the early 12th dynasty, and his detailed 'autobiography' is inscribed on the base of walls that contain the most detailed painted scenes.

WORLDTHROUGHTHELENS-TRAVEL/ALAMY

Tomb wall detail, Tell al-Amarna (below)

⬊ IF YOU LIKE...

If you like **Beni Hasan** (p177) you will also like some of the other tombs along this stretch of the Nile:

- **Tell al-Amarna** (adult/student E£25/15; 8am-4pm Oct-May, to 5pm Jun-Sep) Akhenaten's doomed city has some beautiful 14th-century-BC tombs, the best being No 25, the Tomb of Ay.
- **Tuna al-Gebel** (adult/student E£15/10; 8am-5pm) The necropolis of the ruined city of Hermopolis contains several tombs, none more interesting than the tomb of Petosiris, a High Priest of Thoth from the Ptolemaic period, which shows the influence of Greek culture on ancient Egyptian beliefs.
- **Tombs of Mir** (adult/student E£25/15; 9am-5pm Sat-Wed) Not far from Deir al-Muharraq, these nine Old and Middle Kingdom tombs contain some vivid pagan paintings, in spite of having been used by Coptic hermits.

The Red Monastery, Sohag (opposite)

B.O'KANE/ALA

GETTING THERE & AWAY

A taxi from Minya will cost anything from E£50 to E£100, depending on your bargaining skills and how long you stay at the site. It may also be possible to take a microbus from Minya to Abu Qirqus and a pick-up from there to the ferry landing. Return boat tickets are on a sliding scale from E£5 per person if there are eight or more passengers, to E£15 if you're by yourself.

DEIR AL-MUHARRAQ

Located about 8km southwest of the small rural town of Al-Qusiya, 35km south of Mallawi, is the Coptic complex of Deir al- Muharraq.

Deir al-Muharraq, the **Burnt Monastery**, is a place of pilgrimage, refuge and vows where the strength of Coptic traditions can be experienced. The 120 resident monks believe that Mary and Jesus inhabited a cave on this site for six months and 10 days after fleeing from Herod. Coptic tradition claims the **Church of al-Azraq** (Church of the Anointed) sits over the cave and is the world's oldest Christian church,

consecrated around AD 60. More certai is the presence of monastic life here sinc the 4th century. The current building date from the 12th to 13th centuries.

The **keep** beside the church is an inde pendent 7th-century tower, rebuilt in th 12th and 20th centuries. Its four floors ca serve as a minimonastery, complete wit its own small **Church of St Michael**, a re fectory, accommodation and even buri space behind the altar.

GETTING THERE & AWAY

At the time of writing, the bus from Miny to Asyut had been stopped. If it runs, or you are allowed to come from Asyut, yo will be dropped at Al-Qusiya, about 5 minutes' drive from Asyut. From Al-Qusiy you may be able to get a local microbu (E£3) to the monastery.

SOHAG

pop 190,132

The city of Sohag, 115km south of Asyu is one of the major Coptic Christian area of Upper Egypt.

SIGHTS

The **White Monastery** (Deir al-Abyad; ☺ 7am-dusk), on rocky ground above the old Nile flood level, 12km northwest of Sohag, was founded by Saint Shenouda around AD 400 and dedicated to his mentor, St Bigol. White limestone from Pharaonic temples was reused, and ancient gods and hieroglyphs still look out from some of the blocks.

The **Red Monastery** (Deir al-Ahmar; ☺ 7am-midnight), 4km southeast of Deir al-Abyad, is hidden at the rear of a village. The older of the monastery's two chapels, St Bishoi and St Bigol's, dates from the 4th century AD and contains some rare frescoes.

SLEEPING & EATING

Safa (☎ 230 7701/2; fax 230 7704; Sharia al-Gomhuriyya, West Bank; s/d/tr E£165/193/220; ☒) relatively new West Bank block. Rooms are comfortable and the riverside terrace

is popular in the evening for snacks, soft drinks and water pipes.

Hotel al-Nil (☎ 230 7509; Sharia al-Gamah, East Bank; s/d E£250/325; ☒) The newest and smartest hotel in town, on the east bank near the new museum.

The best food options are in the two main hotels.

GETTING THERE & AWAY

Intercity service taxis don't run yet (though this situation is likely to change) so, apart from private taxi, train remains the easiest way of moving around and there is a frequent service north and south along the Cairo–Luxor main line, with a dozen daily trains to Asyut (1st/2nd class E£31/14) and Luxor (E£21/13).

ABYDOS

As the main cult centre of Osiris, god of the dead, **Abydos** (ancient name Ibdju; adult/student E£30/15; ☺ 7am-6pm) was *the* place to be buried in ancient Egypt. Although there were shrines to Osiris throughout Egypt, each one the supposed resting place of another part of his body, the temple at Abydos was the most important, being the home of his head.

TEMPLE OF SETI I

This great limestone structure, unusually L-shaped rather than rectangular, was dedicated to the six major gods – Osiris, Isis and Horus, Amun-Ra, Ra-Horakhty and Ptah – and also to Seti I (1294–1279 BC) himself.

The temple is entered through a largely destroyed **pylon** and two **courtyards**, built by Seti I's son, Ramses II, who is depicted on the portico killing Asiatics and worshipping Osiris. Beyond is the **first hypostyle hall**, also completed by Ramses II.

CHRISTIANS & PAGANS

Egypt's Christians absorbed both the form and content of the ancient pagan religion. It's impossible to make direct parallels, but the rise of the cult of Mary appears to have been influenced by the popularity of Isis: both were said to have conceived through divine intervention. According to Coptic musicologist Dr Ragheb Moftah, the Coptic liturgy evolved from ancient rites and in it we can hear an echo of ancient Egypt's rituals. Even the physical structure of Coptic churches, with three sacred spaces, the innermost one containing the altar reserved for priests, echoes the layout of earlier pagan temples.

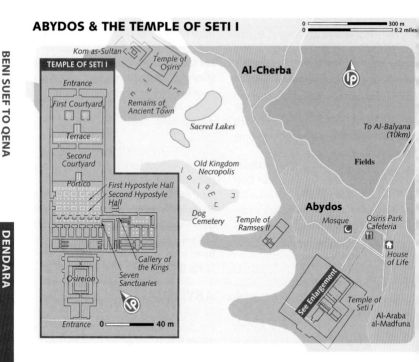

ABYDOS & THE TEMPLE OF SETI I

The **second hypostyle hall**, with 24 sandstone papyrus columns, was the last part of the temple to have been decorated by Seti, although he died before the work was completed. Particularly outstanding is a scene on the rear right-hand wall showing Seti standing in front of a shrine to Osiris, upon which sits the god himself.

THE OSIREION

Directly behind Seti's temple, the Osireion is a weird, wonderful building that continues to baffle Egyptologists, though it is usually interpreted as a cenotaph to Osiris.

SLEEPING & EATING

House of Life (☎ 012 733 0071; www.ancient egyptianhealing.com; opposite Temple of Seti I; B&B/full board per person €15/25) The only hotel functioning at the time of our visit,

this simple Dutch-, Egyptian- and US-ru house overlooking the temple has si rooms, sharing three bathrooms.

Osiris Park Cafeteria (Temple of Seti ⏳ 7am-10pm) Right in front of the templ this is the only reliable option within sigl of the temple.

GETTING THERE & AWAY

A private taxi from Luxor should co around E£300 return, depending o how long you want at the temple. A trai leaves Luxor for Al-Balyana, the close major centre, at 6am and 8.25am (1st/2n class E£18/13, three hours). A private ta from the station to the temple will co about E£50.

DENDARA

Although built at the very end of th Pharaonic Period, the **Temple of Hatho** adult/student E£25/15; ☉ 7am-6pm) at her ult site of Dendara is one of the iconic gyptian buildings, mostly because it re-nains virtually intact, with a great stone oof and columns, dark chambers, under-round crypts and twisting stairways all arved with hieroglyphs.

OURING THE TEMPLE

he inner temple was built by the tolemies, the smaller **inner hypostyle all** again has Hathor columns and walls arved with scenes of royal ceremonials, ncluding the founding of the temple.

BETHUNE CARMICHAEL

Exterior walls of the Temple of Hathor, Dendara

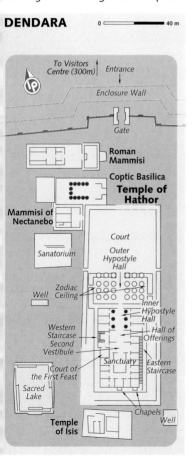

DENDARA

0 —— 40 m

To Visitors Centre (300m)

Entrance

Enclosure Wall

Gate

Roman Mammisi

Coptic Basilica

Temple of Hathor

Mammisi of Nectanebo

Court

Sanatorium

Outer Hypostyle Hall

Zodiac Ceiling

Well

Inner Hypostyle Hall

Hall of Offerings

Western Staircase

Second Vestibule

Sanctuary

Eastern Staircase

Court of the First Feast

Sacred Lake

Chapels

Well

Temple of Isis

Beyond the second hypostyle hall, you will find the **Hall of Offerings** leads to the **sanctuary**, the most holy part of the temple, home to the goddess's statue. A further Hathor statue was stored in the crypt beneath her temple, and brought out each year for the New Year Festival, which in ancient times fell in July and coincided with the rising of the Nile. In the open-air kiosk on the southwestern corner of the roof, the gods awaited the first reviving rays of the sun-god Ra on New Year's Day.

The theme of revival continues in two suites of rooms on the roof, decorated with scenes of the revival of Osiris by his sister-wife, Isis. In the centre of the ceiling of the northeastern suite is a plaster cast of the famous 'Dendara Zodiac', the original now in the Louvre, Paris.

The **exterior walls** feature lion-headed gargoyles to cope with the very occasional rainfall and are decorated with scenes of pharaohs paying homage to the gods. The most famous of these is on the rear (south) wall, where Cleopatra stands with Caesarion, her son by Julius Caesar.

SLEEPING & EATING

The police will not allow you to stay the night in nearby Qena, but even if you could the choices are limited and Dendara is close enough to Luxor for commuting.

If you can get to them (security re stricts movement around the town), tr **Restaurant Hamdi** (Sharia Luxor; dishe E£10-22) and **Restaurant Prince** (Shari al-Gomhuriyya; dishes E£10-20), which bot serve meals of soup, chicken, *kofta* an vegetables. A picnic at the temple migh be preferable.

GETTING THERE & AWAY

A return taxi from Luxor will cost yo about E£200. There is also a day cruise t Dendara from Luxor (see p125). If you ar rive in the nearby town of Qena by train you will need to take a taxi to the templ (E£25 to E£35 to the temple and back wit some waiting time).

↘ ESNA TO
ABU SIMBEL

Feluccas drift on the Nile, Edfu (p197)

IZZET KERIE

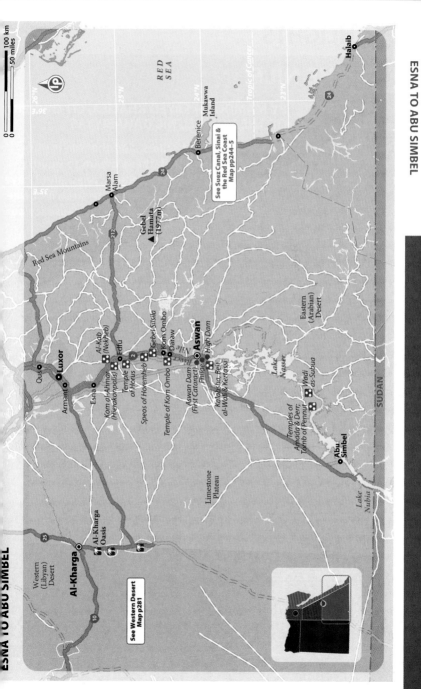

See Suez Canal, Sinai &
the Red Sea Coast
Map pp244–5

See Western Desert
Map p281

HIGHLIGHTS

1 THE NILE

BY MAMDOUH SAYED KHALIFA, CO-OWNER OF THE NOUR EL-NIL DAHABIYYAS

We are a family of sailors, and the Nile is our livelihood. It was my father's dream to build a dahabiyya, like the 19th-century ones, and I have now built four boats. My favourite stretch of Nile is between Edfu and Kom Ombo, because it's so beautiful and the wind is usually good.

⋙ MAMDOUH SAYED'S DON'T MISS LIST

❶ THE LONGEST RIVER

The Nile Basin covers 3.35 million sq km, and although it is shared by 10 countries, Egypt gets the most from it. There is very little rain in this part of the Nile Valley, so without the river there would be nothing. Ancient Egyptians recognised this fact when they likened Egypt to a lotus – the Delta was the flower, and the river and its valley the stem that supported them all. The Nile is particularly beautiful between Luxor and Aswan.

❷ SUNRISE & SUNSET

Spend a few days on and close to the Nile to understand the basics of ancient Egyptian religion. Wake up at dawn to witness the sun come up in all its majesty on the east bank, hear the countryside wake up and see the fishermen already at work. During the day gaze upon the all-important Nile that makes everything possible, until the glowing sun sets over the west bank and everything is put to rest.

Clockwise from top: Boats crowd the Aswan shoreline; Hieroglyphs at the Temple of Kom Ombo (p200); A dahabiyya sailing near Edfu; Shrine at Gebel Silsila (p199); Tour boat on the Nile

CLOCKWISE FROM TOP:JOHN ELK III; LEE FOSTER; GARY BLAKE/ALAMY; MIKE P SHEPHERD/ALAMY; JULIET COOM

CRUISING

. cruise on the Nile is always romantic, ut the cruise ships have become very ig, and feluccas are not everyone's up of tea, so the dahabiyya (house-oat) really offers a good alternative. hey let you travel in style and comfort, nd yet feel very close to the river and fe on the banks.

❺ SWIMMING IN THE NILE

We sailors know where to swim in the Nile – only where the current is strong. In stagnant water you can catch bilharzia.

TEMPLES & MORE TEMPLES

he stretch between Luxor and Aswan as the greatest concentration of well-reserved monuments in the country ncluding the Ptolemaic temples of sna, Edfu and Kom Ombo, but dahabiy-as and feluccas also stop at smaller nd equally interesting sites like Gebel ilsila.

↘ THINGS YOU NEED TO KNOW

When to visit The best time to sail by dahabiyya is during spring or autumn **Where to relax** A dahabiyya trip can be a few days so there is plenty of time to relax on the deck **Avoid crowds** Feluccas and dahabiyyas can moor wherever they want to avoid the cruisers **See also p196 and p308**

THE BEST...

⬎ PLACES TO RELAX

- Walk the whole way from the northern end of **Gebel Silsila** (p199) to the gardens in the south.
- Sail a **felucca** (p206) around the islands in Aswan.
- Sip a cocktail at sunset on the terrace of Aswan's **Old Cataract Hotel** (p208), or a cold beer on the terrace of **Salah ad-Din** (p208).
- Catch the biggest Nile perch on a **fishing safari** (p205) on Lake Nasser.

⬎ PLACES WITH A VIEW

- Kubbet al-Hawa (Dome of the Winds), the tomb of a local sheikh, above the **Tombs of the Nobles** (p205), for stunning Nile views.
- The terrace of the **Old Cataract Hotel** (p208) to see the sunset over Abu.
- The nature reserve south of Aswan town while **birdwatching** (p205) early in the morning.

⬎ WAYS TO BEAT THE CROWD

- Go for a stroll in the gardens of **Elephantine Island** (p203) or wander around its **Abu ruins**.
- Take a motorboat to the temples of **Kalabsha** and **Beit al-Wali** (p214) in their spectacular setting just south of the **High Dam** (p211).
- Visit the interesting **Nubia Museum** (p203) – not many other people do.

Cultural exhibit at the Nubia Museum, Aswan (p203)

IZZET KERI

THINGS YOU NEED TO KNOW

↘ VITAL STATISTICS

- **Telephone codes** Esna (☎ 095), Edfu, Kom Ombo, Aswan and Abu Simbel (☎ 097)
- **Population** 226,013
- **Best time to go** October to April; winter is delightful in Aswan

↘ PLACES IN A NUTSHELL

- **Edfu** (p197) Location of the last temple built on a grand scale.
- **Kom Ombo** (p200) A Ptolemaic temple perched on a bend in the river.
- **Aswan** (p201) A laid-back town where the Nile River is most picturesque.
- **Abu Simbel** (p215) Site of Ramses II's magnificent temple.

↘ ADVANCE PLANNING

- **One month before** Book your accommodation and Nile cruise, particularly if planning your trip during European holiday periods.
- **One day before** Book taxi for the day to visit the temples of Philae and Kalabsha.

↘ RESOURCES

- **Aswan tourist office** (Map p206; ☎ 231 2811, 010 576 7594; Midan al-Mahatta; ⏰ 8am-3pm & 7-9pm Sat-Thu, 9am-3pm & 6-8pm Fri) Helpful with organising trips, and advising on prices for taxis and feluccas.
- **Aswan Guide** (www.aswanguide.com) The official Ministry of Tourism website for Aswan.

↘ EMERGENCY NUMBERS

- **Ambulance** (☎ 123)
- **Police Aswan** (☎ 230 3436)
- **Tourist police Aswan** (☎ 230 3436)

↘ GETTING AROUND

- **Bus** Between Aswan and Abu Simbel.
- **Taxi** For a day trip between Luxor and Aswan, visiting temples on the way.
- **Felucca** For sailing around the islands in Aswan.
- **Dahabiyya** For an intimate cruise on the Nile.
- **Ferry** From the east bank in Aswan to the islands.

↘ BE FOREWARNED

- **Convoy** Travellers no longer have to travel in a police convoy from Luxor to Aswan, but it's still obligatory to join the convoy between Aswan and Abu Simbel.
- **Felucca prices** Check with the Aswan tourist office for official prices per hour or per day.

ITINERARIES

THE CLASSIC ROUTE Three Days

The best way to see the sights along the gorgeous stretch of Ni
between Luxor and Aswan is from a cruiser or dahabiyya. Howeve
if time or money is short you can easily do the trip in a day by ca
stopping at the temples and sights on the way.

Arrange a taxi with driver for the day from Luxor and leave early
the morning, perhaps with a picnic to enjoy at one of the stops alor
the way. Heading south, the first stop is **(1) Esna** (p195), where you ca
walk through the tourist souq to what is left of the Temple of Khnu
and stroll around to see some provincial architecture. Continue sou
along the east bank for the tombs at **(2) Al-Kab** (p197), particularly t
Tomb of Ahmose. More or less halfway between Luxor and Aswan
the town of **(3) Edfu** (p197), where you can visit the Temple of Hor
and then, closer to Aswan, the temple at **(4) Kom Ombo** (p200). Arri
early evening in **(5) Aswan** (p201).

In Aswan, spend time on Elephantine Island visiting the museu
ruins of Abu and walking around the villages. Have lunch in one of t
riverside cafes and visit the Nubia Museum on Aswan's east bank in t
afternoon, followed by the souq. The next day take a half-day tour
(6) Philae (p212), stopping at the High Dam and Unfinished Obelis
then spend the afternoon sailing a felucca around the islands.

THE GREAT OUTDOORS Five Days

Spend a day in **(1) Aswan** (p201) visiting the sights, and take a feluc
around the islands in the late afternoon. Arrange to go out birdwatc
ing the next day in the nature reserves south of the town (see p20
It's wonderful to be on the Nile very early in the morning, gliding alor
the edge of the islands, watching birds and hearing how they fit in
ancient Egyptian history or into Nubian traditions. In the afterno
leave for a three- or four-day fishing cruise (p205) on **(2) Lake Nass
(p215), where you can look for huge Nile perch in its waters, and oth
exotic creatures on its shores, such as crocodiles, snakes and lizard

RELAXED SIGHTSEEING One Week

Follow the Classic Route three-day itinerary for sightseeing en route
Aswan from Luxor, taking in **(1) Esna** (p195), the tombs of **(2) Al-Ka
(p197), **(3) Edfu** (p197), the temple at **(4) Kom Ombo** (p200) and t
sights and activities of **(5) Aswan** (p201). On the morning of day fo
take a minibus to **(6) Abu Simbel** (p215), and book into the Eskale
Hotel for a room and a delicious lunch of fish from the lake and ve
etables from the garden. In the soft afternoon light, stroll over to t
Great Temple of Ramses II after most of the tourists on day trips fro
Aswan have left, and stay on to see the sound and light show. T

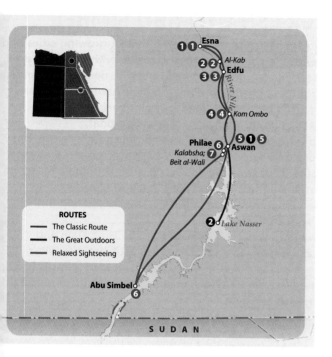

ROUTES
— The Classic Route
— The Great Outdoors
— Relaxed Sightseeing

ext day see the temple in a very different morning light, before the
rowds arrive, and take a wander through the relaxed town.

The next morning return to Aswan, perhaps via the temples of (7)
alabsha and **Beit al-Wali** (p214), if you are in a private taxi or mini-
us. On the last day back in Aswan, go birdwatching (p205) in the
arly morning.

DISCOVER ESNA TO ABU SIMBEL

Where northern Upper Egypt is dominated by fast-growing cities and political problems, the country south of Luxor is both harder and calmer. The Nile is increasingly hemmed in by the desert, its banks lined with well-preserved Graeco-Roman temples at Esna, Edfu and Kom Ombo, its lush fields punctuated by palm-backed villages – it's the ideal place to glide through on a Nile sailing boat.

Aswan may be the regional capital and administrative centre, but this ancient ivory-trading post has a laid-back atmosphere that sets it apart from other tourist centres in Egypt. With the Nubia Museum, ancient remains, a vibrant souq (market), beautiful gardens and a unique Nubian-influenced local culture, it is a fascinating and relaxing place to spend time.

South of Aswan, the land is dominated by the High Dam and its offspring, Lake Nasser, the world's largest artificial lake. Most southerly and spectacular of all is the Great Temple of Ramses II at Abu Simbel, one of ancient Egypt's most awesome structures and a highlight of any visit to Egypt.

HISTORY

The Nile Valley south of Luxor was the homeland of the vulture and crocodile gods, a place of harsh nature and grand landscapes. Its cult places, centres such as Al-Kab and Kom al-Ahmar, date back to the earliest periods of Egyptian history – it was here that the Narmer Palette, the object around which the origins of the 1st dynasty have been constructed, was found; here that one of the earliest-known Egyptian temples, made of wood not stone, was found; and here that recently found Lascaux-type rock carvings have opened a window onto Egypt's remotest past.

Yet most of what one can see between Luxor and Aswan dates from the last period of ancient Egyptian history, when the country was ruled by the descendants of Alexander the Great's Macedonian general, Ptolemy I (323–283 BC). Although they were based in Alexandria and looked out to the Mediterranean, the Ptolemies pushed their way south into Nubia, the land that straddled what is now the border between Egypt and Sudan. They ensured peaceful rule in Upper Egypt by erecting temples in honour of the local gods, building in grand Pharaonic style to appease the priesthood and earn the trust of the people.

Aswan's history was always going to be different. Settlement on Elephantine Island, located in the middle of the Nile at Aswan, dates back to at least 3000 BC. Named Abu (Ivory) after the trade that flourished here, it was a natural fortress positioned just north of the First Nile Cataract, one of six sets of rapids that blocked the river between Aswan and Khartoum. At the beginning of Egypt's dynastic history, in the Old Kingdom (2686–2125 BC), Abu became capital of the first Upper Egyptian nome (province) and developed into a thriving economic and religious centre, its strategic importance underlined by the title accorded to its rulers, Keepers of the Gate of the South. By the end of ancient history, with Egypt part of a larger Roma mpire, the southern frontier town was een as a place of exile for anyone from he north who stepped out of line.

GETTING THERE & AWAY

t the time of writing there are no buses etween Aswan and Luxor. The train tation will only sell tickets for a limited umber of trains between Luxor and swan to foreigners, but they will also tell ou to board any train you want and buy a cket on board for E£6 extra. Service taxis nd minibuses ply the road from Luxor to swan, or ferry passengers between cities long that stretch. With the convoy sys- em no longer in place foreigners are now gain able to travel in a service taxi, or o privatise a taxi for the day, and do the rive between Luxor and Aswan, stopping t the sights on the way. The best way is f course the slow way, sailing a felucca raditional canvas-sailed boat) or a da- abiyya (houseboat), taking in the sights nd the most glorious stretch of river.

There still *is* a convoy system in place etween Aswan and Abu Simbel, and for- eigners are only allowed to travel in an armed convoy that leaves twice a day. The other option is to fly, or to take a cruise on Lake Nasser.

GETTING AROUND

Service taxis and minibuses run between the towns, but the service-taxi station is often outside the town, and/or a few kilo- metres away from the sights. The easiest way is to either privatise a taxi for a day and visit sights en route, or to privatise a taxi once you are in the town and want to go to the sight. Security tightens inevita- bly if there has been any kind of incident in the town, even if it's not necessarily related to tourists or terrorism.

SOUTHERN UPPER EGYPT
ESNA
pop 66,660

Most visitors come to Esna, 54km south of Luxor on the west bank of the Nile, for the Temple of Khnum, but the busy little

JOCHEN TACK/IMAGEBROKER

he lush banks of the Nile between Luxor and Esna

farming town itself is quite charming. Beyond the small bazaar selling mainly tourist souvenirs are several examples of 19th-century provincial architecture with elaborate *mashrabiyyas* (wooden lattice screens). North of the temple is a beautiful but rundown Ottoman caravanserai, the Wekalat al-Gedawi, once the commercial centre of Esna. Opposite the temple is the Emari minaret from the Fatimid period, one of the oldest in Egypt, which escaped the mosque's demolition in 1960. An old oil mill, in the covered souq south of the temple, presses lettuce seed into oil, a powerful aphrodisiac since ancient times. It is now also known for the two Esna locks on the Nile, where cruise boats have to queue up to pass.

The Ptolemaic-Roman **Temple of Khnum** (adult/student E£20/15; ⏰ 6am-5pm Oct-May, to 6pm Jun-Sep) is situated about 200m from the boat landing, at the end of the tourist souq. The temple today sits in a 9m-deep pit, which represents 15 centuries of desert sand and debris, accumulated since it was abandoned during the Roman period. Most of the temple, which was similar in size to the temples of Edfu (see p197) and Dendara (see p180), is still covered. All that was excavated in the 1840s, all you can see now, is the Roman hypostyle hall.

Khnum was the ram-headed creator god who fashioned humankind on his potter's wheel using Nile clay. Construction of the temple dedicated to him was started, on the site of an earlier temple, by Ptolemy VI Philometor (180–145 BC). The Romans added the hypostyle hall that can be visited today, with well-preserved carvings from as late as the 3rd century AD.

The central doorway leads into the dark, atmospheric vestibule, where the roof is supported by 18 columns with wonderfully varied floral capitals in the form of palm leaves, lotus buds and papyrus fans; some also have bunches of grapes, a distinctive Roman touch. The roof is decorated with astronomical scenes, while the pillars are covered with hieroglyphic accounts of temple rituals. On the walls Roman emperors dressed as pharaohs make offerings to the local gods of Esna.

EATING & DRINKING

Few people linger in Esna, as most stop here on the road between Luxor and Aswan. There is nowhere to stay but there are a few *ahwas* (coffeehouses) with a terrace, serving drinks, *sheesha* (water pipe) and some basic food, such as sandwiches with felafel, opposite the temple.

GETTING THERE & AWAY

The busy *kabout* (pick-up trucks) station is beside the canal, and a block further north is the service-taxi and minibus station. A seat in a service taxi or minibus to Luxor is E£3, to Edfu E£3.50 and to Aswan E£10. Arrivals are generally dropped off on the main thoroughfare into town along which *hantour* (horse-drawn carriage) drivers congregate in the hope of picking up a fare. They ask E£10 each way for the five to 10-minute ride to the temple.

DAHABIYYA

There are a number of options for multiday cruising between Esna and Aswan. The dahabiyya (houseboat) operators below all have boats that are beautifully appointed, with an antique feel, tasteful decor and double lateen sails. See also p308 for more on cruising the Nile.

Meroe (☎ 010 657 8322; www.nourelnil.com; 5-night trip per person from €1000; ⏰ 🚢) A replica of a 19th-century dahabiyya indistinguishable from the original, the beautifully finished *Meroe* is the coolest dahabiyya currently on the Nile and is ra

r being owner-operated. It has room for
) passengers in 10 comfortable stylish
hite cabins with private bathroom, and
rge windows overlooking the Nile. The
me owners have three other boats, *El Nil*
0 cabins), *Malouka* and *Assouan* (both
ght cabins). All boats only run from Esna
Aswan (five nights).

La Flâneuse du Nil (☎ in France 00 331 42
16 00; www.la-flaneuse-du-nil.com, in French; 3-
ght trip per person from €640, 4 nights from €790;
:) One of the newcomers, La Flâneuse
as been quickly picked up by several
>-market British tour operators and with
>od reason. The company currently only
as one boat, but it is well fitted and well
n. Like original dahabiyyas, it relies on
ils (or tugs) to move, but does have air-
>n in the seven cabins. Tours are shorter
an some, taking four nights from Esna
Aswan and three nights from Aswan
ick to Esna.

L-KAB

ne little-visited site of **Al-Kab** (adult/stu-
nt E£30/20), ancient Nekheb, is one of the
ost important sites of ancient Egypt. It
as the home of Nekhbet, the vulture
>ddess of Upper Egypt, one of two god-
esses who protected the pharaoh right
ick to the Old Kingdom. The oldest of
e sandstone temples within the walls
edicated to the god Thoth was built by
imses II (1279–1213 BC) and the adjoin-
g Temple of Nekhbet was built during
e Late Period, both reusing blocks
>m much earlier temples from the Early
ynastic Period (from c 3100 BC) and the
iddle Kingdom (2055–1650 BC).

To the northwest of the walls is an
ld Kingdom cemetery. Across the road,
ast the ticket office and cut into the
II at the edge of the valley, are tombs
New Kingdom (1550–1069 BC) local
>vernors. The most important is the

Columns in the Temple of Khnum (opposite)

Tomb of Ahmose (No 2), the 'Captain-
General of Sailors', who fought under
King Ahmose I.

GETTING THERE & AWAY
Al-Kab is 26km south of Esna. The best
way of seeing this site is to take a private
taxi from Esna or Edfu, or on the way from
Luxor to Aswan or vice versa. Dahabiyyas
and some feluccas travelling from Aswan
to Esna stop here too, but not the bigger
cruise boats.

EDFU
pop 69,000

On a rise above the broad river valley, the
Temple of Horus at Edfu, having escaped
destruction from Nile floods, is the most
completely preserved Egyptian temple.

Hypostyle hall in the Temple of Horus, Edfu (below)

JOHN E

The temple's well-preserved reliefs have provided archaeologists with much valuable information about the temple rituals and the power of the priesthood.

Edfu was a settlement and cemetery site from around 3000 BC onwards, as it was the cult centre of the falcon god Horus of Behdet (the ancient name for Edfu), but the **Temple of Horus (Map p199; adult/student E£50/25;** ⏰ **7am-9pm Oct-May, to 10pm Jun-Sep)** you see today is Ptolemaic. Started by Ptolemy III (246–221 BC) on 23 August 237 BC, on the site of an earlier and smaller New Kingdom structure, the sandstone temple was completed some 180 years later by Ptolemy XII Neos Dionysos, Cleopatra VII's father. In conception and design it follows the general plan, scale, ornamentation and traditions of Pharaonic architecture, right down to the Egyptian attire worn by Greek pharaohs depicted in the temple's reliefs.

Today the temple is entered via a long row of shops selling tourist tat, and a new visitors centre with the ticket office, clean toilets, a cafeteria and a room for

showing a 15-minute film on the histo of the temple in English. Beyond th Roman *mammisi* (birth house), with son colourful carvings, the massive 36m-hig **pylon** (gateway) is guarded by two hug but splendid granite statues of Horus as falcon. The walls are decorated with colo sal reliefs of Ptolemy XII Neos Dionysc holding his enemies by their hair befo Horus and about to smash their skull this is the classic propaganda pose of th almighty pharaoh.

Beyond this pylon, the **court of o ferings** is surrounded on three sides k 32 columns, each with different flor capitals. The walls are decorated with r liefs, including the 'Feast of the Beautif Meeting' just inside the entrance, th meeting being that of Horus of Edfu ar Hathor of Dendara, who visited eac other's temples each year and, after tw weeks of great fertility celebrations, we magically united.

A second set of Horus falcon statues black granite once flanked the entrance the temple's first or **outer hypostyle ha**

ut today only one remains. The **inner hypostyle hall** also has 12 columns, and in the top left part of the hall is perhaps this temple's most interesting room: the temple **laboratory**. Here, all the necessary perfumes and incense recipes were carefully brewed up and stored, their ingredients listed on the walls. On either side of the hall, doorways lead into the narrow **passage of victory**, which runs between the temple and its massive protective enclosure walls. Reliefs here show the dramatic re-enactment of the battle between Horus and Seth at the annual Festival of Victory.

The second antechamber gives access to the **sanctuary of Horus**, which still contains the polished-granite shrine that once housed the gold cult statue of Horus. Created during the reign of Nectanebo II (360–343 BC), this statue was reused by the Ptolemies in their newer temple.

GETTING THERE & AWAY

Edfu train station is on the east bank of the Nile, about 4km from town. There are frequent trains heading to Luxor and Aswan throughout the day, although most are 2nd and 3rd class only. To get to the town, you must first take a *kabout* from the train station to the bridge, then another into town.

There are no more buses along the Aswan–Luxor road, so the only other option is to buy a seat in a service taxi or minibus. *Hantours* take passengers from the waterfront to the temple or vice versa for E£10 to E£15, but you may have to bargain.

GEBEL SILSILA

At Gebel Silsila, about 42km south of Edfu, the Nile narrows considerably to pass between steep sandstone cliffs that are cluttered with ancient rock stelae and graffiti. Known in Pharaonic times as Khenu (Place of Rowing), it was an important centre for the cult of the Nile: every year at the beginning of the inundation season sacrifices were made here to ensure the fertility of the land. The quarries were for centuries the main source in Egypt of sandstone for temple building.

The most attractive monuments are on the west bank, where the rocks are carved with inscriptions and there are tiny shrines from all periods, as well as larger chapels. The southern side of the

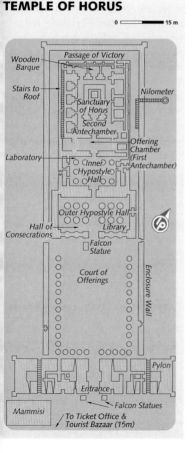

TEMPLE OF HORUS

0 — 15 m

- Wooden Barque
- Passage of Victory
- Stairs to Roof
- Sanctuary of Horus
- Nilometer
- Second Antechamber
- Offering Chamber (First Antechamber)
- Laboratory
- Inner Hypostyle Hall
- Outer Hypostyle Hall
- Library
- Hall of Consecrations
- Falcon Statue
- Court of Offerings
- Enclosure Wall
- Pylon
- Entrance
- Falcon Statues
- Mammisi
- To Ticket Office & Tourist Bazaar (15m)

site is marked by a massive pillar of rock, known as the 'Capstan', so called because locals believe there was once a chain – *silsila* in Arabic, from which the place takes its name – that ran from the east to the west bank. Several stelae, including a large **Stelae of Shoshenq I**, mark the northern limit of the quarry and lead to the **Speos of Horemheb** (adult/student E£30/20; ☽ 7am-8pm), a rock-hewn chapel started by Horemheb (1323–1295 BC) and finished by the officials of the later Ramesside kings.

The best way to get to Gebel Silsila is by felucca or dahabiyya from Aswan to Esna, or the other way around.

KOM OMBO

pop 71,121

In ancient times Kom Ombo was known as Pa-Sebek (Land of Sobek), after the crocodile god of the region. It became important during the Ptolemaic period, when its name was changed to Ombos and it became the capital of the first Upper Egyptian nome during the reign

of Ptolemy VI Philometor. Gold was trade here, but more importantly it was a ma ket for African elephants brought fror Ethiopia, which the Ptolemies needed t fight the Indian elephants of their long term rivals the Seleucids, who ruled th largest chunk of Alexander's former em pire to the east of Egypt.

Standing on a promontory at a ben in the Nile, where in ancient times sacre crocodiles basked in the sun on the rive bank, is the **Temple of Kom Ombo** (Ma p201; adult/student E£30/20; ☽ 7am-8pm Oct-Ma to 9pm Jun-Sep). Unique in Egypt, it has dual dedication to the local crocodile go Sobek and Haroeris, from *har-wer*, mear ing Horus the Elder. This is reflected in th temple's plan: perfectly symmetrical alon the main axis of the temple, there are twi entrances, two shared hypostyle hall with carvings of the two gods on eithe side, and twin sanctuaries. It is assume that there were also two priesthoods. Th left (western) side of the temple was ded cated to Haroeris, the right (eastern) ha to Sobek. The temple's spectacular rive

Temple of Kom Ombo (above)

DONALD C. & PRISCILLA ALEXANDER EASTN

TEMPLE OF KOM OMBO

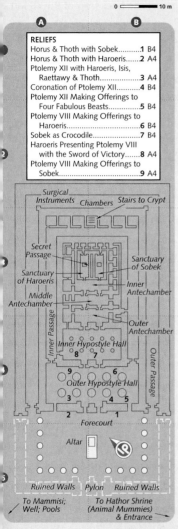

RELIEFS

Horus & Thoth with Sobek..........1 B4
Horus & Thoth with Haroeris......2 A4
Ptolemy XII with Haroeris, Isis,
   Raettawy & Thoth...................3 A4
Coronation of Ptolemy XII..........4 B4
Ptolemy XII Making Offerings to
   Four Fabulous Beasts..............5 B4
Ptolemy VIII Making Offerings to
   Haroeris................................6 B4
Sobek as Crocodile.....................7 B4
Haroeris Presenting Ptolemy VIII
   with the Sword of Victory.......8 A4
Ptolemy VIII Making Offerings to
   Sobek...................................9 A4

Passing into the temple's **forecourt**, where the reliefs are divided between the two gods, there is a double altar in the centre of the court for both gods. Beyond are the shared **inner and outer hypostyle halls**, each with 10 columns. Inside the **outer hypostyle hall**, to the left, is a finely executed relief showing Ptolemy XII Neos Dionysos being presented to Haroeris by Isis and the lion-headed goddess Raettawy, with Thoth looking on. Reliefs in the **inner hypostyle hall** show Haroeris presenting Ptolemy VIII Euergetes with a curved weapon, representing the sword of victory. Behind Ptolemy is his sister-wife and co-ruler Cleopatra II.

From here, three **antechambers**, each with double entrances, lead to the **sanctuaries of Sobek and Haroeris**. The **outer passage**, which runs around the temple walls, is unusual. Here, on the left-hand (northern) corner of the temple's back wall, is a puzzling scene, which is often described as a collection of '**surgical instruments**'. It seems more probable that these were implements used during the temple's daily rituals.

GETTING THERE & AWAY

The best way to visit the temple is to come on a tour or with a private taxi from Luxor or Aswan.

ASWAN

pop 226,013

On the northern end of the First Cataract and marking the country's ancient southern frontier, Aswan has always been of great strategic importance. In ancient times it was a garrison town for the military campaigns against Nubia, its quarries provided the valuable granite used for so many sculptures and obelisks,

...de setting has resulted in the erosion of ...ome of its partly Roman forecourt and ...uter sections, but much of the complex ...as survived and is very similar in layout ...o the other Ptolemaic temples of Edfu ...nd Dendara, albeit smaller.

ESNA TO ABU SIMBEL

and it was a prosperous marketplace at the crossroads of the ancient caravan routes.

Today, slower than most places in Egypt, laid-back and pleasant, it is the perfect place to linger for a few days, rest the eyes and the mind, and recover from the rigours of travelling along the Nile. The river is wide, languorous and stunningly beautiful here, flowing gently down from Lake Nasser, around dramatic black-granite boulders and palm-studded islands. Colourful sleepy Nubian villages

run down to the water and stand o against the backdrop of the desert c the west bank.

INFORMATION

Tourist office (Map p206; ☎ 231 2811, 010 5 7594; Midan al-Mahatta; ☼ 8am-3pm & 7-9pm S Thu, 9am-3pm & 6-8pm Fri) This tourist offic has little material, and still no compute but the manager, Hakeem Hussein, knowledgeable and very helpful. He c deal with most questions, from orga ising a trip and advising on timetabl

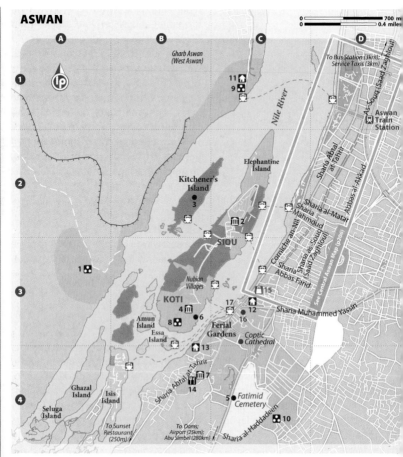

ASWAN

ASWAN

Gharb Aswan
(West Aswan)

To Bus Station (3km);
Service Taxis (3km)

As-Souq (Saad Zaghloul)

Aswan
Train
Station

Nile River

11
9

Elephantine
Island

Kitchener's
Island
3

Sharia Abtal
at-Tahrir

Abbas al-Akkad

2

Sharia al-Matar

Sharia
Mahmoud

SIOU

Corniche an-Nil

Sharia as-Souq (Saad Zaghloul)

See Central Aswan Map (p206)

Nubian
Villages

Sharia
Abbas Farid

KOTI

4   6

15

17   12

Sharia Muhammed Yassin

8

16

Amun
Island
Essa
Island

Ferial
Gardens

Coptic
Cathedral

13

Ghazal
Island
Isis
Island

7
14

5   Fatimid
Cemetery

Seluga
Island

To Sunset
Restaurant
(250m)

To Dams;
Airport (25km);
Abu Simbel (280km)

10

Sharia al-Haddadeen

Sharia Abtal at-Tahrir

0   700 m
0   0.4 miles

o giving an idea of prices for taxis and feluccas.

SIGHTS

THE TOWN & EAST BANK

The **Nubia Museum** (Map p202; ☎ 231 9111; Sharia Abtal at-Tahrir; adult/student E£50/25; ☒ 9am-1pm & 5-9pm) is a showcase of the history, art and culture of Nubia and is a real treat. Established in 1997, in co-operation with Unesco, the museum is a reminder of the history and culture of the Nubians, much of which was lost when Lake Nasser flooded their land after the building of the dams. Exhibits are beautifully displayed in huge halls, where clearly written explanations take you from 4500 BC through to the present day. Among museum highlights are 6000-year-old painted pottery bowls and an impressive quartzite statue of a 25th-dynasty priest of Amun in Thebes with distinct Kushite (Upper Nubian) features. The stunning horse armour found in tombs from the Ballana period (5th to 7th century BC) shows the sophistication of artisanship during this brief ascendancy.

Behind the Nubia Museum is the vast **Fatimid Cemetery** (Map p202), a collection of low mudbrick buildings with domed roofs. Although most tombs are modern, some of the mausolea clustered towards the back of the cemetery go back to the Tulunid period (9th century). The tombs are covered with domes that are built on a drum with corners sticking out like horns, a feature unique to southern Egypt.

In the **Northern Quarries** (Map p202; adult/student E£30/20; ☒ 7am-4pm Oct-May, 8am-6pm Jun-Sep), about 1.5km from town opposite the Fatimid Cemetery, is a huge discarded **Unfinished Obelisk**. Three sides of the shaft, which is nearly 42m long, were completed except for the inscriptions. At 1168 tonnes, the completed obelisk would have been the single heaviest piece of stone the Egyptians ever fashioned. However, a flaw appeared in the rock at a late stage in the process. So it lies where the disappointed stonemasons abandoned it, still partly attached to the parent rock, with no indication of what it was intended for.

THE RIVER

Elephantine Island (Map p202) is the site of ancient **Abu** (meaning both elephant and ivory in ancient Egyptian), both names a reminder of the role the island once played in the ivory trade. As well as being a thriving settlement, Elephantine Island was the main cult centre of the ram-headed god Khnum (at first the god of the inundation, and from the 18th dynasty worshipped as the creator of humankind on his potter's wheel), Satet (Khnum's wife, and guardian of the southern frontier) and their daughter Anket.

The ruins of the original town of Abu and the fascinating **Aswan Museum** (Map p202; adult/student E£25/15; ☒ 8am-5pm Oct-Apr,

8.30am-6pm May-Sep) lie at the southern end of Elephantine Island. The main part of the museum houses a dusty collection of antiquities discovered in Aswan and Nubia, but most of the Nubian artefacts rescued from the temples flooded by Lake Nasser were moved to the Nubia Museum. The modern annexe, however, has a delightful collection of objects, from weapons, pottery and utensils to statues, encased mummies and sarcophagi from predynastic to late Roman times, found in the excavations on Elephantine Island.

A path through the garden behind the museum leads to the evocative **ruins of ancient Abu**. Numbered plaques and reconstructed buildings mark the island's long history from around 3000 BC to the 14th century AD. The largest structure in the site is the partially reconstructed **Temple of Khnum** (plaque Nos 6, 12 and 13). Built in honour of the God of Inundation during the Old Kingdom, it was added to and used for more than 1500 years before being extensively rebuilt in Ptolemaic times. The **Nilometer**

of the Temple of Khnum (No 7) is belo the southern balustrade of the Khnur temple. Built in the 26th dynasty, its ston stairs lead down to a small basin for mea suring the Nile's maximum level. Anothe stairway, with a scale etched into its wal leads to the water from the basin's north ern end. Descending to the river's edg from beneath a sycamore tree near th museum is the **Nilometer of the Sate Temple** (No 10).

Sandwiched between the ruins of Ab and the Mövenpick resort are two colou ful Nubian villages, **Siou** and **Koti**. The shady alleys and gardens make for a tran quil stroll – a north–south path crosse the middle of the island and links the tw villages. At **Animalia** (Map p202; ☎ 231 415 010 545 6420; www.animalia-eg.com; main st, Sio admission E£5, incl guided tour E£10; ☼ 8am-7pr Mohamed Sobhi, a Nubian guide, and h family have dedicated part of their larg house to the traditions, flora and faun and the history of Nubia.

To the west of Elephantine Island **Aswan Botanical Gardens** (Map p202; a

Aswan Botanical Gardens on Kitchener's Island (above)

nission E£15; 🕐 8am-5pm Oct-Apr, to 6pm May-ep), still often referred to by its old name, itchener's Island. The island was given to ord Horatio Kitchener in the 1890s when 1e was commander of the Egyptian army. ndulging his passion for beautiful palms nd plants, Kitchener turned the entire sland into a stunning botanical garden, mporting plants from the Far East, India nd parts of Africa. Avoid coming here n Friday, when the place is invaded by picnicking extended families with stereos. he island is most easily seen as part of a elucca tour.

GETTING THERE & AWAY

wo public ferries (E£1) run to Elephantine sland; the one departing across from gyptAir (Map p202) goes to the Aswan Museum, while the one across from homas Cook (Map p206) goes to Siou.

THE WEST BANK

s with the Botanical Gardens, it is easiest o visit the west bank as part of a felucca our. High up on the west bank stands the elegant **Tomb of Mohammed Shah Aga Khan** (Aga Khan Mausoleum; Map p202; closed to he public), the 48th imam (leader) of the smaili sect, who died in 1957, and of his vife the Begum, who died in 2000. Aswan vas their favourite wintering place, and he family's white villa is in the garden peneath the tomb.

The high cliffs opposite Aswan, just torth of Kitchener's Island, are honey-ombed with the tombs of the governors, he Keepers of the Gate of the South, and ther dignitaries of ancient Elephantine sland. Known as the **Tombs of the Nobles** Map p202; adult/student E£20/10; 🕐 8am-4pm ct-May, to 5pm Jun-Sep), six are open to the ublic. The tombs date from the Old and Middle Kingdoms and most follow a sim-le plan, with an entrance hall, a pillared

room and a corridor leading to the burial chamber. A set of stairs cutting diagonally across the hill takes you up to the tombs from the ferry landing.

A public ferry (E£1) goes from the ferry landing across from the train station on the east bank to West Aswan and the Tombs of the Nobles.

ACTIVITIES
BIRDWATCHING

Local expert, **Mohamed Arabi** (☎ 012 324 0132; www.touregypt.net/featurestories/aswan birding.htm; per person from US$30), is known as the 'Birdman of Aswan' and no bird escapes his eye. He has been taking twitchers and documentary makers for many years, but is also happy to take amateurs out into his small speedboat that glides into the channels between the islands, pointing out the vegetation; sunbirds; hoopoes; purple, squacco, striated and night herons; pied kingfishers; little and cattle egrets; redshanks; and many other birds species.

CRUISES & SAFARIS

Several companies operate cruises and fishing safaris from Aswan, on Lake Nasser. For details about taking a dahabiyya on the river from Esna to Aswan, see p196. For more information on cruising the Nile, see p308.

Kasr Ibrim & Eugénie (☎ 02-516 9653/4/5; www.kasribrim.com.eg; d per person per night on 3- to 4-day trip from US$190; 🕸) Both run by Belle Époque Travel, these boats were the brainchild of Mustafa al-Guindi, a Cairene of Nubian origin who is almost single-handedly responsible for getting Lake Nasser opened to tourists. The boats are stunningly designed: *Eugénie* is modelled on an early-20th-century hunting lodge and *Kasr Ibrim* is all 1930s art deco elegance.

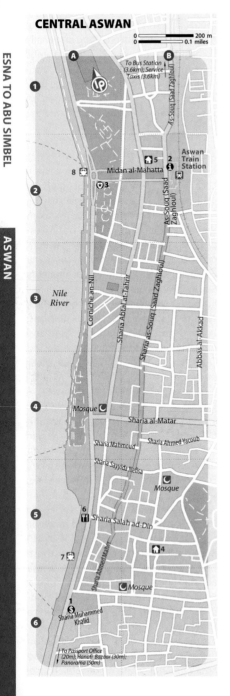

CENTRAL ASWAN

Each has a pool, hammam (bathhouse and fantastic French cuisine.

Ta Seti (☎ 097 231 0907; www.african-angle .net; 3-night trip per person in safari boat from €300 in houseboat from €455) Tim Baily worked i safaris south of the Sahara before setting up African Angler, the first company t run Lake Nasser safaris. He has a staff o skilled guides, expert in the flora, faun and fish life of the lake and owns severa styles of small boat. The two-cabin house boats have toilet and shower, the two bunk safari boat is more basic, while th mothership carries the kitchen and sup plies. There are departures from Aswa each Tuesday.

FELUCCA RIDES

The Nile looks fabulous and magical a Aswan, and few things are more relaxing than hiring a felucca before sunset an sailing between the islands, the deser and the huge black boulders, listening t the flapping of the sail and to Nubian boy singing from their tiny dugouts. The trust worthy **Gelal** (☎ 012 415 4902), who hang out near Panorama Restaurant and th ferry landing, offers hassle-free tours o his family's feluccas at a fixed price (E£3 per boat for an hour, E£35 for a moto boat). According to the tourist office, three- or four-hour tour costs at least E£9 to E£120. A two- to three-hour trip dow to Seheyl Island costs about E£90.

SLEEPING

Prices vary greatly depending on the season; the rates mentioned here are high season, which extends from October through to April, but peaks in December and January. In the low season, and even until early November, you'll have no trouble finding a room at lower prices.

BUDGET

Nuba Nile Hotel (Map p206; ☎ 231 3267; www.nubanile.com; Sharia Abtal at-Tahrir; s/d £60/75; 🞵 🖳 🞵) If the Keylany is full, this friendly family-run hotel is the next best budget option, with clean, comfortable rooms, conveniently located just north of the square in front of the train station and beside a popular *ahwa* and internet cafe. Check the room before you agree, as they vary considerably: some are tiny, others have no windows, but all have private bathrooms, and most have air-con.

Keylany Hotel (Map p206; ☎ 231 7332; www.keylanyhotel.com; 25 Sharia Keylany; s/d/tr US$16.50/24/32; 🞵 🖳) Aswan's best budget hotel has simple but comfortable rooms furnished with pine furniture, and spotless bathrooms with proper showers and hot water. The management and staff are friendly and endlessly helpful. The roof terrace has no Nile view but there is a burlap sunshade and furniture made from palm fronds, and it is a great place to hang out.

MIDRANGE

Aswan has only a small selection of midrange hotels. There's not much to distinguish those at the bottom end of the scale from the better budget places, so if money's tight, look carefully before making a choice.

Beit al-Kerem (Map p202; ☎ 019 239 9443, 12 384 2218; www.betelkerem.com; Gharb Aswan, west bank; s/d incl dinner on 1st night €35/45;

ROBERT HARDING PICTURE LIBRARY LTD/ALAMY
Looking over the Old Cataract Hotel (p208) to the Nile

🞵) This modern hotel overlooking the desert and the Tomb of the Nobles is a great find, offering eight quiet and comfortable rooms with very clean shared bathrooms. The hotel boasts a wonderful rooftop terrace overlooking the Nile and Nubian village, and has a good restaurant (meals €8 to €11). The staff is very friendly and proud to be Nubian. Call ahead and Shaaban will come and fetch you or explain how to get there.

Nile Hotel (Map p202; ☎ 231 4222; www.nilehotel-aswan.com; Corniche an-Nil; s/d/tr US$40/55/73, on Tue & Thu US$45/60/81; 🞵 🖳) A very welcome new hotel in this price range, offering 40 well-appointed rooms with spotless private bathrooms, satellite TV and minibar, all with a window or balcony overlooking the Nile. The staff speak English and are very friendly and helpful. There is a restaurant, a small library with foreign novels and books about Egypt, and a business centre.

TOP END

Sofitel Old Cataract Hotel & Spa (Map p202; ☎ 231 6000; www.sofitel.com; Sharia Abtal at-Tahrir; r from US$250; 🖭 🖳) The grande dame of hotels on the Nile, the Old Cataract brings you back to the days of Agatha Christie, who is said to have written part of her novel *Death on the Nile* here (the hotel featured in the movie). The splendid building, surrounded by well-tended exotic gardens on a rock above the river, commands fantastic views of the Nile and several islands, the ruins of Abu and the desert behind. At the time of writing both the Old and the more modern building of the New Cataract (saved from total demolition by President Mubarak because he wanted to preserve the place where he spent his honeymoon!) have been totally gutted. The hotels are due to reopen in summer 2010 as one deluxe-suite-only hotel with very spacious rooms of contemporary luxury in a Moorish-oriental decor, closer to the hotel's original style.

EATING

Aswan is a sleepy place and most tourists eat on board the cruise boats, but there are a few laid-back restaurants. Outside the hotels, few serve alcohol and few accept credit cards.

Panorama (off Map p206; ☎ 231 6169; Corniche an-Nil; dishes E£8-20) With its pleasant Nileside terrace, this is a great place to chill and sip a herbal tea or fresh juice. It also serves simple Egyptian stews cooked in clay pots, with salad, mezze and rice or chips, or an all-day breakfast.

Golden Pharaoh (Map p202; ☎ 231 0361, 010 229 2910; Corniche an-Nil; mains E£16-45; ☉ 9am-late; 🖭) The newest arrival is

this rather sophisticated eatery with an air-con dining room and a large terrace overlooking the Nile and the city. The menu includes Nubian and international dishes, and the place is already popular with Aswanis.

Salah ad-Din (Map p206; ☎ 231 0361, 01 229 2910; Corniche an-Nil; mains E£40; ☉ noon-late 🖭) This is the best of the Nileside restaurants, with several terraces and a freezing air-conditioned dining room. The menu has Egyptian, Nubian and international dishes, a notch better than most restaurants in Aswan. The service is efficient and the beers are cool (E£12). There is also terrace to smoke a *sheesha*.

Sunset (off Map p202; ☎ 233 0601, 012 16 1480; Sharia Abtal at-Tahrir, in Nasr City; set menu E£45-60; ☉ 9am-3am) This great cafe terrace and restaurant is the place to be at sunset, with spectacular views over the First Cataract. Sit on the huge shady terrace for a mint tea, or enjoy the small selection of excellent grills or pizzas (E£38). Or take a taxi after dark. Very popular with locals at night.

SHOPPING

Sharia as-Souq (Map p206) Aswan's famous market street is a good place to pick up souvenirs and crafts. It appears much like any tourist bazaar but a closer look reveals more exotic elements: handmade Nubian skullcaps (about E£10), colourful scarves (E£20 to E£50), and traditional baskets and trays (E£120 to E£90) in varying sizes are popular. You can also see African masques and enormous stuffed crocodiles. The spices and indigo powder prominently displayed are other good buys, and most of the spice shops sell the dried hibiscus used to make the refreshing drink *karkadai*. However, beware of the safflower that is sold as saffron. The pace is slow particularly in the late afternoon, the air as a slight whiff of sandalwood and, as ancient times, you may feel that Aswan the gateway to Africa.

Hanafi Bazaar (Map p202; ☎ 231 4083; rniche an-Nil; ⏰ 8am-10pm) With its mock haraonic facade, this is the oldest, no oubt also the most dusty, and best baar in town, with genuine Nubian swords,

baskets, amulets, silk kaftans and beads from all over Africa, run by the totally laid-back Hanafi brothers.

GETTING THERE & AWAY
AIR

Daily flights are available with **EgyptAir** (Map p202; ☎ 231 5000; Corniche an-Nil; ⏰ 8am-

WALTER BIBIKOW/JON ARNOLD TRAVEL/PHOTOLIBRARY

Daraw camel market (below)

⬎ IF YOU LIKE...

If you like Aswan's **Sharia as-Souq** (p208), you will definitely like these markets full of local colour:

- **Esna souq** A busy souq with vegetables, fruit, animals and household things on Mondays, right beside the canal north of the tourist souq in Esna (p195).
- **Kom Ombo cattle market** In ancient times, Kom Ombo (p200) was a market where the Ptolemies came for African elephants from Ethiopia, which they needed to fight the Indian elephants of their enemies, the Seleucids. Nowadays, on Thursdays, there is a picturesque cattle market held on the northern outskirts of town, near the railway line.
- **Daraw camel market** Daraw, 8km south of Kom Ombo, is famous for its remarkable camel market *(souq al-gimaal)*. Most of the camels are brought up in caravans from Sudan to just north of Abu Simbel, from where they're trucked in. The rest walk to the market in smaller groups, entering Egypt at Wadi al-Alagi and making their way through the Eastern Desert. Camels are sold here each day of the week, but the main market days are Tuesday and Thursday, when sometimes as many as 2000 camels are brought down from Abu Simbel.

8pm) from Cairo to Aswan (one way E£223 to E£879, 1¼ hours). The one-way trip to Luxor is between E£156 and E£383 and takes 30 minutes. There are three to four flights a day to Abu Simbel, leaving between 6.15am and 9.15am, an hour later in summer.

BOAT
For information on cruisers from Luxor to Aswan, see p132. For dahabiyyas to Aswan from Esna, see p196. See also p308 for more on cruising the Nile.

BUS
The bus station is 3.5km north of the train station, but the tourist office advises against travelling by bus as it is too much of a hassle. At the time of writing, there are no buses to Luxor and travelling by bus to Abu Simbel is restricted to four foreigners per bus. Upper Egypt Bus Co has two daily buses to Abu Simbel (E£25, four hours, departing 8am and 5pm).

SERVICE TAXI
Services taxis and minibuses leave from the bus station, 3.5km north of the train station. A taxi there will cost E£15, or 50 piastres in a communal taxi. A seat in a service taxi or minibus to Luxor costs E£18, to Kom Ombo E£5.50 and to Edfu E£11.

TRAIN
From **Aswan Train Station (Map p206;** ☎ 231 4754) a number of daily trains run north to Cairo, but officially foreigners can only buy tickets in the station for one 1st-class train only (E£165, 14 hours, 6.45pm). However, no one will stop you boarding other trains if you buy the ticket on the train and pay E£6 extra.

Abela Egypt Sleeping Train (☎ 230 2124; www.sleepingtrains.com) has two daily services to Cairo at 5pm and 7pm (single/double cabin per person including dinner

and breakfast US$60/120, children age four to nine years US$45, 14 hours). No that there is no student discount and tic ets must be paid for in US dollars.

GETTING AROUND
TO/FROM THE AIRPORT
The airport is located 25km southwe of town. A taxi to/from the airport cos about E£35 to E£45.

TAXI
A taxi tour that includes Philae, the Hig Dam and the Unfinished Obelisk ne Fatimid Cemetery costs around E£100 E£150 for five to six people. Taxis can al take you on day trips to Daraw and/or Ko Ombo for about E£200. A taxi anywhe within the town costs E£5 to E£10.

ARIADNE VAN ZANDBE

Pillar in the Tombs of the Nobles, Aswan (p205)

AROUND ASWAN

ASWAN DAM

t the end of the 19th century Egypt's fast-rowing population made it imperative o cultivate more agricultural land, which would only be possible by regulating the ow of the Nile. The British engineer Sir William Willcocks started construction of he old Aswan Dam in 1898 above the First ataract. When completed in 1902, it was he largest dam in the world, measuring 441m across, 50m tall and 30m wide, and was made almost entirely of Aswan granite. With the opening of the High Dam, it ow only generates hydroelectricity for a earby factory producing fertilisers, and otherwise serves as a tourist attraction on he way to the High Dam, 6km upstream.

HIGH DAM

gypt's modern example of construction n a monumental scale, the controversial **Aswan High Dam** (As-Sadd al-Ali; Map right) contains 18 times the amount f material used in the Great Pyramid f Khufu and created Lake Nasser, the world's largest artificial lake.

From the 1940s it was clear that the old swan Dam, which only regulated the flow f water, was not big enough to counter the npredictable annual flooding of the Nile. 1 1952, when Gamal Abdel Nasser came o power, plans were drawn up for a new am, 6km south of the old one, but from he start there were political and engineering difficulties. In 1956, after the World Bank efused the promised loan for the project, asser ordered the nationalisation of the Uez Canal, which sparked the Suez Crisis which France, the UK and Israel invaded he canal region. But Nasser got his way and so won additional funding and expertise om the Soviet Union. Work started in 1960 nd was finally completed in 1971.

AROUND ASWAN

ESNA TO ABU SIMBEL

AROUND ASWAN

The dam has brought great benefits to Egypt's farmers, increasing cultivable land by at least 30%. At the same time, the country's power supply has doubled. But there are downsides. The dam has stopped the flow of silt essential to the fertility of the land, and the much higher use of artificial fertilisers has led to increasing salinity of the agricultural areas. The groundwater tables have risen, too, and are damaging many monuments close to the Nile. The now perennially full irrigation canals have led to endemic infection

SAM VAUGHAN/AL

Kiosk of Trajan, Philae

↘ PHILAE (AGILKIA ISLAND)

The romantic aura and the grandeur of the **Temple of Isis** on the island of Philae (fee-*leh*) lured pilgrims for thousands of years, and during the 19th century the ruins became one of Egypt's most legendary tourist attractions. The most important ruins were begun by Ptolemy II Philadelphus (285–246 BC) and added to for the next 500 years until the reign of Diocletian (AD 284–305).

After the completion of the High Dam, the temple would have entirely disappeared had Unesco not intervened. Between 1972 and 1980, the complex was disassembled stone by stone and reconstructed on nearby Agilkia Island.

The boat (E£10) across to the temple leaves you at the base of the **Kiosk of Nectanebo**, the oldest part of the Philae complex. Heading north, you walk down the **outer temple court**, which has colonnades running along both sides; the western one is the most complete, with windows that originally overlooked the island of Bigga. At the end is the entrance of the Temple of Isis, marked by the 18m-high towers of the **first pylon** with reliefs of Ptolemy XII Neos Dionysos smiting enemies.

On the northern tip of the island you'll find the **Temple of Augustus** and the **Gate of Diocletian**; east of the second pylon is the delightful **Temple of Hathor**, decorated with reliefs of musicians (including an ape playing the lute) and Bes, the god of childbirth. South of this is the elegant, unfinished pavilion by the water's edge, known as the **Kiosk of Trajan** (or 'Pharaoh's Bed'), perhaps the most famous of Philae's monuments.

Boats for Philae leave from Shellal south of the old Aswan Dam. Get here by taxi (return E£60) or organised trip from Aswan.

Things you need to know: Temple of Isis (Map p213; adult/child E£50/25; ☼ 7am-4pm Oct-May, to 5pm Jun-Sep); sound and light show (www.soundandlight.com.eg; adult/child E£70/50)

PHILAE (AGILKIA ISLAND)

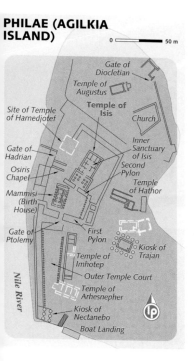

0 —— 50 m

Gate of Diocletian
Temple of Augustus
Temple of Isis
Site of Temple of Harnedjotef
Church
Inner Sanctuary of Isis
Gate of Hadrian
Second Pylon
Osiris Chapel
Temple of Hathor
Mammisi (Birth House)
Gate of Ptolemy
First Pylon
Kiosk of Trajan
Temple of Imhotep
Outer Temple Court
Temple of Arhesnepher
Nile River
Kiosk of Nectanebo
Boat Landing

...ith the bilharzia parasite, until recently huge public health problem.

GETTING THERE & AWAY

...he quickest way to get to the High Dam ...to take a taxi from Aswan (about E£25). ...sually it is combined with a trip to the ...mple of Kalabsha, which is about 3km ...om the western end of the dam and is ...isible from the dam on the western side ...f Lake Nasser.

LOWER NUBIA & LAKE NASSER

...or thousands of years, the First Cataract ...arked the border between Egypt and ...ubia, the land that stretched from ...swan to Khartoum. The Nile Valley on ...e Egyptian side was fertile and continu-...usly cultivated, while the banks further

south in Nubia were more rugged, with rocky desert cliffs and sand separating small pockets of agricultural land.

The building of the Aswan and High Dams irrevocably changed all that, and much of Nubia disappeared under the waters of Lake Nasser. The landscape now is dominated by the contrast of smooth desert and the calm green-brown water of the lake. Apart from the beauty and the peace of the lake itself, the main attraction of this region is the temples that were so painstakingly moved above the floodwaters in the 1960s.

To ancient Egyptians, Nubia was Ta-Sety, the Land of Bowmen, after the weapon for which the Nubians were famous. It was a crucial route for the trade with sub-Saharan Africa, and the source of much-needed raw materials, such as copper, ivory, ebony and gold. Evidence of 10,000-year-old settlements has been found in northern Nubia. At Nabta Playa, located some 100km west of Abu Simbel, archaeologists have recently discovered the remains of houses, sculpted monoliths and the world's oldest calendar, made of small standing stones, dating from around 6000 BC.

Christianity gradually spread to Nubia after the 5th century AD and lasted long after Islam had spread along the Egyptian Nile. In AD 652 Egypt's new Muslim authorities made a peace treaty with the Christian king of Nubia. That treaty lasted more or less until the 13th century, when Egyptians moved south again: the last Christian king of Nubia was replaced by a Muslim in 1305 and most of the population converted to Islam.

Following the completion of the old Aswan Dam in 1902, and again after its height was raised in 1912 and 1934, the water level of the Nile in Lower Nubia gradually rose from 87m to 121m, partially submerging many of the monuments

SAM VAUGHAN/ALA

Temple of Kertassi (below), on the west bank of Lake Nasser

↘ IF YOU LIKE...

If you like **Philae's temples** (p212) you will also like these other temples that were rescued from the rising Nile waters:

- **Kalabsha, Beit al-Wali & Kertassi** (Map p211; adult/student E£30/15; ⊗ 8am-5pm) These temples were transplanted on the west bank of Lake Nasser just south of the High Dam. The late Ptolemaic **Temple of Kalabsha** was dedicated to the Nubian solar god Merwel, known to the Greeks as Mandulis. The **Temple of Beit al-Wali**, mostly built by Ramses II, was cut into the rock and fronted by a brick pylon. On the walls of the forecourt, several fine reliefs detail the pharaoh's victories. Further north are the picturesque remains of the **Temple of Kertassi**, with two Hathor columns and four fine papyrus columns. When the water level is low you can sometimes walk across to the site, otherwise find a motorboat on the western side of the High Dam (around E£30 for the return trip).

- **Wadi as-Subua** (Map p185; adult/student E£35/20) Wadi as-Subua means 'Valley of Lions' in Arabic and refers to the avenue of sphinxes that leads to the Temple of Ramses II. About 1km to the north are the remains of the **Temple of Dakka**, begun by the Upper Nubian Pharaoh Arkamani (218–200 BC) and dedicated to the god of wisdom, Thoth. The nearby **Temple of Maharraqa** is dedicated to Isis and the Alexandrian god Serapis.

- **Amada** (Map p185; adult/student E£35/20) The **Temple of Amada**, built by Tuthmosis III (1479–1425 BC) and his son Amenhotep, is the oldest surviving monument on Lake Nasser, and it has some of the finest and best-preserved reliefs. The rock-cut **Temple of Derr**, built by Ramses II, has well-preserved reliefs illustrating the Nubian campaign of Ramses II. Nearby is the small rock-cut **Tomb of Pennut**, viceroy of Nubia under Ramses VI (1143–1136 BC).

the area and, by the 1930s, totally ooding a large number of Nubian villages. With their homes flooded, some ubians moved north where, with government help, they bought land and uilt villages based on their traditional rchitecture. Most of the Nubian villages ose to Aswan, such as Elephantine, /est Aswan and Seheyl, are made up of eople who moved at this time. Less than 0 years later, the building of the High am forced those who had stayed to nove again. In the 1960s, 50,000 Egyptian ubians were relocated to government-uilt villages around Kom Ombo, 50km orth of Aswan.

ETTING THERE & AWAY

he road to Abu Simbel is open, but oreigners are only allowed to travel in uses or microbuses in a police convoy. bu Simbel can be reached by plane from swan, Luxor or Cairo. For the moment, he rest of the sights can only be reached y boat (see p205), which is in any case ne best way to see Lake Nasser's dramatic nonuments.

AKE NASSER

s the world's largest artificial lake, its atistics are staggering: with an area f 5250 sq km, it is 510km long and be-veen 5km and 35km wide. On average contains some 135 billion cubic metres f water, of which an estimated six bil-on are lost each year to evaporation. Its aximum capacity is 157 billion cubic etres of water, which was reached in 996 after heavy rains in Ethiopia, forc-g the opening of a special spillway at oshka, about 30km north of Abu Simbel, ne first time it had been opened since ne dam was built.

Because the level of the lake fluctuates has been difficult to build settlements around its edges. Instead the lake has become a place for migrating birds to rest on their long journeys north and south. Gazelles, foxes and several types of snake (including the deadly horned viper) live on its shores. Many species of fish live in its waters, including the enormous Nile perch. Crocodiles – some reportedly up to 5m long – and monitor lizards also live in the lake's shallows. For information on boat trips on the lake, see p205.

ABU SIMBEL

The village of Abu Simbel lies 280km south of Aswan and only 40km north of the Sudanese border. Overlooking Lake Nasser, the two **temples of Abu Simbel** (adult/student E£90/45; ⏰ 6am-5pm Oct-Apr, to 6pm May-Sep) are reached by road or, if you are on a cruise boat, from one of the jetties leading directly into the fenced temple compound.

Carved out of the mountain on the west bank of the Nile between 1274 and 1244 BC, the imposing **Great Temple of Ramses II** was as much dedicated to the deified pharaoh himself as to Ra-Horakhty, Amun and Ptah. Over the centuries both the Nile and the desert sands impercep-tibly shifted, and this temple was lost to the world until 1813, when it was redis-covered by chance by the Swiss explorer Jean-Louis Burckhardt. Only one of the heads was completely showing above the sand, the next head was broken off and, of the remaining two, only the crowns could be seen.

Guarding the entrance, three of the four famous colossal Ramses II statues sit majestically, staring out across the water into eternity – the inner left statue col-lapsed in antiquity and its upper body still lies on the ground. The statues, more than 20m high, are accompanied by smaller statues of the pharaoh's mother Queen

Tuya, his wife Nefertari and some of his favourite children. Above the entrance, between the central throned colossi, is the figure of the falcon-headed sun god Ra-Horakhty.

The roof of the large hall is decorated with vultures, which are protective figures symbolising the goddess Nekhbet, and is supported by eight columns, each fronted by an Osiride statue of Ramses II. Reliefs on the walls depict the pharaoh's prowess in battle, trampling over his enemies and slaughtering them in front of the gods. On the north wall is a depiction of the famous Battle of Kadesh (c 1274 BC), now in Syria, where Ramses inspired his demoralised army by his own courage, so that they won the war against the Hittites.

The temple is aligned in such a way that on 22 February and 22 October every year, the first rays of the rising sun reach across the Nile, penetrate the temple and move along the hypostyle hall, through the vestibule and into the sanctuary, where they illuminate the somewhat mutilated figures of Ra-Horakhty, Ramses II and Amun. Ptah, to the left, is never illuminated.

Next to the Great Temple is the much smaller **Temple of Hathor**, with a rock-cut facade fronted by six 10m-high standing statues of Ramses and Nefertari, with some of their many children by their side. Nefertari here wears the costume of the goddess Hathor, and is, unusually, portrayed as the same height as her husband

(instead of coming only up to his knees most consorts were depicted).

A **sound and light show** (www.sou andlight.com.eg; adult/child E£80/45; ☾ show 7pm, 8pm & 9pm winter, 8pm, 9pm & 10pm Ma Sep) is performed nightly.

SLEEPING & EATING

Eskaleh (Beit an-Nubi; ☎ 340 1288, 012 3 0521; d €50-70; ✖ ▯) Part Nubian cultur centre with a library dedicated to Nubia history and culture, part small ecolodg in a traditional Nubian mudbrick hous Eskaleh is definitely the place to stay town and something of a destination its own right, if a bit pricey. Comfortab rooms are simply furnished with local fu niture, and have fans, air-con and goo private bathrooms. Nubian women pre pare delicious home-cooked meals (thre course lunch or dinner E£60) with organ produce from Fikry's garden and fish fro the lake.

GETTING THERE & AWAY

Foreigners travelling from Aswan to Ab Simbel by road must travel in police co voy. Most people opt for a tour and ge the admission and guide included. The are also buses from Abu Simbel to Aswa leaving at 6am, 9.30am, 1pm and 4p from the Wadi el-Nil Restaurant on th main road. Tickets (E£21) are purchase on board. Note that the official limit is fo foreign passengers per bus.

ARIADNE VAN ZANDBE

Pompey's Pillar (p231), in the ancient Rhakotis area of Alexandria

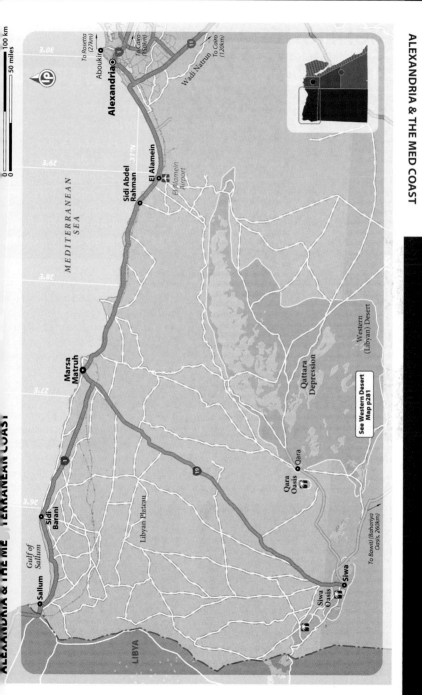

ALEXANDRIA & THE MEDITERRANEAN COAST

HIGHLIGHTS

1   CATACOMBS OF KOM ASH-SHUQQAFA

BY COLIN CLEMENT, PUBLISHER, HARPOCRATES PUBLISHING

This 1st- and 2nd-century AD burial complex is Alexandria's most striking and indeed most Alexandrian archaeological site. Unlike the monstrous monuments of Egypt proper, here there is a human scale and the rich ornamentation, displaying Egyptian, Greek and Roman influences, beautifully jumbled and charmingly badly executed

⬎ COLIN CLEMENT'S DON'T MISS LIST

❶ THE CATACOMBS

Whenever a hole is made in Alexandria, some antiquity is found. This wonderful site was discovered by chance in 1900, when a donkey vanished into the ground, uncovering several levels of catacombs. With three tiers of tombs and chambers cut 35m deep into bedrock, this is the largest known Roman burial site in the country.

❷ THE ROTUNDA

These catacombs most probably started off as a smaller family crypt in

the 2nd century AD. Stairs descende into the central rotunda, which led t the triclinium and on to the main tom chamber. Over the next 300 years th family crypt was expanded into a muc larger funeral complex.

❸ THE TRICLINIUM

The triclinium served as a banquetin hall. Mourners reclined on the benche for the funeral banquet held for th dead when they were buried, then 4 days after the funeral, and then ever anniversary – much as some Egyptiar

Clockwise from top: Sarcophogus reliefs; Colourful tomb interior; Fresco displaying ancient funerary rites; Tom wall carvings showing Graeco-Roman influences

...ll do today. Pottery and shards of ...ne jars were excavated here.

THE PRINCIPAL TOMB

...ost interesting of all is the main ...mb, which has a small antecham- ...er giving way to the inner sanctum. ...e walls are decorated with a typical ...exandrian art mixing different styles ...d religious beliefs. The wonder- ...l high reliefs in the doorway show ...o Anubis figures, representing the ...yptian god of the dead. Strangely, ...ey are dressed as Roman legionar- ...s, and one has the serpent's tail of ...athos Daimon, a Greek divinity.

HALL OF CARACALLA

...the older Hall of Caracalla the mix of ...cient Egypt, Rome and Greece is pal-

...pable. It was once a separate tomb, but the staircase long ago collapsed and it is now part of the larger complex. Beside the hole in the wall made by tomb robbers is a barely visible paint- ing showing both the mummification of the Egyptian god Osiris, and the kidnapping of the Greek Persephone by Hades.

↘ THINGS YOU NEED TO KNOW

How to visit Walk from Pompey's Pillar **Warning** The lower floor is inacces- ...ible because of flooding **See our author's review on p231**

HIGHLIGHTS

↘ ALEXANDRIA NATIONAL MUSEUM

Try to grapple with the immense amount of ancient history made in Alexandria at the city's impressive **Alexandria National Museum** (p229). With a small, thoughtfully selected and well-labelled collection singled out from Alexandria's other museums, it does a sterling job of relating the city's history from antiquity to the modern period. Also see objects found in recent underwater excavations.

↘ BIBLIOTHECA ALEXANDRINA

The original Library of Alexandria was the greatest repository of books and documents in all of antiquity. Ptolemy I established the library in 283 BC as part of a larger research complex known as the Mouseion. Although the new **Bibliotheca Alexandrina** (p234) can't claim the same importance, it has managed to become the city's premier cultural venue.

⬊ ALEXANDRIAN CAFES

Soak in the 19th-century grandeur through a puff of *sheesha* smoke or a kick-start-strong coffee at one of Alexandria's beautiful **period cafes** (p233). Famous literary figures like Lawrence Durrell and the Greek poet Cavafy met here, chatted and pondered the city. Many of these cafes reflect the cosmopolitan city Alexandria once was.

⬊ EL ALAMEIN

Be reminded of the ultimate toll paid by soldiers on all sides of the WWII North Africa campaign at **El Alamein** (p239), where the Allies and General Bernard Law Montgomery defeated Field Marshal Erwin Rommel, the 'Desert Fox'. Winston Churchill famously said 'Before Alamein we never had a victory. After Alamein we never had a defeat'.

⬊ SIDI ABDEL RAHMAN

The coast west of Alexandria is packed with resorts mostly catering to Cairene holidaymakers, but there is so far a lot less development near **Sidi Abdel Rahman** (p239). There is no other reason to come here than the gorgeous white sand and clear turquoise waters, but you'll want to spend a few days.

2 TRAVELPIXS/ALAMY; 3 SIMON FOALE; 4 JOHN WREFORD/ARABIANEYE/PHOTOLIBRARY; 5 PATRICK SYDER; 6 PAVAN ALDO/SIME

Alexandria National Museum (p229); 3 Moat and carved walls of the Bibliotheca Alexandrina (p234); 4 Alexandrian fe, Athineos (p233); 5 El Alamein's Commonwealth War cemetery (p239); 6 Beach, Sidi Abdel Rahman (p239)

THE BEST...

⭘ PLACES TO RELAX

- Walk along the sweeping **Corniche** in Alexandria (p228) and admire the glorious **Eastern Harbour**, in which so much of Alexandria's past has disappeared.
- Take a copy of Lawrence Durrell's *Alexandria Quartet* and read it in your room with sea view at the **Cecil Hotel** (p235), where some of the action is set.
- Wander around town, stopping regularly for a coffee and a pastry at one of Alexandria's many **period cafes** (p233).
- Swim in the transparent turquoise waters of the Mediterranean Sea **beaches** (p240), west of Alexandria.

⭘ PLACES TO EAT FISH

- With tables out in the street, **Qadoura** (p235) is the real thing, serving the freshest fish with bread and mezze, but no menu and no alcohol.

- Owned by Zizi Salem, the retired queen of the Alexandrian belly-dancing scene, **Samakmak** (p235) is definitely one step up from the other fish eateries in the neighbourhood.
- The **Cap d'Or** (p236), one of the only surviving typical Alexandrian bars, is also a good place to eat seafood tapas, such as a squid hotpot and fried calamari, all served with a cold beer.

⭘ PLACES WITH A VIEW

- The delightful terrace of the **Greek Club** (p236) is the best place for a drink at sunset or a wonderful seafood lunch, with full view of the Eastern Harbour.
- Take a diving tour **under the sea** (p234) of the Eastern Harbour to see what might one day be an underwater museum.

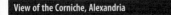

ARIADNE VAN ZANDBERGEN

View of the Corniche, Alexandria

THINGS YOU NEED TO KNOW

↘ VITAL STATISTICS

- **Telephone codes** Alexandria (☎ 03), Marsa Matruh (☎ 046)
- **Population Alexandria** 4.1 million
- **Best time to go** Spring and autumn; winters are cold and summers very crowded

↘ PLACES IN A NUTSHELL

- **Alexandria** (p228) Alexander the Great's city with monuments, a great museum and good cafes.
- **El Alamein** (p239) The scene of a decisive battle in WWII where many were killed and are now buried in the vast War Cemeteries.
- **Sidi Abdel Rahman** (p239) Come here for some of the Egyptian Meds most pristine beaches.
- **Marsa Matruh** (p241) A stopover on the way to Siwa and some good beaches.

↘ ADVANCE PLANNING

- **One month before** Book accommodation ahead, particularly if travelling between June and September.
- **One week before** Check the Bibliotheca Alexandrina website for upcoming events; contact operators to arrange an Alexandria harbour diving tour.

↘ RESOURCES

- **Alexandria main tourist office** (Map p232; ☎ 485 1556; Midan Saad Zaghloul; ☯ 8.30am-6pm)

- **Marsa Matruh tourist office** (☎ 493 1841; cnr Sharia Omar Mukhtar & Al-Corniche)
- **Alex Agenda** Free monthly listings available at many hotels.
- **Alexandria Egypt** (www.alexandria egypt.com) Information and history of the city.
- **Bibliotheca Alexandrina** (www .bibalex.org) News and information about the library.

↘ EMERGENCY NUMBERS

- **Tourist police Alexandria** (☎ 485 0507)
- **Tourist police Marsa Matruh** (☎ 493 5575)

↘ GETTING AROUND

- **Car** The best way for travelling along the coast.
- **Taxi** For getting around the city of Alexandria.
- **Bus** For travelling between cities in the region.
- **Tram** The slow but fun way for getting around Alexandria.

↘ BE FOREWARNED

- **Taxis** There are no meters in Alex taxis so it's best to agree on a price before getting in.
- **Trains** Ones between Cairo and Marsa Matruh only operate in summer.

ITINERARIES

DISCOVERING ALEXANDRIA Two Days

Start day one sipping coffee at one of the city's many time-warp peric cafes (p233), then get a taste of the past at the excellent (1) **Alexandri National Museum** (p229). After the visit head for lunch at the unmis able (2) **Mohammed Ahmed** (p235), deservedly regarded as the kin of *fuul* (fava beans cooked with garlic and garnished with olive oil an spices) and *ta'amiyya*.

Having gotten a view of the city's past, explore the future at th iconic (3) **Bibliotheca Alexandrina** (p234), checking out the arch tecture, and several of its must-see museums and exhibits. Headin along the Corniche, stop at El Qobesi (p236) for the best mango juic ever. Wander the Eastern Harbour around to (4) **Fort Qaitbey** (p234 feeling the echoes of the legendary Pharos. Have a sunset drink at th Greek Club (p236) and have dinner there.

Work off supper by joining the crowds for a leisurely stroll bac along the (5) **Corniche**, or take a taxi to the wonderful seaside *ahw* (coffeehouse) of (6) **Arous al-Zilzila** (p237) opposite the Bibliotheca and relax with a nightcap of *sheesha*, tea and good conversation.

On day two, get an early start with an aromatic and strong Turkis coffee at the gorgeous (7) **Sofianopoulos Coffee Store** (p233). The head to the (8) **Roman Amphitheatre** and **Villa of the Birds** (p23(to see its exquisite ancient mosaics. After a quick pick-me-up me in town, venture to the ancient area of (9) **Rhakotis** (p231) to se Pompey's Pillar and the nearby Catacombs of Kom ash-Shuqqafa. taxi will bring you back to (10) **Midan Ramla** for a stroll around th area. From here you can make your way for a drink and dinner at th atmospheric Cap d'Or (p236), or the more sophisticated expat have of Centro de Portugal (p236).

ANCIENT & MODERN HISTORY Four Days

Spend two days in (1) **Alexandria** visiting the sights as described i the Discovering Alexandria itinerary.

On the third day start with breakfast in one of Alexandria's cafe take a car for the day and head west along the coast to (2) **El Alamei** (p239). Bring a picnic or have a simple sandwich lunch at the cafeteri opposite the War Museum. Visit the War Cemeteries and ponder th cost of war, before heading for a swim at the German War Memoria beach (p240). Spend the night and the next day in (3) **Sidi Abde Rahman** (p239) and return in the evening to Alexandria for a fis dinner at Samakmak (p235).

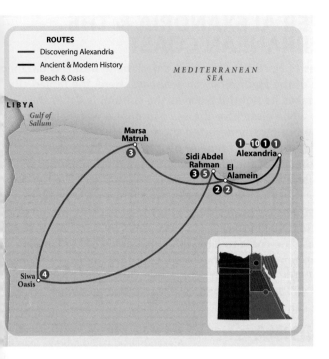

BEACH & OASIS Eight Days

This itinerary allows you to enjoy the best of city, sea and desert.
Follow the Ancient & Modern History itinerary for sightseeing in **(1) Alexandria** and **(2) El Alamein**, but on the fourth day don't return to Alexandria. Instead head for lunch and a dip in the ocean at **(3) Marsa Matruh** (p241) – Cleopatra's Beach, west of town, is particularly lovely. After lunch drive to the lush **(4) Siwa Oasis** (p299). You can spend three days in Siwa, cycling around the sights and the palm groves, taking a tour in the Great Sand Sea (p305), or hanging out in the cafes in Siwa Town. On the eighth day return to Alexandria, stopping at the beach of **(5) Sidi Abdel Rahman** (p239) for a meal and a refreshing swim.

DISCOVER ALEXANDRIA & THE MEDITERRANEAN COAST

The boundaries of Northern Egypt run smack bang into this dazzling 500km stretch of the Mediterranean seaboard. Here, the fabled city of Alexandria takes its rightful place as the cultural jewel in the coastal crown, while elsewhere the sea's turquoise waters lap up against pristine but mostly deserted shores.

Although it was once the home of near-mythical historical figures and Wonders of the World, only fragmented memories of Alexandria's glorious ancient past remain. Today the city is too busy gussying up its graceful 19th-century self to lament what's been and gone, and its streets and cafes buzz with the boundless energy of a new wave of creative youth.

Halfway across the coast to Libya, the memorials of El Alamein loom as solemn reminders of the lives lost during the North Africa campaigns of WWII. And not far off are the white-sand beach distractions of Sidi Abdel Rahman, and Marsa Matruh, which screams into life in the summer months.

ALEXANDRIA

The city of Alexandria (Al-Iskendariyya) is the stuff that legends are made of: the city was founded by none other than Alexander the Great; sassy queen Cleopatra made this the seat of her throne; the entrance to its harbour was marked by the towering Pharos lighthouse, one of the Seven Wonders of the World; and its Great Library of Alexandria was renowned as the ultimate archive of ancient knowledge. Alas, fate dealt the city a spate of cruel blows: today no sign remains of the great Alexander; the city of Cleopatra's day has been mostly swallowed up by the ocean; the Pharos lighthouse collapsed long ago; and the literary treasures of the Great Library were set to numerous torchings.

In the 19th century a cosmopolitan renaissance had Alexandria flirting with European-style decadence, but it was cut short in the 1950s by Nasser's wave of change. The daring new library of Alexandria signalled a brave leap into modernity, the first tentative steps of a city ready to revamp itself for the future. This town is also swooping in on the role of Egypt's culture vulture – legions of young artists and writers are finding their voices and new cutting-edge venues are providing a stage for their prolific output.

HISTORY

The city was initiated with the conquest of Alexander the Great, who arrived from Sinai having had his right to rule Egypt confirmed by the priests of Memphis. Foundations were laid in 331 BC and almost immediately Alexander departed for Siwa to consult the famous oracle, before marching for Persia.

Ptolemy masterminded the development of the new city, filling it with architecture to rival Rome or Athens in a deliberate attempt to establish it as e cultural and political centre of his mpire. Its famed library stimulated me of the great advances of the age: is was where Herophilus discovered at the head, not the heart, is the seat thought; Euclid developed geometry; istarchus discovered that the earth revolves around the sun; and Erastothenes lculated the earth's circumference. A rand tower, the Pharos, one of the even Wonders of the World, was built an island just offshore and acted as oth a beacon to guide ships entering e booming harbour and, at a deeper vel, as an ostentatious symbol of the ty's greatness.

During the reign of its most famous gent, Cleopatra, Alexandria rivalled me in everything but military power – situation that Rome found intolerable nd was eventually forced to act upon. exandria's decline was sealed when the nquering Muslim armies swept into gypt in the 7th century and bypassed lexandria in favour of a new capital further south on the Nile.

During the reign of the Egyptian reformist Mohammed Ali, a new town was built on top of the old one. Alexandria once more became one of the Mediterranean's busiest ports and attracted a cosmopolitan mix of people, among them wealthy Turkish-Egyptian traders, Jews, Greeks, Italians and others from around the Mediterranean. But the wave of anticolonial, pro-Arab sentiment that swept Colonel Gamal Abdel Nasser to power in 1952 also spelled the end for Alexandria's cosmopolitan communities. Since that time the character of the city has changed completely. In the 1940s some 40% of the city's population was made up of foreigners, while today most of its residents are native Egyptians.

SIGHTS
ANCIENT ALEXANDRIA
ALEXANDRIA NATIONAL MUSEUM

The excellent **Alexandria National Museum** (Map p230; ☎ 483 5519; www.alexmuseum.org.eg; 110 Tariq al-Horreyya; adult/student E£35/20; ☯ 9am-4.30pm) sets new

LEE FOSTER

ort Qaitbey (p234) overlooks boats in Alexandria's Eastern Harbour

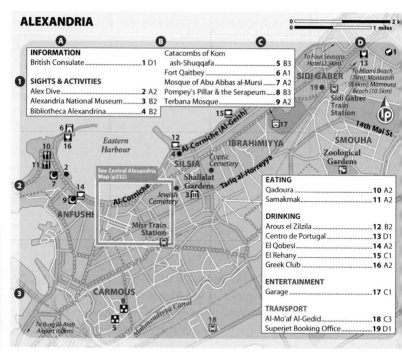

ALEXANDRIA

INFORMATION	
British Consulate **1** D1	
SIGHTS & ACTIVITIES	
Alex Dive...**2** A2	
Alexandria National Museum **3** B2	
Bibliotheca Alexandrina...................**4** B2	

Catacombs of Kom
ash-Shuqqafa.............................**5** B3
Fort Qaitbey **6** A1
Mosque of Abu Abbas al-Mursi **7** A2
Pompey's Pillar & the Serapeum......**8** B3
Terbana Mosque..............................**9** A2

EATING
Qadoura **10** A2
Samakmak.....................................**11** A2

DRINKING
Arous el Zilzila **12** B2
Centro de Portugal........................**13** D1
El Qobesi **14** A2
El Rehany **15** C1
Greek Club **16** A2

ENTERTAINMENT
Garage **17** C1

TRANSPORT
Al-Mo'af Al-Gedid.........................**18** C3
Superjet Booking Office.................**19** D1

benchmarks for summing up Alexandria's past. Housed in a beautifully restored Italianate villa, it stocks several thousand years of Alexandrian history, arranged chronologically over three cryogenically air-conditioned floors.

The ground floor is dedicated to Graeco-Roman times, where highlights include a sphinx and other sculptures found during underwater excavations at Aboukir. The basement covers the Pharaonic Period, with finds from all over Egypt, including an unusual New Kingdom pottery jar with the god Bes and the head of Queen Hatshepsut in painted limestone. The top floor displays artefacts from Islamic and modern periods, with coins, Ottoman weapons and jewels. Well-written panels on the walls provide useful insights into the life, art and beliefs of the Alexandrians through the centuries.

ROMAN AMPHITHEATRE (KOM AL-DIKKA) & GRAECO-ROMAN MUSEUM

While the 13 white-marble terraces of the only **Roman Amphitheatre (Map p23** ☎ 486 5106; Sharia Yousef, off Midan Gomhuriyy adult/student E£20/15; ☉ 9am-5pm) in Egy may not be impressive in scale, they remain a superbly preserved ode to the day of the centurion. Excavations continue to uncover more in the area; in early 201 the ruins of a Ptolemaic-era temple were uncovered along with statues of god and goddesses. In the same complex the captivating **Villa of the Birds (Ma p232)**, a wealthy urban dwelling dating to the time of Hadrian (117–138 AD Redecorated at least four times in antiquity before being destroyed by fire in the 3rd century AD, its multipanel floo mosaic of pigeons, peacocks, quail, pa ts and water hens remains astonishingly ell preserved.

Unfortunately, the wonderful nearby **Graeco-Roman Museum** (Map p232; ☎ 486 520; 5 Al-Mathaf ar-Romani), normally home to one of the most extensive collections of Graeco-Roman art in the world, was closed for restoration at the time of writing.

ANCIENT RHAKOTIS

The massive 30m column that looms over the debris of the glorious ancient settlement of Rhakotis, the original township from which Alexandria grew, is known as **Pompey's Pillar** (Map p230; ☎ 960 1315; Carmous; adult/student E£20/15; ⏰ 9am-4.30pm). The column was named by travellers who remembered the murder of the Roman general Pompey by Cleopatra's brother, but an inscription on the base (presumably once covered with rubble) announces that it was erected in AD 291 to support a statue of the emperor Diocletian. The column rises out of the disappointing ruins of the **Temple of Serapeum**, a magnifi-

cent structure that stood here in ancient times.

A short walk from Pompey's Pillar are the **Catacombs of Kom ash-Shuqqafa** (Map p230; ☎ 484 5800; Carmous; adult/student E£35/20; ⏰ 9am-5pm). This impressive feat of engineering was one of the last major works of construction dedicated to the religion of ancient Egypt. Demonstrating Alexandria's hallmark fusion of Pharaonic and Greek styles, the architects used a Graeco-Roman approach in their construction efforts. The typical Alexandrian-style decoration shows a weird synthesis of ancient Egyptian, Greek and Roman funerary iconography.

From the antechamber a couple of short passages lead to a large U-shaped chamber lined with **loculi** – the holes in which the bodies were placed. After the body (or bodies, as many of the loculi held more than one) had been placed inside, the small chamber was sealed with a plaster slab. For more information on the catacombs, see p220.

WAYNE WALTON

The remains of the Roman Amphitheatre, Alexandria (opposite)

ALEXANDRIA & THE MED COAST

ALEXANDRIA

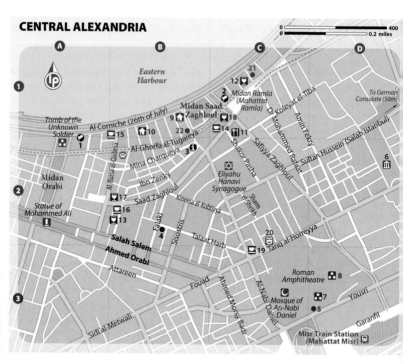

CENTRAL ALEXANDRIA

INFORMATION		
French Consulate	**1**	A2
Italian Consulate	**2**	C1
Main Tourist Office	**3**	B2
Passport Office	**4**	B2
Tourist Police	(see 3)	

SIGHTS & ACTIVITIES		
Amphitheatre Ticket Office	**5**	D3
Graeco-Roman Museum	**6**	D2
Roman Amphitheatre (Kom al-Dikka)	**7**	D3
Villa of the Birds	**8**	D3

SLEEPING		
Cecil Hotel	**9**	B1
Windsor Palace Hotel	**10**	B1

EATING		
China House	(see 9)	
Mohammed Ahmed	**11**	C1

DRINKING		
Athineos	**12**	C1
Cap d'Or	**13**	B2
Délices	**14**	C1
El Tugareya	**15**	B1

Sofianopoulos Coffee Store	**16**	B.
Spitfire	**17**	B1
Trianon	**18**	C
Vinous	**19**	C:

ENTERTAINMENT		
Alexandria Opera House	**20**	C:

TRANSPORT		
EgyptAir	**21**	C
West Delta Booking Office	**22**	B1

CENTRAL ALEXANDRIA & ANFUSHI

Right in the middle of the broad Corniche is the legendary **Cecil Hotel** (Map p232; see also p235), overlooking Midan Saad Zaghloul. Built in 1930, it's an Alexandrian institution and a memorial to the city's belle époque, when guests included Somerset Maugham, Noel Coward and Winston Churchill, and the British Secret Service operated out of a suite on the 1st floor. The hotel was eternalised i Lawrence Durrell's *Alexandria Quartet*.

In Anfushi, the charismatic old Turkis part of town, the beautiful little **Terban Mosque** (Map p230) stands at the junctio of Sharia Faransa and Wekalet al Limor Late-17th-century builders managed t incorporate bits of ancient Alexandri in the mosque's structure, reusing tw classical columns to support the mina ret. Continuing on Sharia Faransa, th street narrows before opening suddenl

ALEXANDRIA & THE MED COAST

ALEXANDRIA

locals enjoying a refreshment in an Alexandrian cafe

DBIMAGES/ALAMY

⬎ ALEXANDRIAN CAFES

Ever since the first half of the 20th century, Alexandria's culture has centred on its cafes, where the city's diverse population congregated to live out life's dramas over pastries and a cup of tea or coffee. Many of these old haunts remain and are definitely worth a visit for nostalgic purposes, historical associations and grand decor, but not always for the food or drink.

As good a place as any to start is by grabbing your first coffee of the day at **Athineos**, opposite Midan Ramla. This place lives and breathes nostalgia. Also facing Midan Ramla is **Trianon**, a favourite haunt of the Greek poet Cavafy, who worked in offices on the floor above. Stop here to admire the 1930s grandeur of its sensational ornate ceiling and grab one of its decent continental-style breakfasts.

After you polish off breakfast, walk around the corner to check out **Delices**. This enormous old tearoom drips with atmosphere and it, too, can whip up a decent breakfast. **Vinous** is an old-school patisserie with more grand art deco styling than you can poke a puff pastry at, but secretly we love it for the period scales labelled with the 'Just' brand.

Finally, if you need one last pick-me-up, head over to the **Sofianopoulos Coffee Store**, a gorgeous coffee retailer that would be in a museum anywhere else in the world.

Things you need to know Athineos (Map p232; ☎ 486 8131; 21 Midan Saad Zaghloul); Trianon (Map p232; 56 Midan Saad Zaghloul; ⏱ from 7am; ✸); Delices (Map p232; 46 Sharia Saad Zaghloul, Attareen; ⏱ from 7am; ✸); Vinous (Map p232; ☎ 486 0956; cnr Sharias al-Nabi Daniel & Tariq al-Horreyya; ⏱ 7am-1am); Sofianopoulos Coffee Store (Map p232; ☎ 484 5469; 21 Sharia Saad Zaghloul; ⏱ 8am-midnight)

on to a *midan* (square) dominated by the stately **Mosque of Abu Abbas al-Mursi** (Map p230), which was originally the tomb of a 13th-century Sufi saint from Murcia in Spain.

FORT QAITBEY

The Eastern Harbour is dominated by the fairy-tale-perfect **Fort Qaitbey** (Map p230; ☎ 486 5106; Eastern Harbour; adult/student E£25/15; ☼ 9am-4pm). Built on a narrow peninsula by the Mamluk sultan Qaitbey in AD 1480, it sits on the remains of the legendary Pharos lighthouse.

EASTERN SUBURBS
BIBLIOTHECA ALEXANDRINA

Alexandria's ancient library was one of the greatest of all classical institutions and while replacing it might seem a Herculean task, the new **Bibliotheca Alexandrina** (Map p230; ☎ 483 9999; www.bibalex.org; Corniche al-Bahr, Shatby; adult/student E£10/5; ☼ 11am-7pm Sun-Thu, 3-7pm Fri & Sat) manages it with aplomb. Opened in 2002, this impressive piece of modern architecture is a deliberate attempt to rekindle the brilliance of the original centre of learning and culture.

The granite exterior walls are carved with letters, pictograms, hieroglyphs and symbols from more than 120 different human scripts. The **Manuscript Museum** contains ancient texts, antiquarian books and maps, including a copy of the only surviving scroll from the ancient library. The **Antiquities Museum** holds some overspill from the Graeco-Roman Museum, including a fine Roman mosaic of a dog that was discovered when the foundations of the library were dug.

BEACHES

If you want to get in the water, there are plenty of public and private beaches

Fort Qaitbey (left)

along Alexandria's waterfront. But th shoreline between the Eastern Harbo and Montazah can be grubby and pack sardine-full in summer, and most loc head for beaches on the North Coast the high season. Women should note th at everywhere but the beaches owned Western hotels, modesty prevails and co ering up when swimming is recommend wear a baggy T-shirt and shorts over yo swimsuit. For more on beaches in t region, see p240.

TOURS & SERVICES

Ann and Medhat Hashem (☎ 012 0 4711; www.muzhela.com) This English exp and her Egyptian husband organise c and driver services starting at arou E£200 per day.

lex Dive (Map p230; ☎ 03-483 2045; www
exandra-dive.com; Corniche, Anfushi) Diving
urs to explore the submerged harbour
:es.

LEEPING

ie summer months of June to September
e the high season in Alexandria, when
alf of Cairo seems to decamp here to
cape the heat of the capital.

Windsor Palace Hotel (Map p232; ☎ 480
23; www.paradiseinnegypt.com; 17 Sharia ash-
ohada; r with sea view US$150) This bejewelled
lwardian gem is an institution unto itself,
wering over the Corniche and keeping
watchful eye on the Med since 1907.
ankfully the wonderful old elevators and
and lobby have been retained, and the
oms boast the sort of old-world, green-
d gold-flavoured pizzazz that wouldn't
e out of place on the *Orient Express*. The
icier rooms have splendid sea views.

Cecil Hotel (Map p232; ☎ 487 7173;
vw.sofitel.com; 16 Midan Saad Zaghloul; s/d
$205/245, with sea view US$265/306) The
storical Cecil Hotel, an Alexandria le-
end, now managed by the international
ofitel chain, has been refitted several
nes over the last couple of decades,
metimes for the better. To that extent
e Cecil very much reflects the city in
hich it stands, where the past has to
e imagined. The big consolation is the
veeping view over the Eastern Harbour,
id the excellent top-floor China House
staurant.

Four Seasons Hotel (off Map p230; ☎ 581
00; www.fourseasons.com/alexandria; 399
rniche, San Stefano; s/d from US$320/350, ste
$800-9000) The much-loved old Casino
n Stefano made way for this grand edi-
e, certainly the most luxurious place to
ay in town, if not the best value (the little
tttles of water in each room cost E£25!). A
ool overlooks the sea, and a tunnel under

the Corniche leads to a private beach and
partially constructed marina. Kids will be
happy, too, with their own pool, babysitting services and entertainment.

EATING

The old and once-grand restaurants, such
as Pastroudis and the Union, have long
closed, leaving central Alexandria something of a culinary wilderness. Many restaurants don't serve alcohol.

Mohammed Ahmed (Map p232; ☎ 483
3576; 17 Sharia Shakor Pasha; dishes E£2-5) Under
no circumstances should you miss this
classic, the undisputed king and still
champion of *fuul* and *ta'amiyya*, filled
day and night with locals downing small
plates of spectacularly good and cheap
Egyptian standards.

China House (Map p232; ☎ 487 7173; Cecil
Hotel, 16 Midan Saad Zaghloul; mains E£30-50;
☺ 11am-11.30pm) Atop the Cecil Hotel, this
highly recommended restaurant serves
scrumptious Asian food beneath a tent
with dangling lanterns and stunning
views over the harbour. The ambience is
breezy, the chicken dumplings and grilled
beef with garlic first-rate, and the banana
fritters unmissable. Beer and Egyptian
wine are served.

Qadoura (Map p230; ☎ 480 0405; 33
Sharia Bairam at-Tonsi; meals E£35-80; ☺ 9am-
3am) Pronounced 'Adora', this is one of
Alexandria's most authentic fish restaurants. Pick your fish from a huge ice-
packed selection, which usually includes
sea bass, red and grey mullet, bluefish,
sole, squid, crab and prawns, and often
a lot more. A selection of mezze is served
with all orders (don't hope for a menu).

Samakmak (Map p230; ☎ 481 1560; 42 Qasr
Ras at-Tin; dishes E£40-90; ☺ 1pm-2am) The fish
is as fresh as elsewhere, but customers
flock to this place for its specials, including crayfish, marvellous crab *tagen* (stew

cooked in a deep clay pot) and a great spaghetti with clams.

DRINKING

Sixty years ago Alexandria was so famous for its Greek tavernas and divey little watering holes that the 1958 movie *Ice Cold in Alex* was entirely based around a stranded WWII ambulance crew struggling through the desert, dreaming of making it back to Alexandria to sip a beer. Times have changed and Alex isn't much of a drinking town anymore; there are few places worth crossing the desert for. Alexandria's cafes and *ahwas* are a different story – see p233.

Centro de Portugal (Map p230; ☎ 542 7599; 42 Sharia Abd al-Kader, off Sharia Kafr Abdou; admission E£10; ❧ 3pm-1am) This hard-to-find expat haven is fully equipped for fun: a garden bar in a leafy patio, an inside bar with darts, foosball and pool, plus a tiny disco complete with mirrored ball. The food menu (dishes E£40 to E£55) sports Western standards, from noodles to pasta to fish, along with the house speciality – pepper steak.

Cap d'Or (Map p232; ☎ 487 5177; 4 Sharia Adbi Bek Ishak; ❧ 10am-3am) The Cap d'Or, just off Sharia Saad Zaghloul, is a top spot to relax, and one of the only surviving typical Alexandrian bars. With beer flowing generously, stained-glass windows, a long marble-topped bar, plenty of ancient memorabilia decorating the walls and crackling tapes of old French *chanson* (type of traditional folk music) or Egyptian hits, it feels very much like an Andalusian tapas bar. Crowds come to drink cold Stella beer, snack on great seafood, or just hang out at the bar and chew the proverbial fat with fellow drinkers.

Spitfire (Map p232; 7 Sharia L'Ancienne Bourse; ❧ 2pm-1.30am Mon-Sat) Just north of Sharia Saad Zaghloul, Spitfire feels almost like

a Bangkok bar – sans go-go girls. It has reputation as a sailors' hang-out and th walls are plastered with shipping-lir stickers, rock-and-roll memorabilia ar photos of drunk regulars. It's a great pla for an evening out in one of the worlc finest harbours, listening to America rock and roll from the 1970s.

Greek Club (Club Nautique Hellenique; M p230; ☎ 480 2690; Corniche, Anfushi; ❧ noo 11pm) The Greek Club is a great pla for a sunset drink, inside its large new restored rooms or, even better, on th wide terrace catching the afternoo breeze or watching the lights on th legendary bay. The menu has a selectic of fresh fish cooked any way you like (grilled with olive oil, oregano and lemc baked or Egyptian style), as well as Gree classics such as moussaka (E£14) ar souvlaki (E£32).

El Qobesi (Map p230; ☎ 486 7860; Corniche; juices E£3-6; ❧ 24hr) El Qobesi h crowned itself the 'king of mango' b take one sip of their juices and you w bow down a loyal peon.

ENTERTAINMENT
MUSIC, THEATRE & DANCE

Bibliotheca Alexandrina (Map p230; ☎ 4 9999; www.bibalex.org; Corniche al-Bahr, Shatl The Bibliotheca Alexandrina is the mo important cultural venue in town no hosting major music festivals, intern tional concerts and performances.

Alexandria Opera House (Map p23 ☎ 486 5106; www.cairoopera.org/sayed_darwi .aspx; 22 Tariq al-Horreyya) The former Say Darwish Theatre has been refurbishe and now houses the city's modestly pr portioned but splendid opera house.

Garage (Map p230; tfetouh@yatfund.o Jesuit Centre, Sharia Bur Said, Sidi Gaber) Th renovated garage of the Jesuit Centre ar maintained by the Young Arab Theat

TRAVELPIXS/ALAMY

Tea for two in an Egyptian *ahwa*

↘ IF YOU LIKE…

If you like Alexandria's traditional **cafes and ahwas** (p233) you will also like these places to watch the world go by:

- **Al-Sheikh Wafik** (off Map p230; Qasr Ras at-Tin; ⊙ 9am-4am) This unassuming and breezy corner cafe has a secret – the best dessert in town. You can get the usual ice cream in several flavours, but the real treats are Egyptian classics such as *couscousy* – a yummy mix of couscous, shredded coconut, nuts, raisins and sugar, topped with hot milk.

- **Arous el Zilzila** (Map p230; Shatby Beach; ⊙ 24hr) This fantastic *ahwa* across from the Bibliotheca Alexandrina is practically unique in Alexandria – you can sip tea and smoke *sheesha* to the sound of waves rolling in, smelling sea air instead of petrol fumes. Directly on the water, it has rustic open-air tables and palm trees with cheerful coloured lights, set around a small curving beach, from where you can hardly hear the traffic.

- **El Rehany** (Map p230; ☎ 590 5521; Corniche, Camp Chesar, cnr Sharia Ismail Fangary) This expansive and breezy Alexandrian classic is reputed to have the best *sheesha* in town, served with a flourish by attentive boys in smart two-toned waistcoats while waiters in black-and-white bring tea in silver urns. There's no sign in English, so look for the place with green awnings, next to the Premiere Wellness and Fitness Centre.

- **El Tugareya** (Map p232; Corniche; ⊙ 9am-late) Although it may not look like much to the uninitiated (it doesn't even sport a sign), this 90-year-old institution is one of the most important *ahwa*s in town. It's an informal centre of business and trade (the name roughly translates to 'commerce'), where deals are brokered in the time-honoured tradition – over a glass of tea. The cafe is separated into multiple rooms, covering a whole block. Look for the green window trim.

Fund, Garage is a breath of fresh air on the city's cultural scene, presenting new performances by local and international youth theatre groups.

GETTING THERE & AWAY

Internationally, Alexandria is served by multiple airlines: **EgyptAir** (Map p232; ☎ 487 3357, 486 5937; 19 Midan Saad Zaghloul; ☽ 8am-8pm), Emirates, Lufthansa, British Airways, British Midland, Air France, and more. Transport to Burg al-Arab airport is via the air-con airport bus (one way E£6 plus E£1 per bag, one hour), leaving from in front of the Cecil Hotel (Map p232) three hours before all departures; confirm the exact bus departure time at the Cecil.

All long-distance buses leave from Al-Mo'af al-Gedid (New Garage; Map p230). West Delta has a convenient city-centre **booking office** (Map p232; ☎ 480 9685; Midan Saad Zaghloul; ☽ 9am-9pm), while Superjet has a less convenient **booking office** (Map p230; ☎ 543 5222; ☽ 8am-10pm) opposite Sidi Gaber Train Station, next to the

large fountain. Superjet has hourly buse to Cairo (E£25, 2½ hours), also stopping a Cairo airport (E£35), from early morning West Delta has hourly departures to Mars Matruh (E£20 to E£35, four hours); man of these buses continue on to Sallu (nine hours) on the border with Liby Four services daily go to Siwa (E£27 t E£35, nine hours) between 8.30am an 10pm.

The main train terminal is **Mahatta Misr** (Misr Train Station; Map p232; ☎ 426 3207 about 1km south of Midan Ramla. Train from Cairo stop first at Mahattat Sidi Gabe (Sidi Gaber Train Station; Map p230), an most locals get off here, but if you're goin to the city centre around Midan Saa Zaghloul, make sure you stay on unt Mahattat Misr. There are more than 1 trains daily between Cairo and Alexandri Special and Spanish trains (1st/2nd clas E£50/35, 2½ hours) are the best trai types, as they make fewer stops. Sea are reserved, and your assigned car an seat should be printed on the ticket – ask conductor for help finding it if needed.

CHRISTINE OSB(

Slow but fun – an Alexandrian tram

GETTING AROUND

s a visitor to Alexandria, you'll rarely use he buses, and while the tram is fun it's ainfully slow. Taxis and microbuses are enerally the best options for getting round.

MEDITERRANEAN COAST

EL ALAMEIN

his small coastal outpost (not a 'city' as he brochures would have you believe) is amed for the decisive victory doled out ere by the Allies during WWII. More than 0,000 soldiers were killed or wounded in he series of desert battles fought nearby vhich helped cement Allied control of orth Africa. The thousands of graves in he Commonwealth, German and Italian var cemeteries in the vicinity of the town re a bleak reminder of the losses.

On the eastern side of town, along side road that leaves the main high-ay at the Greek war memorial, is the **commonwealth War cemetery** (admission ee; 7am-2.30pm, key available outside of these urs). It's a haunting place where more han 7000 tombstones sit on a slope com-anding a sweeping view of the desert. oldiers from the UK, Australia, New ealand, France, Greece, South Africa, East nd West Africa, Malaysia and India who ught for the Allied cause lie here.

A few kilometres west of the cemetery, e **War Museum** (410 0031/21; adult/stu-ent E£20/10; 9am-4pm) has a collection f memorabilia, uniforms and pictorial aterial of each country involved in the attle of El Alamein and the North African ampaigns, and maps and explanations of arious phases of the campaign in Arabic, nglish, German and Italian complement e exhibits.

About 7km west of El Alamein, what looks like a hermetically sealed sandstone fortress overlooking the sea is actually the **German War Memorial**. Inside this unmistakable reminder of war lie the tombs of approximately 4000 German servicemen and, in the centre, a memorial obelisk. About 4km further on, the **Italian Memorial** has a tall, slender tower as its focal point. This was roughly where the front line between the opposing armies ran.

The easiest option for getting to El Alamein is to organise your own car and driver (see Tours & Services, p234). Alternatively, catch any of the Marsa Matruh buses from the Al-Mo'af al-Gedid long-distance bus station in Alexandria (see p238).

SIDI ABDEL RAHMAN

The gorgeous beaches of Sidi Abdel Rahman are the raison d'être for this growing resort hamlet, and with charter flights starting between Europe and nearby El Alamein, (23km east), development is likely to continue.

SLEEPING & EATING

Charm Life (4190061/71; www.charmlifehotels .com; km140 on Alexandria–Marsa Matruh rd, Ghazala Bay; s/d incl breakfast E£1550, 1st child under 12yr stays free) Previously the Mövenpick and possibly to be renamed Ghazala Regency, this resort caters to European families on package tours. The granite-floored rooms are large, but the decor uninspired, the housekeeping variable and the buffet meals bland. The beach, however, is out of this world, with azure water as clear as a pool, and empty stretches of sand.

GETTING THERE & AWAY

The same buses that can drop you at El Alamein en route to or from Marsa Matruh (see p238) can also drop you here.

BLOOMBERG/GETTY IMA

The busy waters of Miami Beach, Alexandria (below)

↘ IF YOU LIKE...

If you like **Sidi Abdel Rahman beach** (p239), you will also like these other Mediterranean beaches:

- **Mamoura Beach, Alexandria** (off Map p230) About 1km east of Montazah is one of Alexandria's better city beaches, with a few small waves rolling in. Despite the entrance fee it's still jammed during high season. So head for the more expensive (E£41 per person or E£80 for a family) but much less crowded private beach with nice frond-type umbrellas.
- **Miami Beach, Alexandria** (off Map p230) This sheltered cove has a waterslide and jungle gym set up in the sea for kids to frolic on, but it can get almost comically crowded during peak season.
- **German Memorial Beach**, El Alamein The sea here is superb, in multiple shades of blue, and you'll feel miles away from Alexandria's teeming beaches. To get to the beach, you can ask the Bedouin keeper at the German War Memorial (p239) to open the gate leading to the sand tracks across the desert.
- **Shaat al-Hanna**, Sidi Abdel Rahman Blissfully uncrowded beach with splendid milky-blue water that's great for swimming, but even here conservative dress for women applies. There's no sign in English; heading west along the Alexandria–Marsa Matruh road the turn-off for the beach is marked by three rusting yellow signs 4.9km after the checkpoint and turn-off for the Marassi Hotel.
- **Agiba Beach** Agiba means 'miracle' in Arabic, and this small but spectacular cove, about 24km west of Marsa Matruh (p241) and accessible only via a path leading down from the clifftop, has dazzlingly clear turquoise water. It's absolutely packed in summer, but the long expanse of accessible beach, 1.5km east of the clifftop is equally beautiful and far less crowded.

MARSA MATRUH

In the summer months of June to September, half of the lower Nile Valley descends on this sleepy Mediterranean town for their holiday spell. The beaches are sardine-packed full of picnicking families, hotels raise their rates to astronomical heights, and buses to and from town overflow. The rest of the year, Marsa Matruh returns to its usual near-comatose state.

The **Lido**, the main beach in town, has decent sand and clear water, but is jam-packed in summer. Possibly the most beautiful piece of coastline in the area is **Cleopatra's Beach**, about 14km west of town around the bay's thin tentacle of land. The sea here is an exquisite hue, and the rock formations are worth a look. You can wade to **Cleopatra's Bath**, a natural pool where legend has imagined the great queen and Mark Antony enjoying a dip, but there's no swimming these days due to the waves and rocks just offshore. For more beaches in the region, see p240.

SLEEPING & EATING

Almaza Bay (☎ 436 0000; www.jaz.travel; north coast 37km east of Matruh; s/d half board low season from €120/160) On a remote stretch of seafront 37km east of town, this resort includes three hotels: Almaza Bay, the Moroccan-themed Oriental, and Crystal, fitted out like a sophisticated New York cocktail bar. Crystal also offers larger family-sized rooms, which have an extra alcove with a crib and pullout couch. The three hotels share a beachfront, and guests can use facilities at any of the three, including sampling the tasty buffets.

Abdu Kofta (☎ 012 314 4989; Sharia al-Tahrir; dishes E£5-60; 🍴) Locals will swear black and blue that this is the best restaurant in town. In the clean and cool 1st-floor room, it serves *kofta* or grilled meat by the weight served with good mezze and salads.

GETTING THERE & AWAY

Twice-weekly flights between Cairo and Marsa Matruh are available with **EgyptAir**

The coast around Marsa Matruh (above)

JOHN ELK III

(☎ 493 6573; Sharia al-Matar) from June to September, leaving Cairo at 3.15pm and returning at 5pm.

West Delta Bus Co (☎ 490 5079) has hourly services to Alexandria from 7am to 2am (E£17 to E£30, four hours). In winter, there are five daily buses to Cairo, again between 7.30am and 2am. Six buses daily head to Siwa (E£13, four hours), between 7am and 2am.

From 15 June to 15 September, there are three **sleeper trains** (www.sleepingtrains.com) weekly (single/double US$60/43, seven

hours) between Cairo and Marsa Matruh. Trains depart Cairo Monday, Wednesday and Saturday, and leave Matruh on the return journey Sunday, Tuesday and Thursday.

GETTING AROUND

Private taxis or pick-ups can be hired for the day, but you must bargain aggressively, especially in summer. Expect to pay E£80 to E£150, depending on the distance. A taxi to the airport will cost around E£7 to E£10.

SUEZ CANAL, SINAI & THE RED SEA COAST

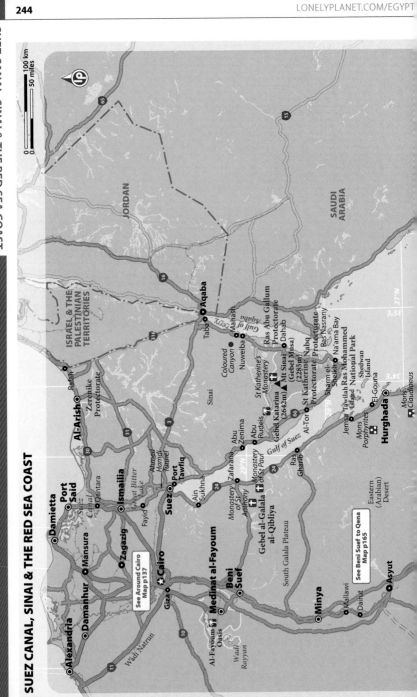

See Around Cairo Map p137

See Beni Suef to Qena Map p165

THINGS YOU NEED TO KNOW

⚓ VITAL STATISTICS

- **Telephone codes** Port Said (☎ 066), Ismailia (☎ 064), southern Sinai (☎ 069), Red Sea coast (☎ 065)
- **Best time to go** All-year-round destination; summers are hot and winters nights are cold

⚓ PLACES IN A NUTSHELL

- **Port Said** (p254) For a glimpse of the Suez Canal.
- **Sharm el-Sheikh** (p258) For choice resorts and good nightlife.
- **Dahab** (p264) For a relaxed atmosphere and good diving.
- **Hurghada** (p272) For a family holiday package.
- **Marsa Alam** (p277) For expert diving.

⚓ ADVANCE PLANNING

- **One month before** Book accommodation and diving courses, particularly if travelling during European holiday periods.

⚓ RESOURCES

- **Hurghada tourist office** (Map p274; ☎ 344 4420; resort strip; ⏱ 9am-8pm Sat-Thu, 2-10pm Fri)
- **Go Red Sea** (www.goredsea.com) Index of dive centres, live-aboards and other information.
- **Red Sea Association for Diving & Watersports** (RSADW; ☎ 344 4802; www.h2o-mag.com; Hurghada) H2O magazine features articles and updates on diving in the region.

- **Virtual Diving Center** (www.redseavdc.com) Detailed descriptions of more than 73 dive sites.
- **St Katherine Protectorate Office** (☎ 347 0032) Located at the tourist village near the entrance to Al-Milga.

⚓ EMERGENCY NUMBERS

- **Ambulance** (☎ 123)
- **Dahab tourist police** (☎ 364 0188)
- **Sharm el-Sheikh tourist police** (☎ 360 0554, 366 0675)

⚓ GETTING AROUND

- **Bus and service taxi** The easiest ways to travel between cities.
- **Train** The slowest way of travelling between the canal cities.
- **Taxi** Good for a day trip from the beach resorts to St Katherine.
- **Ferry** The quickest way to travel between Hurghada and Sharm el-Sheikh.
- **Air** From Cairo to Hurghada and Sharm el-Sheikh.

⚓ BE FOREWARNED

- **Suez Canal** Ships only transit the canal during daylight hours, so visit early in the day to maximise your chances of seeing them.
- **Ferry** Does not always operate between Hurghada and Sharm el-Sheikh, and the crossing can be rough.

ITINERARIES

SINAI BEACHES Three Days

The coast of Sinai has some excellent beaches and good facilitie
and boasts some of the most spectacular coral reefs and marine li
in the world. If you like comfortable hotels, base yourself in Shar
el-Sheikh. If you like simpler accommodation and relaxed bars o
the beach, choose Dahab. Or do the rounds with this itinerary an
experience both scenes.

Spend the first day snorkelling in **(1) Sharm el-Sheikh** (p258), ta
ing in sights like the impressive Near and Middle Gardens, or Ras U
Sid Reef. The second day rent a car or take a tour through your hot
or with one of the many local diving centres to **(2) Ras Mohamme
National Park** (p257), where you'll find plenty of different options f
beaches and dive sites. On the third day drive yourself or take a ta
to **(3) Dahab** (p264) for more fabulous snorkelling and diving – che
out the Lighthouse Reef or Ras Abu Gallum.

THE GREAT OUTDOORS Five Days

This tour takes in trekking in the gorgeous mountainous surroun
ings of St Katherine Protectorate before unwinding on the beach f
a couple of days.

Start off early in the morning in St Katherine's Protectorate, pre
erably before dawn, and climb **(1) Mt Sinai** (p269). Here you ca
survey the place where Moses is believed to have received the Te
Commandments. Come down for breakfast and take a service taxi
visit the beautiful **(2) St Katherine's Monastery** (p268) with its wo
derful icon collection. In the afternoon go to Al-Milga village near
to organise a two-day trek in the **(3) mountains** with Sheikh Mu
(p246), who can arrange a Bedouin guide to show you some of t
cultural and natural sights around the monastery. After your trek, st
at the simple but splendid ecolodge (p269). Lazing on the beach a
snorkelling the reefs of **(4) Dahab** (p264) will be a welcome change f
your next stop – take a service taxi or bus from St Katherine. Shou
you manage to get tired of the beach, you can always organise
camel safari from here.

SAINTS & SEA One Week

Buses connect most of the towns in this itinerary, but you'll need
join a tour or walk for quite a while to get out to the monasteries. T
easiest option is to take your own car.

Rent a car in Cairo and travel to the canal city of **(1) Port Said** (p25
where the best way of seeing the Suez Canal is to take the ferry fro
Port Said to Port Fuad. Continue south for a late lunch and a str

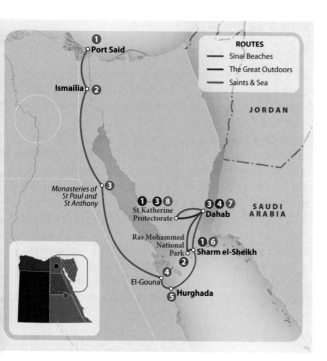

the pleasant colonial town of (2) **Ismailia** (p255), where you can
ay the night.

Pack a picnic for lunch, and head further south early in the morn-
g to the (3) **Monasteries of St Paul and St Anthony** (p271). In the
ternoon drive to (4) **El-Gouna** (p272), where you can swim, enjoy the
each and at night eat in one of the lively town's many restaurants.

On the third day it's a short journey to nearby (5) **Hurghada** (p272).
hile here, book an off-shore diving trip or visit the aquarium. From
urghada, take the ferry to (6) **Sharm el-Sheikh** (p258) and spend the
ext day swimming and snorkelling. There's more beach and sea to
joy for a few hours in laid-back (7) **Dahab** (p264) the next day.

In the late afternoon make for the guest house at St Katherine's
onastery in (8) **St Katherine Protectorate** (p268). While in the pro-
ctorate, climb Mt Sinai early in the morning to enjoy the sunrise,
d visit the monastery. Spend another night at the guest house, and
turn to Cairo the next day.

DISCOVER THE SUEZ CANAL, SINAI & THE RED SEA COAST

One of the world's greatest engineering marvels, the Suez Canal separates mainland Egypt from the Sinai Peninsula, Africa from Asia, and allows transit for more than 20,000 ships a year between the Mediterranean and the Red Sea.

Sinai, a region of stark beauty, has been a place of refuge and curiosity for thousands of years. Wedged between Africa and Asia, it is an intercontinental crossroads *par excellence* – prophets, nomads, exiles and conquerors have all left their footprints here. Sinai is a land of contrasts, from the gorgeous beaches to the barren rows of mountains in the interior, and from the glitzy tourist resorts to traditional Bedouin culture.

The Red Sea is where Moses is said to have parted the waters and set free the Hebrew slaves. These days, famed for its brilliant turquoise waters and splendid coral reefs, the 800km Red Sea coastline is Egypt's most rapidly developing region with more hotels and resorts than anywhere else in the country.

SUEZ CANAL

PORT SAID

If you've ever seen a picture of Port Said it was probably of the striking green domes of the **Suez Canal House**, which was built in time for the inauguration of the canal in 1869. The heart of Port Said is located along the edge of the canal, on and around Sharia Palestine. Here, the waterfront is lined with late-19th-century five-storey buildings complete with wooden balconies, louvered doors and high verandahs in grand belle époque style.

The most enjoyable way to tour Port Said, especially around sunset, is by *hantour* (horse-drawn carriage). There are also plenty of blue-and-white taxis around.

Across the canal from Port Said is the genteel suburb of **Port Fuad**, founded in 1925. The streets near its quay invite a stroll, with their sprawling residences, lush gardens and sloping tiled roofs recall-ing the one-time European presence. Fre ferries from Port Said to Port Fuad off impressive views of the canal and leav about every 10 minutes throughout th day from the terminal at the southwest end of Sharia Palestine.

SLEEPING & EATING

Helnan Port Said (☎ 332 0890; www.heln .com; Sharia Atef as-Sadat; s/d from US$200/40 ⊠ 🖥 🖭) Overlooking the Mediterranea at the north end of town, the five-st Helnan is Port Said's most sophisticate option. Offering low-key luxury rather tha opulent pleasure, the Helnan has we appointed rooms that boast views over th end of the canal and the Mediterranea The hotel is also home to a number of to notch restaurants serving up some of th best eats in town.

GETTING THERE & AWAY

Superjet (☎ 372 1779) has bi-hour buses to Cairo (E£25, three hours) an bus to Alexandria (E£30, four hours) at 30pm daily. The five daily trains going Cairo via Ismailia (2nd-class service £13 to E£18) are slow (five hours) and n at 5.30am, 9.45am, 1pm, 5.30pm and 30pm. There are no 1st-class services. elays on these routes are common. oing by bus is more efficient and more omfortable than taking the non-air-con ains.

MAILIA

mailia (Map pp244–5) was founded and named after Pasha Ismail, who as khedive of Egypt in the 1860s while e Suez Canal was being built. Today, mailia's historic town centre, with its egant colonial streets, expansive lawns d late 19th-century villas, is one of the most peaceful and picturesque neighbourhoods in the country.

More than 4000 objects from Pharaonic and Graeco-Roman times are housed at the small but interesting **Ismailia Museum** (☎ 391 2749; Mohammed Ali Quay; adult/child E£6/3; ☆ 8am-4pm, closed for Fri noon prayers), located on the eastern edge of town. The collection includes statues, scarabs, stelae and records of the first canal, built between the Bitter Lakes and Bubastis by the Persian ruler Darius. There are plenty of taxis around town.

SLEEPING & EATING
Mercure Forsan Island (☎ 391 6316; www .mercure.com; Gezirat Forsan; s/d from US$185/115; ✗ ☐ ☎) About 1.6km southeast of the old centre of town, the four-star Mercure

THE SUEZ CANAL

The Suez Canal represents the culmination of centuries of effort to enhance trade and expand the empires of Egypt by connecting the Red Sea with the Mediterranean Sea. Following the French invasion in 1798, the importance of some sort of sea route south to Asia was recognised. For the first time, digging a canal directly from the Mediterranean Sea to the Red Sea, across the comparatively narrow Isthmus of Suez, was considered. The idea was abandoned, however, when Napoleon's engineers mistakenly calculated that there was a 10m difference between the two sea levels. British reports detected that mistake several years later but it was Ferdinand de Lesseps, the French consul to Egypt, who pursued the Suez Canal idea through to its conclusion. In 1854, de Lesseps presented his proposal to the Egyptian khedive Said Pasha, who authorised him to excavate the canal; work began in 1859.

A decade later the canal was completed amid much fanfare and celebration. Ownership of the canal remained in French and British hands for the next 86 years until, in the wake of Egyptian independence, President Nasser nationalised the Suez in 1956. Today, the Suez Canal remains one of the world's most heavily used shipping lanes, and toll revenues represent one of the largest contributors to the Egyptian state coffers.

Organised trips don't exist and the police do not allow private boats to cruise the canal, for security reasons. Of course, the easiest way to get a fleeting taste of life on the canal is to simply take the free ferry over to Port Fuad from in front of the tourist office on Sharia Palestine in Port Said (p254).

is easily the most attractive hotel in town. Occupying a private island and overlooking a tranquil beach, the Mercure makes for a relaxing getaway and it's surprisingly cheaper than you would imagine – check the web for specials.

George's (☎ 391 8327; 11 Sharia Thawra; dishes E£30-65; ✗) An Ismailia classic, George's has been around since 1950 and serves up seafood dishes amid a cosy British-pub-style ambience.

GETTING THERE & AWAY

East Delta Travel Co (☎ 332 1513) has buses to Cairo (E£20, three hours) every half-hour between 6am and 8pm. Buses to Alexandria (E£30, five hours) leave at 7am, 10.30am and 2.30pm. Buses to Sharm el-Sheikh (E£45 to E£50, six hours) leave throughout the morning, from 6.30am.

SINAI

The majority of international tourists head to the glitzy European-style coastal resorts of Sharm el-Sheikh, of which there are literally hundreds vying for beach spac Most are amenable enough places for sea and-sand holidays, though independer travellers prefer the terminally laid-bac town of Dahab.

Sinai's rugged interior is populated b barren mountains, wind-sculpted can yons and wadis that burst into life wit even the shortest rains. The rocks an desert landscapes turn shades of pin ochre and velvet black as the sun rise and falls, and what little vegetation ther is appears to grow magically out of th rock. Bedouin still wander through th wilderness, and camels are the best wa to travel, with much of the terrain to rocky even for a 4WD.

Whatever captures your fancy, a visi to Sinai will undoubtedly be one of th most memorable parts of your Egyptia travels.

HISTORY

For many people, Sinai is first and foremo the 'great and terrible wilderness' of th Bible, across which the Israelites journeye

Ras Um Sid Reef, Sharm el-Sheikh (p260)

MARK D

in search of the Promised Land, having been delivered from the Egyptian army by the celebrated parting of the Red Sea that allowed the 'Children of Israel' to safely gain access to the dry land of Sinai. It was here that God is said to have first spoken to Moses from a burning bush and it was at the summit of Mt Sinai that God delivered his Ten Commandments to Moses.

Early in the Christian era, Sinai was a place for Christian Egyptians to escape Roman persecution. Monasticism is thought to have begun here as early as the 3rd century AD, with most hermits settling in the caves of Wadi Feiran, on the assumption that Gebel Serbal, located nearby, was in fact the 'Mountain of God'. By the time the Emperor Justinian founded a monastery at the foot of Mt Sinai (Gebel Musa) in the 6th century, it had been decided that this was the mountain on which God had spoken.

GETTING THERE & AWAY

Sinai's international air hub is at Sharm el-Sheikh, which receives regular charters from Europe in addition to local flights. For overland travel, the peninsula is linked to the mainland by the Ahmed Hamdi Tunnel, and by the Mubarak Peace Suspension Bridge, both of which connect to main arteries to Cairo. There are frequent buses connecting Cairo and other destinations with all major towns on the Sinai Peninsula.

RAS MOHAMMED NATIONAL PARK

About 20km west of Sharm el-Sheikh on the road from Al-Tor lies the headland of **Ras Mohammed National Park** (admission per person €5, plus per vehicle €5; ☉ 8am-5pm), Egypt's first national park, named by local fishermen for a cliff that resembles a man's profile. The waters surrounding the peninsula are considered the jewel in the crown of the Red Sea. Most, if not all, of the Red Sea's 1000 species of fish can be seen in the park's waters, including sought-after pelagics, such as hammerheads, manta rays and whale sharks.

You'll need your passport to enter the park. The entrance to the park is about 20km from the reefs. A **visitors centre** (☉ 10am-sunset Sat-Thu) with a restaurant is clearly marked to the left of the main access road in an area known as Marsa Ghoslane.

The park is laid out with colour-coded trails and clearly marked pictograms of what each site offers.

ACTIVITIES

If you're planning to dive in Ras Mohammed, you will need to arrive via a boat tour or a live-aboard, both of which typically depart from Sharm el-Sheikh (p258). If you arrive at the national park by private car, it's possible to hike to a number of wilderness beaches and go snorkelling on a variety of offshore reefs – you will need your own equipment.

SECURITY IN SINAI

In recent years, the region of Sinai has been thrust into the international spotlight following a string of high-profile bombings. It is impossible to offer anything other than blind speculation bordering on irrational fear regarding the possibility of a future terrorist attack in Sinai. It's worth checking your embassy's travel advisory to get an update on the situation before making any plans. The overwhelming majority of travellers to Sinai enjoy their visits without incident.

At the park's laboratory, a pink trail leads to **Khashaba Beach** and a camping area. Yellow arrows lead to the sandy beaches and calm waters of **Marsa Bareika**, excellent for snorkelling and safe for children. Blue arrows take you to **Main Beach**, which gets crowded with day visitors, but remains one of the best places to see vertical coral walls. Brown arrows lead to **Aqaba Beaches**, which border the **Eel Garden**, named after a colony of garden eels 20m down. Just beyond here, orange arrows lead to **Shark Observatory**, a cliff-top area where you can sometimes see sharks as they feed from Ras Mohammed's rich offerings. The red arrows lead to **Yolanda Bay**, another beach with good snorkelling, and green arrows lead to the **Mangrove Channel** and **Hidden Bay** and to **Old Quay**, a spec tacular vertical reef teeming with fish and accessible to snorkellers.

SLEEPING

Camping is permitted in designated areas with permits (€5 per person) availabl from the entrance gate. You'll need t bring all supplies with you; the neares shops are in Sharm el-Sheikh.

GETTING THERE & AWAY

If you don't have a car, you can hire a tax from Sharm el-Sheikh to bring you her but expect to pay at least E£150 for th day. If you don't mind company, the easi est option is to join one of the many da tours by jeep or bus from Sharm el-Sheik and Na'ama Bay, most of which will dro you at the beaches and snorkelling site Expect to pay from E£150.

SHARM EL-SHEIKH & NA'AMA BAY

Known simply as Sharm by package trav ellers the world over, Sinai's largest an most famous beach town has undergon a miraculous transformation in recen years. What was once a small village tha attracted mainly hard-core divers is nov commonly described as Egypt's answe to Las Vegas, drawing in wave upon wav of primarily British and European holiday makers in search of sun and sea.

DANGERS & ANNOYANCES

In 2005, three terrorist bombs explode in Sharm el-Sheikh, killing 88 people an injuring over 200. The worst damage wa in the Sharm Old Market area and nea Ghazala Gardens hotel in Na'ama Bay. I the wake of the bombings, the Egyptia government increased security at a Sharm el-Sheikh hotels and began build ing a fence around the town. The govern

Lion fish, Ras Mohammed National Park (p257)

MARK WEBSTER

A green heron, Sinai

HFS001/ALAMY

⬂ IF YOU LIKE...

If you like **Ras Mohammed National Park** (p257) and **St Katherine Protectorate** (p268), you will also like the other parks and protectorates in the region:

- **Nabq Protectorate** (admission €5; ⌚ 8am-5pm) Nabq straddles 600 sq km of land and sea between the Straits of Tiran and Dahab in Sinai. It has a wonderful mangrove forest, which provides an important habitat for birds and fish. Gazelles, rock hyraxes and Nubian ibexes can also be seen here. It is home to the Bedouin from the Mizena tribe.

- **Ras Abu Gallum Protectorate** (Map pp244-5) This protectorate covers 400 sq km of coastline between Dahab and Nuweiba. It's a fascinating area mixing coastal mountains, narrow valleys, sand dunes and fine-gravel beaches with several excellent diving and snorkelling sites. The Mizena Bedouin live and fish here as they have done for centuries. There is a designated camping area and several walking trails, and you can hire Bedouin guides and camels through the ranger house at the edge of Wadi Rasasah.

- **Wadi Gimal** (Map pp244-5) Extending inland for about 85km south of Marsa Alam, Wadi Gimal is home to a rich variety of bird life, gazelles and stands of mangrove. In ancient times, the surrounding area was the source of emerald, gold and other minerals used in Pharaonic and Roman civilisations. Together with tiny Wadi Gimal Island, Wadi Gimal has been given protected status, and was proposed as a Unesco World Heritage Site.

- **Zerenike Protectorate** (Map pp244-5; ☎ 010 544 2641; per person/car US$5/5; ⌚ park sunrise-sunset, visitors centre 9am-5pm Sat-Thu) Stretched along the Mediterranean coast this 220-sq-km protectorate is a haven for migrating birds, with more than 250 avian species here, including flamingos for most of the year. If you don't have your own transport, it's best to take a taxi from Al-Arish, which can be reached via bus or service taxi from Cairo or Ismailia.

ment has also worked tirelessly to revive tourism to the city. Tourist numbers have since returned to normal and although scars of the attack remain, Sharm is generally considered to be a safe destination. It is overall a relaxed and hassle-free spot, even if you're travelling with young children.

ACTIVITIES
DIVING & SNORKELLING

Sharm's truly exquisite diving has unfortunately been overshadowed by unfettered tourist development. However, offshore dive sites in both Sharm and the adjacent Ras Mohammed National Park are easily accessible by live-aboards, or even from boat trips departing from Dahab.

Snorkelling in the waters around Sharm is excellent. While there are some easily accessed reefs in central Na'ama Bay, it's better to make your way to the more impressive **Near Garden** and **Middle Garden** or the even more beautiful **Far Garden**. The Near Garden is around the point at the northern end of the bay just below the Sofitel hotel, and the Middl and Far Gardens are below the Hyat Regency hotel. All can be reached on foo or you can take a boat organised by on of the diving centres.

Another prime spot for snorkelling i **Ras Um Sid Reef**, near the lighthouse a Sharm el-Sheikh, which is known for it fan corals and plethora of fish, althoug the small beach is parcelled up betwee several resorts and can get quite crowde The popular **Temple** and **Fiasco Reefs** ar within easy swimming distance, and whil they're primarily dive destinations, sno kellers can still get a taste of their flor and fauna.

WATER SPORTS

Most major hotels offer a range of othe water sports, including sailing lesson: windsurfing, parasailing, pedalos, banan boats and glass-bottom boats. Most hote also have beach access – either their ow stretch of waterfront, or by agreemen with another resort. Check when bookin as the beaches of some hotels are fair

The blue waters of Sharm el-Sheikh (p258)

MARK DA

stant (up to 10km) from the hotel itself nd can only be accessed via shuttle.

LEEPING

harm el-Sheikh and the surrounding area as one of the greatest concentrations of

hotels in Egypt. Budget accommodation places are few and far between, with the all-inclusive resort being the standard rather than the exception.

Sanafir Hotel (☎ 360 0197; www.sanafirhotel .com; King of Bahrain St; r from US$80; 🎇 🖳 🐂)

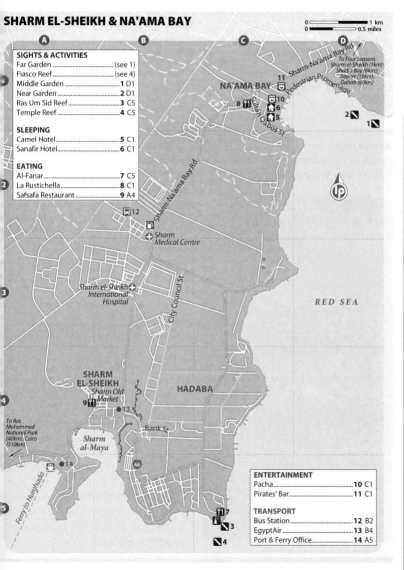

SHARM EL-SHEIKH & NA'AMA BAY

SIGHTS & ACTIVITIES	
Far Garden	(see 1)
Fiasco Reef	(see 4)
Middle Garden	**1** D1
Near Garden	**2** D1
Ras Um Sid Reef	**3** C5
Temple Reef	**4** C5

SLEEPING	
Camel Hotel	**5** C1
Sanafir Hotel	**6** C1

EATING	
Al-Fanar	**7** C5
La Rustichella	**8** C1
Safsafa Restaurant	**9** A4

ENTERTAINMENT	
Pacha	**10** C1
Pirates' Bar	**11** C1

TRANSPORT	
Bus Station	**12** B2
EgyptAir	**13** B4
Port & Ferry Office	**14** A5

RED SEA

Located smack-dab in the nerve centre of Na'ama Bay, the Sanafir was one of the first hotels to be built here. The Sanafir has also expanded its offerings of restaurants, lounges and bars, and with its nearly unbeatable location, Na'ama Bay is literally at your doorstep.

Camel Hotel (☎ 360 0700; www.cameldive.com; King of Bahrain St; s/d from €60/100; 🔀 🖳 🍽) This attractive, small and well-appointed four-star hotel is attached to a dive centre of the same name in the heart of Na'ama Bay. Needless to say, diving is the main attraction here – even the swimming pool is tiered, allowing for open-water skills to be practised in a confined environment. If you're looking to take a course or book dives, you can save if you arrange a package in advance.

Thistlegorm dive site (opposite)

MARK WEBSTER

Four Seasons Sharm el-Sheikh (☎ 36 3555; www.fourseasons.com/sharmelsheikh; Fo Seasons Blvd; r from US$325; 🔀 🔀 🖳 🍽 Unmatched in elegance and sophistic tion, the Four Seasons is an Arabesqu style pleasure palace built aroun palm-ringed courtyards and overlookir the Straits of Tiran.

EATING

As the unashamed tourist capital Sinai, Sharm has hundreds of restauran spanning the culinary globe. Thoug most tourists on all-inclusive package never seem to stray from their resort, it certainly worth venturing outside th hotel walls. Restaurants in Sharm are b no means cheap, but the quality is hig particularly the local seafood.

Safsafa Restaurant (dishes E£20-50; 🔀 A small establishment offering some the freshest and cheapest fish in Shar el-Sheikh (whole fish is priced from E£4 to E£50 per kilogram) – don't skip on th homemade tahini and *baba ghanou* (purée of grilled aubergines with tahir and olive oil).

La Rustichella (pizzas E£25-40, mains E£4 75; 🔀) This Sharm institution serves variety of delectable meals, includin Italian-style seafood dishes, brick-ove roasted pizzas, and a good variety chicken and beef dishes – stop by in th afternoon and cool off with an ice coffe and a creamy gelato.

Al-Fanar (Ras Um Sid; dishes E£40-15 🕑 10am-10.30pm; 🔀) This upmarket re taurant boasts an excellent seafro location at the base of the lighthous cosy alcoves overlooking the wate Bedouin-influenced decor, indoor an outdoor dining, and a large Italian men featuring thin-crust pizza and homemac pasta dishes.

MARK DAFFEY

Blue Hole dive site (below), north of Dahab

≥ IF YOU LIKE...

If you like **diving** in **Sharm el-Sheikh** (p258), you will also like the diving sites slightly further afield. If you don't have your own car and gear, you can access all these sites via a tour with any of the multitude of dive centres in the resort towns:

- Explore the remains of the **Thistlegorm**, one of the top wreck dives in the world. After being sunk by German bombers in October 1941, this WWII British cargo ship lay undisturbed until discovered in 1956 by legendary French diver Jacques Cousteau. The wreck can be accessed by boat or live-aboard, 30km from Sharm el-Sheikh.
- Push your limits by sinking into the deep blue abyss of the **Blue Hole**, which some say is as deep as 130m, Egypt's most infamous dive site, located 6km north of Dahab (p264). Despite their intimidating reputation as danger zones for careless divers, the tops of the reefs are teeming with life, making them fine snorkelling destinations when the sea is calm.
- Visit one of Sinai's most popular dives, the **Canyon**, near Dahab (p264). It's a long, narrow trench perpendicular to the reef shelf, with a multitude of corals and fish.
- Swim with the dolphins in the lagoon or admire the coral ergs at **Sha'ab Samadai** (Dolphin Reef), 8km southeast of Marsa Alam (p277).
- About 125km north of Marsa Alam, dive the steep reef walls of **Elphinstone**, which are covered with soft corals and washed by strong currents ideal for sharks. Legend has it that a large arch in the reef contains the sarcophagus of an unknown pharaoh.

ENTERTAINMENT

With a young resident population and a large number of relatively wealthy tourists, Sharm el-Sheikh has one of Egypt's liveliest bar and club scenes.

Pacha (Sanafir Hotel, King of Bahrain St) The hub of Sharm's nightlife, the Pacha goes wild pretty much every night of the week. Owner Adli Mestakawi also holds Echo Temple Concerts in the desert outside Sharm on Fridays during the high season, bringing big-name singers to play to audiences of thousands under the stars – watch for Pacha's advertising around town to see what's playing.

Pirates' Bar (Hilton Fayrouz Village) A cosy, pub-style bar where divers congregate for an early evening drink or bar meal. Happy hour is from 5.30pm to 7.30pm.

GETTING THERE & AWAY
AIR

Daily flights to Cairo, Luxor and Alexandria are available with **EgyptAir** (☎ 366 1056; www.egyptair.com; Sharm al-Maya; ⏰ 9am-9pm), though prices tend to fluctuate wildly depending on the season and availability. If you book a package holiday in either the UK or Europe, it's likely that your travel agent will arrange a charter flight directly to Sharm for you.

BOAT

Tickets for the high-speed ferry to Hurghada from Sharm el-Sheikh can be bought from various travel agencies in town, or at the port office on days that the ferry runs.

BUS

The bus station is along the Sharm–Na'ama Bay road behind the Mobil petrol station. **Superjet** (☎ 366 1622, in Cairo 02-290 9017) runs buses to Cairo (E£65 to E£75,

five to six hours) at noon, 1pm, 3pm, 5pr and 11pm.

East Delta Travel Co (☎ 366 0660) als has buses to Cairo (E£65 to E£75) at 7am 10am, 11am, noon, 1pm, 2.30pm, 4.30pr and 5.30pm. There are daily buses to Sue (E£35 to E£40, five to six hours) at 7am 9am and 10am; to Dahab (E£15 to E£2(one to two hours) and Nuweiba (E£25 t E£30, three to four hours) at 9am, 2.30pr and 5pm; and to Taba (E£30 to E£35, fou to five hours) at 9am.

GETTING AROUND
TO/FROM THE AIRPORT

Sharm el-Sheikh International Airpor is about 10km north of Na'ama Bay a Ras Nasrany; taxis generally charge fror E£20 to E£25 from the airport to Sharr or Na'ama Bay.

DAHAB

Long hailed as the 'Ko Samui of the Middl East', Dahab has a long history of lurin travellers – and trapping them for day or weeks on end – with its cheap ocean side camps, golden beaches and rug ged mountain backdrop. In recent year Dahab has expanded beyond its humbl origins, and now boasts a smooth fusio of hippie mellowness and resort chic.

Meaning 'gold' in Arabic, a referenc to the area's sandy coastline, Dahab als boasts some of Egypt's most spectacula diving and trekking. A short walk, jee ride or even camel trek will bring you t some of the Red Sea's most memorab dive sites, and a boat can bring you withi easy striking distance of the world-clas reefs in nearby Ras Mohammed Nation Park. Predominantly a Bedouin enclav at its heart, Dahab is also the preferre base for organising guided excursion into the interior deserts, as well as to th lofty heights of nearby Mt Sinai.

IGHTS & ACTIVITIES

ther than just lounging around, snorelling and diving are the most popular ctivities in Dahab. Worthwhile are the eefs off the southern end of Mashraba, st before the lagoon; **Lighthouse Reef**, sheltered snorkelling site at the north-rn tip of Assalah; and the popular **Eel arden**, just north of Assalah, where a plony of eels lives on the sandy seabed. lany dive centres also organise **snorkelng** and **dive safaris** to the nearby Ras bu Gallum and Nabq protectorates, as ell as overnights to Ras Mohammed ational Park (p257).

You can hire snorkelling gear from any of le numerous dive centres for about E£25 p E£40 per day. Keep in mind that some f the reefs have unexpected currents – rownings have occurred in Dahab so eep your wits about you.

Dahab is one of the best places in Sinai p arrange **camel safaris** into the dramatic ountains lining the coast, especially the pectacular Ras Abu Gallum Protectorate ee p259). Itineraries and prices are gen-erally custom designed, but expect to pay from E£75 to E£100 per person for an evening trip into the mountains with dinner at a Bedouin camp, and from about E£300 to E£400 per person per day for a safari including all food and water.

The **Centre for Sinai** (☎ 364 0702; www .centre4sinai.com.eg) is one organisation that tries to promote knowledge of the local culture. **Man & the Environment Dahab** (MATE; ☎ 364 1091; www.mate-info.com) is an environmental education group that helps arrange treks with Bedouin guides. Contact both organisations via telephone or email in order to arrange tours around Sinai.

SLEEPING

Red Sea Relax (☎ 364 1309; www.red-sea-relax.com; Masbat; dm €12, s/d from €35/40; ❄ 🖳 🖭) With a brand-new location a couple of hundred metres from the lighthouse in the north end of the bay, this surprisingly affordable hotel adds the 'Relax' to the Red Sea. The compound is centred on a glistening pool that adds a

JOHN ELK III

The Dahab coastline

touch of resort class, as does the rooftop bar that beckons you with the promise of a fruit smoothie.

Alf Leila (☎ 364 0595; www.alfleila.com; Mashraba; r from US$60; ❄ ▢ ☎) With just eight rooms and four studios that are uniquely designed and decorated, Alf Leila offers individualised attention and service amid truly florid surroundings. While the property is '1001 Arabian Nights' at every turn, the 1st-floor German bakery is an incongruous but wholly welcomed finishing touch.

Nesima Resort (☎ 364 0320; www.nesima -resort.com; Mashraba; s/d/ste €55/65/90; ❄ ▢ ☎) Overlooking the beach in Mashraba, this modest resort is a compromise for those who want resort living without feeling as if they're isolated from the town. With pleasing stone and wood overtones and soaring domes, rooms at Nesima induce calm, relaxed feelings for all who stay here. The most attractive feature of the property is without a doubt the palm-tree-lined infinity-edge pool, which regally overlooks the beach and the boardwalk.

EATING & DRINKING

Funny Mummy (Mashraba; dishes E£35-85) One of the most popular restaurants on the boardwalk, this palm-fringed and pillow-decked spot offers all of your favourite Western and Asian dishes alongside traditional Egyptian delicacies.

Al Capone (at the bridge; dishes E£40-95) Sure, it's packed to the brim with tourists, but the impressive seafood offering, bridgeside location, and the occasional live music and belly dancing make the strangely named Al Capone an obligatory stop.

Lakhbatita (Mashraba; dishes E£45-115) This eccentric beachfront establishment at the southern end of Mashraba is decorated with old Egyptian furniture, and serves

gourmet food drawing on Egyptia Middle Eastern, Asian and Continent. influences.

Tota Dance Bar (Masbat) The centre nightlife in Dahab, this nautically theme drinking spot has free movies from Sunda to Thursday, and turns into an impromptu disco on Friday and Saturday nights – th top deck is a good place to watch the sur set while sipping a cold beer, especiall during the 5pm to 7pm happy hour.

GETTING THERE & AWAY

From the bus station in Dahab City, we southwest of the centre of the action, **Eas Delta Travel Co** (☎ 364 1808) has buses t Sharm el-Sheikh (E£15 to E£20, one to tw hours) departing at 8am, 8.30am, 10am 11.30am, 12.30pm, 2.30pm, 4pm, 5.30pm

ANDERS BLOMQ

Camels stroll the main street of Dahab (p264)

30pm and 10pm. Buses to Nuweiba (£15 to E£20, one hour) leave at 8.30am nd 10.30am, with the 10.30am bus continuing on to Taba (E£35, two hours).

There is a 9.30am bus to St Katherine £20 to E£25, two to three hours), though 's much more convenient to organise a ervice taxi or private vehicle in the late fternoon. Buses heading to Cairo (E£60 o E£70, nine hours) depart at 8.30am, 2.30pm, 2.30pm and 7.30pm.

Service taxis in Dahab are generally nore expensive than buses, and as travllers are a captive market, there's usually ot much room for negotiation.

NUWEIBA

tretched randomly over about 15km, uweiba lacks a defined centre and a coesive ambience, and functions primarily s a port town rather than a travellers' etreat. As a result, Nuweiba has never nanaged to attract the cult following of earby Dahab, or the massive development of Sharm el-Sheikh. Most travellers ass through Nuweiba either on their way o the scenic camps and resorts near the raeli border, or to catch the Aqabaound ferry en route to Petra in Jordan.

SLEEPING & EATING

Nakhil Inn (☎ 350 0879; www.nakhil-inn.com; from US$40; ❄) At the northern end of Tarabin is this charming inn, comprised of attached wooden bungalows, which ront a large patio area, and are strung long a private beachfront. Interiors are a soothing mix of stained woods and natural tiles (a pleasant alternative to much of ne concrete that lines the beachfronts in gypt), and the fireplace-warmed restaurant is wonderfully atmospheric on a cold inter's night.

Cleopatra Restaurant (Nuweiba City; shes E£20-50) One of the more popu-

lar tourist restaurants in Nuweiba City, Cleopatra offers up the bounty of the sea, Lebanese-inspired mezze platters, woodfired pizzas and a few Western fast-food favourites.

GETTING THERE & AWAY
BOAT
There's a so-called 'fast-ferry' service between Nuweiba in Egypt and Aqaba in Jordan, leaving Nuweiba at 3.30pm and in theory taking between one and two hours assuming normal sea conditions. Tickets must be paid for in US dollars (note that these are not always available at the banks in Nuweiba) and can be purchased on the day of departure only at the **ferry ticket office** (☙ 9am), in a small building near the port. Free Jordanian visas can be obtained on the ferry if you have an EU, US, Canadian, Australian or New Zealand passport.

BUS
East Delta Travel Co (☎ 352 0371; Nuweiba Port) has buses to Cairo (E£70 to E£80, seven to eight hours) at 9am, 11am and 3pm going via Taba (E£15 to E£20, one hour); and to Sharm el-Sheikh (E£25 to E£30, three to four hours) at 6.30am, 8.30am, 10am and 4pm going via Dahab (E£15 to E£20, one hour). If you're heading to St Katherine, it's best to arrange a service taxi in Dahab.

NUWEIBA TO TABA
The stunning coastline between Nuweiba and Taba is fringed by aqua waters and rimmed by chains of low, barren mountains.

Basata (☎ 350 0480; www.basata.com; camping per person E£35, huts from E£60, 3-person chalets from US$60) Twenty kilometres north of Nuweiba in the Mahash area is Basata ('simplicity' in Arabic), an ecologically minded and hugely popular travellers' settlement that lives by its name – owner Sherif Ghamrawy's concern for the environment is reflected in the philosophy of the hotel, which uses organically grown produce and recycles its rubbish. There are simple huts sharing facilities, pleasant chalets with electricity and private bathroom, a large camping area, a kitchen (where you can self-cater or arrange to have prepared meals), a bakery and shower blocks.

ST KATHERINE PROTECTORATE

The 4350-sq-km St Katherine Protectorate is a highlight of Sinai's interior and was created in 1996 to counteract the detrimental effects of rapidly increasing tourism on St Katherine's Monastery and the adjacent Mt Sinai.

ST KATHERINE'S MONASTERY

This ancient **monastery** (Map p268; ☎ ⏰ Cairo 02-482 8513; admission free; ⏰ 9am-noo Mon-Wed, Fri & Sun, except religious holiday traces its founding to about AD 33 when the Roman empress Helena ha a small chapel and a fortified refuge fo local hermits built beside what was be lieved to be the burning bush from which God spoke to Moses. In the 6th centur Emperor Justinian ordered a fortress to b constructed around the original chape together with a basilica and a monaster to provide a secure home for the mona tic community that had grown here, an as a refuge for the Christians of souther Sinai. Today St Katherine's is considere one of the oldest continually functionin monastic communities in the world, an its chapel is one of early Christianity's on surviving churches.

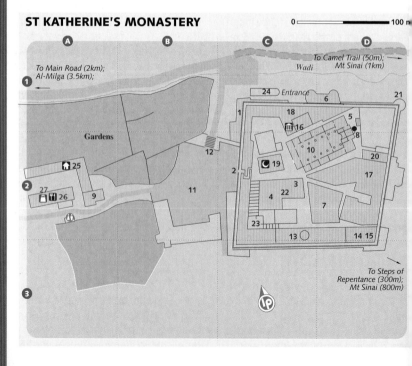

ST KATHERINE'S MONASTERY

Although much of the monastery is closed to the public, it is possible to enter the ornately decorated 6th-century **Church of the Transfiguration**, with its nave flanked by massive marble columns and walls covered in richly gilded icons and paintings. To the left of and below the altar is the monastery's holiest area, the **Chapel of the Burning Bush**. Near the burning bush is the **Well of Moses**, a natural spring that is supposed to give marital happiness to those who drink from it.

Above the well is the superb **Monastery Museum** (adult/student E£25/10), also known as the Sacred Sacristy, which has been magnificently restored. It has displays (labelled in Arabic and English) of many of the monastery's artistic treasures, including some of the spectacular Byzantine-era icons from its world-famous collection, numerous precious chalices and gold and silver crosses.

The least crowded days for visiting the monastery are generally Tuesday and Wednesday, while Saturday and Monday tend to be the most crowded.

MT SINAI
Known locally as Gebel Musa, Mt Sinai is revered by Christians, Muslims and Jews, all of whom believe that God delivered his Ten Commandments to Moses at its summit. The mountain is easy and beautiful to climb, and although you'll invariably be overwhelmed with crowds of other visitors, it offers a taste of the magnificence of southern Sinai's high mountain region. For those visiting as part of a pilgrimage, it also offers a moving glimpse into biblical times. See p296 for more details on climbing the mountain and trekking in the area.

SLEEPING
Al-Karm Ecolodge (Sheikh Awaad; camping/r per person E£25/75) A fine, albeit rugged, base for immersing yourself in the beauty of southern Sinai, the Bedouin-owned Al-Karm Ecolodge, well outside Al-Milga, is in a remote wadi near the small settlement of Sheikh Awaad. It offers simple rooms, solar-heated shared showers, a kitchen and endless tranquillity. To get here, follow the track from Tarfa village, about 20km from St Katherine on the Wadi Feiran road.

Monastery Guesthouse (Map p268; ☎ 347 0353; St Katherine's Monastery; dm per person half board US$25, s/d/tr with bathroom US$40/60/75) A favourite of pilgrims the world over, the Monastery Guesthouse offers well-kept rooms with heaters and blankets to keep out the mountain chill, and a pleasant patio area with views towards the mountains. Meals at the on-site cafeteria are filling and tasty, and lunches can be arranged for a few extra dollars per person.

GETTING THERE & AWAY

St Katherine's Monastery is about 3.5km from the village of Al-Milga (which is where buses from Dahab, Sharm el-Sheikh and Cairo will drop you), and 2km from the large roundabout on the road between the two.

Service taxis usually wait at the monastery for people coming down from Mt Sinai in the morning, and then again around noon when visiting hours end. A lift to the village costs E£10 to E£15. Plan on paying about E£30/45 per person to Dahab/Sharm el-Sheikh. There is a daily bus to Cairo (E£60, six to seven hours) at 6am, and another to Dahab at 1pm (E£20 to E£25, two to three hours), where you can get connections to Nuweiba and Taba. Change buses in Dahab for Sharm el-Sheikh, Hurghada and Luxor.

RED SEA COAST

Surrounded by desert on three sides, the Red Sea was formed some 40 million years ago when the Arabian Peninsula split from Africa, allowing the waters of the Indian Ocean to rush in. Bordered at its southern end by the 25km Bab al-Mandab Strait, the Red Sea is the only tropical sea that is almost entirely closed. No river flows into it and the influx of water from the Indian Ocean is slight. These unique geographical features, combined with the arid desert climate and high temperatures, make the sea extremely salty. It is also windy – on average the sea is flat for only 50 days a year.

In regard to its name (the Red Sea is in fact deep blue), there are two competing schools of thought regarding etymology. Some believe that the sea was named after the surrounding red-rock mountain ranges. Others insist it was named for the periodic algae blooms that tinge the water a reddish-brown. Whatever the spark, it inspired ancient mariners to dub these waters *Mare Rostrum* – the Red Sea.

For independent travellers weary of package tourism, the Red Sea coast can be a frustrating place to visit, though it shouldn't be overlooked altogether

KERSTIN REIGER/IMAGEBROKER/PHOTOLIBRARY

Monastery of St Paul (opposite)

far removed from the coastal scene is the Eastern Desert, which harbours Christianity's two oldest monasteries, plus traces of Pharaonic, Roman and other settlements. And, if you do happen to find yourself in any of the Red Sea's coastal resort towns, you'll find the diving here truly is world-class.

RED SEA MONASTERIES

The Coptic monasteries of St Anthony and St Paul (Map pp244–5) are Egypt's and Christianity's oldest monasteries, and are among the holiest sites in the Coptic faith. In fact, the establishment of the religious community of St Anthony's, hidden in the barren cliffs of the Eastern Desert, marks the beginning of the Christian monastic tradition.

Both monasteries are open daily throughout the year (St Anthony's from 7am to 5pm, St Paul's from 8am to 3pm), except during Advent and Lent, when they can only be visited on Friday, Saturday and Sunday. During Holy Week they are closed completely to visitors. For inquiries or to confirm visiting times, contact the monasteries' Cairo headquarters: **St Paul's** (☎ 02-2590 0218; 26 Al-Keneesa al-Morcosia) or **St Anthony's** (☎ 02-2590 6025; 26 Al-Keneesa al-Morcosia), located off Clot Bey, south of Midan Ramses in Cairo. If you don't have your own vehicle, the easiest way to visit the monasteries is to join an organised tour from Cairo or Hurghada (any hotel or travel agency can organise these).

MONASTERY OF ST ANTHONY

This historic monastery traces its origins to the 4th century AD when monks began to settle at the foot of Gebel al-Galala al-Qibliya, where their spiritual leader, Anthony, lived. The oldest part of the monastery is the **Church of St Anthony**, built over the saint's tomb and containing one of Egypt's most significant collections of Coptic wall paintings. Perched about 300m – 1158 wooden steps – above the monastery on a nearby cliff is the **Cave of St Anthony**, where Anthony spent the final 40 years of his life. The climb up is hot and steep and takes about half an hour if you're reasonably fit.

MONASTERY OF ST PAUL

St Paul's monastery dates to the 4th century, when it began as a grouping of hermitages in the cliffs of Gebel al-Galala al-Qibliya around the site where St Paul had his hermitage. Paul, who was born into a wealthy family in Alexandria in the mid-3rd century, originally fled to the Eastern Desert to escape Roman persecution. The heart of the monastery complex is the **Church of St Paul**, which was built in and around the cave where

THE FATHER OF MONASTICISM

St Paul is honoured as the earliest Christian hermit, but St Anthony is considered the Father of Monasticism. Anthony, born around AD 251, sought solitude and spiritual salvation in a cave in the Eastern Desert. Word of his holiness soon spread and flocks of disciples arrived and formed the first Christian monastic community.

The number of Anthony's followers grew rapidly, and within decades the whole Byzantine Empire was alive with monastic fervour, which by the next century had spread throughout Europe. When St Anthony died at the age of 105, the location of his grave became a guarded secret.

Paul lived. The **fortress** above the church was where the monks retreated during Bedouin raids.

There is no official accommodation for the general public at either monastery, although male pilgrims are allowed to spend the night in dormitories with written consent from the monasteries' Cairo headquarters.

EL-GOUNA

The brainchild of Onsi Sawirie, the Egyptian multibillionaire who heads the Orascom conglomerate, El-Gouna (Map pp244-5) was largely built from the ground up during the 1990s. Boasting more than a dozen hotels, several golf courses, countless shopping malls and the odd casino, El-Gouna serves up heaping amounts of family fun, albeit the homogenised, vacation-community variety.

El-Gouna is a veritable paradise for water sports. The various activity centres inside the resorts offer a laundry list of activities including sailing, ocean kayaking, boogie-boarding, parasailing, jet-skiing, windsurfing, kitesurfing, waterskiing and many, many others. Offshore, you'll find a good number of excellent snorkelling and diving sites.

SLEEPING

Dawar el-Omda (☎ 358 0063; www.dawar elomda-elgouna.com; Kafr El-Gouna; s/d half board from US$115/125; ✗ ☼ ☲) This tastefully decorated four-star resort eschews European design in favour of classic Egyptian lines and arches. Although there's no beach, shuttle boats can whisk you away to the sands, and you're within easy walking distance of El-Gouna's retail shopping hubs.

Sheraton Miramar (☎ 354 5606; www .starwoodhotels.com/sheraton; El-Gouna; s/d half board from US$175/215; ✗ ☼ ☐ ☲) A five-

star, pastel-coloured, postmodern desert fantasy, the Sheraton was designed by well-known architect Michael Graves and is one of the signature properties of El-Gouna. Accommodation of varying levels of opulence incorporates a dreamlike mix of Arabian, Nubian and Egyptian design motifs.

GETTING THERE & AWAY
AIR
Several domestic charter companies serve El-Gouna, though most international flights touch down in Hurghada, about 20km south along the main coastal highway.

BUS
El-Gouna Transport buses travel three times daily between the Hilton Ramses in Cairo, El-Gouna and Hurghada (E£85 to E£95, five hours), best booked a day in advance.

TAXI
Taxis run frequently between El-Gouna and Hurghada, with fares ranging from E£60 to E£75, depending on your destination.

GETTING AROUND
The El-Gouna sprawl is readily accessible by a fairly comprehensive network of local buses – a daily bus pass will only cost you E£5. Tuk-tuks also scan the streets for potential fares; prices for these are highly variable, around E£3 to E£10.

HURGHADA
Once an isolated and modest fishing village, the Hurghada coast area has metamorphosed into a sprawling collection of more than 100 hotels, and is today Egypt's most popular resort destination for foreign travellers. Not surprisingly, the reefs close

shore have been degraded by illegal ndfill operations and irresponsible reef se. To be fair, Hurghada was put on the ap because of its superb diving, and there e some incredible offshore sites here. If ou want to combine a diving holiday with visit to Luxor and other Nile Valley sites, urghada is a convenient destination.

If you don't want to put your head nder the water, you can still get an idea f some of the life in the Red Sea at the quarium (☎ 354 8557; Corniche, Ad-Dahar; adission E£5; ☼ 9am-10pm). Although there is me easily accessible coral at the south-n end of the resort strip, the best reefs e offshore, and the only way to see them to take a boat and/or join a snorkelling r diving excursion. For any boat excurion, take your passport with you as you'll eed to show it at the port.

LEEPING

asmine Village (☎ 346 0460; www.jasmine llage.com; s/d all-inclusive from US$65/85; ☼ 🖵 🏊) Another oldie but a goodie, ne Jasmine Village has also found a home among families trying to save a quick buck. Guests stay in one of 400-plus bungalow-style rooms, which look out onto a proper beach, a stunning coral reef and the open ocean.

Oberoi Sahl Hasheesh (☎ 344 0777; www.oberoihotels.com; Sahl Hasheesh; ste from €200; ✂ 🍴 🖵 🏊) Peaceful, exclusive and opulent beyond your imagination, the Oberoi features palatial suites decorated in minimalist Moorish style. Each individually decorated accommodation comes complete with sunken marble baths, walled private courtyards – some with private pools – and panoramic sea views. Located a few kilometres south of the resort strip.

EATING

Portofino (Sharia Sayyed al-Qorayem, Ad-Dahar; dishes E£25-50; 🍴) A Hurghada institution, Portofino serves authentic Italian wood-fired pizzas and homemade pastas as well as a few staple Egyptian dishes including homemade tahini and *baba ghanoug*.

Chez Pascal (Sharia Sayyed al-Qorayem, Ad-Dahar; meals E£30-65; 🍴) This charming,

Walking on the beach at El-Gouna (opposite)

FRANS LEMMENS

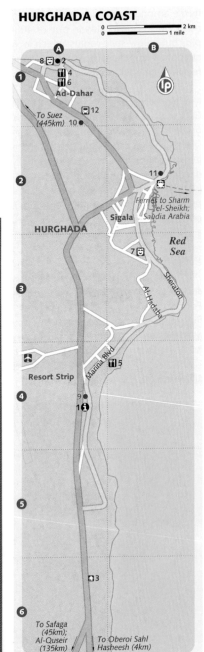

HURGHADA COAST

European-style bistro is a good spot f
eclectic cuisine served amid bright an
clean surroundings – the perfect place t
savour a Turkish coffee and indulge in
bit of people-watching.

Little Buddha (Marina Blvd, resort strip; mai
E£45-75) This is one of Hurghada's most we
known Asian restaurants. The cuisine her
is a fusion of sushi spreads, Chinese-sty
seafood dishes and plenty of rice an
noodle concoctions to round things out

ENTERTAINMENT

The centre of nightlife in Hurghada is th
Papas Bar (www.papasbar.com; Sharia Sherato
Sigala), a popular Dutch-run bar attache
to Rossi Restaurant in Sigala. Under th
same management is **Papas II** (ww
.papasbar.com; Corniche, Ad-Dahar), with a da
wooden interior, cold beers and live mus
several nights weekly.

GETTING THERE & AWAY

EgyptAir (☎ 344 3592/3; www.egyptair.con
resort strip) has daily flights to Cairo an
Sharm el-Sheikh, though prices tend t
fluctuate greatly depending on the se
son and availability.

▲ diver spots a hawksbill turtle, Red Sea

MARK WEBSTER

Ferry tickets to Sharm el-Sheikh are sold at the **International Fast Ferries office** (orniche, Sigala).

Upper Egypt Bus Co (☎ 354 7582; off aria an-Nasr, Ad-Dahar) has 10 daily buses Cairo (E£60 to E£70, six to seven hours). here are also regular daily departures to ıez (E£35 to E£40, four to five hours) and ıxor (E£30 to E£35, five hours) via Safaga £10, one hour). Finally, there a few daily epartures to Al-Quseir (E£20 to E£25, two three hours), Marsa Alam (E£30 to E£35, ıur to five hours) and Shalatein (E£55, ıne hours).

ETTING AROUND

O/FROM THE AIRPORT

ıe airport is close to the resort strip. A ıxi to downtown Ad-Dahar will cost be- ween E£25 and E£30.

IICROBUS

l-Gouna Transport (☎ 354 1561) operates route (E£5 to E£10) between El-Gouna, d-Dahar and the end of Sharia Sheraton Sigala about every halfhour, beginning at 9am. Flag the bus down at any point along the way.

TAXI

Taxis from Ad-Dahar to the start of the resort strip (around the Marriott hotel) charge about E£15. Travelling from the bus station to the centre of Ad-Dahar, expect to pay between E£5 and E£10.

AL-QUSEIR

The historic city of Al-Quseir was founded during Pharaonic times as the launching point for boats sailing to Punt, a fabled site in eastern Africa that was the alleged source of rare and exotic trade products. Although nothing remains of this ancient trading port, Al-Quseir's long history and sleepy present lend it a charm absent from other towns along the coast of the Red Sea.

The 16th-century Ottoman **fortress** (admission E£10; ⏰ 9am-5pm) is Al-Quseir's most important historical building. Just across from the fortress is the 19th-century **shrine** of a Yemeni sheikh, Abdel Ghaffaar

NOMADS OF THE EASTERN DESERT

The southern Red Sea may seem empty and inhospitable, but the area has been home to nomadic Ababda and Besharin tribes for millennia. Members of the Beja, a nomadic tribe of African origin, they are thought to be descendents of the Blemmyes, the fierce tribesmen mentioned by classical geographers. Until well into the 20th century, the extent of the territory in which they roamed was almost exactly as described by the Romans, with whom they were constantly at war some 2000 years earlier.

The Ababda and Besharin lived a nomadic lifestyle that hardly changed until the waters of Lake Nasser rose and destroyed their traditional grazing lands. While most Besharin, many of whom do not speak Arabic, live in Sudan, most of the Arabic-speaking Ababda are settled in communities in the Nile Valley between Aswan and Luxor. A small number continue to live in their ancestral territory, concentrated in the area from Marsa Alam to Wadi Gimal, as well as on the eastern shores of Lake Nasser.

If you spend time in the region, you'll still likely see the traditional Ababda hut, or hear Ababda music, with its rhythmic clapping and drumming and heavy use of the five-stringed lyre-like *tamboura*. At the centre of Ababda social life is *jibena* – heavily sweetened coffee prepared from fresh-roasted beans.

With the rapid expansion of tourism along the southern Red Sea, long-standing Ababda lifestyles have become increasingly threatened. Tourism has begun to replace livestock and camels as the main source of livelihood, and many Ababda men now work as guards or labourers on the resorts, while others have started working with travel companies, offering camel safaris to tourists.

al-Yemeni, which is marked by an old gravestone in a niche in the wall.

SLEEPING & EATING

Al-Quseir Hotel (☎ 333 2301; Sharia Port Said; s/d E£135/165; ✖) This charismatic hotel has six simple but spacious rooms in a renovated 1920s merchant's house on the seafront. With its original narrow wooden staircase, high wooden ceilings and latticework on the windows, it's full of atmosphere, and staying here is a pleasure. There are also good views from the seafront rooms, and a tiny restaurant – order ahead for meals.

Mövenpick Sirena Beach (☎ 333 2100; www.moevenpick-quseir.com; r from US$105; ✖ 💻 🐾) This low-set, domed ensemble 7km north of the town centre is top o the line in Al-Quseir, and one of the be resorts along the coast, though it's sur prisingly more affordable than you migh imagine. Its amenities include exceller food and the usual five-star facilities, Subex diving centre, quiet evenings an a refreshing absence of the glitz so com mon in other resort hotels. The manage ment is known for its environmental conscious approach.

Restaurant Marianne (☎ 333 438 Sharia Port Said; dishes E£15-50) One of the be places in town to sample the bounty the Red Sea, this local favourite serve up some seriously delicious seafoo Opening hours are irregular.

GETTING THERE & AWAY

The bus and service-taxi stations are next to each other about 3km northwest of the Safaga road.

Buses run to Cairo (E£80 to E£85, 10 to 11 hours) and Hurghada (E£20 to E£25, three hours), departing at 6am, 7.30am, 9am, 7pm and 8.30pm. Buses to Marsa Alam (E£10 to E£15, two hours) are at 7am, 9am, 7pm and 8pm.

GETTING AROUND

Microbuses go along Sharia al-Gomhuriyya, with some also going to the bus and service-taxi stations. Fares are between 50pt and E£1, depending on the distance travelled. Taxis also cover this route, with fares averaging a few pounds per ride.

MARSA ALAM

Until very recently, only serious divers accessed this far-flung destination, though tourist numbers in Marsa Alam are on the rise, perhaps due to growing dissatisfaction with traditional resort destinations such as Hurghada. At present, the area around Marsa Alam is home to a collection of highly recommendable ecolodges and, for the time being, only a handful of upmarket luxury resorts.

SLEEPING

Shaqra Ecolodge (☎ in Cairo 03-3337 9942; www.redsea-divingsafari.com; Marsa Shagra; tents/chalets per person €35/50) This simple place owned by Hossam Helmi – lawyer, committed environmentalist and diving enthusiast – was one of the first ecolodges along the southern Red Sea coast, and remains the best. It offers simple but spotless and comfortable accommodation in a choice of two-bed tents sharing bathroom facilities or stone chalets with en suite – all designed to be as kind to the environment as possible – plus first-rate diving (dives from €30). Nondivers in search of beautiful vistas and tranquillity are welcome, too.

GETTING THERE & AWAY

The Marsa Alam International Airport is 67km north of Marsa Alam along the

MARK WEBSTER

A feeding dugong, Red Sea

Al-Quseir road. There is no public transport, so you'll need to arrange a transfer in advance with your hotel.

Buses from Shalatein pass Marsa Alam en route to Edfu (E£35, three to four hours) at around 7am and 9am daily. There are four daily buses to Al-Quseir (E£10 to E£15, two hours) and Hurghada (E£30 to E£35, four to five hours), departing at 5am, 12.30pm, 2.30pm and 5pm. To Cairo direct, the fare is E£85 to E£90 (10 to 11 hours).

EASTERN DESERT

The Eastern Desert – a vast, desolate area rimmed by the Red Sea Mountains to the east and the Nile Valley in the west – was once crisscrossed by ancient trade routes and dotted with settlements that played vital roles in the development of many of the region's greatest civilisations. Today the desert's rugged expanses are filled with fascinating footprints of this history, including rock inscriptions, ancient gold and mineral mines, wells and watchtowers, and religious shrines and buildings. Indeed, it is one of the highlights of any visit to the Red Sea coast, and a world apart from the commercialised coastline.

Although second-rate travel agencies occupy every corner of the tourist hub of Hurghada (p272), it is recommended that you book a tour through **Red Sea Desert Adventures** (☎ 012 399 3860; www.redsea desertadventures.com; Marsa Shagra).

Tours start at approximately €40 per person, though they vary depending on the specifications of your uniquely catered tour, the size of your party and the time of year. In order for the necessary permits to be organised for multiday desert safaris, try to book at least one month in advance.

ICONOTEC/AL

Cleopatra's Bath (Spring of the Sun), Siwa Oasis (p301)

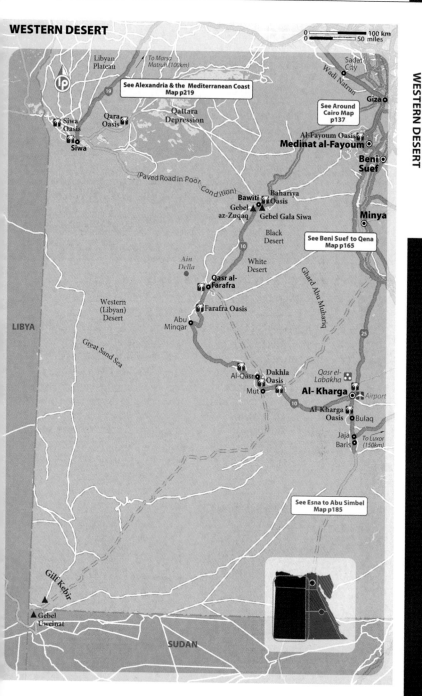

WESTERN DESERT

0 — 100 km
0 — 50 miles

Libyan Plateau

To Marsa Matruh (100km)

Sadat City

Wadi Natrun

See Alexandria & the Mediterranean Coast Map p219

Giza

Qattara Depression

See Around Cairo Map p137

Siwa Oasis

Qara Oasis

Al-Fayoum Oasis
Medinat al-Fayoum

Beni Suef

Siwa

(Paved Road in Poor Condition)

Bawiti

Bahariya Oasis

Gebel az-Zuqaq

Gebel Gala Siwa

Minya

Black Desert

See Beni Suef to Qena Map p165

White Desert

Aïn Della

Ghard Abu Muharriq

Qasr al-Farafra

Western (Libyan) Desert

Farafra Oasis

LIBYA

Abu Minqar

Great Sand Sea

25

Al-Qasr

Dakhla Oasis

Qasr el-Labakha

Mut

Al-Kharga

Airport

Al-Kharga Oasis

Bulaq

Jaja

Baris

To Luxor (150km)

See Esna to Abu Simbel Map p185

Gilf Kebir

▲ Gebel Uweinat

SUDAN

HIGHLIGHTS

1 THE WHITE DESERT

BY WAEL ABED, OWNER OF AL TARFA DESERT SANCTUARY AND CO-OWNER OF ZARZORA EXPEDITIONS

The desert is the best of Egypt. Mysterious, beautiful, remote, it is a world away from the Nile valley. When you come here, life takes on a different meaning, concerns have a different proportion. Come to the desert to learn a differen way of living, of seeing, and of thinking.

↘ WAEL ABED'S DON'T MISS LIST

❶ AIN DELLA (SPRING OF SHADE)

I love going to Ain Della, but you can only get here with a guide who must apply for a special military permit. This picturesque spring about 120km from Qasr al-Farafra is surrounded by splendid cliffs on the north and east and dunes to the south and west. This is the Western Desert at its best.

❷ WHITE DESERT PROTECTORATE

As you travel in this 300-sq-km area your imagination starts to work an you recognise wind-eroded rock for mations shaped like all sorts of animal and birds. At different times of the day they take on different colours from white and light pink, to flaming orang and deep purple. You can spend day going through the sands here for fos sils, bits of quartz and different deep black iron pyrites.

Clockwise from top: Sunrise over the White Desert; The Black Desert; Bizarre inselbergs (rock formations) in the White Desert

❷ LANDMARKS

The two flat-topped mountains known as the **Twin Peaks** are another favourite destination, and the view from the top of the surrounding symmetrical hills, all shaped like giant ant hills, is spectacular. The steep escarpment of **Naqb as-Sillim** (Pass of the Stairs), the main pass into and out of the Farafra Depression, marks the end of the White Desert. **Crystal Mountain** is a large quartz rock.

❸ INSELBERGS

Here in Egypt we have our own modest and whiter version of Arizona's Monument Valley. Out of the desert sands rise these amazing white inselbergs, strange wind-eroded chalk sculptures that take on all colours in the course of the day.

❺ BLACK DESERT

Driving between Farafra and Bahariya, you notice the desert suddenly changes from the white chalk towers in the White Desert, into the Black Desert.

↘ THINGS YOU NEED TO KNOW

When to go At sunrise or sunset for colours; or under a full moon, when it's ghostly and arctic-like **Where to camp** In the shade of the inselbergs in the White Desert **Be warned** Go with an experienced tour operator **More safari info** See p310 **See our author's review on p295**

HIGHLIGHTS

↘ SIWA OASIS

Stroll, cycle or hang out in the seriously laid-back oasis of **Siwa** (p299). Isolated from the rest of Egypt for so many centuries, the locals still speak their own Berber dialect. This is where Alexander the Great came for the Oracle, which named him as son of Amun, and where today more and more travellers come looking for one of the most romantic spots in Egypt.

↘ GREAT SAND SEA

Arrange a 4WD and venture in the vast expanse of the rolling sand dunes of the **Great Sand Sea** (p305) near Siwa. You don't need to penetrate far into the desert in order to feel the isolation, beauty and enormous scale of this amazing landscape. And if you are lucky the guide will take you for a swim in one of the lakes surrounded by dunes.

WESTERN DESERT

HIGHLIGHTS

⬊ GARDENS

Think about oases and you think about palms, hundreds of thousands of them, heavy with dates. Oases gardens will produce olives and other fruit and, in the shade they provide, some crops, but palms themselves are a mainstay of oasis life – providing juice for fermenting into alcohol, trunks for roof beams, and dried fronds for beds, chairs and boxes.

⬊ AL-QASR

There is something magical about **Al-Qasr** (p293), a magic that isn't found anywhere else in the region. Here you will find the traditions of oasis life still strong and important, the old houses still inhabited, and life lived as it was when the oases were separated by sand, not by tarmac.

⬊ BAHARIYA OASIS

In case you need convincing that the desert can be a surprising place, head to Bawiti in Bahariya Oasis and visit the **museum** (p296). The golden mummies are evidence that Bahariya wasn't always the outpost it is today. The **Oasis Heritage Museum** (p297), with its scenes of traditional life, is another highlight.

2 SARA-JANE CLELAND; 3 ARIADNE VAN ZANDBERGEN; 4 MICHELE FALZONE/AGE FOTOSTOCK/PHOTOLIBRARY; 5 JOHN ELK III; 6 LEANNE LOGAN

Mudbrick minaret, Siwa Oasis (p299); 3 Dunes in the Great Sand Sea (p305); 4 Palm gardens; 5 The town of l-Qasr (p293); 6 Clay figures in the Oasis Heritage Museum, Bahariya Oasis (p297)

THE BEST...

⭢ PLACES TO RELAX

- **Palm gardens** (p299) Siwa's greatest attraction is the oasis itself, with more than 300,000 palm trees, 70,000 olive trees and many fruit orchards.
- **Great Sand Sea** (p305) Just beyond the fringe of Siwa is one of the world's great dune fields.
- **Al-Qasr** (p293) This old town in Dakhla Oasis is one of the best places to go for traditional oasis life.

⭢ PLACES TO STAY

- **Al Tarfa Desert Sanctuary** (p293) An award-winning luxury camp from desert traveller Wael Abed.
- **Under the Moon Camp** (p298) A beautiful camp near the Ain Gomma spring with powerful desert views.
- **Nature Camp** (p298) A great ecolodge with thatch huts overlooking the desert.

- **Shali Lodge** (p303) A simple but beautiful mudbrick hotel set in a palm grove.
- **Adrère Amellal** (p304) One of Egypt's most amazing hotels – in its own oasis on the edge of the Great Sand Sea.

⭢ SPRINGS

- **Ain Gomma** (p298) With cool and crystal-clear water, this small spring is surrounded by the desert expanse on all sides – the views are amazing.
- **Bir Wahed** (p301) A freshwater lake and bubbling hot spring on the edge of the Great Sand Sea.
- **Cleopatra's Bath** (p301) The 'Spring of the Sun' lies at the heart of Siwa Oasis.

The hotel Adrére Amellal, Siwa Oasis (p304)

THINGS YOU NEED TO KNOW

↘ VITAL STATISTICS

- **Telephone codes** Al-Kharga, Dakhla and Farafra (☎ 092), Bahariya (☎ 02), Siwa (☎ 046)
- **Population Siwa** 22,000
- **Best time to go** Spring and autumn; summers are very hot and winters cold; March to April there's the chance of desert storms

↘ OASES IN A NUTSHELL

- **Al-Kharga** (p290) The capital of the Western Desert, but least picturesque of the oases.
- **Dakhla** (p291) One of the most interesting oases, particularly its Qasr area.
- **Farafra** (p293) The smallest and least touched of the oases.
- **Bahariya** (p296) The closest oasis to Cairo and the beginning of the desert circuit.
- **Siwa** (p299) The most isolated of Egypt's oases, near the Libyan border.

↘ ADVANCE PLANNING

- **One month before** Book accommodation, particularly if travelling during European holiday periods. Also arrange desert safaris as permits need to be organised.

↘ RESOURCES

- **Bahariya tourist office** (Bawiti; ☎ 3847 3035/9, 012 373 6567; ⊙ 8am-2pm Sat-Thu, plus 7-9pm Nov-Apr) Run by the eager and helpful Mohamed Abd el-Kader, also contactable by email (mohamed_kader26@hotmail.com). In the centre of town.

- **Siwa tourist office** (Map p303; ☎ 460 1338, 010 546 1992; mahdi_hweiti@yahoo.com; Siwa Town; ⊙ 9am-2pm Sat-Thu, plus 5-8pm Oct-Apr) Mahdi Hweiti is very knowledgeable and can help arrange trips to surrounding villages or the desert.

↘ EMERGENCY NUMBERS

- **Ambulance** (☎ 123)
- **Bahariya tourist police** (☎ 3847 3900)
- **Siwa tourist police** (☎ 460 2047)

↘ GETTING AROUND

- **Air** From Cairo to Al-Kharga
- **Bus** To travel between the oases.
- **4WD** For trips into the sand dunes or the White Desert.
- **Cycle** Around the oasis of Siwa.
- **Walk** Around the palm groves and gardens in the oases.

↘ BE FOREWARNED

- **Permits** These are needed to venture off the beaten track from Siwa. Mahdi Hweiti at the Siwa tourist office can arrange permissions quite quickly (but not on Friday), as well as the permit needed from Siwa to Bahariya. Bring your passport.
- **Desert safety** Never venture on your own into the desert and always carry plenty of water.

ITINERARIES

THE QUICK ESCAPE Three Days

Rent a car or take a bus and leave Cairo via the desert route
the morning, passing the (1) **Pyramids of Giza** (p79). Head f
(2) **Bahariya Oasis** (p296) and, if you're coming by car or tour, st
and have a picnic on the way. Check into your hotel before wande
ing around the oasis town of Bawiti, and arrange a tour of the loc
sights below through your hotel or tourist office if you don't hav
your own vehicle.

The next morning visit the local museum, the mount of Qarat Qa
Salim, and the rock-cut tombs of Zed-Amun-ef-ankh and his so
Bannentiu. Also stop by the Oasis Heritage Museum, where Mahmou
Eed has arranged displays of traditional village life. In the late afte
noon go for a swim in (3) **Bir al-Ghaba** (p297), about 15km northea
of Bawiti.

Finally, explore nearby Gebel Dist, the pyramid-shaped mounta
that can be seen from almost everywhere in the oasis, and take a d
in the spectacular spring of (4) **Ain Gomma** (p298) before headir
back to Cairo.

CITIES & SIWA OASIS Five Days

Spend day one in (1) **Cairo** (p65) visiting the Egyptian Museum ar
Islamic Cairo. The next day arrange a taxi and make a full day
going to the (2) **Pyramids of Giza** (p79) and the vast cemetery
(3) **Saqqara** (p147). Start early on day three and either drive
take a bus or train from Cairo to (4) **Alexandria** (p228) to take
the Alexandria National Museum, the Roman Amphitheatre and th
Catacombs of Kom ash-Shuqqafa. Have dinner at a local seafood re
taurant and spend the night at the Cecil Hotel (p235).

Leaving Alexandria, head for (5) **Siwa Oasis** (p299), arriving in th
late afternoon in time for a stroll in sleepy Siwa Town, which has se
eral wonderful traditional crafts shops and a few cafes. In town th
next day, visit the small House of Siwa Museum, the mudbrick fortre
of Shali, and the Temple of the Oracle at Aghurmi, east of town, th
famous oracle visited by Alexander the Great. Be sure to fit in a to
of the dunes of the (6) **Great Sand Sea** (p305), and include dip in th
spring of Bir Wahed at its edge.

OASES HOP One Week

The easiest way to tour the desert and oases is with a personalise
tour (see p310). Otherwise, you can travel between oases by bus, ar
take taxis to get around.

Start from Cairo and follow the first two days of the Quick Escar
itinerary at (1) **Bahariya Oasis** (p296). On day three take a tour fro

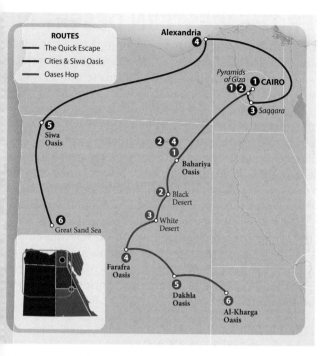

ahariya to the **(2) Black Desert** (p296), and the **(3) White Desert** 295), with its strange wind-eroded white rock formations – a great ace for camping out at night. In the morning head for **(4) Farafra asis** (p293) and its town of Qasr al-Farafra. Continue in the after- on to Al-Qasr in **(5) Dakhla Oasis** (p291) and stay at one of the eautiful hotels there. Explore the fascinating old town of Al-Qasr in e morning, and the sights of nearby Mut in the afternoon, such as e wonderful Ethnographic Museum and the old town, where the tadel commands great views. The next day drive to **(6) Al-Kharga asis** (p290), where you can explore the Museum of Antiquities and e Necropolis of Al-Bagawat. On your final day, take the newish road the Upper Egyptian city of Luxor, from where you can return to airo by air or road.

DISCOVER THE WESTERN DESERT

It's more ancient than the Pyramids, more sublime than any temple. Nearly as vast as your imagination, Egypt's Western Desert stretche: from the Nile and the Mediterranean to the Sudanese and Libyan borders, rolling far into Africa oblivious to any lines drawn on the map. The Great Sand Sea starts here, a formidable khaki ocean undulating with some of the largest sand dunes on earth.

This desolate region is punctuated with five major oases boasting freshwater sources and supporting islands of verdant greenery. The valley floors lie speckled with crumbling Roman forts, once towerin protectively over ancient caravan routes as they wound their way across North Africa. Flourishing palm plantations engulf medieval towns, and it's here out west that you will find the eerie rock formations of the White Desert. Nearby, you can explore the charre mountains of the Black Desert, and bathe in innumerable crystal-clear springs. Away from the popular desert circuit road lies happily isolated Siwa, a tranquil paradise of springs and ancient ruins thick carpeted with date palms.

HISTORY

The ancient Egyptians understood the nature of the desert, which they saw as being synonymous with death and exile. Seth, the god of chaos who killed his brother Osiris, was said to rule here. Despite their fears, it is believed the ancient Egyptians did maintain links with the oases throughout the Pharaonic era, although so far, with the exception of Dakhla Oasis, there is scant evidence of this before the Third Intermediate Period. (1069–945 BC)

The oases enjoyed a period of great prosperity during Roman times, when new wells and improved irrigation led to a vast increase in the production of wheat and grapes for export to Rome. When the Romans withdrew from Egypt, the trade routes became unsafe and were a target for attacking nomadic tribes. The fortified villages built to defend the population can still be seen in Dakhla (Al-Qasr, Balat) and Siwa (Shali).

AL-KHARGA OASIS

As the closest of the oases to the Ni Valley, Al-Kharga used to have the une: viable role as a place of banishment f mischievous Nile Valley citizens.

AL-KHARGA

The busy city of Al-Kharga is the large town in the Western Desert and also th poster child of the government's effor to modernise the oases.

Designed to resemble the architectu of nearby Bagawat, Al-Kharga's two-store **Museum of Antiquities** (Sharia Gamal Abc Nasser; adult/student E£30/15; ☺ 8am-5pm) housed in a cavernous, well-lit buildir made from local bricks.

It may not look like much from afar, b the **Necropolis of Al-Bagawat** (Map p29 adult/student E£30/15; ☺ 8am-5pm Oct-Apr, 8a 6pm May-Sep) is one of the earliest survivir and best-preserved Christian cemeteri

AL-KHARGA OASIS

0 _____ 15 km
0 _____ 10 miles

To Asyut (205km)
Al-Munira
Monastery of Al-Kashef
Al-Kharga Airport
Necropolis of Al-Bagawat
Temple of Hibis
Al-Kharga
Temple of An-Nadura
Train Station
Hamadalla Sahara City
To Mut (Dakhla Oasis; 147km)
Qasr al-Ghueita
Al-Haytan
Qasr az-Zayyan
Spring
Bulaq
Darb al-Arba'een (Forty Days Rd)
To Luxor (225km)
Jaja
Baris al-Gedida
Baris
Darb al-Arba'een
Qasr ad-Dush

SLEEPING & EATING

Pioneers Hotel (☎ 792 9751-3; www.solymar
.com; Sharia Gamal Abdel Nasser; s/d half board from
€66/84; ❄ ▣ ▣) While the salmon-pink,
low-rise construction is reminiscent of a hol-
lowed-out sponge cake, the hotel does offer
a level of comfort that was until recently
unimaginable in the oases: a swimming
pool, fitness area, outdoor cafe, billiards
and a children's playground all connected
by ridiculously lush grass. Located about
400m north of Midan Nasser in town.

Pizza Ibn al-Balad (Midan Sho'ala; pizzas
E£10-30) Strike us down if this place doesn't
serve some of the best darned *fiteer*
(Egyptian pizza/pancake) in the oases. In
the southern part of town.

GETTING THERE & AWAY

The Petroleum Service Company has
Sunday flights on a 15-seat plane, leaving
Cairo at 8am and returning from Al-Kharga
at 4pm (E£500 one way, 1½ hours).

Upper Egypt Bus Co (☎ 792 4587; Sharia
Mohammed Farid) operates buses to Cairo
(E£60, eight to 10 hours) daily at 6am,
9pm, 10pm, 11pm and midnight. There
are several buses bound for Asyut (E£16,
three to four hours) leaving daily at 6am,
7am, 9am, 11am, noon, 2pm, 10pm and
12.30am. Buses to Dakhla (E£16, three
hours) leave daily at 5am, 11am, 2pm,
11pm, 1am and 3.30am.

There's no bus service to Luxor. If heading that way, you can either catch a bus to
Asyut and change there, or hire a private
taxi. Thanks to the new road, special taxis
can get you to Luxor (via Jaja) in three hours,
but will set you back E£350 to E£400.

DAKHLA OASIS

Lush palm groves and orchards support
traditional villages, where imposing,
ancient mudbrick forts still stand guard

the world. About 3km north of town
nd 1km north of the well-preserved
mestone **Temple of Hibis**, it's built on
e site of an earlier Egyptian necropolis,
ith most of the 263 mudbrick tombs ap-
earing to date from the 4th to the 6th
enturies AD.

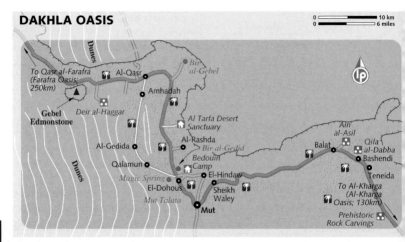

DAKHLA OASIS

over the townships and allude to their less tranquil past. At the centre of the oasis lies the town of Mut.

MUT

Dakhla's wonderful **Ethnographic Museum** (Sharia as-Salam; admission E£5; 8am-2pm Sat-Thu), attached to Dar al-Wafdeen Government Hotel, is only opened on request: ask at the tourist office or at the **Cultural Palace** (☎ 782 1311; Sharia al-Wadi), where the museum's manager can be found.

Most houses in the **old town** of Mut have no outside windows, thus protecting against intruders and keeping out the heat and wind of the desert. From the top of the hill, at the **old citadel**, there are great views of the new town and the desert beyond.

SLEEPING & EATING

Bedouin Oasis Village (☎ 782 0070, 012 669 4893; s/d E£70/150, full board E£100/200) This hilltop hotel at the north end of Mut has the most character of any place in town, with a deluge of domes, arches and vaults.

Abu Mohamed Restaurant (☎ 7⁊ 1431; Sharia as-Sawra al-Khadra; meals E£5-2⁊ 🖳) Abu Mohamed, brother of Ahme⁊ Hamdy touts, cooks and serves in th⁊ simple roadside restaurant, northwest ⁊ Midan al-Tahrir. Cold beer, internet an⁊ bike hire (E£10 per hour) are available.

Ahmed Hamdy's Restaurant (☎ 7⁊ 0767; Sharia as-Sawra al-Khadra; meals E£10-3⁊ On the main road into town is Ahme⁊ Hamdy's popular place serving del⁊ cious chicken, kebabs, vegetables and⁊ few other small dishes inside or on th⁊ terrace.

GETTING THERE & AWAY

Upper Egypt Bus Co (☎ 782 4366; Midan Gamaa) runs buses at 7.30pm and 8.30p⁊ to Cairo (E£55, eight to 10 hours) via ⁊ Kharga Oasis (E£16, one to two hours) an⁊ Asyut (E£25, four to five hours).

GETTING AROUND

Most places in Dakhla are linked b⁊ crowded pick-ups, Peugeots or micr⁊ buses, but working out where they all g⁊ requires a degree in astrophysics.

ROUND MUT

OT SPRINGS

here are several hot sulphur pools
ound the town of Mut, but the easiest
 reach is **Mut Talata** (Mut Three). Set
nong breathtaking desert scenery, **Bir
-Gebel** (Mountain Spring; admission E£10) has
een turned into a day-trip destination
here blaring music and hundreds of
hoolchildren easily overwhelm any am-
ence it might have had. It's best to come
 the evening, when it's quieter and the
ars blaze across the night sky.

L-QASR

he old town is built on the ancient foun-
ations of a Roman city and is thought to
e the one of the oldest inhabited areas
 the oases. The gateway of a temple to
oth is now the front of a private house,
d inscribed blocks from the temple
ve been used in other local buildings.
There are 37 lintels in the village, the
rliest of which dates to the early 16th
ntury. One of the finest is above the
mb of Sheikh Nasr ad-Din inside

the old mosque, which is marked by a
restored 12th-century mudbrick minaret.
Adjoining it is **Nasr ad-Din Mosque**, with
a 21m-high minaret.

SLEEPING

Al-Qasr Hotel (☎ 787 6013; r E£30) The ever-
helpful Mohamed captains this great little guest house, which sits above a cafe
near the old town. The simple rooms with
shared bathroom are fine for the price, and
some even boast views on to Al-Qasr.

Al Tarfa Desert Sanctuary (Map
p292; ☎ 910 5007/8/9; www.altarfa.com; s/d full
board from €390/510; ♨ ☐ ☒) The tradition-
ally inspired decor is tasteful and impec-
cably rendered, down to the smallest
detail, from the museum-quality embroidered bedspreads to the mud-plastered
walls that don't show a single crack.

FARAFRA OASIS

Though light on tourist infrastructure
or any real tourist attractions, Farafra's
proximity to the White Desert (only 20km

assageway in the old town of Al-Qasr (above)

JOHN ELK III

DANIELA DIRSCHERL/WATERFRAME - UNDERWATER IMAGES/PHOTOLIB

Desert Lodge (below), Dakhla Oasis

↘ IF YOU LIKE...

If you like **Al Tarfa Desert Sanctuary** (p293), you will also like some of these other wonderful desert hotels:

- **Hamadalla Sahara City** (Map p291; ☎ 092-762 0240; Kharga–Dush rd; s/d E£130/160; ⊠) Shimmering like a mirage, 15km south of Al-Kharga, it has domed bungalows with neat, agreeable rooms and private bathrooms. Hard to get to without your own wheels, but the desert views are impressive.
- **Bedouin Camp & El-Dohous Village** (Map p292; ☎ 092-785 0480; www.dakhla bedouins.com; s/d E£100/120) The Bedouin Al-Hag Abdel Hameed built this curving mudbrick hotel in Dakhla Oasis, with everything from cave rooms to regular two-storey abodes, all decorated with local crafts.
- **Desert Lodge** (☎ 092-772 7061/2, in Cairo 02-2690 5240; www.desertlodge.net; s/d/tr half board €75/120/175; ⊠ ☐ ☎) This thoughtfully designed, ecofriendly mudbrick fortress is on a hilltop overlooking the old town of Al-Qasr in Dakhla Oasis, with a good restaurant, a hot spring and a painting studio.
- **Aquasun Farafra** (Map p295; ☎ 012 7807 999; www.raid4x4egypt.com; Bir Sitta; s/d half board €35/50; ⊠ ☎) Built beside Bir Sitta (from which piping-hot water fills the hotel pool) and nestled in its own idyllic oasis, Aquasun has 21 chalet-style rooms. Owner Hisham Nessim is a long-time desert-safari operator.
- **Al-Babinshal** (Map p303; ☎ 046-460 1499; www.siwa.com; s/d/tr E£260/340/420) This extraordinary mudbrick hotel is grafted on to the front of Shali's fortress, and a maze of tunnels and stairways connects the spacious and cool cavelike rooms, making it impossible to tell where the hotel ends and the fort begins.

vay), and its torpid pace of life and ex-
nsive palm gardens, manage to draw
small trickle of travellers each year.
asr al-Farafra is the only real town in
e oasis.

Badr Abdel Moghny is a self-taught art-
t whose gift to his town has become its
nly real sight. **Badr's Museum** (☎ 751
91, 012 170 4710; donation E£10; ☽ 8.30am-
nset), surrounded by a desert garden, is
orth seeing for the enthusiasm that Badr
uts into his work, much of which records
aditional oasis life.

LEEPING & EATING

l-Badawiya Safari & Hotel (☎ 751
60, 012 214 8343; www.badawiya.com; off main
ahariya–Dakhla rd; s/d €25/35, villas with air-con
5/55; ☐ ☎) Al-Badawiya has a wide
hoice of stylishly designed and tradi-
onally themed rooms and is dotted with

cushioned sitting areas, has a refreshing
pool, and boasts more than its fair share
of arches and domes.

A trio of restaurants in the centre
of town, Wembe al-Waha, Hussein's
Restaurant and Samir Restaurant serve
the typical Egyptian variety of grilled
dishes for similar prices (about E£20 for
a full meal, including rice, salad, beans,
tahini and bread).

GETTING THERE & AWAY

There are Upper Egypt Bus Co buses travelling from Farafra to Cairo (E£45, eight to
10 hours) via Bahariya (E£25, three hours)
at 10am and 10pm. Buses from Farafra to
Dakhla (E£25, four hours) originate in
Cairo and leave at around 2pm to 3pm
and around 2am.

Microbuses to Dakhla (E£20, three to
four hours) and Bahariya (E£20, three
hours) leave from the town's main inter-
section when full (not often), so you're
better off going early in the morning.
Rare service taxis to Dakhla cost E£20, to
Al-Kharga E£30.

FARAFRA OASIS TO BAHARIYA OASIS

The stupefying desert formations between the Farafra and Bahariya Oases are
responsible for attracting more travellers
to this far-flung corner of Egypt than any
other sight.

WHITE DESERT

Upon first glimpse of the White Desert
(Sahra al-Beida; Map p295) dream-
scape, you'll feel like a modern Alice
fallen through the desert looking glass.
Blinding-white spires of rock sprout almost supernaturally from the ground,

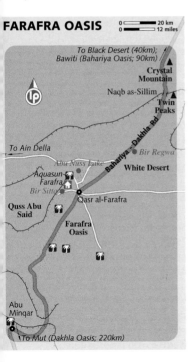

FARAFRA OASIS

0 _____ 20 km
0 _____ 12 miles

To Black Desert (40km);
Bawiti (Bahariya Oasis; 90km)

Crystal Mountain

Naqb as-Sillim

Twin Peaks

To Ain Della

Abu Nuss Lake

Bir Regwa

White Desert

Aquasun
Farafra
Bir Sitta

Qasr al-Farafra

Quss Abu Said

Farafra Oasis

Abu Minqar

To Mut (Dakhla Oasis; 220km)

Interesting rock formations, White Desert (p295)

of the mountains, which have spread layer of black powder and rubble ov the peaks and plateaus, it's a mesmeri ing landscape straight out of Hades.

GETTING THERE & AWAY

Ordinary vehicles are able to drive th first kilometre or so off the road into th White and Black Deserts, but only 4W vehicles can advance deeper into eith area. There are plenty of safari outfits th can take you around the sights; enquire the tourist office (p287) in Bawiti.

BAHARIYA OASIS

Bahariya is one of the more fetching the desert-circuit oases, and at just 365k from Cairo is also the most accessibl Surrounded on all sides by towering ridge much of the oasis floor is covered by ve dant plantations of date palms and pool marked with dozens of refreshing spring

During the Pharaonic era, the oasis was centre of agriculture, producing wine sol in the Nile Valley and as far away as Rom

BAWITI

Until recently, Bawiti was a quiet town de pendent on agriculture, but it's gainin a new lease on life as more people hea to the desert or come to see the Golde Mummies.

SIGHTS & ACTIVITIES

Since the discovery of the Golde Mummies in the 1990s, growing interes in Bahariya's ancient past has led to th opening of a new **museum** (Sharia al-Matha Bawiti; 8am-2pm). Some of the 10 mum mies on show are richly decorated an while the motifs are in some ways crud the painted faces show a move away from stylised Pharaonic mummy decoration to wards Fayoum portraiture.

each frost-coloured lollipop licked into an ever odder shape by the dry desert winds. As you get further into the 300-sq-km White Desert Protectorate, you'll notice that the surreal shapes start to take on familiar forms: chickens, ostriches, camels, hawks and other uncanny shapes abound. They are best viewed at sunrise or sunset, when the sun turns them hues of pink and orange, Salvador Dali–like, or under a full moon, which gives the land-scape a ghostly, arctic, whipped-cream appearance. See also p282.

BLACK DESERT

The change in the desert floor from beige to black, 50km south of Bawiti, signals the beginning of the Black Desert (Sahra Suda; Map p281). Formed by the erosion

BAHARIYA OASIS

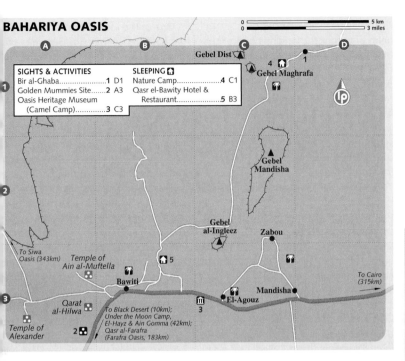

SIGHTS & ACTIVITIES		SLEEPING
Bir al-Ghaba.....................**1** D1	Nature Camp..................**4** C1
Golden Mummies Site......**2** A3	Qasr el-Bawity Hotel &
Oasis Heritage Museum	Restaurant..................**5** B3
(Camel Camp).............**3** C3	

The small mount of **Qarat Qasr Salim**, amid the houses of Bawiti northeast of the town centre, is likely to have been built upon centuries of debris. There are two well-preserved 26th-dynasty tombs here that were robbed in antiquity and reused as collective burial sites in Roman times. The rock-cut **Tomb of Zed-Amun-ef-ankh** (☽ 8.30am-4pm) is a fascinating glimpse of Bahariya in its heyday. Next to it lies the **Tomb of Bannentiu** (☽ 8.30am-pm), Zed-Amun-ef-ankh's son.

You can't miss Mahmoud Eed's **Oasis Heritage Museum** (Map p297; ☎ 3847 3666; www.camelcamp.com; Bahariya-Cairo rd; admission €5-10; ☽ no set opening times), about 2km east of the town's edge on the road to Cairo: this hilltop bastion is announced by massive clay camels gazing longingly into the street.

One of the most satisfying springs to visit is **Bir al-Ghaba** (Map p297), about 15km northeast of Bawiti. It's quite a trek to get out here, but there is nothing quite like a moonlit hot bath on the edge of the desert.

For those without their own vehicles, there are numerous **tours** on offer that will take in the sights of Bawiti and around. Your hotel will be able to recommend an operator, or you can check at the tourist office.

SLEEPING & EATING

It makes sense to sort out accommodation in Bawiti before you arrive, especially in high season due to the fray of touts that swarm each bus arrival.

Old Oasis Hotel (☎ 012 232 4425; www.oldoasissafari.com; by El-Beshmo springs; s/d/tr E£90/120/180, with air-con E£120/180/220; ▣)

Astute owner Saleh Abdallah is at the helm of this hotel, which is one of the most charming places to stay in Bawiti town. The Old Oasis Hotel sits above a pretty, shaded garden of palm and olive trees and has 13 simple but impeccable fan rooms, as well as a few fancier stone-wall air-con rooms. A large pool receives steaming hot water from the nearby spring; the run-off waters the hotel garden and its fountain.

Popular Restaurant (meals E£20; ⏰ 5.30am-10pm) Name it popular, and they will come. The irrepressible Bayoumi serves the usual selection of chicken, soup, rice and vegetable dishes, though quality seems to be slipping while prices are creeping up. There's cold beer too. Located in the town centre.

GETTING THERE & AWAY

Upper Egypt Bus Co (☎ 3847 3610; Sharia Misr; ⏰ roughly 9am-1pm & 7-11pm) runs from Bawiti to Cairo (E£30, four to five hours) at 6.30am, 10am and 3pm from the kiosk near the post office. If you're heading to Farafra (E£20, two hours) and Dakhla (E£40, four to five hours), you can hop on one of the buses headed that way from Cairo.

There are no service taxis to Siwa, so you will have to hire a private 4WD for the rough journey (permit required).

AROUND BAWITI

Gebel Dist is an impressive pyramid-shaped mountain that can be seen from most of the oasis. A local landmark, it is famous for its fossils – dinosaur bones were found here in the early 20th century, disproving the previously held theory that dinosaurs only lived in North America. In 2001 researchers from the University of Pennsylvania found the remains of another huge dinosaur, *Paralititan stromeri*.

One of the most magnificent spring we have yet seen is **Ain Gomma**, a fa distance away at 45km south of Bawiti.

SLEEPING & EATING

Under the Moon Camp (off Map p297; ☎ 0 423 6580; www.helaltravel.com; El-Hayz; huts s/d ha board E£90/180, bungalows half board E£140/24 Isolated in the small oasis hamlet of E Hayz, 45km south of Bawiti, this beautif camp features several round, stone hut (no electricity) and some new mudbric bungalows (with lights) scattered around garden compound. The lovely Ain Gomm spring (above) is nearby and there's a co spring pool right in the camp, with powe ful desert views. Helal, the Bedouin own who once trained Egyptian military uni in desert navigation, runs highly recom mended safari trips and arranges free pic ups from Bawiti.

Nature Camp (Map p297; ☎ 847 2184, 01 337 5097; naturecamps@hotmail.com; Bir al-Ghab r half board per person E£100) At the foot Gebel Dist, Nature Camp sets new stan ards for environmentally focused budg accommodation. The peaceful cluster candlelit and intricately designed thatc huts looks out onto the expansive dese beside Bir al-Ghaba. The food is very goo (meals E£25) and the owner, Ashraf Lotf is a skilled desert hand.

Qasr el-Bawity Hotel & Restaurar (Map p297; ☎ 3847 1880; www.qasrelbawi .com; s/d/ste half board from €50/80/120; ☒ ☎ The relatively new Qasr el-Bawity offe some of the swankiest accommodatio in Baharia. With a finely trained eye fc environmentally friendly design, this plac has sumptuous rooms finished in coc stonework and sporting ornate dome roofs, fine furniture and arty, frilly touche There are two pools (one natural and on chlorinated) and the restaurant here i suitably good.

SIWA OASIS

Set against a backdrop of jagged sandstone hills, backed by the rolling silica ocean of the Great Sand Sea and carpeted thick with palm groves, this is the archetypal oasis. Siwa's very isolation helped protect a unique society that until today stands apart from mainstream Egyptian culture. Originally settled by Berbers (roaming North African tribes), Siwa was till practically independent only a few hundred years ago. Even today local traditions and Siwi, the local Berber language, dominate.

The hectares of palm groves invite casual strolling, numerous comfortable and cushioned cafes are perfect for chilling and meeting fellow travellers, and dozens of clear springs practically beg for you to dip your toes.

HISTORY

The oldest monuments in the oasis, including the Temple of the Oracle, date from the 26th dynasty, when Egypt was invaded by the Assyrians. Siwa's Oracle of Amun (p301) was already famous then, and Egyptologists suspect that it dates back to the earlier 21st dynasty, when the Amun priesthood and oracles became prominent throughout Egypt. Such was the fame of Siwa's oracle that it threatened the Persians, who invaded Egypt in 525 BC and ended the 26th dynasty. One of the Western Desert's most persistent legends is of the lost army of Persian king Cambyses, which was sent to destroy the oracle and disappeared completely in the desert.

The young conqueror Alexander the Great led a small party on a perilous eight-day journey across the desert in 331 BC. It is believed that the priests of Amun, who was the supreme god of the Egyptian pantheon and later associated with the Greek god Zeus, declared him to be a son of the god.

The end of Roman rule, the collapse of the trade route and the gradual decline in the influence of oracles in general all contributed to Siwa's gentle slide into

SARA-JANE CLELAND

Idyllic Siwa Oasis vista

WESTERN DESERT

SIWA OASIS

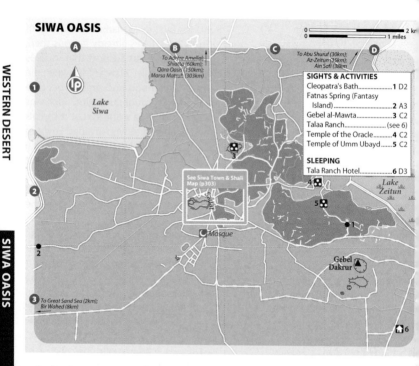

obscurity. The Siwans finally converted to Islam around the 12th century, and gradually built up wealth trading date and olive crops along the Nile Valley, and with Libyan Fezzan and the Bedouins.

The oasis is now home to just over 20,000 Siwans and nearly 2000 Egyptians.

SIGHTS & ACTIVITIES

Strolling through the palm groves or relaxing over a cup of tea as the towns-people go about their languid paces seems to be the order of the day. Occasional visits to the wonderful springs in the area offer further distractions, and bicycles are a suitably geared form of transport that can be rented nearly everywhere.

SIWA TOWN

Siwa is a pleasant little town centred on a market square, where roads lead off into the palm groves in nearly every directio Around the corner from the local cour cil offices is the small **House of Siw Museum** (Map p303; adult/student E£10/ ⏱ 9am-2.30pm Sun-Thu), which contains modest display of traditional clothin jewellery and crafts typical of the oasis.

The centre of the town is dominate by the spectacular organic shapes of th remains of the 13th-century mudbric **Fortress of Shali** (Map p303). Built fro a material known locally as *kershef* (larg chunks of salt from the lake just outsid town, mixed with rock and plastered i local clay), the labyrinth of huddled build ings was originally four or five storeys hig and housed hundreds of people. Now on a few buildings around the edges are o cupied or used for storage, including th **King Fuad mosque** (Map p303) with it old, chimney-shaped minaret.

GHURMI

efore Shali was founded in the 13th entury, Siwa's main settlement was at ghurmi, 4km east of the present town of wa. It was here that in 331 BC Alexander he Great consulted the oracle (see p299) t the 26th-dynasty **Temple of the Oracle** Map p300; adult/student E£25/15; ☯ 9am-5pm). hough treasure hunters have been at vork here and the buttressed temple was oorly restored in the 1970s, it remains an vocative site, steeped in history. About 00m further along the track stands he remains of the almost totally ruined **emple of Umm Ubayd** (Map p303).

GEBEL AL-MAWTA

, small hill at the northern end of Siwa own, **Gebel al-Mawta** (Map p300; adult/ tudent E£25/15; ☯ 9am-5pm) – whose name heans Mountain of the Dead – is honey-ombed with rock tombs, most dating ack to the 26th dynasty, Ptolemaic and oman times. The best paintings are in he **Tomb of Si Amun**, where beautifully oloured reliefs portray the dead man,

thought to be a wealthy Greek landowner or merchant, making offerings and praying to Egyptian gods.

HOT & COLD SPRINGS

Siwa has no shortage of active, bubbling springs hidden among its palm groves. Following the track that leads to the Temple of the Oracle and continuing past the Temple of Umm Ubayd, will lead you to the most famous spring, **Cleopatra's Bath** (Spring of the Sun; Map p300). The crystal-clear natural spring water gurgles up into a large stone pool, which is a popular bathing spot for locals. There's a similar but slightly more secluded pool at **Fatnas Spring** ('Fantasy Island'; Map p300), the small island in the salty Birket Siwa (Lake Siwa) accessible across a narrow causeway. This is an idyllic place to watch the sunset.

A favourite excursion among local guides is the cold freshwater lake at **Bir Wahed** (off Map p300), 15km away on the edge of the Great Sand Sea. Once over the top of a high dune, you come to a hot

PATRICK SYDER

The ruins of the Fortress of Shali (opposite)

DANIELA DIRSCHERL/WATERFRAME - UNDERWATER IMAGES/PHOTOLIBR/

Qasr al-Ghueita (below)

↘ IF YOU LIKE...

If you like the **Temple of the Oracle** (p301) you will also like some of the other
ancient monuments scattered in the desert sands:

- **Qasr al-Ghueita** (Map p291; adult/student £30/15; ☾ 8am-5pm Oct-Apr, 8am-6pm May-
  Sep) This imposing Roman mudbrick fortress has survived millennia and still
  dominates the road to Baris. Its name means 'Fortress of the Small Garden',
  as it was the centre of a fertile agricultural community. The garrison's outer
  walls enclose a 25th-dynasty sandstone temple, dedicated to Amun, Mut
  and Khons.

- **Qasr el-Labakha** (Map p281) Amid a desertscape of duney desolation is a
  micro-oasis some 40km north of Al-Kharga. Scattered among sandy swells
  and rocky shelfs are the remains of a towering four-storey Roman fortress,
  two temples, and a vast necropolis where over 500 mummies have been
  unearthed (you can still see human remains in the tombs).

- **Qila al-Dabba** (Map p292; adult/student £25/15; ☾ 8am-5pm Oct-Apr, to 6pm May to Sep)
  Located 35km east of Mut is Balat's ancient necropolis. The five mastabas
  (mudbrick structures above tombs that were the basis for later pyramids),
  the largest of which stands over 10m high, date back to the 6th dynasty.
  Four are ruined, but one has been restored and is now open to the public.
  You may need to find a guardian in the nearby buildings to get access.
  You'll need a private vehicle to get here.

- **Deir al-Haggar** (Map p292; adult/student £25/15; ☾ 8am-sunset) This restored
  Roman sandstone temple is one of the most complete Roman monuments
  in Dakhla. Dedicated to the Theban triad of Amun, Mut and Khons, as well
  as Horus, it was built between the reigns of Nero (AD 54–68) and Domitian
  (AD 81–96).

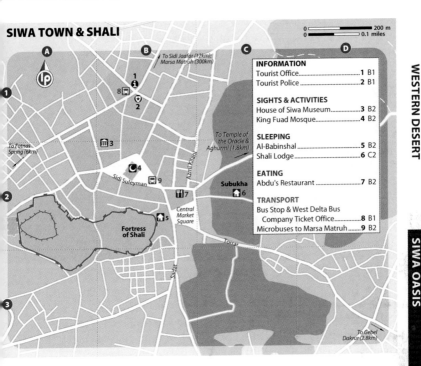

SIWA TOWN & SHALI

INFORMATION	
Tourist Office	1 B1
Tourist Police	2 B1

SIGHTS & ACTIVITIES	
House of Siwa Museum	3 B2
King Fuad Mosque	4 B2

SLEEPING	
Al-Babinshal	5 B2
Shali Lodge	6 C2

EATING	
Abdu's Restaurant	7 B2

TRANSPORT	
Bus Stop & West Delta Bus Company Ticket Office	8 B1
Microbuses to Marsa Matruh	9 B2

spring, the size of a large jacuzzi, where sulphurous water bubbles in a pool and runs off to irrigate a garden. Bir Wahed can only be reached by 4WD, so if you don't have your own, you'll need to hire a guide and car.

TOURS

The tourist office (Map p303) can be a great help in organising tours around the oasis. All desert trips require permits, which cost US$5 plus E£11 and are usually obtained by your guide from the tourist office. Prices and itineraries vary, but one of the most popular trips takes you to the desert hot spring at Bir Wahed, on the edge of the Great Sand Sea. Most trips are done by 4WD, so ensure that the vehicle is roadworthy before you set out and, as with any desert trip, that you have enough water.

Camels were recently introduced to the oasis to do desert trips. Sherif Fahmy of the **Tala Ranch** (Map p300; ☎ 010 588 6003; talaranchsiwa@hotmail.com; Gebel Dakrur) can arrange camel tours to watch the sunset from the sand dunes or a longer desert safari, though prices are a bit steep at E£350 for a day and night or E£150 per half-day.

SLEEPING

Shali Lodge (Map p303; ☎ 460 1299; info@eqi .com.eg; Sharia Subukha; s/d/tr E£260/340/420) This tiny, beautiful mudbrick hotel, owned by environmentalist Mounir Neamatallah, nestles in a lush palm grove about 100m from the main square. The large, extremely comfortable rooms have lots of curving mudbrick goodness, exposed palm beams, rock-walled bathrooms and cushioned sitting nooks.

Baskets of vegetables, Siwa Oasis

ARIADNE VAN ZANDBERGE

Adrére Amellal (off Map p300; ☎ in Cairo 02-2736 7879; www.adrereamellal.net; Sidi Jaafar, White Mountain; s/d incl all meals, drinks & desert excursions US$415/550, ste from US$750; ⚓) Backed by the dramatic White Mountain (called Adrére Amellal in Siwi), this impeccable desert retreat lies coddled in its own oasis, with stunning views over the salt lake of Birket Siwa and the dunes of the Great Sand Sea beyond. It offers the ultimate in spartan chic, as gourmet dinners are eaten under the stars or in salt-encrusted chambers. The swimming pool is an ancient stone natural spring and the rooms and suites are palatial, yet simple and beautiful.

Tala Ranch Hotel (Map p300; ☎ 010 588 6003; www.talaranch-hotel.com; s/d E£300/400) This low-key ecoresort offers a very different experience of Siwa, with six stylish and comfortable rooms on the edge of the desert. It promises generous helpings of hush and is as relaxing as things get, with the camels, the desert and the wind as the only distractions. Sherif can organise camel trips or safaris for guests, while

his wife, Siham, prepares commendable Egyptian food served in a Bedouin tent (four-course dinner E£120).

EATING

Abdu's Restaurant (Map p303; ☎ 460 1243 central market sq; dishes E£5-30; ⏰ 8.30am midnight) This is the longest-running res taurant in town and remains the bes eating option around, with a huge men of breakfast, pasta, traditional dishes, veg etable stews, couscous, roasted chicken and fantastic pizza whipped to your table by the efficient service.

GETTING THERE & AWAY

Buses depart from the bus stop opposite the tourist police station. There are three daily buses to Alexandria (E£33 to E£35 eight hours), stopping at Marsa Matruh (E£15, four hours); these leave at 7am 10am and 10pm. There's an extra daily bus leaving at 3pm in the winter and 5pm in the summer. There's a daily service jus to Marsa Matruh at 1pm. Buses to Cairo (E£60) leave only on Monday, Thursday and

Saturday, at 8pm. More frequent but less comfortable microbuses going to Marsa Matruh leave from the main square.

A new road linking the oases of Siwa and Bahariya was under construction, but funds dried up and any finishing date is now a distant mirage. There are no buses or service taxis here, but Siwan drivers are willing to make the 10-hour trip for about E£1300 per car.

GETTING AROUND

Bicycles are one of the best ways to get around and can be rented from several sources, including most hotels and a number of shops dotted around the town centre.

Donkey carts, *careta*s, are a much-used mode of transport for Siwans and can be a more amusing, if slower, way to get around than bicycles or cars.

BEYOND SIWA

GREAT SAND SEA

One of the world's largest dune fields, the Great Sand Sea straddles Egypt and Libya, stretching over 800km from its northern edge near the Mediterranean coast south to Gilf Kebir. Covering a colossal 72,000 sq km, it contains some of the largest recorded dunes in the world, including one that is 140km long. Crescent, *seif* (sword) and parallel wavy dunes are found here in abundance and have challenged desert travellers for hundreds of years. The Great Sand Sea is not a place to go wandering on a whim, and you will need military permits as well as good preparation. Guides will take you to the edges of the Great Sand Sea from Siwa and many safari outfits will take you on expeditions that skirt the area (see p310).

WESTERN DESERT

BEYOND SIWA

EGYPT IN FOCUS

ACTIVITIES

Hot-air balloons float above Luxor (p124)

MARK DAFF

Most people who visit Egypt come to see the monuments, and have hardly any time to do anything else. But, with large stretches of coast, a wide expanse of oasis-dotted desert and the enchanting Nile River, Egypt has a wealth of possibilities for things to do besides visiting tombs and temples.

BALLOONING

Hot-air ballooning in the early-morning light is a great way to see the Nile, the Theban mountains and the monuments on the West Bank of Luxor. See p124 for details.

BIRDWATCHING

Egypt is an ornithologist's delight. One of the prime birdwatching spots is Lake Qarun in the Al-Fayoum region (p154), where species include the spoonbill and the marsh sandpiper. In Aswan twitchers can go out at dawn with 'bird guide' Mohamed Arabi (p205) to spot sunbirds, hoopoes, herons and kingfishers, among other species. For more information, check out www.birdinginegypt.com.

CRUISING THE NILE

A cruise on the Nile has always ranked among the world's most exciting and most romantic travel experiences. The combination of the world's longest river, extraordinary monuments, the stunningly fertile valley, the light, the heat and the joy of slow travel all adds up to one of the highlights of any trip to Egypt.

DAHABIYYAS

By the Middle Ages, it was estimated that there were as many as 36,000 ships on the Nile. Some were simple, lateen (triangular) sailed cargo boats, called feluccas; others were called dahabiyyas, described as lavishly decorated, two-masted wooden boats with private cabins and bathrooms.

Although dahabiyyas (houseboats) are now relatively rare, there is a good choice of boats and operators. Some are privately chartered for honeymooners, extended families or groups of friends. They carry small numbers of passengers, so a dahabiyya is the most luxurious way to sail between towns and see the monuments without crowds. Most dahabiyyas also have flexible itineraries and personalised service.

See p196 for recommended dahabiyya operators sailing between Esna and Aswan.

NILE TRAVEL READS

- **Flaubert in Egypt** by Gustave Flaubert
- **A Winter on the Nile: Florence Nightingale, Gustave Flaubert and the Temptations of Egypt** by Anthony Sattin
- **A Thousand Miles Up the Nile** by Amelia B Edwards
- **The Histories** by Herodotus
- **Old Serpent Nile: A Journey to the Source** by Stanley Stewart

EGYPT IN FOCUS

ACTIVITIES

CRUISERS

A cruise remains the easiest way to see the Nile in comfort on a midrange budget and can be ideal for families with older children who want to splash in a pool between archaeological visits, or for people who want to combine sightseeing with relaxation. The downside is that monuments are almost always seen with large groups and the itineraries are generally inflexible.

Like Egyptian hotels, cruisers range from slightly shabby to sumptuous, but almost all have some sort of pool, a large rooftop area for sunbathing and watching the scenery, a restaurant, bar, air-con, TV, minibars and en-suite bathrooms.

Large cruisers stick to itineraries on the busy Luxor–Aswan stretch of the Nile. See p132 for recommended operators. For cruises on Lake Nasser, see p205.

FELUCCAS

For many travellers, the only way to travel on the Nile is slowly, on board a traditional felucca. Except for swimming, this is as close as you can get to the river, zigzagging from one bank to the other, watching the seemingly timeless activity on the land. While more intimate and less expensive than other cruising options, feluccas have limited facilities (no toilets, for instance). Still, a felucca trip can make a great family holiday, especially with older kids.

Most multiday journeys begin at Aswan and go to Kom Ombo (two days), Edfu (three days) or Esna (four days). It's easiest to make arrangements through your hotel. Alternatively, cut out the middle man and negotiate directly with boat captains in Aswan. The Aswan tourist office is also a good source of advice.

EGYPT IN FOCUS

ACTIVITIES

LEFT: JEAN-BERNARD CARILLET; RIGHT: MARK WEBSTE

Left: Camels strut the beach in Dahab (p264); Right: Stunning marine life, Ras Mohammed National Park (p257)

Of course you don't have to be on the water for days to get a feel for the Nile – ther are ample opportunities to escape on a felucca for a few hours in Cairo (p82), Luxo (p125) and Aswan (p206), and elsewhere along the river.

DESERT SAFARIS

Going on safari in the Western Desert can be one of the most rewarding experience Egypt has to offer. Included among the Western Desert's more challenging routes are the Great Sand Sea (p305) and remote Gilf Kebir (in Egypt's southwest corner), where you'll find the Cave of the Swimmers – made famous by *The English Patient*. Here also is Gebel Uweinat, a 2000m-high peak trisected by the Egyptian, Libyan and Sudanese borders. These expeditions require extensive organisation, quality equipment and plenty of experience to properly execute.

The following safari operators have solid international reputations, are among the more reliable in Egypt and will treat the desert with the respect it deserves. **Hisham Nessim** (☎ 012 780 7999; www.raid4x4egypt.com) is a rally driver and owner of the Aquasun hotels in Farafra and Sinai; he has the full equipment. **Peter Gaballa** (www.egyptoffroa .com) organises expert self-drive trips or trips with a driver to all parts of the Western Desert. **Zarzora Expedition** (☎ 02-761 8105; www.zarzora.com) is captained by Ahmed Al Mestekawi, a retired colonel who used to conduct military desert patrols.

Sinai safaris are easier to arrange, from either Dahab or Nuweiba.

A growing number of travellers are choosing to combine an Eastern Desert safar (p278) with a diving holiday on the Red Sea coast.

DIVING & SNORKELLING

Many visitors to Egypt rarely have their heads above water. No wonder, as some of the bes diving in the world is to be found along the Sinai Peninsula and Red Sea coast. In 198 panel of scientists and conservationists chose the northern portion of this 1800km-long body of water as one of the Seven Underwater Wonders of the World. Here divers will find coral mountains, shallow reefs swarming with brightly coloured fish, sheer drop-offs disappearing into unplumbed depths and coral-encrusted shipwrecks, all bathed in an ethereal blue hue. One of the jewels is Ras Mohammed National Park in Sinai, home to the 'Holy Trinity' of Shark Reef, Eel Garden and Yolanda Bay.

The strongest appeal of the Red Sea is that you can tailor your diving holiday to your own travelling style. Independent travellers spend more time than they planned in the backpacker-friendly village of Dahab, and to a lesser extent Nuweiba, while package tourists enjoy the creature comforts in the resort towns of Sharm el-Sheikh, Hurghada and El-Gouna. If you want to maximise your underwater time, there's no better option than a week on a dive safari. Many of the hotels in the region also run diving tours and rent out equipment.

It isn't necessary to dive to enjoy the marine life of the Red Sea. You can see plenty with just a snorkel, mask and flippers. Along the Sinai coast the reefs are only 15m out, and in some places you don't need to go out of your depth to be among shoals of brightly coloured fish. In most places on the Red Sea coast you need to take a boat out to snorkel.

Diving tours in Alexandria (p234) are a less colourful option, but they allow you to see the sunken ancient monuments in the Eastern Harbour.

THE BEST

JOHN ELK III

Sunset in the White Desert (p282)

NATURE SPOTS

- **Lake Qarun** (p156)
- **Siwa Oasis** (p299)
- **St Katherine Protectorate** (p246)
- **Wadi Rayyan Protected Area** (p158)
- **White Desert** (p282)

FISHING

Angling is seen more as a means of living than a leisure pastime in Egypt, but sport fishing does occur on Lake Nasser, where **African Angler** (☎ 097 231 0907; www.african angler.net) can take you on 'big game' fishing safaris for Nile perch and other fish. There is also an annual International Fishing Tournament every February in Hurghada; for more details check with the **Egyptian Angling Federation** (www.egaf.org).

HORSE RIDING

Horse riding is possible in Cairo around the Pyramids, but avoid the touts hanging around and head straight for the stables in Nazlet as-Samaan (p79), the village near the Sphinx. In Luxor there are stables on the West Bank just up from the local ferry landing; the best one being Nobi's (p124), which provides the best horses, insurance and riding hats. There are also stables at the Sinai resorts of Sharm el-Sheikh, Dahab and Nuweiba that rent out steeds to tourists by the hour.

CULTURE

LEE FOST

Locals relax on the banks of the Nile, Esna (p195)

To the Arab world, Cairo is Mother of the World, particularly when it comes to film, TV, music and theatre. While little of this culture has had any impact on the West, a great many Egyptian actors and singers are superstars and revered cultural icons to Arabic speakers around the world.

ART

Since the 1990s many young artists who lived and studied abroad have come bac to Egypt with some remarkable work that is now internationally acclaimed. Cairo' **Townhouse Gallery of Contemporary Art** (Map pp66-7; ☎ 2576 8086; www.thetownhous gallery.com; 10 Sharia Nabrawy, Downtown) has led the way in promoting contemporary art, and many other galleries now show contemporary work from the best Egyptian artists.

CINEMA

In the halcyon years of the 1940s and '50s, Cairo's film studios turned out more tha 100 movies annually, filling cinemas throughout the Arab world. These days, restrictiv censorship has meant that many Egyptian films are of a lesser quality. One directo bucking this trend is Yousef Chahine (1926–2008), Egypt's Fellini who was honoure at Cannes in 1997 with a lifetime achievement award.

LITERATURE

Nobel Prize–winner Naguib Mahfouz's (1911–2006) masterpiece *The Cairo Trilogy* is a sag of family life, rich in colour and detail, that has him compared to Dickens and Zola.

RECOMMENDED LISTENING

- **Layli Nahari by Amr Diab** The most catchy album by Egypt's heart-throb.
- **Inta Omri by Umm Kolthum** An absolute classic; also try *Alf Layla wa-Layla* and *Al-Atlal.*
- **Al-Darb fil Iraq by Shaaban Abdel Rahim** *Shaabi*est of *shaabi* singers.
- **Taam al-Beyout by Mohammed Mounir** The thinking-person's pop star, a Nubian who fuses traditional Arabic music with jazz.
- **Zakhma by Ahmed Adawiyya** The title means 'crowded'.

The Map of Love, by Ahdaf Soueif, an Egyptian writer living in London, was short-listed for he prestigious Booker prize. The blockbuster *The Yacoubian Building,* by Alaa al-Aswany, is bleak and utterly compelling snapshot of contemporary Cairo and Egypt seen through he stories of the occupants of a Downtown building.

MUSIC

he 1940s and '50s were the golden days of Arab classical music, when a rushing tide of ationalism made Cairo the virile heart of the Arab-speaking world. Umm Kolthum (see 69) was the most famous Arab singer of the 20th century. Her protracted love songs and *asa'id* (long poems) were the very expression of the Arab world's collective identity.

In the 1970s Ahmed Adawiyya set the blueprint for a new kind of music known as *l-jeel* (the generation), or Egyptian pop. Head of the pack in this genre today is Amr iab, often described as the Arab world's Ricky Martin. Adawiyya's legacy also spawned *haabi* music (the word for popular), much cruder than *al-jeel,* with often satirical or olitically provocative lyrics.

BELLY DANCING

omb paintings show that Egyptian romen were already dancing in Pharaonic mes. This continued in medieval times rhen *ghawazee* dancers travelled and erformed with storytellers and poets. ineteenth-century European travellers, uch as French author Gustave Flaubert, rere lured by these exotic dancers, who red their erotic fantasies.

Belly dancing was imbued with glam-ur with the advent of Egyptian cinema, nd a handful of dancers – such as Samia amal and Tahia Carioca – became su-erstars. Many high-profile local dancers ave now donned the veil and stopped ancing, leaving the scene to foreign belly ancers.

THE BEST

EDDIE GERALD

Cairo Opera House entrance (p88)

PLACES FOR CULTURE

- **Cairo Opera House** (p88)
- **Bibliotheca Alexandrina** (p234)
- **Alexandria Opera House** (p236)
- **El Sawy Culture Wheel, Cairo** (p89)
- **Makan, Cairo** (p89)

↘ FAMILY TRAVEL

PHILIP & KAREN SMI

Kids scaling a sand dune in Sharm el-Sheikh (p258)

Egypt is a very child-friendly country, particularly in the big tourist destinations such as Luxor and Sharm el-Sheikh, and having kids in tow is a great icebreaker with locals. There's a lot to keep the under-aged contingent happy – pyramids and tombs can be explored by junior archaeologists, felucca rides please aspiring pirates and beach outings are always popular.

EATING WITH KIDS

Egyptians often eat out as a family group and you'll see children dining with their parents in restaurants until the early hours. Waiters are uniformly accepting of children anwill go out of their way for them. Egypt's cuisine is very child friendly, being simple yevaried: kebabs (particularly *shish tawouq*) are perennial favourites and roast chicken iusually a safe bet. And of course the snack foods tend to go down a treat, particularl*fiteer*, *kushari* and *ta'amiyya*. Plenty of fresh juices and soft drinks are always availablto quench the thirst, too.

Some restaurants have high chairs, but they're in the minority. Kids menus are usuallonly seen at Western-style hotel restaurants.

FACILITIES & HEALTH

One has to be aware that there is little child-safety awareness in Egypt. Seat belts ansafety seats are rarely seen in the back seats of cars and taxis; if you're renting a caremember to specify that you want them. Also, don't expect felucca or other boa perators to have children's life jackets. If you don't want to travel without them, bring our own.

Another potential worry is the high incidence of diarrhoea and stomach problems hat hit travellers in Egypt. If children get sick, they tend to dehydrate more quickly han adults and, given the country's dry climate, it is crucial to keep giving them liquids, ven if they just throw them up again. It's worth having rehydration salts on hand, which are available at all pharmacies (ask or Rehydran) and usually cost less than a lollar for a box of six sachets. These can prevent a bad case of the runs from turning into something more serious.

Formula is readily available in pharmacies, and supermarkets stock disposable nappies. Babysitting facilities are usually available in top-end hotels.

THINGS TO SEE & DO

Bookshops at most five-star hotels in the major tourist centres stock a wide variety of Egyptology-related children's books hat will help kids relate to what they're seeing. Locally produced history books, such as Salima Ikram's *The Pharaohs,* are excellent and reasonably priced.

> ## ⬎ THE NITTY GRITTY
>
> - **Change facilities** Hardly anywhere apart from a few five-star hotels.
> - **Cots** Available in some midrange and in most five-star hotels.
> - **Health** Watch out for dehydration, bring sunblock and protect from sun.
> - **High chairs** Only in five-star hotels.
> - **Nappies** Widely available.
> - **Strollers** Bring your own fold-up stroller
> - **Transport** No life jackets on boats, no seat belts in taxis.

Children are usually fascinated visiting tombs and temples because the wall decorations are very visual, like ancient cartoons. They love drawing sculptures in a museum, or wrapping up like a mummy with toilet paper, all easy ways to relate to what they ee on the way.

Apart from antiquities, there are the ever-popular camel or donkey rides. And horse iding can be great fun – Nobi's stables on Luxor's West Bank (p124) and around the Pyramids in Cairo (p79) have plenty of horses docile enough for young people, and hard hats in all sizes.

It pays to stay in a hotel with a swimming pool, so kids can swim during the heat of the day.

FOOD & DRINK

An egyptian banquet including felafel, bread and dips

CHRISTINE OSBOR

Egypt's culinary heritage may not be as sophisticated as the rich cuisines of countries like Lebanon, Turkey or Morocco, but the food is good, fresh and honest peasant fare that packs an occasional – and sensational – knockout punch. Whether you're a hard-core carnivore or a devoted vegetarian, you'll never fail to find cheap and hearty fare in Egypt.

FOOD
MEZZE
Mezze (starters), always bursting with colour and flavour, are the perfect start to a mea and more often than not they are a meal in themselves. Simplicity is the key to Egyptia mezze, which consist of pulses and crunchy fresh ingredients (including herbs), ofte tossed in oil and lemon juice. Mezze are eaten with *'aish* (bread), which locals use i lieu of cutlery to scoop up dips and salads.

The most common mezze are *baba ghanoug* (smoked aubergine dip), *hummu* (creamy lemony chickpea dip), *tahina* (sesame paste), *besara* (broad-bean puree), *salat baladi* (oriental salad of chopped tomatoes, cucumber, onion and pepper), *tabboule* (bulgur wheat, parsley, garlic and tomato with lemon), *kibbeh* (fried patty of mince lamb, bulgur wheat and pine seeds) and *wara einab* (stuffed vine leaves).

SOUPS
Hearty soups are also big on the menu and often eaten as a main course. Favourite are *shorba ads* (lentil soup served with wedges of lemon) and *fuul nabbed* (broad-bea

oup). Typically Egyptian is *molokhiyya*: a green leafy vegetable, known in the West as mallow, made into a tasty soup with a glutinous texture and earthy flavour, and served with roast chicken or rabbit. It inspires an almost religious devotion among locals.

MEATS

Kofta (skewers of grilled spicy minced lamb) and *kebab* (grilled skewers of chunks of lamb; the chicken equivalent is called *shish tawouq*) are two of the most popular dishes in Egypt. Two other favourites are cooked in earthenware pots: *daoud basha,* meatballs cooked with pine nuts and tomato sauce; and *fatta*, layers of rice, crispy pita and chunks of lamb topped with a garlicky-vinegary tomato sauce, so rich you might have to retire after eating.

Firekh (chicken) roasted on a spit is a commonly spotted dish, and in restaurants is typically ordered by the half. *Hamam* (pigeon) is also extremely popular, and is best served as *tagen* with onions and tomatoes and stuffed with cracked wheat.

SEAFOOD

In Alexandria, along the Red Sea and in Sinai, you'll undoubtedly join the locals in falling for the marvellous array of fresh seafood on offer. Local favourites are *kalamaari* (squid); *balti* (fish about 15cm long, flattish and grey with a light belly); and the larger, tastier *bouri* (mullet). You'll also commonly find sea bass, bluefish, sole, *subeit* or *gambari* (shrimp) on restaurant menus. The most popular ways to cook fish are to bake them with salt, grill them over coals or fry them in olive oil.

STREET FOOD

The national stars of Egyptian street food are *fuul* and *ta'amiyya,* both things of joy when eaten fresh, particularly at breakfast or as a sandwich. *Fuul,* an unassuming

LEFT: RICHARD I'ANSON; RIGHT: PHIL WEYMOUTH

Left: Spices for sale; Right: A tricky bread delivery through the streets of Cairo

peasant dish of slow-cooked fava beans made with garlic and garnished with parsley, olive oil, lemon and cumin, is the national dish. *Ta'amiyya* (better known outside Cario as felafel) is mashed broad beans, green herbs and spices rolled into balls and deep fried. Almost as popular is *shwarma*, strips of compressed lamb or chicken, sliced from a vertical spit, and served with garnish in pita bread.

Kushari is also common. It's a delicious and filling mix of noodles, rice, lentils and fried onions, served with a spicy tomato sauce, and some garlicky vinegar on the side. The local variation of the pizza is *fit-eer,* which has a thin, flaky pastry base. Try it topped with salty haloumi cheese, or even with a mixture of sugar-dusted fruit.

THE BEST

VERONICA GARBE

Nile perch with rice and salad

EGYPTIAN RESTAURANTS

- **Sofra** (p129)
- **Salah ad-Din** (p208)
- **Khan el-Khalili Restaurant & Mahfouz Coffee Shop** (p86)
- **Citadel View** (p86)
- **Abou El Sid** (p86)

DESSERTS & SWEETS

The prince of local puds is undoubtedly *omm ali,* layers of crunchy bread soaked i cream and milk, topped with nuts and raisins, and baked in the oven. *Muhalabiyya,* delicious concoction of rice flour, milk, sugar and rose water topped with pistachios an almonds, is as popular as *ruz bi laban* (rice pudding). But more often than not desse is a plate of seasonal fresh fruit, a refreshing finale to any meal.

Best of all are the pastries, particularly *kunafa,* an angel-hair pastry stuffed with wicl edly rich clotted cream *(eishta),* or nuts; and baklava (filo pastry stuffed with hone and nuts).

DRINKS

HOT DRINKS

Shai (tea) usually comes as a teabag in a cup, with sugar on the side, sometimes serve with mint *(bi-na'na),* or with milk *(b'laban).*

Arabic coffee *(ahwa;* the word is also used for coffeehouse) is a thick, strong, Turkisl style brew served in small cups. *Ahwa mazboot* comes with a moderate amount of suga if you don't want any sugar ask for *ahwa saada.* These days, European-style cafes se espresso, cappuccino or instant coffee (always called *neskaf).*

Also popular are herbal teas such as *karkadai* (a brew of hibiscus leaves drunk hot o cold), *yansoon* (aniseed), *hilba* (fenugreek), in winter *sahlab* (a warming drink made wit iris root powder, milk and chopped nuts) and in summer fresh *limoon* (lime juice).

ALCOHOLIC DRINKS

Most Muslims don't drink alcohol, but it is widely available in hotels and touristy area 'Stella' beer, brewed in Cairo for more than 100 years, is a yeasty and highly drinkabl

VEGETARIANS & VEGANS

Though it's quite usual for people in the Middle East to eat meals with plenty of vegetables, the concept of vegetarianism is quite foreign; but it's not difficult to order vegetable-based dishes. You'll find that you can eat loads of mezze and salads, *fuul, kushari, ta'amiyya,* the occasional omelette or oven-baked vegetable *tagens* with okra and eggplant. If your diet enables you to eat fish, note that fresh seafood is nearly always available in tourist towns and along the coasts.

The main cause of inadvertent meat eating in Egypt is meat stock, often used to make otherwise vegetarian *tagens* and soups.

ger, although the taste can vary enormously by batch. There's also the more upmarket tella Meister (a light lager) and Stella Premium, but most locals just stick to the unfussy asic brew, or its worthy 'competitor' Saqqara.

There's a growing viticulture industry around Alexandria, with Grand de Marquise by ar the best of a lacklustre bunch. They produce an antipodean-style red and a chablis-tyle white. Obelisk has a quaffable cabernet sauvignon, a Pinot blanc and a dodgy rosé. he country's oldest winery, Gianaclis, produces three decidedly headache-inducing pples: red Omar Khayyam, rosé Rubis D'Egypte and dry white Cru des Ptolémées.

VATER & JUICES

n Egyptian proverb says that if you drink water from the Nile you will always come ack to Egypt, but it's best not to try. Don't even *think* of drinking from the tap in Egypt – he dreaded 'Pharaoh's revenge' is enough to ruin any traveller's day. Cheap bottled vater is readily available in even the smallest towns.

Juice stands are recognisable by the hanging bags of netted fruit (and carrots) that dorn their facades and are an absolute godsend. Standard juices *(asiir)* include *moz* banana), *guafa* (guava), *limoon* (lemon), *manga* (mango), *bortuaan* (orange), *gazar* carrot), *rumman* (pomegranate), *farawla* (strawberry) and *asab* (sugar cane). Make ure to choose a clean venue.

HISTORY

Mist over the Nile at Luxor

IZZET KERIB

Egypt's history is as rich as the land, as varied as the landscape, as lively as the character of its people. And it is as long as the Nile. While much of Europe was still wrapped in animal skins and wielding clubs, Egyptians enjoyed a sophisticated life, dedicated to maintaining order in the universe and to making the most of their one great commodity, the Nile.

THE OLD KINGDOM

Narmer, the king credited with uniting the north (Lower) and south (Upper) of Egypt, is believed to have lived around 3100 BC, at the beginning of what is known as the 1st dynasty, although most of what is known about him comes from a single object – the Narmer Palette in the Egyptian Museum.

More certain is the existence of a pharaoh named Zoser (Djoser), who reigned 2667–2648 BC. The second king of the 3rd dynasty, Zoser was buried in the world's oldest monumental stone building, the Step Pyramid in Saqqara.

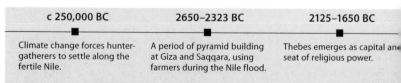

c 250,000 BC	2650–2323 BC	2125–1650 BC
Climate change forces hunter-gatherers to settle along the fertile Nile.	A period of pyramid building at Giza and Saqqara, using farmers during the Nile flood.	Thebes emerges as capital and seat of religious power.

From this time, Egyptian society quickly evolved to such a degree that each pharaoh expected to be buried in a pyramid and there was sufficient manpower, organisation and wealth to provide one. Within a century of Zoser's reign and his architect Imhotep's great achievement in Saqqara, Pharaoh Khufu (Cheops) was being buried in the largest pyramid of them all, the Great Pyramid at Giza.

THE NEW KINGDOM

A thousand years after Cheops was laid to rest in his pyramid, Ahmose, a prince of Thebes (Luxor), defeated the Hyksos, a western Asian tribe that had invaded the Nile Valley. The New Kingdom Ahmose created, with its power base in Luxor, was to be one of the most glorious in Egyptian history. Under Queen Hatshepsut (1473–1458 BC), Egyptians travelled south to the 'Land of Punt', perhaps modern-day Somalia or Yemen. Hatshepsut's stepson and successor, Tuthmosis III (1479–1425 BC), was a warrior-king in the Napoleonic mould and expanded the Egyptian empire into Syria.

The New Kingdom reached its peak soon after Tuthmosis' death. So too did the power of the priests of Thebes. In an attempt to break the priestly grip on their court, in the 1340s BC Pharaoh Amenhotep IV and his wife Nefertiti created a new sun-worshipping religion and a new capital at Tell al-Amarna. Their son, or son-in-law, Tutankhamun, died young but lived long enough to return the capital to Thebes and be buried in the Valley of the Kings by a grateful priesthood.

The late flowering of this glorious epoch occurred under Pharaoh Seti I (1294–1279 BC), who built the temple at Abydos, and his son Ramses II (1279–1213 BC). Ramses lived long enough to complete a number of important works, including the temple at Abu Simbel, to fight the Hittites at Kadesh (in modern-day Syria) and father scores of children.

> ### THE PHARAOH'S CURSE
>
> In November 1922, archaeologist Howard Carter discovered a tomb doorway with seals intact in Luxor's Valley of the Kings. Some days later when his benefactor, Lord Carnarvon, arrived, he broke into the Tomb of Tutankhamun. The mass of treasure found inside was bound to excite international interest, especially at a time of economic boom and of fledgling mass communication. Lord Carnarvon's death soon after – and the untimely deaths of several other people connected with the discovery – led many to speculate that the pharaoh had placed a curse on all who disturbed his rest. Coincidence? Who can tell…

1650–1550 BC	1550–1186 BC	1352–1336 BC
■	■	■
The Hyksos from western Asia bring great technological and social innovations.	The empire expands into Syria and down the Red Sea during the New Kingdom.	Akhenaten's short-lived experiment with monotheism ends when Tutankhamun returns the capital to Thebes.

A visitor at the Mosque of Ibn Tulun, Islamic Cairo (p77)

IZZET KERI

ALEXANDER & HIS SUCCESSORS

Egyptians had become used to foreign rule long before Alexander the Great and h
army arrived on the Nile in 331 BC. The Libyans had invaded in the 10th century BC, th
Assyrians had sacked Thebes in 663 BC and the Persian king Cambyses had conquere
the country in 525 BC. But Alexander was different. In a hurry to conquer Persia an
the East, he stayed a short time in Egypt, but long enough to found the new capital c
Alexandria, be crowned pharaoh in Memphis and ride to Siwa to consult the Oracl
of Amun.

On Alexander's death in 323 BC, his general Ptolemy I seized power and created a
independent kingdom in Egypt and a dynasty that lasted less than 300 years. The la:
of the Ptolemaic rulers, a queen called Cleopatra VII (51–30 BC), fell, with her lover Mar
Antony, in the face of overwhelming force from Rome.

CHRISTIAN EGYPT

According to Coptic tradition, Christianity arrived in Egypt in AD 45 when St Mar
converted an Alexandrian cobbler called Ananias. The early days of the religion wer
full of persecution. St Mark was executed for speaking out against the worship of th
city's pagan god Serapis, and so many Christians died during the first centuries, pa
ticularly under Emperor Diocletian, that the Coptic Church calendar is called the Era c

1184–1153 BC	945–715 BC	663 BC
Ramses III defeated external threats and internal dissent, but the empire ends with his death.	Libyan settlers take power in the Delta, while the Egyptian Nile is divided among a series of princes.	Ashurbanipal, King of the Assyrians, attacks Egypt, sacks Thebes and loots the Temple of Amun.

Martyrs. The change came in 313, when the emperor Constantine converted to Christianity. In 324, Christianity was made the imperial religion.

Egypt's Christians played a decisive role in the evolution of the young religion, with Copts insisting on the oneness of Father and Son, an idea enshrined in what became known as the Nicene Creed. Copts also argued against allowing pagans to continue worshipping their own gods and, in 391, Emperor Theodosius issued an edict that banned people from visiting pagan temples or even from looking at pagan statues. But at the Council of Chalcedon in 451, Egyptians refused to accept that Jesus had one person but two natures, which seemed to them a revival of polytheism. As a result, the Egyptians split with the rest of Christianity, their patriarch was excommunicated and their principal city, Alexandria, was sacked.

❯ IBN TULUN

Of the many short-lived dynasties to rule Egypt after the Arab invasion, few were as brief or glorious as that of Ahmed ibn Tulun. In the 9th century, Egypt was ruled from Baghdad. Turkish general Ibn Tulun was appointed governor of Egypt in 868 and set about building a capital worthy of his master, and himself. Little of that city remains now beyond the Mosque of Ibn Tulun (p77), but you can gauge how magnificent it might have been from the mosque's scale, artistry and symmetry.

THE COMING OF THE ARABS

In 629, a messenger travelled to the emperor in Byzantium (now Istanbul) from Arabia. He had been sent by a man named Mohammed to reveal a new religion, Islam. The messenger was murdered on the way. Ten years later, Arab armies invaded Egypt.

Under their brilliant general Amr ibn al-As, the Arabs swept through a badly defended and ill-prepared Egypt, and defeated the Byzantine army near Babylon. Alexandria opened its gates without a fight.

Amr didn't force Egyptians to convert to the new religion: he encouraged them to do so. Nor did he destroy the capital of Alexandria. Instead, he built a new one near the site of the Roman fort at Babylon, at a place called Fustat. Over the next 300 years, waves of Arabs, Kurds and Iraqis washed through the new capital, each adding their own mark – and district. In 969, the Fatimid caliphs arrived from Tunis and built a palace-city that included the university-mosque of Al-Azhar and was called Al-Qahira (Cairo), 'the Victorious'.

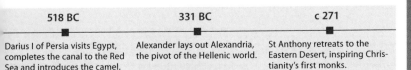

518 BC	331 BC	c 271
Darius I of Persia visits Egypt, completes the canal to the Red Sea and introduces the camel.	Alexander lays out Alexandria, the pivot of the Hellenic world.	St Anthony retreats to the Eastern Desert, inspiring Christianity's first monks.

LEFT: JOHN ELK III; RIGHT: SARA-JANE CLELA

Left: Statue of Mohammed Ali, Alexandria; Right: Iron grille in the Mosque of Mohammed Ali, Islamic Cairo (p76)

THE MAMLUKS

Most rulers of this new city relied on friends and relatives to provide security. One o
the last rulers of the Ayyubid dynasty created by Saladin (Salah ad-Din), a man name
Sultan as-Salih, was so despised that he bought slaves from the land between the Ura
and the Caspian to guarantee his protection. These men were formed into a permaner
Turkic slave-soldier class, which came to rule Egypt.

These Mamluks – their name means 'owned' or 'slave' – owed allegiance to the
original owner, the emir. New purchases maintained the groups. Forbidden to bequeat
their wealth, Mamluks spent huge amounts on building exquisite mosques, school
and tombs. During their 267-year reign (1250–1517), the city was the intellectual an
cultural centre of the Islamic world.

NAPOLEON IN EGYPT

When Napoleon and his musket-armed forces blew apart the scimitar-wielding Mamlu
cavalry at the Battle of the Pyramids in 1798, he dragged Egypt into the age of geo
politics. Napoleon wanted both to revive Egypt's glory and to strike at British interest
in the region, particularly the land route to India.

During Napoleon's time in Egypt, he established a French-style government, re
vamped the tax system, introduced Africa's first printing press, implemented pub

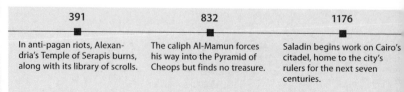

391	832	1176
In anti-pagan riots, Alexandria's Temple of Serapis burns, along with its library of scrolls.	The caliph Al-Mamun forces his way into the Pyramid of Cheops but finds no treasure.	Saladin begins work on Cairo's citadel, home to the city's rulers for the next seven centuries.

c works projects, and introduced new rops and a new system of weights and easures. His army of scholars and artts studied Egypt's monuments, crafts, rts, flora and fauna, as well as its society nd people, and stimulated the study of gyptian antiquities.

However, relations between the occuied and occupier deteriorated rapidly nd there were regular uprisings against ne French in Cairo. When the British anded an army at Aboukir in 1801, the rench agreed to an armistice and eparted.

HE ALBANIAN MERCENARY

he power vacuum left by the French was oon exploited by an Albanian lieutenant n the Ottoman army, Mohammed Ali, ho became governor of Egypt within ve years of the French evacuation.

> ### THE ROSETTA STONE
>
> Now the most viewed exhibit at London's British Museum, the Rosetta Stone was unearthed in 1799 by a French soldier at Fort St Julien near Rosetta. The lower half of a granitic stele, the stone contains a trilingual decree issued by the priests of Memphis on 27 March 196 BC, the anniversary of the coronation of Ptolemy V (205–180 BC), honouring the 13-year-old pharaoh with his own cult in return for tax exemptions and other perks. It provided Frenchman Jean François Champollion with the key he needed to decipher hieroglyphs. Champollion published his important work in 1822.

Mohammed Ali's long reign (he died in 1848) is pivotal in the history of the ountry. He modernised the army, built a navy, built roads, cut a new canal linking lexandria with the Nile, introduced public education, improved irrigation, built a arrage across the Nile and began planting Egypt's fields with the valuable cash rop, cotton. His heirs continued the work, which culminated in Ali's grandson, hedive (Viceroy) Ismail, opening the Suez Canal in 1869 to great fanfare and an udience that included European royalty, such as the Empress Eugenie of France.

But Ismail had taken on too much debt, made himself dependent on Europeans, nd eventually was pressured to abdicate. Foreign involvement in Egyptian afairs created great resentment and led a group of Egyptian army officers to move gainst the new khedive. In 1882, under the pretext of restoring order, the British ombarded Alexandria, and defeated a nationalist Egyptian army.

HE VEILED PROTECTORATE

he British were primarily concerned with the Suez Canal and the passage to their ndian empire and were happy for the heirs of Mohammed Ali to remain on the throne,

1250	1468	1517
■	■	■
Mamluk slave warriors grace the capital with some of its most impressive and beautiful monuments.	Sultan Qaitbey's reign brings stability and wealth to the country.	Turkish sultan Selim I executes the last Mamluk sultan and makes Egypt a Turkish province.

THE BEST

ARIADNE VAN ZANDBERGEN

Relief featuring Tuthmosis III, Luxor Museum (p114)

MUSEUMS

- **Egyptian Museum, Cairo** (p65)
- **Luxor Museum** (p114)
- **Coptic Museum, Cairo** (p71)
- **Alexandria National Museum** (p229)
- **Bawiti Museum, Western Desert** (p296)

although real power was in the hands the British Agent, Sir Evelyn Baring. Egyp became known as the 'veiled protecto ate', colonisation by another name.

Egyptian desire for self-determinatic led to riots in 1919. It also found its voic in Saad Zaghloul, the most brilliant of a emerging breed of young Egyptian polit cians, who said of the British, 'I have n quarrel with them personally but I war to see an independent Egypt'. The Britis allowed the formation of a nationalist p litical party, called the Wafd (Delegation and granted Egypt its sovereignty. Britis 'advisors' remained and their troop num bers grew dramatically during WW when Rommel threatened to overru Alexandria. But the Germans did not brea through and the British maintained a mil tary and political presence in Egypt afte the end of the war.

INDEPENDENT EGYPT

After years of demonstrations, strikes and riots against foreign rule, an Anglo-Egyptia showdown over a police station in the Suez Canal zone provided the spark that ignite the capital. On 26 January 1952, known as Black Saturday, foreign-owned shops an businesses were torched by mobs.

Although the smoke cleared, the sense of agitation remained against the British an also against the Egyptian monarchy, which was seen as too weak to resist this outsid intervention. A faction within the Egyptian officer corps, known as the Free Officer planned a coup. On 26 July 1952, King Farouk, descendant of the Albanian Mohamme Ali, departed from Alexandria harbour on the royal yacht, leaving Egypt to be ruled b Egyptians for the first time since the pharaohs.

The leader of the Free Officers, Colonel Gamal Abdel Nasser, was elected presiden in the 1956 elections. Wanting to return some of Egypt's wealth to its much-exploite peasantry, he dispossessed the country's landowners and moved against the hug foreign community, many of whom sold up and shipped out. On 26 July that yea Nasser nationalised the Suez Canal to finance the building of a great dam that woul

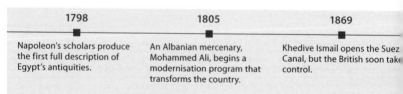

1798	1805	1869
Napoleon's scholars produce the first full description of Egypt's antiquities.	An Albanian mercenary, Mohammed Ali, begins a modernisation program that transforms the country.	Khedive Ismail opens the Suez Canal, but the British soon take control.

control the flooding of the Nile and boost Egyptian agriculture. The British, French and Israelis responded by sending troops to retake the canal, but they were forced to retreat after the UN and US applied pressure. Nasser emerged from the conflict a hero of the developing world.

NEIGHBOURS & FRIENDS

Relations with Israel had been hostile ever since Israel's founding in 1948. Egyptian soldiers had fought alongside Palestinians against the newly proclaimed Jewish state and ended up on the losing side.

Simmering anger between the neighbours flared up in 1967. Israel struck first, in June 1967, and when the shooting stopped six days later, Israel controlled all of the Sinai Peninsula and had closed the Suez Canal (which didn't reopen for another eight years). A humiliated Nasser offered to resign, but the Egyptian people wouldn't accept this move and he remained in office until his death from a heart attack in 1970.

While Nasser had looked to the Soviet Union for inspiration, Anwar Sadat, another of the Free Officers and Egypt's next president, looked to the US. Sadat believed that to deal with Israel, he needed bargaining power. On 6 October 1973, the Jewish holiday of Yom Kippur, he launched a surprise attack across the Suez Canal. Egypt's army crossed

JANE SWEENEY

The blue straight line of the Suez Canal (p254)

1902	1922	1952
Inauguration of the Aswan Dam, Asyut Barrage, and the Egyptian Museum on Cairo's Midan Tahrir.	Britain grants Egypt independence, but maintains a large military presence on the Suez Canal.	Nasser and his fellow Free Officers overthrow King Farouk and establish the Republic of Egypt.

PHIL WEYMOU

Tea, *sheesha* and the daily news, part of modern life in a Cairo cafe

the supposedly impregnable Israeli line of fortifications. Although these initial gains were later reversed, Egyptian pride was restored and Sadat's negotiating strategy had succeeded. In 1978, he and the Israeli premier signed the Camp David Agreement, in which Israel agreed to withdraw from Sinai in return for Egyptian recognition of Israel's right to exist.

The consequences were far reaching. The Arab world accused Sadat of betrayal for talking to Israel, and on 6 October 1981 at a parade commemorating the 1973 war, Sadat was assassinated by one of his soldiers, a member of an Islamist group.

MUBARAK & THE RISE OF THE ISLAMIST MOVEMENT

Sadat's successor, Hosni Mubarak, another of the Free Officers and former vice president, is less flamboyant than Sadat and less charismatic than Nasser. Mubarak's achievement has been to balance relations abroad and at home. While he rehabilitated Egypt in the eyes of the Arab world without abandoning the treaty with Israel, he also managed to keep the lid on the Islamist extremists at home. In the early 1990s the lid blew off.

Whatever caused the development of Islamist groups such as the Muslim Brotherhood – social and economic problems or religious fanaticism – the result included a campaign of violence against foreign tourists. The violence peaked in 1997 with a fire-bomb attack on a tour bus outside the Egyptian Museum in Cairo, and the massacre of holidaymakers

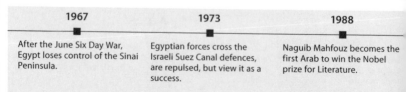

1967	1973	1988
After the June Six Day War, Egypt loses control of the Sinai Peninsula.	Egyptian forces cross the Israeli Suez Canal defences, are repulsed, but view it as a success.	Naguib Mahfouz becomes the first Arab to win the Nobel prize for Literature.

the Temple of Hatshepsut in Luxor. The brutality – and its success at deterring foreign visitors, a valuable source of income – destroyed grassroots support for militants. The Muslim Brotherhood declared a ceasefire the following year.

In 2005 President Mubarak bowed to growing international pressure to hold a proper presidential election. With the Muslim Brotherhood banned and the leader of the popular and secular Ghad (Tomorrow) party, Ayman Nour, arrested and jailed on forgery charges (the validity of which were questioned by local human rights organisations and the US), Mubarak won 89% of the vote. In subsequent parliamentary elections that November, the Muslim Brotherhood managed to win 88 seats in the 444-seat national parliament, six times the number they had previously held.

EGYPT TODAY

More than economic downturn or domestic terrorism, the biggest challenge facing President Mubarak is the passing of time. One of the few surviving Free Officers who overthrew the monarchy in 1952, Mubarak is an old man with failing health. But media censorship in Egypt has not made it easy for critics to press the issue.

When the national paper *Al-Dastur* ran rumours of the president's ill health in September 2007, the editor was arrested for damaging the public interest, and some US$350 million was withdrawn from the Egyptian stock market by nervous foreign investors. Legally, presidential power passes to the vice president, but Mubarak has always refused to appoint one. Many rumours surround the president's son, Gamal Mubarak, but the succession is far from clear.

Whoever takes the helm, there is no denying that Egypt is in serious economic crisis, and has been for many years. The national economy has had to cope with a massive growth in population, rise in unemployment, and decline in the value of the Egyptian currency. Lower taxes, reduced energy subsidies and increased privatisation have facilitated a higher GDP and a booming stock market, but the living standards for the average Egyptian have not kept pace. In response, the masses have taken to the streets over stagnant wages and rising commodity prices, a threatening combination that has been further aggravated by the global economic slowdown.

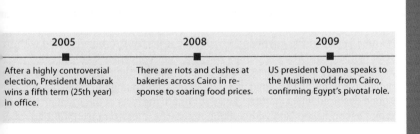

2005	2008	2009
After a highly controversial election, President Mubarak wins a fifth term (25th year) in office.	There are riots and clashes at bakeries across Cairo in response to soaring food prices.	US president Obama speaks to the Muslim world from Cairo, confirming Egypt's pivotal role.

PHARAONIC EGYPT

Carving at the museum in Saqqara (p138)

IZZET KER

Ancient Egypt saw 30 royal dynasties ruling from c 3100 BC over a 3000-year period. As the world's first nation-state, predating the civilisations of Greece and Rome by several millennia, Egypt was responsible for some of the most important achievements in human history. It was where writing was invented, the first stone monuments erected and an entire culture set in place, which remained largely unchanged for thousands of years. All this was made possible by the Nile River, which brought life to this virtually rainless land.

PHARAONIC WHO'S WHO

Egypt's Pharaonic history is based on the regnal years of each king, or pharaoh, a word derived from *per-aa,* meaning palace. Among the many hundreds of pharaohs who ruled Egypt over a 3000-year period, the following are some of the names found most frequently around the ancient sites.

Narmer c 3100 BC First ruler of a united Egypt after he conquered the north (Lower Egypt, Narmer from south (Upper) Egypt is portrayed as victorious on the famou Narmer Palette in the Egyptian Museum. He is perhaps to be identified with th semimythical King Menes, founder of Egypt's ancient capital city Memphis.

Zoser (Djoser) c 2667–2648 BC As second ruler of the 3rd dynasty, Zoser wa buried in Egypt's first pyramid, the world's oldest monumental stone building, de signed by the architect Imhotep. Zoser's statue in the foyer of the Egyptian Museur shows a long-haired king with a slight moustache, dressed in a tight-fitting robe.

neferu c 2613–2589 BC The first pharaoh of the 4th dynasty, and held in the highest steem by later generations, Sneferu was Egypt's greatest pyramid builder. He was responsible for four, and his final resting place, the Red (Northern) Pyramid at Dahshur, as Egypt's first true pyramid and a model for the more famous ones at Giza.

hufu (Cheops) c 2589–2566 BC As Sneferu's son and successor, Khufu was second pharaoh of the 4th dynasty. He is best known for Egypt's largest pyramid, e Great Pyramid at Giza, and his only surviving likeness is Egypt's smallest royal culpture, a 7.5cm-high figurine in the Egyptian Museum. The gold furniture of his other Hetepheres is also in the museum.

hafre (Khephren, Chephren) c 2558–2532 BC Khafre was a younger son of Khufu ho succeeded his half-brother to become fourth ruler of the 4th dynasty. He built e second of Giza's pyramids. He is best known as the model for the face of the reat Sphinx, but his diorite statue in the Egyptian Museum is equally stunning.

lenkaure (Mycerinus) c 2532–2503 BC As the son of Khafre and fifth pharaoh f the 4th dynasty, Menkaure built the smallest of Giza's three huge pyramids. He also well represented by a series of sculptures in the Egyptian Museum, which how him with the goddess Hathor and deities representing various administrative ivisions of Egypt.

epi II c 2278–2184 BC As fifth pharaoh of the 6th dynasty, Pepi II was a child at is accession; his delight with a dancing pygmy was recorded in the Aswan tomb f his official Harkhuf. As one of the world's longest-reigning monarchs (96 years), epi contributed to the decline of the Pyramid Age.

lontuhotep II c 2055–2004 BC As overlord of Thebes, Montuhotep II reunited gypt and his reign began the Middle Kingdom. He was the first pharaoh to build funerary temple at Deir al-Bahri, in hich he was buried with five of his ives and a daughter, with further ives and courtiers buried in the surounding area.

esostris III (Senwosret, Senusret) 1874–1855 BC The fifth pharaoh of e 12th dynasty, Sesostris III reorganed the administration by taking power om the provincial governors (nomarhs). He strengthened Egypt's frontiers nd occupied Nubia with a chain of foresses, and is recognisable by the stern, areworn' faces of his statues. His female elatives were buried with spectacular ewellery.

menhotep I c 1525–1504 BC As second pharaoh of the 18th dynasty, menhotep I ruled for a time with is mother Ahmose-Nofretari. They ounded the village of Deir el-Medina

FEMALE PHARAOHS

From early dynastic times it seemed common practice that when the pharaoh died and his heir was too young, his wife would be appointed regent. Quite often they declared themselves pharaoh later on.

Hatshepsut, the most famous female pharaoh, became regent to her stepson Tuthmosis III in 1479 BC, and later declared herself pharaoh. Nefertiti, wife of the rebel pharaoh Akhenaten, is often depicted wearing kingly regalia.

In 51 BC, at the age of 17, Cleopatra came to the throne with her brother Ptolemy XIII. She first married Julius Caesar, whose son she bore, and later on Mark Antony.

for the workers who built the tombs in the Valley of the Kings. Amenhotep I ma have been the first king to be buried there.

Hatshepsut c 1473–1458 BC As the most famous of Egypt's female pharaohs, Ha shepsut took power at the death of her brother-husband Tuthmosis II and initial ruled jointly with her nephew-stepson Tuthmosis III. After taking complete contr she undertook ambitious building schemes, including obelisks at Karnak Temp and her own spectacular funerary temple at Deir al-Bahri.

Tuthmosis III c 1479–1425 BC As sixth pharaoh of the 18th dynasty, Tuthmos IIII expanded Egypt's empire with a series of foreign campaigns into Syria. He bu extensively and his tomb was the first in the Valley of the Kings to be decorated

Amenhotep III c 1390–1352 BC As ninth pharaoh of the 18th dynasty, Amenhote III's reign marks the zenith of Egypt's culture and power. He is the creator of Lux Temple and the largest ever funerary temple marked by the Colossi of Memno and his many innovations, including Aten worship, are usually credited to his so and successor Amenhotep IV (later 'Akhenaten').

Akhenaten (Amenhotep IV) c 1352–1336 BC Changing his name from Amenhote to distance himself from the state god Amun, Akhenaten relocated the royal capit to Amarna with his wife Nefertiti . While many still regard him as a monotheist an benign revolutionary, evidence suggests he was a dictator whose reforms we political rather than religious.

Nefertiti c 1338–1336 BC (?) Nefertiti ruled with her husband Akhenaten, an while the identity of his successor remains controversial, this may have bee Nefertiti herself, using the throne name 'Smenkhkare'. Also controversial is th suggested identification of her mummy in tomb KV 35 in the Valley of the King

Tutankhamun c 1336–1327 BC Tutankhamun was the 11th pharaoh of the 18t dynasty, and his fame is based on the great quantities of treasure discovered i

ANDERS BLOMQ

Akhenaten, Nefertiti (see above) and the kids, Egyptian Museum, Cairo (p65)

his tomb in 1922. Most likely the son of Akhenaten by minor wife Kiya, Tutankhamun reopened the traditional temples and restored Egypt's fortunes after the disastrous reign of his father.

Horemheb c 1323–1295 BC As a military general, Horemheb restored Egypt's empire under Tutankhamun and after the brief reign of Ay eventually became king himself, marrying Nefertiti's sister Mutnodjmet. His tomb at Saqqara was abandoned in favour of a royal burial in a superbly decorated tomb in the Valley of the Kings.

Seti I c 1294–1279 BC The second pharaoh of the 19th dynasty, Seti I continued to consolidate Egypt's empire with foreign campaigns. He is best known for building Karnak's Hypostyle Hall, a superb temple at Abydos and a huge tomb in the Valley of the Kings. His mummy in the Egyptian Museum is one of the best preserved.

HEALTH

With an average life expectancy of around 35 years, ancient Egyptians took health care seriously. Wind-blown and sand-damaged eyes, teeth and lungs were common problems; bites from snakes and scorpions were dangers; parasitic worms lurked in water; and flies spread diseases. By 2650 BC there were dentists and doctors, with specialists in surgery, gynaecology and even veterinary practice, trained in the temple medical schools.

Magic was also used to combat illness or injury, and spells were recited and amulets worn to promote recovery. A magical mix of honey, sour milk and crocodile dung was recommended as a contraceptive.

Ramses II c 1279–1213 BC Son and successor of Seti I, Ramses II fought the Hittites at the Battle of Kadesh and built temples including Abu Simbel and the Ramesseum, once adorned with the statue that inspired Shelley's poem 'Ozymandias'.

Ramses III c 1184–1153 BC As second pharaoh of the 20th dynasty, Ramses III was the last of the warrior kings, repelling several attempted invasions portrayed in scenes at Medinat Habu. Buried in a finely decorated tomb in the Valley of the Kings, his mummy was the inspiration for Boris Karloff's *The Mummy*.

Taharka 690–664 BC As fourth pharaoh of the 25th dynasty, Taharka was one of Egypt's Nubian pharaohs and his daughter Amenirdis II high priestess at Karnak, where Taharka undertook building work. A fine sculpted head of the ruler is in Aswan's Nubian Museum. He was buried in a pyramid at Nuri in southern Nubia.

Alexander the Great 331–323 BC During his conquest of the Persian Empire, the Macedonian king Alexander invaded Egypt in 331 BC. Crowned pharaoh at Memphis, he founded Alexandria, visited Amun's temple at Siwa Oasis to confirm his divinity and after his untimely death in Babylon in 323 BC his mummy was eventually buried in Alexandria.

Ptolemy I 323–283 BC As Alexander's general and rumoured half-brother, Ptolemy seized Egypt at Alexander's death and established the Ptolemaic line of pharaohs. Ruling in traditional style for 300 years, they made Alexandria the greatest capital of the ancient world and built many of the temples standing today, including Edfu, Philae and Dendara.

Cleopatra VII 51–30 BC As the 19th ruler of the Ptolemaic dynasty, Cleopatra VI ruled with her brothers Ptolemy XIII then Ptolemy XIV before taking power hersel A brilliant politician who restored Egypt's former glories, she married Julius Caesa then Mark Antony, whose defeat at Actium in 31 BC led to the couple's suicide.

THE GODS

Religion suffused almost every aspect of the ancient Egyptians' lives and gave thei culture its incredible coherence and conservatism. They believed their gods would tak care of them, and each pharaoh was regarded as the gods' representative on earth ruling by divine approval.

Osiris was the King of the Underworld, and he was also the first mummy, created b his wife-sister Isis, the Goddess of magic. Isis and Osiris magically produced their so Horus, the falcon god of the sky. Pharaohs associated themselves with Horus, and thu considered Isis their symbolic mother.

Ra was the supreme sun god, who travelled through the skies in a boat, sinking down into the underworld each night before re-emerging at dawn to bring light. Hi daughter, Hathor, the goddess of love and pleasure, was the patroness of music an dancing. Amun, the local god of Thebes, later became the sun god Amun-Ra, King o the Gods.

The jackal or jackal-headed Anubis was the God of mummification, patron of em balmers and guardian of cemeteries. Thoth was the god of wisdom and writing, an patron of scribes. Important, too, was Hapy, the god of the Nile flood, represented a a man with breasts. The Nile flood was controlled by Khnum the ram-headed god wh created life on his potter's wheel. The sky goddess Nut swallowed the sun each evening to give birth to it each morning.

EVERYDAY LIFE IN ANCIENT EGYPT
FASHIONS & COSMETICS

In ancient Egypt clothes were generally linen, made from the flax plant before th introduction of cotton during the rule of the Ptolemies (323 BC–30 BC). The most com mon garment was the loincloth, but men also wore a linen kilt, sometimes pleated The female garments were dresses, most wrapped sari-like around the body, although there were also V-neck designs cut to shape.

Wigs and hair extensions were also popular and date back to c 3400 BC, as does th use of henna as a hair dye *(Lawsonia inermis)*. The clergy had to shave their heads fo ritual purity, and children's heads were partially shaved to leave only a side lock of hai as a symbol of their youth.

Egyptian perfumes were famous throughout the ancient world for their strength and quality. Oils perfumed with flowers and spices were used to protect the skin from the drying effects of the sun. Powdered green malachite and black galena (kohl) wer used as eye make up. Crushed red ochre was used to shade lips and cheeks.

ANCIENT EGYPTIAN FOOD

The staple food was bread. Onions, leeks, garlic and pulses were eaten in great quan tities along with dates, figs, pomegranates and grapes. Spices, herbs, nuts and seed were added to food, along with oil extracted from native plants and imported almonds and olives. Cows provided milk for drinking and making butter and cheese, but meat was only eaten regularly by the wealthy and by priests. The wealthy enjoyed wine, but most people drank barley beer.

AGRICULTURE

The majority of ancient Egyptians were farmers, whose lives were based around the annual cycle of the Nile. When the flood waters covering the valley floor receded (by October), farmers planted their crops in the silt left behind, using irrigation canals to distribute the flood waters where needed and to water their crops until harvest time, in April. Agriculture was so fundamental to life in both this world and the next that it was one of the main themes in tomb scenes. Hieroglyphs are now known to have been first developed c 3250 BC as a means of recording produce.

SCRIBES & WRITING

A huge civil service of scribes worked on the pharaoh's behalf to record taxes and organise workers. In a society where less than 1% were literate, scribes were regarded as wise and were much admired. They were taught to read and write in the schools attached to temples where written texts were stored and studied. The temples formed the heart of every settlement as a combination of town hall, college, library and medical centre.

Hieroglyphs, meaning 'sacred carvings' in Greek, are the pictorial script used by the ancient Egyptians. Recent discoveries at Abydos dating to around 3250 BC make this the earliest form of writing yet found, even predating that of Mesopotamia. They were in constant use for more than 3500 years until the last example was carved at Philae temple on 24 August AD 394. Evolving from a handful of basic signs, more than 6000 hieroglyphs have been identified, although less than 1000 were in general use.

FRANS LEMMENS

Decorations inside a coffin, Egyptian Museum, Cairo (p65)

MUMMIFICATION

After a long process of experimentation, and a good deal of trial and error, the Egyptians seem to have finally cracked mummification around 2600 BC. All the organs were removed except the kidneys, which were hard to reach, and the heart, considered to be the source of intelligence. The brain was generally removed by inserting a metal probe up the nose and whisking until it had liquefied sufficiently to be drained out the nose.

All was covered with natron salt (a combination of sodium carbonate and sodium bicarbonate) and left to dry out for 40 days, after which it was washed, purified and anointed with a range of oils, spices and resins. All parts were then wrapped in layers of linen, with the appropriate amulets set in place over the various parts of the body as priests recited the necessary incantations. The internal organs were placed in Canopic jars, and the wrapped body with its funerary mask was placed inside its coffin.

ARCHITECTURE

The survival of so many pyramids, temples and tombs has created a misleading impression of the Egyptians as a morbid bunch obsessed with religion and death, when they actually loved life so much that they went to enormous lengths to ensure it continued for eternity.

TEMPLES

There were two types of temples in ancient Egypt. The stone cult temples, usually located on the Nile's east bank, were houses of the spirits of the gods, where daily rituals were performed on behalf of the pharaoh, who was high priest of every temple.

The funerary or mortuary temple usually built on the Nile's west bank, was where the pharaoh's soul was commemorated and sustained with offerings. These include Ramses III's temple at Medinat Habu (p123), Amenhotep III's once-vast temple marked by the Colossi of Memnon (p117) and the best known example built by Hatshepsut into the cliffs of Deir al-Bahri (p117).

➤ THE BEST

IZZET KERIBAR

Wall carving detail, Medinat Habu (123)

EGYPTIAN TEMPLES

- Medinat Habu (p123)
- Temples of Karnak (p109)
- Luxor Temple (p112)
- Abydos (p166)
- Philae (p212)
- Great Temple of Ramses II, Abu Simbel (p215)

TOMBS

PYRAMIDS

By around 3100 BC the mound of sand heaped over a grave was replaced by a more permanent structure of mudbrick whose characteristic bench-shape is known as a mastaba. As stone replaced mudbrick, the addition of further levels to increase height created the pyramid, the first built at Saqqara for Zoser (p148).

ts stepped sides soon evolved into the familiar smooth-sided structure, with the Pyramids of Giza (p79) the most famous examples.

ROCK-CUT TOMBS

With little room for grand superstructures along many of the narrow stretches beside the Nile, an alternative type of tomb developed: cut tunnel-fashion into the cliffs that border the river. These simple rock-cut tombs consisting of a single chamber gradually developed into more elaborate structures complete with an open courtyard, offering a chapel and entrance facade carved out of the rock, with a shaft leading down into a burial chamber. The most impressive rock-cut tombs were those built for the kings of the New Kingdom (1550–1069 BC), who relocated the royal burial ground south to the religious capital Thebes (modern Luxor), to a remote desert valley on the west bank, now known as the Valley of the Kings (see p118).

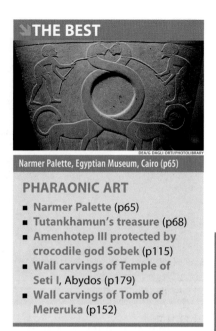

THE BEST

DEA/G DAGLI ORTI/PHOTOLIBRARY

Narmer Palette, Egyptian Museum, Cairo (p65)

PHARAONIC ART

- **Narmer Palette** (p65)
- **Tutankhamun's treasure** (p68)
- **Amenhotep III protected by crocodile god Sobek** (p115)
- **Wall carvings of Temple of Seti I, Abydos** (p179)
- **Wall carvings of Tomb of Mereruka** (p152)

ART

The majority of art and artefacts produced in ancient Egypt were for religious and funerary purposes. Despite their breathtaking beauty, these pieces would have been hidden away from public gaze, either within a temple's dark interior or buried in a tomb with the dead. Artists regarded the things they made as a job rather than art, and only very occasionally signed their work.

The Egyptians believed it was essential that the things they portrayed had every relevant feature shown as clearly as possible, so they could be magically reanimated to sustain the spirits of both the gods and the dead. Figures needed a clear outline, with a profile of nose and mouth to let them breathe, and the eye shown whole as if seen from the front, to allow the figure to see. This explains why eyes were often painted on the sides of coffins (to allow the dead to see out) and why hieroglyphs such as snakes or enemy figures were sometimes shown in two halves – to prevent them causing damage when reactivated. The vast quantities of food and drink offered in temples and tombs were duplicated on surrounding walls to ensure a constant supply for eternity.

EGYPT IN FOCUS

RELIGION

⬊ RELIGION

WAYNE WALT

Eid al-Fitr prayers mark the end of Ramadan

It is clear that ancient Egyptians were deeply religious, and that most of their life was governed by their beliefs. In that sense little has changed; Islam now permeates Egyptian life. It's manifested not in a strictly authoritarian manner as in Saudi Arabia (Egyptians love enjoying themselves too much for that), but it's there at an almost subconscious level. Ask after someone's health and the answer is *'Alhamdulallah'* (Fine. Praise to God). Arrange to meet tomorrow and it's *'inshallah'* (God willing).

A MUSLIM MAJORITY

Ninety percent of Egyptians are Sunni Muslims. Adam, Abraham (Ibrahim), Noah, Mose and Jesus are all accepted as Muslim prophets (note Jesus is recognised as a prophet an not as the son of God). The essence of Islam is the Quran and Prophet Mohammed, wh was the last and truest prophet to deliver messages from Allah (God) to the people.

BEGINNINGS OF ISLAM

Islam was founded by Mohammed (AD 570–632), who was illiterate and is said t have received his first divine message at 40. The revelations continued and were late transcribed to become the holy Quran. Nothing in the Quran has been changed an it is considered to be the direct word of Allah. Even non-Arab Muslims read the Qura in Arabic, and not in translation, because it is considered the language of Allah. In 62

Mohammed and his followers retreated to Medina, and this Hejira (migration) marks the start of the Muslim calendar.

FIVE PILLARS OF ISLAM

Islam means 'submission' and this principle is visible in the daily life of Muslims. The faith is expressed by observance of the five 'pillars of Islam':

- Publicly declare that 'there is no god but God, and Mohammed is His Prophet'.
- Pray five times a day: at sunrise, noon, mid-afternoon, sunset and night. It is perfectly permissible to pray at home or elsewhere; only the Friday midday prayer need be conducted in the mosque.
  Give *zakat* (alms) for the propagation of Islam and to help the needy.
  Fast during daylight hours during the month of Ramadan.
- Complete the hajj (pilgrimage to Mecca).

IZZET KERIBAR

Mosque of Abu al-Haggag, Luxor (p114)

THE BEST

MOSQUES

- **Mosque of Ibn Tulun**, Cairo (p77)
- **Mosque-Madrassa of Sultan Hassan**, Cairo (p77)
- **Al-Azhar Mosque**, Cairo (p73)
- **Mosque of Abu al-Haggag**, Luxor (p114)
- **Terbana Mosque**, Alexandria (p232)

COPTIC CHRISTIANITY

Egyptian Christians are known as Copts. The term is the Western form of the Arabic *qibt,* derived from the Greek *aegyptios* (Egyptian). Before the arrival of Islam, Christianity was the predominant religion in Egypt. St Mark, companion of the apostles Paul and Peter, began preaching Christianity in Egypt around AD 45, and although it did not become the official religion of the country until the 4th century, Egypt was one of the first countries to embrace the new faith.

Egyptian Christians split from the Orthodox Church of the Eastern (or Byzantine) Empire, of which Egypt was then a part, after the main body of the church described Christ as both human and divine.

The Coptic Church is ruled by a patriarch (presently Pope Shenouda III), other members of the religious hierarchy and an ecclesiastical council of laypeople. It has a long history of monasticism and can justly claim that the first Christian monks, St Anthony and St Pachomius, were Copts.

MODERN COPTS

The Coptic language, which has its origins in Egyptian hieroglyphs and Ancient Greek, is still used in religious ceremonies, sometimes in conjunction with Arabic for the benefit of the congregation.

EGYPT IN FOCUS

RELIGION

↘ THE BEST

JULIET COOMBE

Inside St Katherine's Monastery, Sinai (p268)

CHRISTIAN SITES

- **Coptic Monasteries of Wadi Natrun** (p159)
- **St Paul's and St Anthony's monasteries** (p271)
- **Coptic Museum & Hanging Church** (p71)
- **Burnt Monastery** (p178)
- **St Katherine's Monastery** (p268)

The Copts have long provided something of an educated elite in Egypt, filling many important government and bureaucratic posts. Furthermore, they've always been an economically powerful minority.

COPTIC ART

Coptic art has a strong tradition of textile and painting, which can be seen as a direct continuation of ancient Egyptian traditions. The art of textile-making was inherited from the ancient Egyptians, particularly loom and tapestry weaving. Religious illustration also started in ancient Egypt when pharaohs started adorning papyrus texts with liturgies and prayers. Like their forebears, Coptic artisans used bright colours for vignettes, and striking black ink for all texts.

The early Coptic wall paintings were Christian themes painted on top of Pharaonic reliefs covered in plaster when ancient temples were converted into churches. Later some of the finest Coptic wall paintings depicted spiritual scenes awash with vibrant colours and accented with gold.

OTHER CREEDS

There are about one million members of other Christian denominations in Egypt, from Anglicans and Roman Catholics of the Latin rite to the whole gamut of the fragmented Middle Eastern rites including Armenian, Syrian, Chaldean, Maronite and Melkite.

Egypt was also once home to a significant number of Jews. The first 40 years of the 20th century constituted something of a golden age for Egyptian Jews as their numbers reached an all-time peak of 80,000, and they came to play a bigger role in society and the affairs of state. However, with the creation of Israel in 1948, and Gamal Abdel Nasser's nationalisation program, a long exodus followed. Today, it's estimated there are no more than 200 Jews left in Egypt.

RELIGIOUS FESTIVALS
RAMADAN

Although it is the Islamic month of fasting, Ramadan is also considered a month of feasting. Many Egyptian Muslims fast during the day, and then feast through the night until sunrise. The combination of abstinence and lack of sleep means that tempers are often short. The evening meal during Ramadan, called *iftar* (breaking the fast), is always a celebration. Although non-Muslims are not expected to fast, it is considered impolite to eat or drink in public during fasting hours.

BECCA POSTERINO

Sufi dancing from the Al-Tannoura Egyptian Heritage Dance Troupe (p89)

MOULIDS

A cross between a funfair and a religious festival, a *moulid* celebrates the birthday of a local holy person. There are both Islamic and Christian *moulids* and they are often a colourful riot of festivities attended by hundreds of thousands of people. In the midst of the chaos, barbers perform mass circumcisions, snake charmers induce cobras out of baskets, and children are presented at the shrine to be blessed and the sick to be cured.

In the evenings at an Islamic *moulid,* Sufis hold hypnotic *zikr*s (literally 'remembrance'), a long session of dancing, chanting and swaying usually carried out to achieve oneness with God.

Most *moulid*s last for about a week and climax with the *leila kebira* (big night). Much of the infrastructure is provided by 'professional' *mawladiyya,* or *moulid* people, who spend their lives going from one *moulid* to another.

SHOPPING

Scenes of a souq in Luxor

IZZET KERIBA

Egypt is a shopper's dream – from traditional papyrus scrolls and original artwork to handmade jewellery and the obligatory hookah, there is no shortage of trinkets and souvenirs on sale in souqs across the country. While a good portion of tourist offerings tend to be low quality, anyone with a discerning eye can pick out the diamonds in the rough.

WHERE TO GO

The undisputed shopping capital of Egypt is Cairo's Khan al-Khalili (p73), which is as much a tourist circus as one of the Middle East's most fabled and historic markets. The main drag is full of tourist junk, but veer off into the smaller alleys to hunt for more interesting buys. The street behind Al-Azhar Mosque also has some fine shops.

Other top-notch shopping areas include Luxor (p131), for souvenirs and crafts. Luxor is also famous for its beautiful alabaster work, which is available from workshops along the main road on the West Bank. The souq in Aswan (p208) is good for crafts plus spices and more exotic items. Also, be on the lookout for traditional Siwan, Bedouin and Nubian handicrafts when travelling through the Western Desert, Sinai and Aswan, respectively.

BARGAINING

Bargaining is part of everyday life in Egypt. It can be a hassle but remember it's a game, not a fight. Shop around to get an idea of the price, or decide how much you would be happy paying and simply walk away if you can't get the price you want, which can often help close the deal. Note it's considered very bad form to offer an amount, have the shopkeeper agree and then to change your mind. See p354 for more haggling tips.

⬂ DIRECTORY & TRANSPORT

DIRECTORY

ACCOMMODATION

Egypt offers visitors the full spectrum of accommodation: hotels, flotels (Nile cruisers), all-inclusive resorts, pensions, B&Bs, youth hostels, camping grounds and even ecolodges.

Prices cited in this book are for rooms available in the high season and include taxes. Breakfast is included in the room price unless indicated otherwise in the review. We have roughly defined budget hotels as any that charge up to E£120 for a room, midrange as any that charge between E£120 and E£600 and top end as those that charge E£600 or more for a room. However, there is some variation in pricing brackets throughout the book as certain destinations are pricier than others.

Be advised that rates often go up by around 10% during peak times, including the two big feasts (Eid al-Fitr and Eid al-Adha; see p352), New Year (20 December to 5 January) and sometimes for the summer season (approximately 1 July to 15 September).

Also note that just because a hotel has its rates displayed it doesn't mean they aren't negotiable. In off-peak seasons and during the middle of the week, haggling will often get you significant discounts, even in midrange places.

Resorts in Egypt typically offer half board (two meals), full board (three meals) or all-inclusive rates that usually include most drinks as well as some activities. Although prices are given throughout the book for all-inclusive resorts, it's worth booking these accommodation options in advance as considerable discounts are sometimes available.

Hotels rated three stars and up generally require payment in US dollars, which

⬆ BOOK YOUR STAY ONLINE

For more accommodation reviews and recommendations by Lonely Planet authors, check out the on-line booking service at www.lonely planet.com. You'll find the true, insider lowdown on the best places to stay. Reviews are thorough and independent. Best of all, you can book online.

officially is illegal though no one seems to be paying much attention. Upmarket hotels are increasingly accepting credit-card payments, but you shouldn't take this as a given. A number of hotels, particularly along the coasts, list prices in euros, which is in response to the weakening dollar and the large European clientele. You can pay in other currencies but be advised that exchange fees sometimes apply.

HOTELS
BUDGET

The two-, one- and no-star hotels form the budget group. Generally, the prices quoted include breakfast, but don't harbour any great expectations – more often than not, it's usually a couple of pieces of bread, a frozen patty of butter, a serving of jam, and tea or coffee. Competition among the budget hotels in cities such as Cairo and Luxor is fierce, which is good news for travellers as it leads to an overall improvement in standards and services offered.

MIDRANGE

Egypt has a great range of budget and top-end hotels, but midrange options are surprisingly limited. This is particularly so in Cairo and Alexandria, where foreign nvestment is channelled into top-end accommodation. In these cities local establishments often pitch themselves as midrange establishments but end up offering no-star facilities at three-star rates. Also, beware the extras: sometimes you'll be charged extra for the fridge, air-con and satellite TV in your room – before agreeing to take the room, always confirm what the quoted cost actually covers. This is particularly important when it comes to taxes, which are as high as 24% in many midrange and top-end establishments.

TOP END

Visitors are spoilt for choice when it comes to top-end hotels in Egypt. While prices and amenities are usually up to international standards, in some instances service and food can fall short. As always, it's a good idea to inspect your room before handing over any hard-earned cash.

CLIMATE

Egypt's climate is easy to summarise: hot and dry, with the exception of the winter months of December, January and February, which can be quite cold in the north. Average temperatures range from 20°C (68°F) on the Mediterranean coast to 26°C (80°F) in Aswan. Maximum temperatures for the same places can get up to 31°C (88°F) and 50°C (122°F), respectively. At night in winter the temperature sometimes plummets to as low as 8°C in Cairo and along the Mediterranean coast. In the desert it's even more extreme – often scorching during the day and bitterly cold at night.

Alexandria receives the most rain, approximately 19cm a year, while far to the south in Aswan the average is about 10mm over five years. Al-Kharga in the Western Desert once went 17 years without any rain at all.

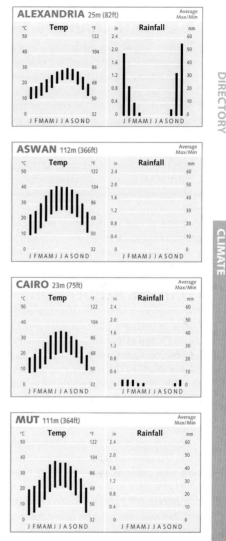

Between March and April the khamsin (a dry, hot wind) blows in from the parched Western Desert at up to 150km/h. The sky becomes dark orange and choked with dust and, even when everyone closes all doors and windows tightly, the inside of every house is covered with

⚓ CLIMATE CHANGE & TRAVEL

Travel – especially air travel – is a significant contributor to global climate change. At Lonely Planet, we believe that all who travel have a responsibility to limit their personal impact. As a result, we have teamed with Rough Guides and other concerned industry partners to support Climate Care, which allows people to offset the greenhouse gases they are responsible for with contributions to energy-saving projects and other climate-friendly initiatives in the developing world. Lonely Planet offsets all staff and author travel.

For more information, turn to the responsible travel pages on www.lonely planet.com. For details on offsetting your carbon emissions and a carbon calculator, go to www.climatecare.org.

a patina of grit so that they resemble undisturbed tombs.

For more information on the best time to visit Egypt, see p44.

CUSTOMS REGULATIONS

The duty-free limit on arrival is 1L of alcohol, 1L of perfume, 200 cigarettes and 25 cigars. On top of that, once in the country, you can buy another 3L of alcohol plus a wide range of other duty-free articles, but this must be done within 24 hours of arrival at one of the special Egypt Free shops in the arrival and departure areas of the airport.

Sometimes the Customs Declaration Form D is given to arriving tourists to list all digital cameras, jewellery, cash, travellers cheques and electronics (laptop computers, MP3 players, video cameras etc). No one seems to be asked for this form on departure, and few tourists are given it on arrival. However, travellers are sometimes asked to declare their digital camera, and some have reported being hit with a hefty 'import tax'.

There are prohibited and restricted articles, including books, printed matter, motion pictures, photographs and materials that the government considers 'subversive or constituting a national risk or incompatible with the public interest. Articles for espionage and explosive are banned.

DANGERS & ANNOYANCES

The incidence of crime, violent or otherwise, in Egypt is negligible compared with most Western countries. Most visitors and residents would agree that Egyptian towns and cities are safe to walk around in the day or night. Unfortunately, the hassle factor often means that this isn't quite the case for an unaccompanied foreign woman – for details, see p358.

Apart from the issues discussed here, you should be aware that the Egyptian authorities take a hard view of illegal drug use (see p352).

Terrorist acts against foreign tourists in 1997, 2004, 2005, 2006 and 2009 resulted in a great many deaths, and have led to the government giving security the highest possible priority – after all, the income derived from tourism constitutes an extraordinary 20% or so of the country's GDP.

While further incidents may occur at some point in the future, we'd say that Egypt is presently no more or less dangerous than any other country, your own included.

THEFT

Theft never used to be a problem in Egypt but it seems to be becoming a bigger one. In the past couple of years we've received a stream of letters from readers concerning money disappearing from locked rooms, even hotel safes. Our advice is to keep your cash and valuables on your person at all times.

There are also a few areas where pickpockets are known to operate, notably on the Cairo metro and the packed local buses from Midan Tahrir to the Pyramids. Tourists aren't the specific targets, but be careful how you carry your money in crowded places.

Generally though, unwary visitors are parted from their money through scams, and these are something that you really do have to watch out for.

DISCOUNT CARDS
STUDENT CARDS

Proof of student status is required before an International Student Identity Card (ISIC) will be issued. That proof must be a university ID card or letter from your own college or university. You'll also need one photo, a photocopy of the front page of your passport and E£65. There are no age limits. Most of Cairo's backpacker hotels and budget travel agencies can get the cards.

SCAMS, HUSTLES & HASSLE

Egyptians take hospitality to strangers seriously. You'll receive a steady stream of *salaam*s (greetings) and the odd *ahlan wa sahlan* (hello/welcome) inviting you to sit and have *shai* (tea). A lot of this is genuine, particularly in rural areas.

But in more touristy places – notably around the Egyptian Museum and Pyramids in Cairo, and all around Luxor – a cheery 'Hello, my friend' is doublespeak for 'This way, sucker'.

Be warned that you'll become a magnet for instant friends who just happen to have a papyrus factory they'd like to show you. You'll be showered with helpful advice such as 'the museum is closed, take *shai* with me while you wait' – of course the museum isn't closed and refreshments will be taken at a convenient souvenir shop. As an English-speaker you might be asked to spare a moment to check the spelling of a letter to a relative in the USA, and while you're at it how about some special perfume for the lady…

It's all pretty harmless but it can become very wearing. Everyone works out a strategy to reduce the hassle to a minimum but about the only way to deal with unwanted attention is to be polite but firm, and when you're in for a pitch cut it short with 'Sorry, no thanks'.

There are also countless irritating scams. The most common involves touts who lie and misinform to get newly arrived travellers into hotels for which they get a commission.

If you do get stung, or feel one more 'Excuse me, where are you from?' will make you crack, it's best to take a deep breath – by acting rudely or brusquely you may offend one of the vast majority of locals who is only trying to help a guest to the country.

It's worth having a student card as it entitles you to a 50% discount on admission to nearly all the antiquities and museums, as well as significant reductions on train travel.

EMBASSIES & CONSULATES

Most embassies and consulates are open from around 8am to 2pm Sunday to Thursday. The addresses of some of the foreign embassies and consulates in Egypt are in the following list.

Australia (Map pp66-7; ☎ 02-2575 0444; 11th fl, World Trade Centre, 1191 Corniche el-Nil, Cairo)

Canada (Map pp66-7; ☎ 02-2791 8700; 26 Sharia Kamal el-Shenawy, Cairo)

Denmark (Map pp66-7; ☎ 02-2739 6500; www.ambkairo.um.dk/da; 12 Hassan Sabry, Zamalek, Cairo)

France Cairo (Map pp66-7; ☎ 02-2394 7150; www.ambafrance-eg.org; 29 Sharia el-Fadl); Alexandria (Map p232; ☎ 03-487 5615; 2 Midan Orabi, Mansheyya)

Germany Cairo (Map pp66-7; ☎ 02-2728 2000; www.kairo.diplo.de; 8 Hassan Sabry, Zamalek); Alexandria (off Map p232; ☎ 03-4867 503; 9 Sharia el-Fawateem, Azarita)

Ireland (Map pp66-7; ☎ 02-2735 8264; www .embassyofireland.org.eg; 22 Hassan Assem, Zamalek, Cairo)

Italy Cairo (Map pp52-3; ☎ 02-2794 3194; 15 Sharia Abdel Rahman Fahmy, Garden City); Alexandria (Map p232; ☎ 03-487 9470; 25 Sharia Saad Zaghloul)

Netherlands (Map pp66-7; ☎ 02-2739 5500; http://egypt.nlembassy.org; 18 Sharia Hassan Sabry, Zamalek, Cairo)

New Zealand (Map pp52-3; ☎ 02-2461 6000; www.nzembassy.com; lvl 8, North Tower, Nile City Towers, 2005C Corniche el-Nil, Cairo)

Spain (Map pp66-7; ☎ 02-2735 6462; Embe speg@mail.mae.es; 41 Sharia Ismail Mohammed, Cairo)

UK Cairo (Map pp52-3; ☎ 02-2791 6000; 7 Shari Ahmed Ragheb, Garden City); Alexandria (Map p230; ☎ 03-546 7001/2; Sharia Mena, Rushdy)

USA (Map pp66-7; ☎ 02-2797 3300; http:/ cairo.usembassy.gov; 8 Sharia Kamal el-Din Salah Garden City, Cairo)

FOOD

In this book, budget eateries are usually defined as those where you can get a meal (no drinks) for less than E£15 Midrange restaurants serve up main courses for under E£75 and often serve alcohol. Top-end joints are usually in five-star hotels, serve up main courses for over E£75, almost always serve alcohol and require diners to dress for dinner. Tipping is appreciated in budget places, advisable in midrange places and essential in all top-end restaurants.

For more information about eating out in Egypt, see p316.

GAY & LESBIAN TRAVELLERS

Homosexuality is no more or less prevalent in Egypt than elsewhere in the world but it's a lot more ambiguous than in the West. Men routinely hold hands, link arms and give each other kisses on greeting but don't misread the signals: this is not

---

TRAVEL ADVISORIES

Australian Department of Foreign Affairs (☎ 1300 139 281; www.smart traveller.gov.au)

British Foreign Office (☎ 0845-850-2829; www.fco.gov.uk/travel)

Canadian Department of Foreign Affairs (☎ 800-267 6788; www.dfait -maeci.gc.ca)

US State Department (☎ 888-407 4747; http://travel.state.gov)

ay behaviour; it's just the local take on nale bonding.

Beyond this a strange double standard oes on whereby an Egyptian man can ndulge in same-sex intercourse but not onsider himself gay because only the assive partner is regarded as such. So it's ot uncommon for foreign male visitors o receive blatant and crudely phrased ropositions of sex from Egyptian men.

While there is no mention of homosexality in the Egyptian penal code, some tatutes criminalising obscenity and pubc indecency have been used against gay nen in the past. In May 2001, 55 Egyptian nen were arrested when police raided a loating bar/restaurant moored on the lile in Cairo.

There are no national support groups r gay- or lesbian-information lines at resent. The premier gay and lesbian gypt site is www.gayegypt.com.

HEALTH

revention is the key to staying healthy while travelling in Egypt. Infectious disases can and do occur here but these are sually associated with poor living conitions and poverty, and can be avoided with a few precautions.

BEFORE YOU GO

's tempting to leave planning to the ast minute – don't! Many vaccines don't nsure immunity for the first two weeks o visit a doctor four to eight weeks bere departure. Ask your doctor for an nternational Certificate of Vaccination also known as the yellow booklet), which sts all the vaccinations you've received.

INSURANCE

nd out in advance if your insurance plan vill make payments directly to providers r reimburse you later for overseas health expenditures (in many places doctors expect payment in cash). It's also worth ensuring your travel insurance will cover repatriation home or to better medical facilities elsewhere. Your insurance company may be able to locate the nearest source of medical help, or you can ask at your hotel.

RECOMMENDED VACCINATIONS
The World Health Organization (WHO) recommends that all travellers, regardless of the region they are travelling in, should be vaccinated against diphtheria, tetanus, measles, mumps, rubella and polio, as well as hepatitis B.

INTERNET RESOURCES
There is a wealth of travel health advice on the internet. For further information, the **Lonely Planet** (www.lonelyplanet.com) website is a good place to start. The **World Health Organization** (www.who.int/ith) publishes a superb book, *International Travel and Health*, which is revised annually and is available online at no cost. Another website of general interest is **MD Travel Health** (www.mdtravelhealth.com), which provides complete travel health recommendations for every country, updated daily, also at no cost.

IN EGYPT
AVAILABILITY & COST OF HEALTH CARE
Care can be excellent in private hospitals and those associated with universities but patchier elsewhere. Reciprocal payment arrangements with other countries rarely exist and you should be prepared to pay for all medical and dental treatment. Medical care is not always readily available outside major cities. Medicine, and even sterile dressings or intravenous fluids, may need to be bought from a pharmacy.

DIRECTORY

HEALTH

DISEASES

Malaria

Malaria is found in certain parts of some oases; risk varies seasonally. Risk of malaria in most cities is minimal but check with your doctor if you are considering travelling to any rural areas.

Schistosomiasis (Bilharzia)

This is spread by the freshwater snail. It causes infection of the bowel and bladder, often with bleeding. It is caused by a fluke and is contracted through the skin from water contaminated with human urine or faeces. The Nile is known to be a source of bilharzia, but paddling or swimming in *any* suspect freshwater lakes or slow-running rivers should be avoided. A blood test can detect antibodies if you have been exposed, and treatment is then possible in specialist travel or infectious-disease clinics.

Standards of dental care are variable and there is an increased risk of hepatitis B and HIV transmission via poorly sterilised equipment.

For minor illnesses such as diarrhoea, pharmacists, who are well qualified, can often provide valuable advice and sell over-the-counter medication.

ENVIRONMENTAL HAZARDS

HEAT ILLNESS

Heat exhaustion occurs following heavy sweating and excessive fluid loss with inadequate replacement of fluids and salt. Symptoms include headache, dizziness and tiredness. You're already dehydrated by the time you feel thirsty – aim to drink sufficient water so that you produce pale diluted urine. The treatment of the salt loss component consists of taking in salty fluids such as soup or broth, and adding a little more table salt to food than usual.

Heatstroke is much more serious. This occurs when the body's heat-regulating mechanism breaks down. Excessive rise in body temperature leads to sweating ceasing, irrational and hyperactive behaviour and eventually loss of consciousness and even death. Rapid cooling by spraying the body with water and fanning is an ideal treatment. Emergency fluid and electrolyte replacement by intravenous drip is usually also required.

INSECT BITES & STINGS

Mosquitoes may not carry malaria but can cause irritation and infected bites. They also spread dengue fever. Using DEET-based insect repellents will prevent bites.

Sandflies are located around the Mediterranean beaches. They usually only cause a nasty itchy bite but can also carry a rare skin disorder called cutaneous leishmaniasis. Bites may be prevented by using DEET-based repellents.

Scorpions are frequently found in arid or dry climates. They can cause a painful bite, which is rarely life-threatening.

TRAVEL HEALTH WEBSITES

It's usually a good idea to consult your government's travel health website before departure, if one is available.

Australia (www.dfat.gov.au/travel)
Canada (www.travelhealth.gc.ca)
UK (www.dh.gov.uk)
USA (www.cdc.gov/travel)

WATER

Tap water is not safe to drink throughout Egypt. Stick to bottled water or boil water for 10 minutes, use a filter or use water-purification tablets. Do not drink water from rivers or lakes, as it may contain bacteria or viruses that can cause diarrhoea or vomiting.

TRAVELLING WITH CHILDREN

All travellers with children should know how to treat minor ailments and when to seek medical treatment. Make sure the children are up to date with routine vaccinations, and discuss possible travel vaccinations well before departure as some vaccines are not suitable for children aged under one year.

In hot, moist climates any wound or break in the skin may lead to infection. The area should be cleaned and then kept dry and clean. Remember to avoid contaminated food and water. If your child is vomiting or experiencing diarrhoea, lost fluid and salts must be replaced. It may be helpful to take re-hydration powders with you, to be re-constituted with boiled water. Ask your doctor about this.

Children should be encouraged to avoid dogs or other mammals because of the risk of rabies and other diseases. Any bite, scratch or lick from a warm-blooded, furry animal should immediately be thoroughly cleaned. If there is any possibility that the animal is infected with rabies, immediate medical assistance should be sought.

HOLIDAYS

Egypt's holidays and festivals are primarily Islamic or Coptic religious celebrations, though all holidays are celebrated equally by the entire population regardless of creed.

The Hejira (Islamic calendar) is 11 days shorter than the Gregorian (Western) calendar, so Islamic holidays tend to fall 11 days earlier each Western year. The 11-day rule is not entirely strict though as the holidays can fall from 10 to 12 days earlier. The precise dates are known only shortly before they fall as they're dependent upon the sighting of the moon. See the Islamic Holidays table (p352) for the approximate dates of the major holidays for the next few years.

The following list details public holidays in Egypt:

New Year's Day 1 January – Official national holiday but many businesses stay open.

Coptic Christmas January – Coptic Christmas is a fairly low-key affair and only Coptic businesses are closed for the day.

Coptic Easter March/April – The most important date on the Coptic calendar although it doesn't significantly affect daily life for the majority of the population.

Sham an-Nessim March/April – A Coptic holiday with Pharaonic origins, it literally means 'smell of the breeze'. It falls on the first Monday after Coptic Easter and is celebrated by all Egyptians, with family picnics and outings.

Sinai Liberation Day 25 April – Holiday celebrating Israel's return of Sinai in 1982 (Sinai only).

May Day 1 May – Official national holiday.

Liberation Day 18 June

Revolution Day 23 July – Official national holiday commemorating the date of the 1952 coup, when the Free Officers seized power from the puppet monarchy.

Wafa'a el-Nil 15 August – Literally 'the flooding of the Nile'.

ISLAMIC HOLIDAYS

HEJIRA YEAR	MOULID AN-NABI	RAMADAN STARTS	EID AL-FITR	EID AL-ADHA	RAS AS-SANA
1431	26.02.10	11.08.10	10.09.10	16.11.10	18.12.10
1432	15.02.11	01.08.11	30.08.11	06.11.11	26.11.11
1433	15.02.12	20.07.12	19.08.12	26.10.12	15.11.12

Note that dates can vary slightly.

Coptic New Year 11 September; 12 September in leap years

Armed Forces Day 6 October – Official national holiday celebrating Egyptian successes during the 1973 war with Israel. The day is marked by military parades and air displays and a long speech by the president.

Suez Victory Day 24 October

Victory Day 23 December

ISLAMIC HOLIDAYS

For more details on these holidays and festivals, see the Calendar (p46).

Eid al-Adha Also known as Eid al-Kebir. Marks the time of the hajj (pilgrimage to Mecca). If you want to travel within Egypt at this time, book your tickets well in advance.

Ras as-Sana Islamic New Year's Day. The entire country has the day off but celebrations are low-key.

Moulid an-Nabi Birthday of the Prophet Mohammed.

Ramadan Observant Muslims fast for a month during daylight hours.

Eid al-Fitr A three-day feast marking the end of Ramadan.

INSURANCE

A travel insurance policy to cover theft, loss and medical problems is a good idea. There is a wide variety of policies available, so check the small print. Some policies specifically exclude 'dangerous activities', which can include scuba diving, motorcycling and trekking.

Worldwide travel insurance is availabl at www.lonelyplanet.com/travel_ser ices. You can buy, extend and claim or line anytime – even if you're already o the road.

INTERNET ACCESS

The good news is that Egypt has taken u the internet in a big way, and there ar internet cafes throughout the countr Unfortunately, outside Cairo, Alexandri and tourist destinations in the Sinai an along the Red Sea coast, internet conne tions can be infuriatingly slow at times a result of too much demand on insu ficient international bandwidth. In recer years, a surprising number of wireles hotspots have been appearing in majo tourist destinations.

LEGAL MATTERS

Foreign travellers are subject to Egyptia laws and get no special consideration. you are arrested you have the right t telephone your embassy immediate (see p348).

One of the first signs visitors see whe entering the country via Cairo airport is prominent billboard warning that the po sible penalty for drug use in Egypt is han ing. Executions for such offences hav been taking place since 1989 and you get no exemption from penalties just be cause you're a tourist – be very careful.

MOHAMMED, MUHAMMAD...MU7AMMAD?

People have been wrestling Arabic into Roman letters for centuries, and now the rise of mobile phone and internet communication in the Middle East has spawned another method. Once you get over the confusion that it involves numbers, the so-called 'Arabic chat alphabet' might be the most sensible transliteration system to come along in a while. All the sounds peculiar to Arabic have been assigned a number, based very loosely on their shape in Arabic. A 3 for the back-of-the-throat letter *ayn* is the most common, so you could type 'Assalaam 3aleikum!' as a greeting. A 7 represents the aspirated 'h' ('Al-7amdulillah!'), and a 9 is the emphatic 's'. The system is popping up in ads, names of cool clubs and the like. Who knows – if it really catches on, we might be using it in the next edition of this book.

With that said, travellers tend to take a lax attitude towards smoking hashish in Sinai, particularly in the backpacker-friendly towns of Dahab and Nuweiba. Although you will no doubt be offered drugs during your travels, and will come across other travellers who are indulging, trust us – there are far better places to spend your golden years than rotting away in an Egyptian prison.

MAPS

The pick of the country maps available commercially is the Kümmerly & Frey map, which covers all of Egypt on a scale of 1:950,000. The same company also produces a map of Sinai and a pictorial (but fairly useless) map of the Nile. Similarly good is the Freytag & Berndt map, which includes a plan of the Pyramids of Giza and covers all of Egypt except the western quarter, at a scale of 1:1,000,000. It includes insets of Cairo and central Alexandria.

Nelles Verlag has one of the most complete, though dated, general maps of Egypt (scale 1:2,500,000) including a map of the Nile Valley (scale 1:750,000) and a good enlargement of central Cairo.

Map of Egypt (scale 1:1,000,000), published by Macmillan, includes a map of the Nile Valley and a map of the country, plus good maps of Cairo and Alexandria and a variety of enlargements and temple plans.

MONEY

The currency is the Egyptian pound (E£) – in Arabic, a *guinay*. One pound consists of 100 piastres (pt). There are notes in denominations of 5pt, 10pt and 25pt, but these are rarely spotted. The 50pt, E£1, E£5, E£10, E£20, E£50 and E£100 notes are widely used. There's also a rarely seen E£200 note. There are 10pt, 20pt, 5pt, 50pt and E£1 coins, but they seem to be almost nonexistent and are sometimes thought of as collector's items.

As a good rule of thumb in Egypt, make sure you hoard small change wherever possible. Also, be sure to cash out large bills in upscale establishments, even if they initially appear unwilling.

Because of the dire state of the national currency, many tour operators and hotels will only accept payment in American dollars or euros. To be on the safe side, it's a good idea to travel around Egypt with a modest supply of dollars.

Exchange rates for a range of foreign currencies are given on the inside front cover of this book.

ATMS

It's possible to travel in Egypt now relying solely on plastic as ATMs are becoming more and more widespread. Tourist-friendly cities such as Cairo, Alexandria, Luxor, Sharm el-Sheikh and Hurghada are saturated with cash dispensers, and you'll also find them in Alexandria, Dahab, Nuweiba and Aswan.

Of the numerous types of ATM in Egypt, the vast majority are compatible with Visa, MasterCard and any Cirrus or Plus cards. ATMs at Banque Misr, CIB, Egyptian American Bank (EAB), National Bank of Egypt and HSBC are particularly reliable.

CREDIT CARDS

Amex, Visa, MasterCard and Diners Club are becoming more useful in Egypt. Generally speaking, they are accepted quite widely in foreign-friendly hotels, shops and restaurants, though away from tourist establishments, they are far less common and in remote areas they remain useles In many places you will be charged a pe centage of the sale (anywhere betwee 3% and 10%) to use them.

Make sure you retain any receipts t check later against your statements a there have been cases of shop owner adding extra zeros.

Visa and MasterCard can be used fo cash advances at Banque Misr and th National Bank of Egypt, as well as a Thomas Cook offices.

INTERNATIONAL TRANSFERS

Western Union, the international money transfer specialist, operates jointly i Egypt with Misr America Internationa Bank and IBA business centres.
Cairo (☎ 02-2755 5165) Downtown (Ma pp66-7; 19 Qasr el-Nil, Cairo); Garden City (Ibrahim Naguib, Garden City)

THE ART OF BARGAINING

Even in shops where prices are clearly marked, many Egyptians will still try to shave something off the bill. Of course, when buying in souqs, such as Cairo's Khan al-Khalili, bargaining is imperative unless you are willing to pay well over the odds.

The first rule is never to show too much interest in the item you want to buy. Second, don't buy the first item that takes your fancy. Wander around and price things up, but don't make it obvious; otherwise, when you return to the first shop, the vendor knows that it's because he or she is the cheapest.

Decide how much you would be happy paying and then express a casual interest in buying. The vendor will state a price. So the bargaining begins. You state a figure somewhat less than the one you have fixed in your mind. The shopkeeper will inevitably huff about how absurd that is and then tell you the 'lowest' price. If it is not low enough, then be insistent and keep smiling. Tea or coffee might be served as part of the bargaining ritual but accepting it doesn't place you under any obligation to buy. If you still can't get your price, walk away. This often has the effect of closing the sale in your favour. If not, there are thousands more shops in the bazaar.

If you do get your price or lower, never feel guilty – no vendor, no matter what they may tell you, ever sells below cost.

Luxor (Map pp96-7; ☎ 095-372 292; Mina Palace Hotel, Corniche an-Nil, Luxor)

MONEYCHANGERS

Money can be officially changed at Amex and Thomas Cook offices, as well as commercial banks, foreign exchange (forex) bureaus and some hotels. Rates don't tend to vary much, especially for the US dollar but, if you're keen to squeeze out the last piastre, note that the forex bureaus generally offer slightly better rates than the banks, and usually don't charge commission.

Egyptian pounds can be changed back into hard currency at the end of your stay at some banks, forex bureaus, and Thomas Cook and Amex offices.

It is also possible to have money wired to you from home through Amex. This service operates through most Amex branches, and can be used by anyone, regardless of whether you have an Amex card or not.

TAXES

Taxes of up to 25% will be added to your bill in most upmarket restaurants. There are also hefty taxes levied on four- and five-star accommodation – these have been factored into the prices we have cited.

TRAVELLERS CHEQUES

While there is no problem cashing well-known brands of travellers cheques at the major banks such as Banque Misr or the National Bank of Egypt, many forex bureaus don't take them. Cheques issued on post office accounts (common in Europe) or cards linked to such accounts cannot be used in Egypt.

Banks can have a small handling charge on travellers cheques, usually a few Egyptian pounds per cheque. Always ask about commission as it can vary. Forex bureaus that take cheques tend not to charge any commission.

In addition, Amex and Thomas Cook travellers cheques can also be cashed at their offices, found in Cairo, Alexandria, Luxor, Aswan, Hurghada and Sharm el-Sheikh. A small handling charge usually applies.

SOLO TRAVELLERS

Other than where common sense dictates – for example, don't go wandering off into the desert on your own, don't go snorkelling or diving unaccompanied – there is nowhere in Egypt that can't be travelled solo – if you are a man, that is. Solo travel for women is slightly more difficult (see p358 for more information and tips for women), but is still viable as long as you use sensible caution and dress appropriately.

TELEPHONE

The country code for Egypt is ☎ 20, followed by the local area code (minus the zero), then the number. Local area codes are given at the start of each city or town section. The international access code (to call abroad from Egypt) is ☎ 00. For directory assistance call ☎ 140 or ☎ 141. The most common mobile phone prefixes in Egypt are ☎ 010 and ☎ 012.

Two companies sell phonecards in Egypt. Menatel has yellow-and-green booths, while Nile Tel's are red and blue. Cards are sold at shops and kiosks and come in units of E£10, E£15, E£20 and E£30. Once you insert the card into the telephone, press the flag in the top left corner to get instructions in English.

INTERNATIONAL CALLING CARDS

The following cards can be accessed through these Cairo numbers: AT&T (☎ 02-2510 0200) and MCI (☎ 02-2795 5770).

MOBILE PHONES

Egypt's mobile-phone network runs on the GSM system.

There are two main mobile-phone companies in Egypt: **MobiNil** (☎ 02-2574 7000; www.mobinil.com) and **Vodafone** (☎ 16888; www.vodafone.com.eg, www.mobileconnect .vodafone.com). Both sell convenient prepaid cards from their many retail outlets across the country.

TIME

Egypt is two hours ahead of GMT/UTC and daylight-saving time is observed (it begins on the last Thursday in April and ends on the last Thursday in September). So, without allowing for variations due to daylight saving, when it's noon in Cairo it is 2am in Los Angeles, 5am in New York and Montreal, 10am in London, 1pm in Moscow, and 7pm in Melbourne and Sydney.

TOILETS

Public toilets, when they can be found, are bad news. Some toilets are of the 'squat' variety. Only in midrange and top-end hotels will toilet paper be provided; most toilets simply come equipped with a water squirter for washing yourself when you're finished. If you do use toilet paper, put it in the bucket that's usually provided.

In cities it's a good idea to make a mental note of all Western-style fast-food joints and five-star hotels, as these are where you'll find the most sanitary facilities.

TOURIST INFORMATION

The **Egyptian Tourist Authority** (www .egypt.travel) has tourist information offices throughout the country, some of which are better than others. The usefulness of the offices depends largely on the staff. The Cairo, Aswan, Luxor, Dakhla, Siwa, Alexandria and Suez offices are staffed by people who have strong local knowledge and who will go out of their way to hel you. Government-produced referenc materials, such as maps and brochure tend to be out of date and too general.

TRAVELLERS WITH DISABILITIES

Egypt is not well equipped for traveller with a mobility problem. Ramps are fev and far between, public facilities don necessarily have lifts, curbs are high (ex cept in Alexandria, which has wheelchai friendly sidewalks), traffic is lethal an gaining entrance to some of the ancien sites – such as the Pyramids of Giza c the tombs on the West Bank near Luxor is all but impossible due to their narrov entrances and steep stairs.

Despite all this, there is no reaso why intrepid travellers with disabilitie shouldn't visit Egypt. In general you'll fin locals quite willing to assist with any diff culties. We have heard excellent reports c **Egypt for All** (www.egyptforall.com; 334 Shari Sudan, Mohandiseen, Cairo), an Egyptian com pany specialising in travel arrangement for travellers who are mobility impaired

See the website **Access-Able Trave Source** (www.access-able.com) for genera information for travellers with disabili ties. Before leaving home, travellers ca also get in touch with their nationa support organisation. Ask for the 'trave officer', who may have a list of travel ager cies that specialise in tours for peopl with disabilities.

Access, The Foundation for Accessi bility by the Disabled (☎ 516-887 579 PO Box 356, Malverne, NY 11565, USA)

CNFLRH (☎ 01 53 80 66 66; 236 Rue de Tolbia Paris, France)

Radar (☎ 020-7250 3222; www.radar.or uk; 12 City Forum, 250 City Rd, London EC1V 8A UK) Produces holiday fact-packs tha cover planning, insurance, useful o anisations, transport, equipment and specialised accommodation.

Society for the Advancement of Travel for the Handicapped (SATH; ☎ 212-447 7284; www.sath.org; 347 Fifth Ave, o 610, New York, NY 10016, USA)

VISAS & PERMITS

Most foreigners entering Egypt must obtain a visa. The only exceptions are citizens of Guinea, Hong Kong and Macau. There are three ways of doing this: in advance from the Egyptian embassy or consulate in your home country, at an Egyptian embassy abroad or, for certain nationalities, on arrival at the airport. This last option is the cheapest and easiest of the three.

Visas are available on arrival for nationals of all western European countries, the UK, the USA, Australia, all Arab countries, New Zealand, Japan and Korea. At the Cairo airport, the entire process takes only 20 minutes or so, and costs US$15. No photo is required.

Nationals from other countries must obtain visas in their countries of residence. Processing times and costs for visa applications vary according to your nationality and the country in which you apply.

If you are travelling overland, you can get a visa at the port in Aqaba, Jordan before getting the ferry to Nuweiba. However, if you are coming from Israel, you *cannot* get a visa at the border unless you are guaranteed by an Egyptian Travel Agency. Instead, you have to get the visa beforehand at either the embassy in Tel Aviv or the consulate in Eilat.

A single-entry visa is valid for three months and entitles the holder to stay in Egypt for 40 days.

SINAI ENTRY STAMPS

It is not necessary to get a full visa if your visit is confined to the area of Sinai be-

tween Sharm el-Sheikh and Taba (on the Israeli border), including St Katherine's Monastery. Instead you are issued with an entry stamp, free of charge, allowing you a 15-day stay. Note that this does not allow you to visit Ras Mohammed National Park. Points of entry where such visa-free stamps are issued are Taba, Nuweiba (port), St Katherine's airport and Sharm el-Sheikh (airport or port).

VISA EXTENSIONS & RE-ENTRY VISAS

Six-month and one-year extensions of your visa for tourist purposes can easily be obtained at passport offices, and only cost a few dollars. If you don't have a multiple-entry visa, it's also possible to get a re-entry visa that is valid to the combined expiry dates of your visa and any extensions.

In Cairo all visa business is carried out at the **Mogamma** (Map pp66-7; Midan Tahrir, Downtown; ⏰ 8am-1.30pm Sat-Wed), a 14-storey Egypto-Stalinist monolith that is rumoured to be closing at some point in the near future.

On the 1st floor, go to window 12 for a form, fill it out and then buy stamps from window 43 before returning to window 12 and submitting your form with the stamps, one photograph, and photocopies of the photo and visa pages of your passport (photos and photocopies can be organised on the ground floor).

Generally speaking, applications are processed overnight, though same-day service is sometimes possible if you drop your passport off very early in the morning.

Passport and visa offices elsewhere in the country:

Alexandria (Map p232; ☎ 482 7873; 25 Sharia Talaat Harb; ⏰ 8.30am-2pm Mon-Thu, 10am-2pm

Fri, 9-11am Sat & Sun) Does visa extensions, usually on the same day.

Aswan (off Map p206; ☎ 231 2238; Corniche an-Nil; ⏳ 8.30am-1pm Sat-Thu) For visa extensions. At the southern end of the Corniche.

Hurghada (Sharia an-Nasr, Ad-Dahar; ⏳ 8am-2pm Sat-Thu) For visa extensions and re-entry visas.

Ismailia (☎ 391 4559; Midan al-Gomhuriyya; ⏳ 8am-2pm Sat-Thu)

Luxor (Map p96-7; ☎ 238 0885; Sharia Khalid ibn al-Walid; ⏳ 8am-8pm Sat-Thu, 2-8pm for information only)

Minya (☎ 236 4193; 2nd fl, above main post office; ⏳ 8.30am-2pm Sat-Thu) Off Sharia Corniche an-Nil.

Port Said (left wing, 4th fl, Governorate Bldg, Sharia 23rd of July; ⏳ 8am-2pm Sat-Thu)

Suez (Sharia al-Horreyya; ⏳ 8.30am-3pm) Issues visa extensions.

TRAVEL PERMITS

Military permits issued by either the Ministry of Interior or Border Police are needed to travel in the Eastern Desert south of Shams Allam (50km south of Marsa Allam), on or around Lake Nasser, off-road in the Western Desert and on the road between the oases of Bahariya and Siwa. These can be obtained through a safari company or travel agency at least a fortnight in advance of the trip.

WOMEN TRAVELLERS

Egyptians are conservative, especially on matters concerning sex and women – Egyptian women that is, not foreign women.

An entire book could be written from the comments and stories of women travellers about their adventures and misadventures in Egypt. You're almost certain to hear chat-up lines such as 'I miss you like the desert misses the rain', which might be funny if they weren't so constant and intimidating. Most of the incidents are nonthreatening nuisances, like a fly buzzing in your ear: you can swat it away and keep it at a distance, but it's always out there buzzing around.

The presence of foreign women presents, in the eyes of some Egyptian men, a chance to get around local cultural norms with ease and without consequences. This belief is reinforced by distorted impressions gained from Western TV and by the clothing worn by some female tourists. As a woman traveller you may receive some verbal harassment at the very least. Serious physical harassment and rape do occasionally occur, but more rarely than in most Western countries.

ATTITUDES TOWARDS WOMEN

Some of the biggest misunderstandings between Egyptians and Westerners occur over the issue of women. Half-truths and stereotypes exist on both sides: many Westerners assume all Egyptian women are veiled, repressed victims, while a large number of Egyptians just see Western women as sex-obsessed and immoral.

For many Egyptians of both genders, the role of a woman is specifically defined: she is mother and matron of the household. The man is the provider. However, as with any society, generalisations can be misleading and the reality is far more nuanced. There are thousands of middle- and upper-middle-class professional women living in Egypt who, like their counterparts in the West, juggle both work and family responsibilities. Among the working classes, where adherence to tradition is the strongest, the ideal may be for women to concentrate on the home and family, but economic reality means that millions of women are forced to work (but are still responsible for all the domestic chores).

TIPS FOR WOMEN TRAVELLERS

- Wear a wedding ring. Generally, Egyptian men seem to have more respect for a married woman.
- If you are travelling with a man, it is better to say you're married rather than 'just friends'.
- Avoid direct eye contact with an Egyptian man unless you know him well.
- Be careful in crowds and other situations where you are crammed between people.
- On public transport, sit next to a woman if possible. On the Cairo metro the first compartment is reserved for women only.
- If you're in the countryside (off the beaten track) be extra conservative in what you wear.
- Remember that even innocent, friendly talk can be misconstrued as flirtation by men unused to close interaction with women.
- If you need help for any reason (directions etc), ask a woman first.
- Be wary when horse or camel riding. It's not unknown for a guy to ride close to you and grab your horse, among other things.
- Only on private beaches in the top-end resorts along the Red Sea and in southern Sinai are you likely to feel comfortable stripping down to a bikini. Along the Mediterranean coast and in oasis pools, swim in shorts and a T-shirt at the minimum, though even then you'll likely attract male onlookers. Egyptian women rarely go swimming at public beaches; when they do, they swim fully clothed, scarf and all.
- If you do get harassed, don't expect people to be ashamed or apologise if you call them out – all the advice to ignore is really wiser.
- Being befriended by an Egyptian woman is a great way to learn more about life in Egypt and have someone totally nonthreatening to guide you around. Getting to know an Egyptian woman is, however, easier said than done – seize on whatever opportunities you get.

The issue of sex is where the differences between Western and Egyptian women are most apparent. Premarital sex (or, indeed, any sex outside marriage) is taboo in Egypt. However, as with anything forbidden, it still happens. Nevertheless, it is the exception rather than the rule – and that goes for men as well as women.

For women, however, the issue is potentially far more serious. With the possible exception of the upper classes, women are expected to be virgins when they marry and a family's reputation can rest upon this point. In such a context the restrictions placed on a girl – no matter how onerous they may seem to a Westerner – are to protect her and her reputation from the potentially disastrous attentions of men.

WHAT TO WEAR

Away from the Sinai and Red Sea beaches, Egyptians are quite conservative about dress. As with anywhere, take your cues from those around you: if you're in a rural area and all the women are in long, concealing dresses, you should be conservatively dressed. If you're going out to a hip Cairo nightspot, you're likely to see middle- and upper-class Egyptian girls in the briefest designer gear and can dress accordingly – just don't walk there.

It is particularly important to cover up when visiting mosques and churches – you'll find that carrying a shawl to use as a head covering will come in very useful, particularly when visiting areas such as Islamic and Old Cairo.

Unfortunately, although dressing conservatively should reduce the incidence of harassment, it by no means guarantees you'll be left alone. Although it may or may not be comforting, Egyptian women get verbal and physical harassment as well – it's not just because you're foreign.

TRANSPORT

GETTING THERE & AWAY

ENTERING THE COUNTRY

If you enter the country via Cairo International Airport, there are a few formalities. After walking past the dusty-looking duty-free shops, you'll come to a row of exchange booths. If you haven't organised a visa in advance, you'll need to pay US$15 to receive a visa stamp (see p357). You then fill in one of the pink immigration forms available on the benches in front of the immigration officials before queuing to be processed.

Although formalities vary depending on which border you're crossing, generally speaking it's fairly straightforward to enter Egypt by land or sea.

Regardless of the means by which you enter Egypt, it is important to have a passport that is valid for at least six months from the date that you enter the country.

AIR

AIRPORTS & AIRLINES

Egypt has quite a few airports, but onl seven of these are official international ports of entry: Cairo, Alexandria, Luxo Aswan, Hurghada, Sharm el-Sheikh and Marsa Alam. Most air travellers ente Egypt through Cairo, Alexandria or Sharr el-Sheikh, while the other airports tend to be used by charter and package-dea flights only.

Egypt's international and national car rier is **EgyptAir** (MS; ☎ national call centre 090 70000; www.egyptair.com; ☉ 8am-8pm), whic has its hub at Cairo International Airport

AIRLINES FLYING TO/FROM EGYPT

Air France (AF; ☎ in Cairo 02-2770 6262 www.airfrance.com)

Alitalia (AZ; ☎ in Cairo 02-2578 5823; ww .alitalia.com)

British Airways (BA; www.britishairway .com) Cairo (☎ 02-2480 0380); Cairo Inter national Airport (☎ 02-2269 1690)

BMI (BMI; ☎ in UK 0870 6070 555; www.flybm .com)

El Al Israel Airlines (LY; ☎ in Cairo 02-73 1620; www.elal.com)

Emirates Airlines (EK; www.emirates.com ☎ in Cairo 02-19899)

KLM (KL; ☎ in Cairo 02-2770 6251; www .klm.com)

Lufthansa (LH; ☎ in Cairo 02-19380; www .lufthansa.com)

Royal Jordanian (RJ; ☎ in Cairo 02-257 0875; www.rj.com)

Singapore Airlines (SQ; ☎ in Cairo 02-374 2879; www.singaporeairlines.com)

LAND

ISRAEL & THE PALESTINIAN TERRITORIES

The two official borders with Israel and the Palestinian Territories are Rafah and Taba. At the time of research, the Rafah order crossing, which services a direct route from Cairo to Tel Aviv via the Gaza Strip, was closed.

The border crossing at Taba is used for the majority of travel between Egypt and Israel and the Palestinian Territories. Travellers make their way to Taba from destinations across Egypt, and then walk across the border, which is open 24 hours. An Israeli visa is not required for most nationalities. Keep in mind that there are no buses operating in Israel and the Palestinian Territories on Friday evenings or before sundown Saturday, the Jewish holy day of Shabbat.

Heading back to Egypt, you must have a visa in advance unless your visit is limited to eastern Sinai or you have prearranged your entry with an Egyptian tour operator (see also p357). At the **border crossing** (☎ 08-637 2104, 636 0999) you'll need to pay a 68NIS fee to leave. Once you've crossed the border, you'll need to pay an Egyptian entry tax of E£30 at a booth about 1km south of the border on the main road. Alternatively, you can pick up a free Sinai-only entry permit (see p357).

TOURS

There are countless possibilities for organised tours in Egypt, with a plethora of agencies dealing with everything from guided trips and overland safaris to Nile cruises and dive trips. See pp308-11 and individual destination sections for details.

It pays to shop around. When considering a tour, ask what the price includes (ie flights, admission fees, food etc) – some companies include these in their prices, while others don't – you need to be aware of what you're paying for when you compare prices.

Following is a list of specialist operators that organise Egypt packages tailored for travellers looking for more than just two weeks in the sun.

AUSTRALIA

Intrepid Travel (☎ 03-8602 0500; www .intrepidtravel.com) Highly regarded small-group tours with an emphasis on responsible tourism. Also has offices in the UK, North America, Europe and South Africa.

Peregrine Adventures (☎ 03-9663 8611; www.peregrineadventures.com) An agent for the UK's Dragoman, Exodus and the Imaginative Traveller.

EGYPT

Abercrombie & Kent (☎ in the US 800-554-7094, 630-954-2944, www.akegypt.com) Offers first-class packages using top-end hotels, domestic flights and its own custom-built Nile cruisers.

Experience Egypt (☎ 02-3302 8364; www.experience-egypt.com; 42 Sharia Abu el-Mahassen el-Shazly, Mohandiseen, Cairo) Part of Lady Egypt Tours. Organises small-group tours of Sinai, Alexandria and the Nile Valley that are marketed in the UK and Canada.

UK

Bales Tours (☎ 0870 752 0780; www.bales worldwide.com) Runs upmarket tours using five-star accommodation.

Egypt On The Go (☎ 020-7371 1113; www .egyptonthego.com) Tours of Egypt and PADI diving-course holidays. Also has an Australian office.

Exodus (☎ 0870 240 5550; www.exodus .co.uk) Includes Nile cruises and tours around Sinai and through the Western Desert.

Explore Worldwide (☎ 0800 227 8747; www.exploreworldwide.com) A variety of short and long itineraries.

Hayes & Jarvis (☎ 0870 366 1636; www .hayes-jarvis.com) A respected Egypt specialist.

Imaginative Traveller (☎ 0800 316 2717; www.imaginative-traveller.com) Small-group tours. Also has offices elsewhere, including the US.

Wind, Sand & Stars (☎ 020-7359 7551; www.windsandstars.co.uk) A Sinai specialist that organises trips involving climbing and walking, desert camping, bird-watching and snorkelling.

USA & CANADA

Bestway Tours & Safaris (☎ 604-264 7378; www.bestway.com) Canadian company offering small-group tours, including a tour from Siwa to Ghadames in Libya and one visiting Egypt, Israel and the Palestinian Territories, and Jordan.

GETTING AROUND

Egypt has a very extensive public and private transport system, and you can travel just about anywhere in Egypt relatively cheaply.

AIR

EgyptAir (www.egyptair.com) is the main domestic carrier, and flights are a surprisingly cheap and convenient means of bypassing countless hours on buses or trains. Prices can increase dramatically during the high season (October to April), and high demand means that it's wise to book as far in advance as possible.

BOAT

No trip to Egypt is complete without a trip down the Nile River. Egyptians have been plying these muddy waters for countless generations, and you can still take the trip on a felucca (a traditional sailing vessel) or opt for a modern steamer or cruise ship. See p308 for details.

Travellers heading to Sinai can bypa hours of bumpy roads and frustratin police checkpoints by taking the speec boat from Hurghada to Sharm el-Sheik (p275).

BUS

Buses service just about every city, tow and village in Egypt. Ticket prices are ger erally comparable with the cost of 2nc class train tickets.

Relatively comfortable, air-con 'delux buses travel between Cairo, Alexandri Ismailia, Port Said, Suez, St Katherine Monastery, Sharm el-Sheikh, Hurghad and Luxor. Tickets cost a bit more tha those for standard buses but they'r still cheap. The best of the deluxe bu companies is **Superjet** (☎ in Cairo 02-229 9017) – try to travel with them when ever possible. You should also alway carry your passport as buses are ofte stopped at military checkpoints for ran dom identity checks.

It is advisable to book tickets in ac vance, at least on very popular route (such as from Cairo to Sinai) and thos with few buses running (from Cairo t the Western Desert).

CAR & MOTORCYCLE

Driving in Cairo is a crazy affair, so thin seriously before you decide to drive ther (see also p93). Driving elsewhere in Egyp isn't so bad, and in some areas it's the bes way to get around. Avoid intercity drivin at night. An International Driving Permit i required and you can be hit with a heav fine if you're caught without one. Driver should be over the age of 25.

HIRE

Several international car-hire agencie have offices in Egypt, including **Avi** (www.avisegypt.com), **Budget** (www.budge

POLICE CONVOYS

Prior to 2009, tourists travelling by road in the Nile Valley, and along parts of the Red Sea coast, were forced to join a police-escorted convoy. A legacy of the Islamist insurgency of the 1990s, which reached its height with the 1997 massacre at the Temple of Hatshepsut in Luxor, the convoy system was introduced by the Egyptian government to give foreign tourists a sense of personal security.

Now, after more than a decade of having your itinerary dictated by a frustratingly rigid schedule, and having to keep up with notoriously lead-footed police, it is possible to travel independently throughout an increasingly large swath of Egypt.

Note that police convoys still operate between Aswan and Abu Simbel.

com), **Europcar** (www.europcar.com/car-egypt html) and **Hertz** (www.hertzegypt.com). Their ates match international charges and inding a cheap deal with local agencies s virtually impossible – it's advisable to make arrangements via the web before you arrive.

ROAD RULES

Driving is on the right-hand side. The official speed limit outside towns is 90km/h though it is often less in some areas) and 00km/h on four-lane highways, such as the Cairo–Alexandria Desert Hwy. If you're caught speeding, the police will confiscate your driving licence and you have to go to the traffic headquarters in the area to get it back – a lengthy and laborious process.

Many roads have checkpoints where police often ask for identity papers, so make sure you've got your passport and International Driving Permit on hand or you may be liable for a US$100 on-the-spot fine.

When driving through the countryside, keep in mind that children and adults are likely to wander onto your path, even on main roads. If you do have an accident, get to the nearest police station as quickly as possible and report what happened.

LOCAL TRANSPORT

As well as the local transport services described here, some cities and towns have their own options – most are variations on the pony-and-trap theme.

BUS & MINIBUS

Cairo and Alexandria are the only cities with their own bus systems. Taking a bus in either place is an experience far beyond simply getting from A to B. The scene inside the bus in this case usually resembles a *Guinness World Record* attempt on the greatest number of people in a fixed space. Taking a minibus is an easier option. Passengers are not allowed to stand (although this rule is frequently overlooked), and each minibus leaves as soon as every seat is taken.

METRO

Cairo is the only city in Egypt with a metro system (for details, see p93).

MICROBUS

A slightly bigger version of the service taxi, the *meecrobus* is a Toyota van that would normally take about 12 people, but in Egypt takes as many as 22. Privately owned and usually unmarked, they shuttle around all the larger cities.

In Cairo, you might have occasion to use a microbus to get out to the Pyramids, while in Alexandria they shuttle the length of Tariq al-Horreyya and the Corniche to Montazah, and in Sharm el-Sheikh they carry passengers between Old Sharm, Na'ama Bay and Shark's Bay.

PICK-UP

Toyota and Chevrolet pick-up trucks cover a lot of the routes between the smaller towns and villages off the main roads. The general rule is to get 12 people inside the covered rear of the truck, often with an assortment of goods squeezed in on the floor.

Covered pick-up trucks are also sometimes used within towns as local taxis. This is especially so in some of the oases towns, on Luxor's West Bank and in smaller places along the Nile.

SERVICE TAXI

Travelling by *servees* is one of the fastest ways to go from city to city. Drivers con-gregate near bus and train stations an tout for passengers by shouting the destination. When the car's full, it's of A driver won't leave before his car is fu unless you and/or the other passenge want to pay for all of the seats. Fares a usually cheaper than either the buse or trains and there are no set departu times – you just turn up and find a car.

TAXI

Almost every second car in Egypt (wheth labelled or not) is a taxi, and they are b far the most convenient way of gettin about. Stand at the side of the road, stic your hand out, shout your destinatio and get ready for some potential Ind race-car driving.

As a general rule, taxi etiquette is tha you get in knowing what to pay, an when you arrive you get out and han the money through the window. Wit that said, if a driver suspects you don know what the correct fare is, you're fa game for fleecing. Since most traveller

'TAXI!'

Taxis are at once a blessing and a curse. They're a remarkably convenient and affordable way of getting around the city, but they can also be a frequent source of unpleasantness when it comes to paying the fare. The problem stems from the unmetered system of payment, which can lead to discontent. Passengers frequently feel that they've been taken advantage of (which they often have), while drivers are occasionally genuinely aggrieved by what they see as under-payment. So why don't the drivers use the meter? Because they were all calibrated at a time when petrol was ludicrously cheap. That time has long passed and any driver relying on his meter would now be out of pocket every time he came to fill up.

Taxi driving is far from being a lucrative profession. Which isn't to say that the next time you flag a taxi for a short hop across town and the driver declares '10 pounds' that you should smile and say 'OK'. But it might make it easier to see that it was probably worth his while trying. After all, from the point of view of the local taxi driver, if you can afford to make it all the way to Egypt, you can probably afford to pay a bit more than the going rate.

n Egypt don't speak fluent Arabic, it's probably best to agree on a price before getting into the taxi.

Often when it comes to bargaining, a driver will demand absurd amounts of money – don't be intimidated and don't be drawn into an argument. It's nothing but bluster; the driver is likely playing on the fact that you're a *khwaga* (foreigner) and don't know better. Eventually, the driver will probably accept your offer if it's appropriate, though you can always walk away if you feel like you're being taken advantage of and try again with another taxi.

TRAIN

Although trains travel along more than 5000km of track to almost every major city and town in Egypt, the system is badly in need of modernisation (it's a relic of the British occupation). Most services are grimy and battered and are a poor second option to the deluxe bus. The exceptions are the *Turbini* and *Espani* services from Cairo to Alexandria, and the tourist and sleeping trains from Cairo down to Luxor and Aswan – on these routes the train is the preferred option over the bus.

If you have an International Student Identification Card (ISIC), discounts are granted on all fares, except those for the sleeping-car services.

CLASSES & SERVICES

Trains with sleeper cars are the most comfortable and among the fastest in Egypt. The cars, which are run by Abela Egypt, are the same as those used by trains in Europe. At least one sleeper train travels between Alexandria, Cairo, Luxor and Aswan daily. For details, see the Getting There & Away sections of those cities.

The Abela sleeper trains are 1st class only and reservations must be made in advance. Compartments come with a seat that converts into a bed, a fold-down bunk (with clean linen, pillows and blankets) and a small basin with running water. Beds are quite short and tall people may spend an uncomfortable night as a result. It is worth requesting a middle compartment, as those at the ends of the carriages are located near the toilets and can sometimes be noisy. Shared toilets are generally clean and have toilet paper. Airline-style dinners and breakfasts are served in the compartments but you should not expect a gourmet eating experience. Drinks (including alcohol) are served by the steward.

↘ GLOSSARY

abd – servant of
abeyya – woman's garment
abu – father, saint
ahwa – coffee, coffeehouse
ain – well, spring
al-jeel – a type of music characterised by a hand-clapping rhythm overlaid with a catchy vocal; literally 'the generation'

ba'al – grocer
bab – gate or door
baksheesh – alms, tip
baladi – local, rural
beit – house
bey – leader; term of respect
bir – spring, well
burg – tower
bustan – walled garden

calèche – horse-drawn carriage
caravanserai – merchants' inn; also called *khan* and *wikala*
centrale – telephone office

dahabiyya – houseboat
darb – track, street
deir – monastery, convent
domina – dominoes

eid – Islamic feast
emir – Islamic ruler, military commander or governor; literally 'prince'

fellaheen – (singular: fellah) peasant farmers or agricultural workers who makes up the majority of Egypt's population; 'fellah' literally means 'ploughman' or 'tiller of the soil'

galabiyya – man's full-length robe
gebel – mountain

gezira – island
guinay – pound (currency)

hajj – pilgrimage to Mecca; all Muslim should make the journey at least onc in their lifetime
hammam – bathhouse
hantour – horse-drawn carriage
Hejira – Islamic calendar; Moham med's flight from Mecca to Medina i AD 622

ibn – son of
iconostasis – screen with doors an icons set in tiers, used in Eastern Chris tian churches
iftar – breaking the fast after sundow during the month of *Ramadan*

kershef – building material made o large chunks of salt mixed with rock an plastered in local clay
khamsin – a dry, hot wind from th Western Desert
khan – merchants' inn; also calle *caravanserai* and *wikala*
khanqah – *Sufi* monastery
khedive – Egyptian viceroy under Otto man suzerainty
khwaga – foreigner
kuttab – Quranic school

madrassa – school, especially one as sociated with a mosque
mahattat – station
mammisi – birthhouse
maristan – hospital
mashrabiyya – ornate carved woode panel or screen; a feature of Islami architecture

mastaba – mudbrick structure in the shape of a bench above tombs, from which later pyramids developed; Arabic word for 'bench'

matar – airport

midan – town or city square

mihrab – niche in the wall of a mosque that indicates the direction of Mecca

minbar – pulpit in a mosque

Misr – Egypt (also means 'Cairo')

moulid – saints' festival

muezzin – mosque official who calls the faithful to prayer

mugzzabin – *Sufi* followers who participate in *zikrs*

muqarnas – stalactite-like stone carving used to decorate doorways and window recesses

oud – a type of lute

piastre – Egyptian currency; one Egyptian pound consists of 100 piastres

qala'a – fortress

qasr – castle or palace

Ramadan – the ninth month of the lunar Islamic calendar during which Muslims fast from sunrise to sunset

ras – headland

sabil – public drinking fountain

servees – service taxi

shaabi – popular music of the working class

sharia – road or street

sharm – bay

sheesha – water pipe

souq – market

speos – rock-cut tomb or chapel

Sufi – follower of any Islamic mystical order that emphasises dancing, chanting and trances to attain unity with God

tahtib – male dance performed with wooden staves

tarboosh – the hat known elsewhere as a fez

towla – backgammon

umm – mother of

wadi – desert watercourse, dry except in the rainy season

waha – oasis

wikala – merchants' inn; also called *caravanserai* and *khan*

zikr – long sessions of dancing, chanting and trances usually carried out by *Sufi mugzzabin* to attain unity with God.

⬇ PHARAONIC GLOSSARY

akh – usually translated as 'transfigured spirit', produced when the ka (soul) and ba (spirit) united after the deceased entered the afterlife

Ammut – composite monster of the underworld who was part crocodile, part lion, part hippo and ate the hearts of the unworthy dead

ankh – similar to a cross with a looped top, often seen in Pharaonic art and said to symbolise life; also called 'key of life'

ba – usually translated as 'spirit', which appeared after death as a human-headed bird, able to fly to and from the tomb and into the afterlife

Book of the Dead – modern term for the collection of ancient funerary texts designed to guide the dead through the afterlife, partly based on the earlier *Pyramid Texts* and *Coffin Texts*

Canopic jars – containers usually made of limestone or calcite to store the preserved entrails of mummies

cartouche – the protective oval shape (from the French word for cartridge), which surrounded the names of kings and queens and occasionally gods

cenotaph – a memorial structure set up in memory of a deceased king or queen, separate from their tomb

Coffin Texts – funerary texts developed from the earlier *Pyramid Texts*, which were then written on coffins

coregency – a period of joint rule by two pharaohs, usually father and son

cult temple – religious building(s) designed to house the spirits of the gods and accessible only to the priesthood, usually on the Nile's east bank

deshret – 'red land', referring to barren desert

djed pillar – the symbolic backbone of Osiris, bestowing strength and stability and often worn as an amulet

false door – the means by which the soul of the deceased could enter and leave the world of the living to accept funerary offerings brought to their tomb

funerary (mortuary) temple – the religious structures where the souls of dead pharaohs were commemorated and sustained with offerings, usually built on the Nile's west bank

Heb-Sed festival – jubilee ceremony of royal renewal and rejuvenation, usually celebrated after 30 years' rule

Heb-Sed race – part of the *Heb-Sed festival* when pharaohs undertook physical feats to demonstrate their prowess

hieratic – ancient shorthand of *hieroglyphs* used for day-to-day transactions

hieroglyphs – Greek for 'sacred carvings', referring to ancient Egypt's formal picture writing used mainly for tomb and temple walls

hypostyle hall – imposing section of temple characterised by densely packed monumental columns

ka – usually translated as 'soul', this was a person's 'double', which was created with them at birth and which lived on after death, sustained by offerings

kemet – 'black land', referring to the fertile areas along the Nile's banks

king lists – chronological lists of king's names kept as an historical record

lotus (water lily) – the heraldic plant of Upper (southern) Egypt

mammisi – the Birth House attached to certain Late Period and Graeco-Roman temples and associated with the goddesses Isis and Hathor

mastaba – Arabic word for bench, used to describe the mudbrick tomb structures built over burial chambers and from which pyramids developed

naos – sanctuary containing the god's statue, generally located in the centre of ancient temples

natron – mixture of sodium carbonate and sodium bicarbonate used to dry out the body during mummification; used by the living to clean linen, teeth and skin

nemes – the yellow-and-blue striped headcloth worn by pharaohs, such as on Tutankhamun's golden death mask

nomarch – local governor of each of Egypt's 42 nomes

nome – term for Egypt's 42 provinces

obelisk – monolithic stone pillar often gilded to reflect sunlight around temples and usually set in pairs

Opening of the Mouth ceremony – the culmination of the funeral, performed on the mummy of the deceased by their heir or funerary priest using spells and implements to restore their senses

Opet festival – celebration held at Luxor Temple to restore the powers of the pharaoh at a meeting with the god Amun

papyrus – the heraldic plant of Lower (northern) Egypt

pharaoh – term for an Egyptian king derived from the ancient Egyptian word for palace, per-aa

pylon – gateway with sloping sides forming the entrance to temples

Pyramid Texts – funerary texts inscribed on the walls of late Old Kingdom pyramids and restricted to royalty

sarcophagus – large stone coffins used to house the mummy and its coffin(s)

scarab – the sacred dung beetle believed to propel the sun's disc through the sky in the same way the beetle pushes a ball of dung across the floor

Serapeum – vast network of underground catacombs at Saqqara in which the Apis bulls were buried, later associated with the Ptolemaic god Serapis

serdab – from the Arabic word for cellar, a small room in a mastaba tomb containing a statue of the deceased to which offerings were presented

shabti (or ushabti) – small servant figurines placed in burials to undertake any manual work in the afterlife

sidelock of youth – characteristic hairstyle of children and certain priests in which the head is shaved and a single lock of hair allowed to grow

solar barque – the boat in which the sun god Ra sailed through the heavens, with actual examples buried close to certain pyramids for use by the spirits of the pharaohs

Uraeus – an image of the cobra goddess Wadjet worn at the brow of royalty to symbolically protect them by spitting fire into the eyes of their enemies

Weighing of the Heart (The Judgement of Osiris) – the heart of the deceased was weighed against the feather of Maat with Osiris as judge; if light and free of sin they were allowed to spend eternity as an akh; if heavy it was eaten by Ammut and they were damned forever

⇘ BEHIND THE SCENES

THE AUTHORS
ANTHONY SATTIN

Coordinating author, This is Egypt, Egypt's Top 25 Experiences, Egypt's Top Itineraries, Planning Your Trip, Luxor, Esna to Abu Simbel, Beni Suef to Qena

Anthony's latest book is *A Winter on the Nile: Florence Nightingale, Gustave Flaubert and the Temptations of Egypt*. His other highly-acclaimed books include *The Pharaoh's Shadow*, a travel book about Egypt, and *The Gates of Africa*, an account of the search for Timbuktu. Anthony is a regular contributor to the *Sunday Times* and *Condé Nast Traveller*, and his work has also appeared in *Vanity Fair, GQ* and a range of other publications. He has lectured widely, appeared in many television documentaries and presents features for BBC radio. He is the editor of Lonely Planet's *A House Somewhere: Tales of Life Abroad* and has contributed to Lonely Planet's *Morocco* and *Algeria* guidebooks.

Author thanks Alexandra Stock, Colin Clement, Horus, Zoltan Mahrazi, Jane Akshar, Mamdouh Sayed Khalifa, Salima Ikram, Nabil Naguib, Khairy Ibrahim, Wael Abed, Richard Launayy, Mennat Allah Farouk and Wagdy Soliman.

MICHAEL BENANAV
Western Desert

Michael cut his adventure-travelling teeth in Egypt back in 1998, and his experiences were so bizarre he figured he'd better start writing about them. Since then, he's authored the highly praised books *Men of Salt: Crossing the Sahara on the Caravan of White Gold*, for which he joined a working camel caravan on its mission schlepping salt to Timbuktu; and *Joshua & Isadora: A True Tale of Loss and Love in the Holocaust*, which took him through the vodka-soaked villages of rural Ukraine. He also writes and photographs for the *New York Times* and other publications. When he's not in some remote nook of Asia or Africa, he can often be found walking in the hills behind his home in northern New Mexico.

LONELY PLANET AUTHORS

Why is our travel information the best in the world? It's simple: our authors are passionate, dedicated travellers. They don't take freebies in exchange for positive coverage so you can be sure the advice you're given is impartial. They travel widely to all the popular spots, and off the beaten track. They don't research using just the internet or phone. They discover new places not included in any other guidebook. They personally visit thousands of hotels, restaurants, palaces, trails, galleries, temples and more. They speak with dozens of locals every day to make sure you get the kind of insider knowledge only a local could tell you. They take pride in getting all the details right, and in telling it how it is. Think you can do it? Find out how at lonelyplanet.com.

MATTHEW D FIRESTONE

Cairo, Around Cairo, Suez Canal, Sinai & the Red Sea Coast

Matthew is a trained anthropologist and epidemiologist, though he abandoned a promising academic career in favour of spending his youth living out of a backpack. With his best explorer's hat and hiking boots on hand, Matthew blazed a trail across the Middle East in the footsteps of Indiana Jones. Although a brief excursion to Petra failed to reveal the final location of the Holy Grail, Matthew's travels brought him from the depths of the Red Sea to the heights of Mt Sinai. He may not have found eternal life but at least he found a bit of adventure – and a whole lot of sand.

THOMAS HALL

Alexandria & the Mediterranean Coast

After a childhood in Mexico, Brazil, and the suburban Chicago of *Risky Business*, Tom attended the University of California, San Diego, and most likely graduated with Literature and Writing degrees. After ingloriously eking out a living as a trivia writer and musician, he moved to San Francisco and failed to strike it rich in the internet gold rush, though he made up for it with voracious consumption of vegetarian burritos. Spending 18 months in Egypt, Tom became a connoisseur of seriously good *sheesha* and learned to appreciate *fuul* and *ta'amiyya*. After working for Lonely Planet in Oakland and Melbourne, Tom now lives in London.

CONTRIBUTING AUTHORS

Dr Joann Fletcher wrote the Pharaonic Egypt section. As a research and teaching fellow at the University of York, where she teaches Egyptian archaeology, Joann undertakes scientific research on everything from mummification to ancient perfumes. She is the Egyptologist for several UK museums and designed the UK's first nationally available Egyptology qualification. Having excavated at a number of sites in Egypt, including the Valley of the Kings, Joann regularly appears on TV, has contributed to the BBC History website and has written a number of books.

Dr Caroline Evans wrote the Health section. Having studied medicine at the University of London, Caroline completed general practice training in Cambridge. She is the medical adviser to Nomad Travel Clinic, a private travel-health clinic in London, and is also a GP specialising in travel medicine. Caroline has acted as expedition doctor for Raleigh International and Coral Cay expeditions.

THIS BOOK

This 1st edition of *Discover Egypt* was coordinated by Anthony Sattin, and researched and written by him, Matthew D Firestone, Michael Benanav and Thomas Hall. This guidebook was commissioned in Lonely Planet's Melbourne office, and produced by the following:

Commissioning Editors Sasha Baskett, Shawn Low
Coordinating Editor Laura Crawford
Coordinating Cartographer Jolyon Philcox
Coordinating Layout Designer Carol Jackson
Managing Editor Annelies Mertens

Managing Cartographers Adrian Persoglia, Herman So
Managing Layout Designers Sally Darmody, Celia Wood, Indra Kilfoyle
Assisting Editors Helen Koehne, Angela Tinson
Assisting Cartographers Diana Duggan, Birgit Jordan
Assisting Layout Designers Nicholas Colicchia, Jim Hsu, Paul Iacono, Jacqui Saunders
Cover Naomi Parker, lonelyplanetimages.com
Internal Image Research Aude Vauconsant, lonelyplanetimages.com
Project Manager Glenn van der Knijff
Language Content Branislava Vladisavljevic

Thanks to Glenn Beanland, Yvonne Bischofberger, Jessica Boland, Brigitte Ellemor, Bruce Evans, Ryan Evans, Joshua Geoghegan, James Hardy, Jane Hart, Laura Jane, Kerrianne Southway, Lyahna Spencer, Simon Tillema

Internal photographs p4 Camels and guides, Aswan, Shania Shegedyn; p10 Tourists riding camels at the Pyramids of Giza, Richard I'Anson; p12 Men outside tents in the souq area of Islamic Cairo, Phil Weymouth; p31 Street in Khan al-Khalili, Cairo, Mark Daffey; p39 Camel and pyramid, Giza, Holger Leue; p3 & p50 Interior of the Mosque of Mohammed Ali, Cairo, Richard I'Anson; p3 & p95 Balloon ride over Luxor, Shania Shegedyn; p3 & p135 Camel handler, Birqash camel market, Sara-Jane Cleland; p3 & p163 Nile River, Beni Suef, Josef Niedermeier/imagebroker; p3 & p183 Hieroglyph column detail at the Temple of Kom Ombo, Shania Shegedyn; p3 & p217 Man selling vegetables in a market, Alexandria, Ariadne Van Zandbergen; p3 & p243 Crowd watching the sunrise, summit of Mt Sinai, Mark Daffey; p3 & p279 Dune in the Great Sand Sea, Western Desert, Ariadne Van Zandbergen; p306 Market stalls and customers, Siwa Oasis, Ariadne Van Zandbergen; p343 Traffic in downtown Cairo, Elliot Daniel

All images are copyright of the photographer unless otherwise indicated. Many of the images in this guide are available for licensing from Lonely Planet Images: www.lonelyplanetimages.com.

SEND US YOUR FEEDBACK

We love to hear from travellers – your comments keep us on our toes and help make our books better. Our well-travelled team reads every word on what you loved or loathed about this book. Although we cannot reply individually to postal submissions, we always guarantee that your feedback goes straight to the appropriate authors, in time for the next edition. Each person who sends us information is thanked in the next edition and the most useful submissions are rewarded with a free book.

To send us your updates – and find out about Lonely Planet events, newsletters and travel news – visit our award-winning website: lonelyplanet.com/contact.

Note: we may edit, reproduce and incorporate your comments in Lonely Planet products such as guidebooks, websites and digital products, so let us know if you don't want your comments reproduced or your name acknowledged. For a copy of our privacy policy visit lonelyplanet.com/privacy.

↘ INDEX

---

000 Map pages
000 Photograph pages

INDEX

B–C

INDEX

O–S

000 Map pages
000 Photograph pages

INDEX

T–W

INDEX

GREENDEX

GREENDEX

Going 'green' is a relatively new concept in Egypt but there are some trailblazers worth supporting. The following have been selected by Lonely Planet authors because they demonstrate an active sustainable-tourism policy, are involved in conservation or environmental education, or are operated with a view to maintaining and preserving regional identity and culture.

We want to keep developing this content. If you think we've omitted someone or if you disagree with our choices, send us your feedback at www .lonelyplanet.com/contact. And for more information, see www.lonelyplanet .com/responsibletravel.

accommodation

Adrére Amellal (Siwa Oasis) 304
Al Tarfa Desert Sanctuary
   (Al-Qasr) 293
Al-Babinshal (Siwa) 294
Al-Karm Ecolodge (St Katherine
   Protectorate) 269
Basata (Nuweiba to Taba) 267-8
Desert Lodge (Al-Qasr) 294
Eskaleh (Abu Simbel) 216
Mövenpick Sirena Beach
   (Al-Quseir) 276
Nature Camp (Bahariya Oasis)
   298

Shali Lodge (Siwa Town)
   303
Shaqra Ecolodge (Marsa Alam)
   277
Tala Ranch Hotel (Siwa Oasis) 304
Under the Moon Camp
   (Bahariya Oasis) 298

activities & tours

Centre for Sinai 265
Man & the Environment (Dahab)
   265
Red Sea Desert Adventures
   278

national parks & protectorates

Nabq Protectorate 259
Ras Abu Gallum Protectorate 259
Ras Mohammed National Park
   257-8
Wadi Rayyan & Wadi al-Hittan
   158-9
Zerenike Protectorate 259

organisations

Man & the Environment 265
Red Sea Association for Diving &
   Watersports 251

MAP LEGEND

ROUTES

Tollway	One-Way Street
Freeway	Mall/Steps
Primary	Tunnel
Secondary	Pedestrian Overpass
Tertiary	Walking Tour
Lane	Walking Tour Detour
Under Construction	Walking Path
Unsealed Road	Track

TRANSPORT

Ferry	Rail/Underground
Metro	Tram
Monorail	Cable Car, Funicular

HYDROGRAPHY

River, Creek	Canal
Intermittent River	Water
Swamp/Mangrove	Dry Lake/Salt Lake
Reef	Glacier

BOUNDARIES

International	Regional, Suburb
State, Provincial	Marine Park
Disputed	Cliff/Ancient Wall

AREA FEATURES

Area of Interest	Forest
Beach, Desert	Mall/Market
Building/Urban Area	Park
Cemetery, Christian	Restricted Area
Cemetery, Other	Sports

POPULATION

◎ **CAPITAL (NATIONAL)**	◉ **CAPITAL (STATE)**
● **LARGE CITY**	● **Medium City**
● **Small City**	○ Town, Village

SYMBOLS

Sights/Activities

	Buddhist
	Canoeing, Kayaking
	Castle, Fortress
	Christian
	Confucian
	Diving
	Hindu
	Islamic
	Jain
	Jewish
	Monument
	Museum, Gallery
	Point of Interest
	Pool
	Ruin
	Sento (Public Hot Baths)
	Shinto
	Sikh
	Skiing
	Surfing, Surf Beach
	Taoist
	Trail Head
	Winery, Vineyard
	Zoo, Bird Sanctuary

Information

	Bank, ATM
	Embassy/Consulate
	Hospital, Medical
	Information
	Internet Facilities
	Police Station
	Post Office, GPO
	Telephone
	Toilets
	Wheelchair Access

Eating

	Eating

Drinking

	Cafe
	Drinking

Entertainment

	Entertainment

Shopping

	Shopping

Sleeping

	Camping
	Sleeping

Transport

	Airport, Airfield
	Border Crossing
	Bus Station
	Bicycle Path/Cycling
	FFCC (Barcelona)
	Metro (Barcelona)
	Parking Area
	Petrol Station
	S-Bahn
	Taxi Rank
	Tube Station
	U-Bahn

Geographic

	Beach
	Lighthouse
	Lookout
	Mountain, Volcano
	National Park
	Pass, Canyon
	Picnic Area
	River Flow
	Shelter, Hut
	Waterfall

LONELY PLANET OFFICES

Australia

Head Office
Locked Bag 1, Footscray, Victoria 3011
☎ 03 8379 8000, fax 03 8379 8111
talk2us@lonelyplanet.com.au

USA

150 Linden St, Oakland, CA 94607
☎ 510 250 6400, toll free 800 275 8555,
fax 510 893 8572
info@lonelyplanet.com

UK

2nd fl, 186 City Rd,
London EC1V 2NT
☎ 020 7106 2100, fax 020 7106 2101
go@lonelyplanet.co.uk

Published by Lonely Planet
ABN 36 005 607 983

Printed through Colorcraft Ltd, Hong Kong
Printed in China

Mixed Sources
Product group from well-managed
forests and other controlled sources
www.fsc.org Cert no. SGS-COC-005002
© 1996 Forest Stewardship Council